D1564890

FUTURES MARKETS

FUTURES MARKETS

Darrell Duffie

PRENTICE HALL, Englewood Cliffs, New Jersey 07632

Library of Congress Cataloging-in-Publication Data

Duffie, Darrell.
  Futures markets / Darrell Duffie.
    p. cm.
  Bibliography: p.
  Includes index.
  1. Futures market. I. Title.
HG6024.A3D84 1989   88-8032
332.64'4—dc19   CIP

Editorial/production supervision and
  interior design: *Anthony Calcara*
Cover design: *Ben Santora*
Manufacturing buyer: *Ed O'Dougherty*

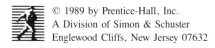 © 1989 by Prentice-Hall, Inc.
A Division of Simon & Schuster
Englewood Cliffs, New Jersey 07632

Printed in the United States of America

10 9 8 7 6 5 4 3 2 1

ISBN 0-13-345604-8

Prentice-Hall International (UK) Limited, *London*
Prentice-Hall of Australia Pty. Limited, *Sydney*
Prentice-Hall Canada Inc., *Toronto*
Prentice-Hall Hispanoamericana, S.A., *Mexico*
Prentice-Hall of India Private Limited, *New Delhi*
Prentice-Hall of Japan, Inc., *Tokyo*
Simon & Schuster Asia Pte. Ltd., *Singapore*
Editora Prentice-Hall do Brasil, Ltda., *Rio de Janeiro*

To Denise

OVERVIEW

CONTENTS

PREFACE

This book presents futures markets from the broadest perspective suitable for a one semester course in business schools and economics programs. The goal is to provide a survey of both practical and conceptual interest, from the mechanics of futures trading to the theoretical determination of futures prices in a general equilibrium setting, with a great deal in between. The student should come away with an understanding of the behavior of futures markets, and how to use them in making business decisions.

The coverage is best surmised by looking over the Table of Contents. Although futures contracts are the most prominent form of forward agreement in the world today, other forward agreements such as swaps, futures options, and various forward markets (such as oil, foreign exchange, and U.S. Treasury bills) are also actively traded, and receive some attention here. Departing from many other treatments, the emphasis of this book is a unified treatment of principles and techniques common to futures markets of all types, rather than concentrating on particular commodity or financial futures. For example, instead of chapter titles such as "Stock Index Futures," "Energy Futures," and so on, the chapters are organized along functional lines, with coverage of specific contract types via numerous examples and student exercises.

Each chapter has a traditional breakdown into a main body of discussion, a set of exercises, notes to the literature, and appendices containing supplementary material. The second page of each chapter contains an outline of that chapter. For the reader's convenience, each time a new specialized term is introduced, it is set in italics to indicate this fact. Examples are set between horizontal markers.

The prerequisite knowledge is essentially the basics of investment theory and U.S. security markets at the level of William Sharpe's text: *Investments*. In terms of mathematical preparation, those readers familiar with statistical linear regression theory will not find the material demanding. In any case, all the requisite mathematics beyond undergraduate algebra and calculus are developed here from scratch.

This book is based on lecture notes that I have used over the last few years for an MBA course on futures markets at the Graduate School of Business at Stanford University, whose support has been indispensable.

I am grateful for discussions with, or information from, Myron Scholes, Bill Beaver, and Ken Singleton (Stanford University); Joe Texido and Gene Flood (Morgan Stanley); Pattie Dunn and Jeremy Evnine (Wells Fargo Investment Advisers); Bill Jahnke (Vestek Systems); Eric Chai (Shell Development Company); Scott Roberts (Shell Oil Company); Bill Wilson (North Dakota State University); Matthew Jackson (Northwestern University); Ronald Anderson (Columbia University); Robert Levin and Ray Melkomian (New York Mercantile Exchange); Victor Attanasio (New York Futures Exchange); Steve Youngrin and Todd Petzel (Chicago Mercantile Exchange); Dana Kellerman (Chicago Board of Trade); Frank Jones (Kidder, Peabody); Kim Jackson (Packers); George Hutchings (INTEX); Pat Apfelbaum (Commodity Futures Trading Commission); Bruno Solnik (Centre HEC–ISA); Mary McCalley (Futures Magazine); Joshua Sommer (International Risk Control, Inc.); Remy Chaudhuri (Stanford University); John Wyche (Sumitomo Bank); Suzy Akers, and Masayuki Katsuyama. In particular, I have drawn on research developed with some valued colleagues: Matthew Jackson, Wayne Shafer, Peter DeMarzo, Bill Zame, and Richard Stanton.

The secretarial assistance of Jill Fukuhara and Renee Gibb, as well as the computational help of Matthew Jackson, John Wyche, Stephen Fan, and Joshua Sommer are especially appreciated. At Prentice-Hall, Carole Freddo, Anthony Calcara, Paul Feyen, Teresa Fernandez and (especially) Scott Barr have all been helpful and friendly. Finally, I am thankful for the editorial comments of Scott Barr (Prentice-Hall) and several reviewers: Thomas O'Brien (University of Connecticut), Mark Rzepczynski (University of Houston), Susan Cheng (Columbia University), Jerome Duncan, Jr. (Hofstra University), Raymond Chiang (University of Miami), Alan Tucker (University of Tennessee), Gerald Gay (Georgia State University), and Avi Kamara (University of Washington). I myself retain all responsibility for errors, and would be pleased to learn of any.

Darrell Duffie
Graduate School of Business, Stanford University

1

OVERVIEW

This chapter gives a brief overview of futures markets as well as the contents of this book. It is broken into five sections: an introduction, a review of the history of futures markets, some discussion of their current institutional structure, a summary of currently traded futures contracts, a synopsis of the key practice of marking a futures position to market, and a brief discussion of the pricing of futures.

1. INTRODUCTION

From the simplest perspective, a *futures contract* is an agreement between two parties to make a particular exchange at a particular future date. Significant throughout our study of futures contracts is the lag in time between the agreement to trade and the trade itself. For example, a futures contract made on June 30 could call for the purchasing agent to pay $400, the *futures price*, on September 30 in exchange for an ounce of gold delivered on September 30. A *spot* sale on June 30, in contrast, might call for the payment of $380, the *spot price* (also known as the *cash price*), on June 30 in immediate exchange for an ounce of gold.

Forward contracts comprise a general family of agreements to make exchanges at one or more future dates. A futures contract, as distinct from most forward contracts, is usually retraded through time at a central market called a *futures exchange*, which has special institutional procedures designed to enable many different agents to efficiently deal in the same contract. Among these special procedures, two are important enough to state immediately. First, each exchange has a clearinghouse that stands behind the performance of contracts traded on that exchange, largely freeing each trader from the risk of individual default of the other side of the trade. Second, the extent of

1

Chapter Outline

individual defaults is reduced by mandatory margin accounts, a form of performance bond that is regularly adjusted for losses and gains according to a contractually prescribed formula. This margin adjustment procedure is called "resettlement," and normally occurs on a daily basis. Although, technically speaking, a futures contract is a special type of forward contract, "futures contracts" and "forward contracts" are often thought of as distinct classes of securities, differing principally in that forward contracts do not have daily resettlement. According to this common usage, our opening example actually illustrates a gold forward contract at a *forward price* of $400 per ounce. This book is concerned with forward contracts in general, but its title and contents reflect the fact that futures transactions dominate other forms of forward agreements by almost all reasonable measures of interest.

Futures contracts serve many purposes. Beyond their obvious role of facilitating the exchange of commodities and financial instruments, futures contracts are essentially insurance contracts, providing protection against uncertain terms of trade on spot markets at the future date of delivery. In the example given above, the purchaser of the gold futures contract could be a jewelry manufacturer worried about the uncertain cost of required future gold inputs. The same futures contract could have been sold by a gold producer that prefers to fix in advance the price it will receive for future gold production, or alternatively, by an investor with no spot commitments in gold who is willing to sell gold futures merely as a form of investment. Because the institutional arrangement of a futures market is in many cases more convenient for trade than that of the corresponding spot market, futures contracts are sometimes also used as a substitute for spot transactions. Futures contracts are useful even to those who do not trade them, since futures prices are publicly available indicators of future demand and supply conditions.

Our goal is to reach a broad understanding of futures markets, especially the behavior of the various agents that use, operate, and regulate these markets. In this chapter we first look briefly at the history of futures markets, and then turn to the basic structure of present-day futures markets in the United States. After reviewing the various agents involved and their contractual links, we will take a more detailed view of the institutional structure of the market in Chapters 2 and 3. Chapters 4 through 7 supply a convenient analytical framework with which to study and use futures contracts. Chapter 8 gives an overview of the closely related markets for options and futures options. Finally, Chapter 9 reviews the design and regulation of futures contracts.

2. HISTORY

It is believed that futures trading may date back to India at about 2000 B.C., and that it subsequently appeared in Greco–Roman times. The trading methods of modern futures markets probably trace their origins to the medieval fairs of France and England dating from the twelfth century. There are examples of organized forward markets in Europe and Japan in the 17th and 18th centuries. Rice was traded for future delivery in Osaka, for example, beginning in the 1730s. The modern form of futures markets, however, originates in the mid-19th-century United States, especially in the grain markets of Chicago. The Chicago Board of Trade, established in 1848, became an active exchange for trade of agricultural commodities, especially corn and wheat. Trading was both spot and forward, or as it was then called, "to arrive." Because of spot price uncertainty, which was heightened by the Crimean and Civil Wars, trading in forward contracts became increasingly popular. It became common to trade and re-trade the forward contracts themselves. By the time the Chicago Board of Trade established its General Rules in 1865, the organized trading of forward contracts had become the first essential example of modern futures markets. The New York Cotton Exchange, established in 1870, governed cotton futures trading shortly afterward. Trading in many other agricultural commodities followed.

Manipulation of futures markets was initially commonplace; "plungers," as they were known, attempted to corner or squeeze certain markets, often successfully. A famous case is "Black Friday," the day in 1869 on which the price of gold collapsed. The corner organized by Jay Gould and Jim Fisk was broken when President Grant ordered the sale of gold from the U.S. Treasury.

Because of impressions that speculative futures trading caused financial instability and undue spot price fluctuation, state and federal legislators repeatedly resisted, or attempted to abolish, futures trading. Finally, the Grain Futures Act of 1922 set up the licensing and regulation of futures exchanges, officially known as "contract markets," by a board designated by the Secretary of Agriculture. Regulation was extended to traders and brokerage firms by the Commodities Exchange Act of 1936. Amendments followed in 1968 and in the Commodity Futures Trading Act of 1974, which established the Commodity Futures Trading Commission (CFTC) as the new independent regulatory commission in charge of futures markets. The role and authority of the CFTC are described in Chapter 9.

The introduction of financial futures contracts in the 1970s brought trading volume to previously unheard-of levels and entirely changed the character of futures markets. Markets for options, stocks, bonds, index funds, foreign currencies, and other securities have been profoundly affected by the introduction of related futures contracts as well as futures options. Active financial futures markets have been introduced in foreign countries, notably England and Japan. Program trading, a wide array of new futures contracts as well as futures options, lower transaction costs, increased trading volume, expanded trading hours, electronic trading, and domestic and international intermarket links continue to tie all of these financial markets into a remarkably tight and efficient financial trading network.

3. THE BASIC STRUCTURE OF U.S. FUTURES MARKETS

A basic contractual structure of a typical U.S. futures market is illustrated in Figure 1.1. Although there are variations to this structure, we shall proceed as though this pattern is more a rule than an example, and refer readers to the Notes at the end of the chapter for sources with further information.

Exchange Corporation

Most futures exchanges are nonprofit firms, incorporated as *membership associations* and operated for the benefit of their members, who are generally

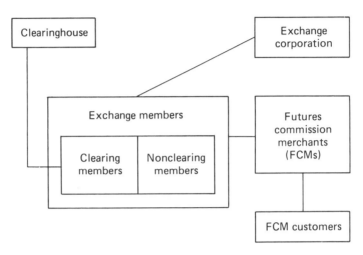

Figure 1.1   The Basic Contractual Structure of a Futures Market

engaged in their own businesses related to futures trading. The basic purpose of an exchange is to provide an organized marketplace, with uniform rules and standardized contracts. Like any corporation, a futures exchange has shareholders, a board of directors, and executive officers. The business of an exchange is generally managed by the officers with the advice and assistance of a staff and various committees made up of members. The actual decision-making power of an exchange, however, usually resides with the committees, which are typically extensive and active. An exchange may operate markets for spot commodities, options, and other financial securities in addition to futures contracts, and may provide other goods and services (such as price information) to the public. An exchange funds its operations by membership dues and by fees for services provided, which may include transactions fees per contract traded on the exchange.

Exchange Members

The essence of a futures market is its exchange members. Although membership is limited to individuals, these individual members often act on behalf of firms such as brokerage houses, investment banks, or commodity dealers and producers. The total number of members of an exchange is limited. Mem-

berships are themselves available for sale on the floor of an exchange and
are often substantial and risky investments. The value of membership lies
mainly in the privileges it conveys for trading contracts directly on the floor
of the exchange, with immediacy and low transactions fees. Recent prices for
memberships, or *seats* (as they are sometimes called), on major U.S. futures
exchanges are shown in Table 1.1, along with each exchange's annual volume
of transactions.

TABLE 1.1   Active U.S. Futures Markets—1987

Exchange	Symbol	Volume[a]	Seat Price[b]
Chicago Board of Trade	CBT	93,565,124	$382,500
Chicago Mercantile Exchange	CME	68,082,277	380,000
Coffee Sugar and Cocoa Exchange	CSCE	5,480,535	58,000
Commodity Exchange, Inc.	CMX	16,821,132	145,000
Kansas City Board of Trade	KCBT	1,484,482	40,000
Mid America Commodity Exchange	MCE	2,260,180	na
Minneapolis Grain Exchange	MGE	300,977	7,000
Chicago Rice and Cotton Exchange	CRCE	13,891	na
New York Cotton Exchange	NYCE	2,127,545	46,000
New York Futures Exchange	NYFE	3,222,533	100
New York Mercantile Exchange	NYME	20,178,017	165,000
Philadelphia Board of Trade	PBOT	10,161	na

[a] Annual volume in contracts, Sept. 1986 to Sept. 1987, *CFTC Annual Report, 1987*.
[b] As published in *The Wall Street Journal*, January 18, 1988 (na = not available).

Those members, nominees of members, and other individuals who actually have and use floor trading privileges are *traders*. Several basic categories
of traders serve to distinguish their reasons for trade, and often distinguish
as well a particular variety of trading privileges and special transactions fees.
Although the terminology varies, one possible classification is:

1. *Floor brokers*, who typically execute orders placed with them from
   off the floor of the exchange or by other traders.
2. *Day traders*, who trade on their own accounts and eliminate their
   contract positions each day before the end of trading.
3. *Scalpers*, who trade for their own accounts, are often charged relatively low transaction fees, and specialize in contract positions held
   over short intervals of time.
4. *Position traders*, who trade on their own accounts and may hold
   contracts over a period of days or weeks.

Although floor brokers sometimes trade on their own accounts, their basic role is in the chain of transactions services allowing the public at large to buy or sell contracts. Floor brokers profit mainly from fees for this service. Traders in the other categories attempt to profit from price movements, either by small price advantages that may appear for very short periods of time, or via some understanding of the general formation of spot and futures market prices combined with the information continually coming onto the floor of the exchange. Some succeed; some do not. Collectively, however, they meet a critical need for *liquidity*, the ability of the market to act as a reliable and efficient mechanism for quickly taking or offsetting contract positions.

Trading is conducted on the floor of an exchange, mainly in the form of an *open outcry auction* described in Chapter 2.

Futures Commission Merchants

A *futures commission merchant (FCM)* is an intermediary between its customers, drawn from the public at large, and the floor brokers of a futures exchange. An FCM acts as an agent for customers, placing orders and maintaining accounts, as will be described in detail in the next chapter. In so doing, an FCM is regulated by the *Commodity Futures Trading Commission* (CFTC), as are the exchanges and their members, among other parties.

Figure 1.1 shows a distinction between an exchange member and an FCM. In fact, an FCM often maintains a membership on the exchange, typically held in the name of one of its officers. (As already noted, exchanges generally allow only individuals to be members.) Some FCMs provide futures services, in return for fees, as a principal line of business; some do so in addition to providing other financial or commodity services.

Customers

Customers may establish futures accounts with an FCM. Large customers, such as producers, commodity merchants, exporters, and investment banks, may bypass FCMs by purchasing an exchange membership, which allows them to trade directly at the futures exchange, with corresponding immediacy and lower transactions costs. In many cases, a member will place some orders with an independent broker in order to disguise the source of the trade.

Clearinghouse

Like an exchange corporation, a *clearinghouse* is typically a nonprofit incorporated membership association. The members of a clearinghouse usually form a subset of the members of the associated exchange corporation, although in rare cases a clearing corporation is established independently of any particular exchange in order to serve one or more exchanges. Although most U.S. futures exchanges have their own clearing operations, the clearing operations of several different exchanges can be consolidated within a single clearing corporation. The International Commodities Clearing House (ICCH), for example, clears for most of the futures exchanges in England. Currently, the Intermarket Clearing Corporation clears for the New York Futures Exchange and the Philadelphia Board of Trade.

In some instances, a clearing membership association is not separately incorporated, but organized as a division within the exchange corporation. In order to insulate the exchange from the legal liability of the clearing corporation, however, this practice is often avoided.

The basic function of a clearinghouse is to *clear* futures contracts, as follows. A clearing member, say an FCM, may establish a number of new contract positions for different customer accounts during the course of a trading day. At the end of the day, these positions are *cleared*, that is, *recorded* by the clearinghouse. At this point the clearinghouse assumes certain responsibilities for the performance of the contracts. In so doing, the clearinghouse requires that the FCM maintain a margin account with the clearinghouse as collateral against default, according to a formula discussed in Chapter 3. The clearinghouse also monitors the financial integrity of its members, sometimes requiring corrective action. Finally, the clearinghouse maintains a guarantee fund to cover defaults. By these measures—*record keeping, margin requirements, financial oversight of members,* and a *guarantee fund*—a clearinghouse supports the financial integrity of a futures market.

Clearing Members

All futures contracts must be cleared. Those exchange members that are not clearing members must maintain an account with a clearing member for this purpose. Exchange members may usually become clearing members by purchasing a clearing membership. This avoids clearing through other members and the associated fees and margin requirements.

4. CURRENT U.S. FUTURES MARKETS

An extensive list of the world's futures markets appears in Appendix 9D. Table 1.1 shows the currently active U.S. futures exchanges. The futures contracts offered by each, and the associated volumes of trade in 1987, are shown in Appendix 1A. The largest current exchange by most measures, including volume, is the Chicago Board of Trade, although its degree of dominance has been somewhat diminished. The various types of contracts traded on U.S. futures markets are often grouped into the two major categories, *commodities* and *financials*, and further subdivided as indicated in Tables 1.2 and 1.3.

TABLE 1.2   U.S. Commodity Futures Groups

Commodity Group	Commodity Type
GRAINS	Corn Oats Rice Wheat
OIL AND MEAL	Soybean Complex
LIVESTOCK	Pork Commodities Beef Commodities
ENERGY	Heating Oil Gasoline Crude Oil Propane Gas
METALS	Gold Silver and Silver Coins Platinum Palladium Copper Aluminum
FOREST PRODUCTS	Lumber
TEXTILES	Cotton
FOODSTUFFS	Cocoa Coffee Orange Juice Potatoes Sugar Corn Syrup

For each type of contact, trade can occur for delivery at different specific dates in the future. For example, the Chicago Board of Trade offers a "corn contract," summarized in Table 1.4, which is actually a series of contracts for delivery each December, March, May, July, and September. This contract calls for delivery of a particular quantity and grade of corn, with substitutions allowed at prearranged price differentials, at specific "regular" locations (with discounts for irregular locations). The contract design also includes position limits, daily price limits, and quotation conventions, according to detailed

TABLE 1.3   U.S. Financial Futures Groups

Financial Group	Instrument Type
INTEREST RATES	Treasury Bonds Treasury Bills Treasury Notes GNMA Commercial Paper (CDs) Eurodollars Municipal Bonds Corporate Bonds 30 Day Interest Rates
FOREIGN CURRENCIES	French Francs British Pounds Japanese Yen Deutsche Marks Swiss Francs Mexican Pesos Canadian Dollars Australian Dollars European Currency Units (ECUs)
INDICES	S&P Indices Value Line Indices NYSE Index Amex Major Market Indices NASDAQ Indices Over–the–Counter Indices CPI–W Index U.S. Dollar Index CRB (Commodity) Index Russel Stock Indices Institutional Stock Index CBOE 250 Stock Index

legal specifications. The contract design attempts to reduce to the greatest possible extent any ambiguities as to the nature of a delivered contract. Although an extremely small fraction of contracts purchased are actually held until delivery, uncertainty as to the terms of a futures contract reduces the quality of the insurance it provides, and thus its popularity. In particular, the availability of a standard grade of the deliverable asset in a supply large enough to inhibit price manipulation has been considered a key ingredient in contract design, as discussed in more detail in Chapter 9. Appendix 9D summarizes the contract designs of the commonly traded futures contracts.

Certain contracts, including many financial futures, are based on *cash delivery* rather than physical delivery. In this case, the holder of a contract at the delivery date receives funds based on a formula specified in the contract design. This allows, for example, the design of a futures contract that

TABLE 1.4   Chicago Board of Trade: Corn Futures Contract

Basic Trading Unit	5,000 bushels
Deliverable Grade	U.S. No. 2 Yellow corn—see Exchange Rules and Regulations for exact specifications
Price Quotation	Cents and quarter cents per bushel
Minimum Fluctuation	1/4 cent per bushel ($12.50 per contract)
Daily Price Limit	10 cents per bushel ($500 per contract) above and below the previous day's settlement price
Contract Months	March, May, July, September, and December
Trading Hours	9:30 a.m. to 1:15 p.m. (Chicago time)
Last Trading Day	Seventh business day preceding the last business day of the month
Last Delivery Day	Last business day of the month
Ticker Symbol	C
Date Trading Began	January 2, 1877

Source: Board of Trade of the City of Chicago.

promises to pay an amount based on economic variables for which no underlying deliverable asset even exists, such as an inflation index.

5. MARKING TO MARKET

A "futures price" is something of a misnomer, for it is not a price at all. Rather, purchasing or selling futures contracts means making a legal commitment to accept a particular series of cash flows called *variation margin* during the period the contracts to deliver (or accept delivery) are held. One may *offset* one's position, that is, sell the number of contracts previously purchased or buy the number of contracts previously sold, at any time before delivery. Some of the cash flows are positive, or *collects*; some are negative, or *pays*. These cash flows are calculated using a formula presented in Chapter 3, and are based on daily changes in the *settlement price* of the contract, which is announced at the end of each trading day as a representative price at the close of trade. For the simplest case, *100 percent variation*, the variation margin payment on any particular day is the number of contracts held (which may be negative if constracts are sold) multiplied by the change in futures settlement price from the previous day. That is, letting f_t denote the futures settlement price for day t, any account holding n contracts collects $n(f_{t+1} - f_t)$ dollars (or pays, if the amount is negative) after the new settlement futures price f_{t+1} is announced, collects $n(f_{t+2} - f_{t+1})$ when the contract is again resettled at the futures price f_{t+2}, and so on, until the position is offset (or delivery occurs). In this way, each futures account is said to be *marked to market*. The process of collecting and paying variation margin is called *resettlement*. Variation margins are normally more complicated, however, than the simple case of 100 percent variation margin outlined here. Resettlement procedures are described in more detail in Chapter 3.

Example: Acme Metals purchased 10 Comex gold contracts for June delivery at 11 a.m. on Monday at a futures price of $400 per ounce. This means essentially that Acme Metals became legally obligated to make daily payments (or accept daily payments) determined as follows. Each contract is for 100 ounces. Acme's FCM requires 100 percent variation margin. At the close of trading on Monday, the futures price settles at $395. On Tuesday morning, Acme Metals is therefore required to pay its FCM 100 percent of the change in the futures price multiplied by the number of ounces purchased for future delivery, for a pay of

$$(\$400 - \$395) \times 100 \times 10 = \$5,000.$$

Tuesday's settlement price is $397; on Wednesday morning, Acme Metals therefore collects ($397 − $395) × 100 × 10 = $2,000. On Wednesday at 2 p.m., Acme offsets its position by selling 10 contracts at a futures price of $401, an appreciation of $4 over Tuesday's settlement price, generating an additional payment to Acme of $4,000 on Thursday morning.

By purchasing 10 contracts, Acme received a total cumulative profit of $1,000 (before commission charges) by the time its position was offset on Thursday. This reflects the total change in price from execution on Monday at $400 per ounce to offset on Wednesday at $401 per ounce. Anyone familiar with the time value of money recognizes a distinction, however, between a one time payment of $1,000 on Thursday and the actual series of payments on Tuesday, Wednesday, and Thursday that totaled $1,000.

Futures contracts are marked to market in order to limit default risk. If cumulative price changes were to be paid only when positions are offset, the cash amounts involved could represent a substantial risk to the payees. By staging the payments daily, through the device of marking a futures position daily to market, default risk is lessened. A good analogy is the system of watertight bulkhead doors sealing off the compartments of a submarine; a leak usually costs the loss of at most one compartment. In Chapters 2 and 3 we outline other safeguards used in futures markets for protecting the integrity of the market as a whole from individual risks.

Short and Long Futures Positions

Selling a futures contract is synonymous with *taking a short position*; buying a futures contract means taking a long position. More generally, a *futures position* in a given contract is the cumulative total to date of the number of contracts purchased less the number of contracts sold. A positive total is a *long position*; a negative total is a *short position*. That is, a net position of -100, for example, is called a short position of 100. A short futures position profits whenever the futures price goes down; a long position profits whenever the futures price goes up. Other than this obvious distinction, there is essentially no difference between the concepts or practicalities of short and long positions.

Example: To illustrate the simple symmetry between short and long futures positions, we repeat the calculations of the previous example, changing only one fact: Acme's original position is short 10 gold contracts rather than long 10. The price decline from Monday's execution at $400 per ounce to Monday's settlement at $395 per ounce generates a collect (rather than a pay) of

$$(\$400 - \$395) \times 100 \times 10 = \$5,000.$$

In other words, the previous example involving a $5,000 loss to a long position of 10 contracts here translates into a $5,000 profit to a short position of 10 contracts. Equivalently, we can think of a short position of 10 contracts as a net position of -10. (The finance industry, however, prefers not to use negative signs!)

Continuing to reverse the pays and collects of the previous example, Tuesday's settlement price of $397 requires a pay from Acme of $2,000 (the $2 rise in settlement price multiplied by the short position of 10 contracts at 100 ounces each). Acme closes out its position on Wednesday by purchasing 10 contracts at a futures price of $401, an increase of $4 over Tuesday's settlement price, for a loss by Acme of $4,000. The total loss over the three days is $1,000, precisely the opposite of the $1,000 gain generated by the long position in the previous version of the example.

6. A FORMULA FOR FUTURES PRICES?

Chapter 4 discusses the determination of futures prices. The general answer given is that futures prices are whatever they must be in order to equate demand and supply. Only by adopting restrictive assumptions concerning the behavior of individual agents in the market can this vague answer be made precise by deriving formulas for supply and demand. There is, however, a simple answer that can be told in certain cases.

Example: Suppose that gold is selling at $450 per ounce, interest rates are 10 percent per year, and the gold futures price for delivery in one year is $500 per ounce. An astute investor could devise the following strategy: sell one futures contract, buy one ounce of gold, and finance the spot gold cost by borrowing $450 until the delivery date, one year hence. For purposes of this example, let us ignore daily resettlement payments and assume that the contract is entirely settled at delivery. In one year's time, neglecting any costs for storing the gold and commission charges, the investor can deliver the ounce of stored gold against the short futures position, collect the $500 futures price originally agreed upon, and pay off the amount due on the loan, $450 plus $45 interest, for a net profit of $5. The investor's strategy involves no costs and no risk! This is called *arbitrage*. Clearly, this is such an attractive proposition that the arbitrage strategy could be scaled up for arbitrarily large profits, so that markets could not clear at these prices. We have deduced, neglecting several details, that the market clearing futures price can be no more than $495, the amount due at delivery, with interest, if the spot price of an ounce of gold is borrowed today.

Now let us turn this example into a more general formula. Let $f_{t,T}$ denote the futures price at time t for delivery of an asset at time T, and let $B_{t,T}$ denote the amount payable at time T on a riskless loan of 1 dollar made at time t. Equivalently, $1/B_{t,T}$ is the price at time T of a riskless discount bond maturing at T with a face value of \$1. Suppose the deliverable asset can be purchased at time t at the spot price, s_t. For simplicity, let us ignore the fact that futures positions are resettled daily, assume that the asset can be stored costlessly, and also neglect transactions costs.

From a theoretical point of view, an *arbitrage* is a financial strategy yielding a riskless profit and requiring no investment. For theoretical purposes, we always presume that prices adjust quickly enough to preclude arbitrage. We intend to show that, under this assumption, $f_{t,T} \le s_t B_{t,T}$.

Suppose that $f_{t,T} > s_t B_{t,T}$. An arbitrageur takes a short position of one futures contract at time t, and maintains the position until delivery at T. The arbitrageur also buys the underlying asset at time t, and stores it until T in order to make delivery as required by the terms of the futures contract. The cost s_t of the asset at time t is borrowed and repaid with interest at T, when the total amount due on the loan is $s_t B_{t,T}$. The net cash flow at time T is the futures price $f_{t,T}$ received for delivery of the stored asset, net of the loan payment $s_t B_{t,T}$, for a net riskless profit of $f_{t,T} - s_t B_{t,T}$. This is an arbitrage if $f_{t,T} > s_t B_{t,T}$. Since we assume that arbitrage is impossible, this proves our claim that $f_{t,T} \le s_t B_{t,T}$.

Does the reverse argument show that $f_{t,T} \ge s_t B_{t,T}$? The answer is, "Yes, but only if the asset can be short sold at its market price s_t." *Short selling* the asset at its market price s_t means borrowing the asset at time t from some agent that already owns it, selling the borrowed asset at the current price s_t, and finally returning the asset (somehow) to the asset lender at an agreed date. If $f_{t,T} < s_t B_{t,T}$, the following strategy is an arbitrage:

1. Take a long futures position of one contract at time t.

2. Sell the asset short at time t for s_t, with the asset to be returned to its lender at time T.

3. Lend the proceeds of the short sale risklessly until time T, when $s_t B_{t,T}$ is received on the loan.

4. At time T, return the asset sold short by accepting delivery on the futures contract.

This strategy generates a net cash flow at time T of $s_t B_{t,T} - f_{t,T}$, the loan proceeds less the payment made on the futures contract. If $s_t B_{t,T} > f_{t,T}$, this is an arbitrage profit, which is again assumed to be impossible. Thus, if the strategy outlined above is possible, we know that $s_t B_{t,T} \le f_{t,T}$. Based on the opposite arbitrage possibility, we would then conclude that $f_{t,T} = s_t B_{t,T}$, a tidy formula indeed! Since $B_{t,T}$ is a number larger than 1, whenever this

formula applies, we can conclude that the futures price should be larger than
the spot price. Since $B_{t,T}$ gets closer and closer to 1 as the current date t
gets closer and closer to the delivery date T, the futures price should also get
closer to the spot price as the delivery date approaches. This convergence of
the spot and futures prices at delivery is shown in Figure 1.2.

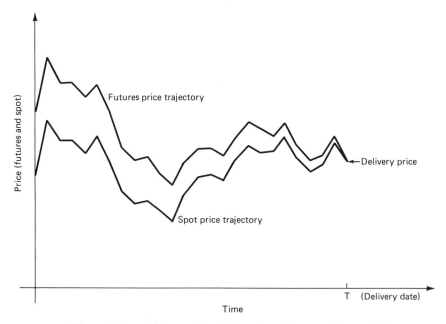

Figure 1.2   Arbitrage–Free Trajectories of Spot and Futures Prices

In many cases, step 2 of the above strategy is not possible; an asset
cannot typically be sold short at its market price. In addition to the price of
the asset, the agent lending the asset to the short seller from time t until time
T may want some compensation for giving up the right to use or sell the asset
during the interim. Thus our tidy formula for the futures price, $f_{t,T} = s_t B_{t,T}$,
need not be correct. A number of financial assets as well as gold, however,
can be short sold at prices close to their spot prices, and for these types of
futures contracts, simple modifications to the *arbitrage formula* $f_{t,T} = s_t B_{t,T}$
work fairly well, as we shall see in Chapter 5.

Aside from the possibility of short sales, one must also consider storage costs, dividends payable to the asset holder, transactions costs, and the fact that the futures position is marked to market. Some of these complexities can be dealt with, as shown in Chapter 5, and our simple formula can be extended in several practical ways. In general, however, there is no simple formula for futures prices. The general question of how futures prices are determined is examined in Chapter 4.

EXERCISES

1.1 Suppose the spot price for gold is $400 per ounce, while the futures price for delivery in one year is $435 per ounce. The interest rate on one year loans is 7 percent. Ignoring storage and transactions costs, does this represent an arbitrage opportunity? Why? Suppose the futures price of gold is, instead, $420 per ounce. Assuming gold can be short sold at a transactions cost of $5 per ounce, describe an arbitrage strategy.

1.2 Suppose the spot price for Swiss francs $0.60 per franc, while the futures price for delivery in one year is $0.59 per franc. Must this represent an arbitrage opportunity? Why, or why not?

NOTES

Our outline of the historical development of futures markets is based in part on Chapter 4 of Hieronymus (1977) and Chapter 1 of Markham (1987). Markham gives additional sources, and notes that the Futures Industry Association traces the origins of futures trading back to 2000 B.C., "when the merchants of what is now Bahrein Island took goods on consignment for barter in India." Rees (1972) provides an extensive history of Britain's commodity markets, including early European trading techniques. Section 1.3 is constructed from a number of sources, including interviews, Hieronymus (1977), the *Commodity Trading Manual* for the Chicago Board of Trade (1985), and Edwards (1984), a study of the clearing operation. Section 1.4 is compiled from the *Commodity Trading Manual* (1985) and various unpublished sources.

Additional introductory information on futures markets can be found in Carlton (1984), Erickson and Steinhart (1985), Kamara (1982), and Telser and Higginbotham (1977).

Appendix 1A: Active U.S. Futures Contracts

TABLE 1.5   Active U.S. Futures Contracts—1987

Exchange	Contract Type	Volume[a] (Contracts)
Chicago Board of Trade	Wheat	1,812,532
	Corn	7,177,029
	Oats	262,497
	Soybeans	6,560,196
	Oil, Soybean	3,732,146
	Meal, Soybean	3,409,222
	T–Bonds	61,147,076
	T–Notes, 6.5–10-Year	4,782,680
	GNMA (Mortgages) CDR	9,870
	Silver, 1000 Tr. oz.	510,842
	Silver, 5,000 Tr. oz.	5,437
	Gold (1 kg.)	167,322
	Gold (100 Tr. oz.)	7,582
	Stock Index, Maxi MM	2,556,912
	Stock Index, Instit.	173
	Bonds, Muni	1,423,608
	Total	93,565,124
Minneapolis Grain Exchange	Wheat	294,855
	Wheat, White	224
	Corn Syrup, HF	5,898
	Total	300,977
New York Mercantile Exchange	Oil, Heating Number 2	3,898,337
	Potatoes, Maine	11,860
	Oil, Crude (Sweet)	12,809,021
	Palladium	147,521
	Platinum	1,471,290
	Gasoline, Leaded	1,806
	Gasoline, Unleaded	1,834,908
	Propane Gas	3,274
	Total	20,178,017
Coffee, Sugar and Cocoa Exchange	Cocoa	845,405
	Sugar Number 11	3,543,852
	Sugar Number 12	173
	Sugar Number 14	74,087
	Coffee C	1,017,008
	CPI–W Index	10
	Total	5,480,535

[a]These data, for the period September 30, 1986, to September 30, 1987, were compiled from the *CFTC Annual Report, 1987*

TABLE 1.5   (Continued)   **Active U.S. Futures Contracts—1987**

Exchange	Contract Type	Volume[a] (Contracts)
Mid America Commodity Exchange	Wheat	200,519
	Corn	330,898
	Oats	6,647
	Soybeans	447,521
	Soybean Meal (New)	2,615
	Soybean Meal (Old)	101
	T-Bonds	862,706
	T-Bills, US 90 Days	25,340
	Hogs, Live	51,495
	Cattle, Live	40,392
	Platinum	5,448
	Silver, 1–Bar	7
	Silver, NY Delivery	8,163
	Copper	26
	Copper (High GR)	139
	Gold, NY Delivery	19,260
	Dollars, Canadian	7,978
	Franc, Swiss	99,803
	Mark, Deutsche	82,137
	Pound Sterling	11,416
	Yen, Japanese	57,569
	Total	2,260,180
Chicago Rice and Cotton Exchange	Cotton	0
	Rice, Rough	13,891
	Total	13,891
Commodity Exchange, Inc.	Silver	4,761,811
	Copper	2,203,984
	Gold	9,843,980
	Aluminum	11,357
	Total	16,821,132
Kansas City Board of Trade	Wheat	845,624
	Value Line Stock Index	611,548
	Mini Value Line Stock Index	27,310
	Total	1,484,482
New York Futures Exchange	Stock Index, NYSE	3,092,511
	CRB Index	119,594
	Index, Russel 2000	3,294
	Index, Russel 3000	7,134
	Total	3,222,533

TABLE 1.5   (Continued)   Active U.S. Futures Contracts—1987

Exchange	Contract Type	Volume[a] (Contracts)
Chicago Mercantile Exchange (incl. IMM)	T–Bills	1,697,900
	Hogs, Live	2,122,828
	Pork Bellies	1,178,355
	Cattle, Live New	4,848,001
	Cattle, Feeder	514,212
	Lumber	430,288
	Gold, 100 Tr. oz.	239,599
	Gold, 5000 Tr. oz.	22,687
	Dollars, Canadian	885,572
	Franc, French	9,661
	Franc, Swiss	5,227,193
	Mark, Deutsche	6,056,744
	Pound Sterling	2,376,445
	Yen, Japanese	4,683,459
	Dollars, Australian	46,656
	CDs, 90–Day	122
	Eurodollars (3-Month)	17,846,626
	Stock Index, S&P 500	19,892,507
	S&P OTC 250	12
	European Currency Unit	3,410
	Total	68,082,277
New York Cotton Exchange and Associates	Cotton Number 2	1,320,799
	Orange Juice	210,452
	Propane Gas	8,670
	Dollar Index	295,994
	Eurpean Currency Unit	52,722
	U.S. Treasury Notes	238,908
	Total	2,127,545
Philadelphia Board of Trade	Stock Index, Over-the-Counter	87
	Franc, Swiss	4,424
	Mark, Deutsche	4,681
	Pound, Sterling	790
	Yen, Japanese	101
	Dollar, Canadian	128
	Dollar, Australian	37
	Total	10,161
ALL EXCHANGES	GRAND TOTAL	213,546,854

2

TRADING FUTURES

In this, the first of two chapters reviewing the operation of futures markets, we aim at trading procedures. We start with their focal point, the futures auction, then turn to price reporting and orders, and finally review clearing and delivery procedures.

1. THE FUTURES AUCTION

The trading of futures contracts in the United States, as regulated by the Commodity Futures Trading Commission (CFTC), presently occurs only on the trading floors of registered futures exchanges by several different types of auctions, now to be described. By regulation, no exchange can be made by private negotiation (except as noted in Appendix 2A). The objective of any of these auctions is to match buyers and sellers, or more explicitly, to allow pairs of traders to make a specific-size trade in a specific futures contract at a specific price. The possible objectives of a trader participating in a futures auction are:

- To benefit from positions taken on the trader's own account.
- To fill an order for another account as a transaction service, in return for commissions or wages.

Positions taken on the trader's own account can benefit the trader by acting as a hedge against some other risk, or by producing expected profits (that outweigh the associated risk), or both. We later review the various types of orders and order-handling procedures.

The Open Outcry Auction

By far the best known method of trading futures contracts, and the method that accounts for the vast majority of transactions today, is the *open outcry*

Chapter Outline

auction. Conducted in *trading pits*, designated areas on the trading floor of the exchange, this often hectic and dramatic auction places the traders of a particular contract face-to-face, allowing any trader to make an offer "by open outcry" to buy or sell an announced number of contracts at an announced price.

A trading pit—or *ring*, as it is sometimes called (see Figure 2.1)—is generally a polygonal or circular platform with one or more concentric rings of steps dropping toward the center; hence "pit." One pit is often dedicated to the exchange of a certain *contract type* (that is, a particular commodity or financial instrument), and the traders of a given delivery date for that contract type are sometimes informally grouped in a corresponding area of the pit. The *nearby contract*, that is, the contract with the earliest delivery date, is often the most actively traded, and is therefore often traded on the topmost step of the pit, as close as possible to the phone desks of the futures commission merchants. In other cases, the pit is divided as a pie is divided into slices, with the trading in different delivery dates located in corresponding "slices" of the pit. For purposes of ticker and wallboard display, bidding information is collected by exchange employees in a *pulpit*, also known as a *rostrum*, usually located on the fringe of the pit as indicated in Figure 2.1.

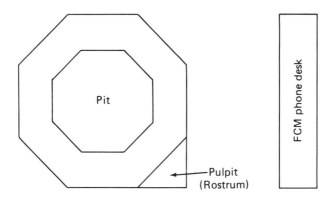

Figure 2.1   A Typical Trading Pit

By regulation, a trader announcing a *bid* (proposal to buy) or *offer* (proposal to sell) must do so both vocally (calling out the price and number of contracts) and by hand signals. (Of course, regulations are not always precisely followed.) The price quoted for a given contract type is generally given in terms of a convenient *unit size*, such as bushels for grains, ounces for gold, or barrels for oil, even though one contract may represent multiple units (for example, 5,000 bushels of corn). A typical convention for vocalizing an offer is

"*n* at *p*,"

for example "three at thirty," for a proposal to sell *n* contracts at a unit price of *p*. The corresponding convention for vocalizing a bid is

"*p* for *n*,"

meaning a proposal to buy *n* contracts at a unit price of *p*. Because of the usually high noise level, the order of calling price and quantity is reversed in this way between bids and offers in order to reduce confusion. For brevity and speed, only the fractional part of the price is usually called out, since the price generally moves through whole number levels gradually enough to preclude ambiguity. The minimum fractional price fluctuation, or *tick*, is specified in the contract design. For example, the minimum price fluctuation for grains is often a quarter of a cent per bushel. The tick for each contract type is shown in Appendix 9D.

Bids and offers are also given by hand signals. The following conventions are used at the Chicago Mercantile Exchange:

1. An offer is indicated by facing the palm of the hand outward, away from the proposer; a bid is signaled by facing the palm of the hand inward, toward the proposer.

2. Price quotes are given with the hand directly in the front of the trader's body. Prices are in terms of the number of ticks above the current whole number of the price. Volume signals are made with the hand away to one side of the body; the number signaled refers to the number of contracts.

3. The numbers 0 through 5 are indicated by the number of fingers shown pointing upward, as illustrated in Figure 2.2a. The numbers 6 through 9 are shown as 5 plus the number of fingers pointing horizontally, as illustrated in Figure 2.2b.

Bids and offers must be made openly in this fashion for the benefit of all traders in the pit; trade must occur with the first trader to signal acceptance. If two or more traders simultaneously accept a bid or offer, the trade (if more than a single contract) must be shared among them. Traders must be silent if they are not prepared to bid or offer at prices comparable to or better than the best current prices (the highest bid or lowest offer).

At the culmination of a trade, the trader on each side records the number of contracts, the contract type, the delivery date (by the symbol for the delivery month, as indicated in Table 2.1), the price, the name of the clearing firm of the member on the opposite side of the trade, and the initials of the trader on the opposite side. Traders may wear color-coded clothing or letter-coded badges in order to identify their status and firm, according to the convention of the exchange. On some exchanges, each half hour of the trading period is assigned a different letter of the alphabet, which is prominently displayed on the trading floor. This letter signal, the *time bracket*, would then also be recorded with each trade. All orders received from outside the exchange must also be time-stamped as they reach the order desk of the FCM handling the

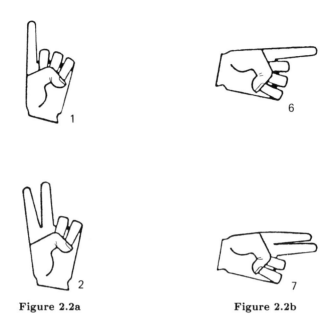

Figure 2.2a   Figure 2.2b

Figure 2.2   Open Outcry Hand Signals

TABLE 2.1   Delivery Month Symbols

Delivery Month	Current Year Symbol	Following Year Symbol
January	F	A
February	G	B
March	H	C
April	J	D
May	K	E
June	M	I
July	N	L
August	Q	O
September	U	P
October	V	R
November	X	S
December	Z	T

order; this is a CFTC regulation.

If made on the personal account of the trader, the trade is recorded on a trading card such as that illustrated in Figure 2.3. On the card shown (similar to that used at the Chicago Mercantile Exchange), the "CARS" column is for the number of contracts traded. (In days past, the routine size of a contract was one railway carload.) The "BK" column is for the time bracket. Figure 2.3 depicts the side of the card on which contracts bought are recorded; on the opposite side of the card (not shown) the word SELLER appears in place of the word BUYER.

BUYER			DATE	
CARS	MO.	SELLER	PRICE	BK

Figure 2.3   A Floor Trader's Card (BUYER Side)

If the trade is executed for a customer, the information is recorded on a multipart order ticket such as that illustrated in Figure 2.4. We will discuss customer orders in more detail later in the chapter.

Each trade is recorded twice, once by each side; any discrepancies, or *out*

AJAX COMMODITIES—ORDER FORM						
Exchange: CBOT					Order No.: A001872	
CXL	BUY	Quant.	Month	Commodity	Price	Qualification
X	2		DEC	T-BOND	MKT	
CXL	SL	Quant.	Month	Commodity	Price	Qualification

Special Instructions: Duration:

Account No.:   36254-7   Execution Price:
Customer Name: John Poor
Associated Person: 15   92-30

Figure 2.4   A Sample Customer Order

trades, are handled with the clearing procedure, which is described later in the chapter.

Price Limits

Each exchange, subject to the approval of the CFTC, sets limits at the end of each trading session on the prices at which trades may occur on the following trading day. Trading outside of these *price limits* is prohibited, with the obvious potential for an excess supply of a contract at its lower price limit or an excess demand at its upper limit. Price limits are thought by some to provide a measure of financial integrity at times of extreme fluctuations in market conditions, although there is controversy over this point. Some exchanges have *variable price limits*, allowing price limits during a given trading session to expand according to sometimes complicated formulas. The Chicago Board of Trade, for example, expands the price limits of one contract when a certain number of related contracts hit their respective price limits, according to a rigorously given criterion. Some contracts do not have price limits at all. Price limits are discussed further in Appendix 5A and in Chapter 9.

The Opening Call and the Close

Many exchanges begin trading on the floor of the exchange each day with an *opening call* for each contract. The opening call establishes an *opening price* or *opening range* for prices by posting traders' initial bids and offers as well as the actual prices and quantities traded. After traders have had the opportunity to execute trades at the opening call, the continuous open outcry auction may begin. At most exchanges, a separate opening call is held in each pit for each delivery date in succession before continuous trading by open outcry begins. The opening call is intended to allow an orderly start of trading and filling of orders that request execution at the opening range.

A *closing range* is similarly established as the range of prices at the end of the trading period for a given contract. A trader filling a large order at the close may request that the closing range include all prices of transactions occurring while that order is filled.

The *settlement price* is a representative price from the closing range, generally as close as possible to the midpoint of the closing range. The settlement price, which is similar in concept to the *closing price* on a stock exchange, is used to determine margin requirements and price limits. Since the settlement price is so important, a special *settlement committee* of each futures exchange is usually given responsibility for choosing it.

The opening and closing of trade in a given contract are signaled with a bell; trading is forbidden before the opening bell or after the closing bell. Daily trading hours vary by contract, as indicated in Appendix 9D.

Board Trading

On some exchanges, trades in the least active contracts occur by *board trading*, that is, by posting bids or offers on boards outside the pits. The contract type, delivery date, quantity, and price are posted under "BUY" or "SELL," and remain posted until canceled or matched by another bid or offer, at which time a contract is constituted and recorded by an exchange employee on a sales board, along with the identities of buyer and seller. Bids and offers must first be made in the pits by open outcry, for all to hear and observe, before being transferred to a trading board.

Electronic Trading

Another form of futures auction, not currently in use on the United States exchanges, is *electronic trading*. With this form of auction, bids and offers are made electronically by traders, perhaps physically removed from one another, and matched by computer, in the manner of board trading. The International Futures Exchange, *INTEX*, is an electronic futures exchange operated as a Bermuda corporation, with trading from computer terminals located throughout the world, including several U.S. locations. Clearing for INTEX is done by the International Commodities Clearing House Limited, ICCH, the common clearinghouse of British futures markets. There are currently joint plans by Reuters Holdings and the Chicago Mercantile Exchange to introduce an electronic trading system, to be called *Globex*, for executing trades after normal trading hours at the International Monetary Market. Globex (previously known as Post-Market-Trading) is currently slated to commence in mid–1989. If approved by the CFTC, the system will initially handle only foreign currency futures and futures options. Other exchanges may eventually list some of their contracts on Globex.

There is also a proposal by the Tokyo Stock Exchange for electronic trading of the TOPIX contract, a stock index futures contract based on the Tokyo Stock Exchange Index.

The advent of electronic trading promises efficiencies in clearing and back office operations, access to markets by physically distant traders, as well as improvements in the speed and fairness of order execution. Since electronic trading will be based on a different type of auction than the traditional open outcry format, however, there is no guarantee that it can improve the overall efficiency of the markets. There may also be some resistance to the introduction of electronic trading by exchange members who have a vested interest in the current market system.

Exchange for Physicals

Although it is widely believed that CFTC regulations require every futures trade executed in the United States to be passed through the futures pit of a registered exchange, there is an important exception: *exchange for physicals* (EFP), a procedure that allows a futures trade to be negotiated outside of the pits, provided the two sides of the trade simultaneously trade a like amount of the underlying asset. The exchange-for-physicals procedure is reviewed in more detail in Appendix 2A.

2. REPORTING PRICES AND OTHER INFORMATION

The immediate availability of market information to traders and customers is an important requirement for a successful futures exchange. Individuals are obviously reluctant to trade with those who may have superior market information. The key pieces of market information are prices and volumes of trade. The *volume of trade* over a given period of time is the total number of contracts traded during that time. *Open interest* is defined as the sum of all long positions (as defined in Section 1.5), or equivalently, the sum of all short positions.

Pit Reporting

Reporters, employees of the exchange, are located at the rostrums or pulpits adjacent to each pit, and record the times and prices of bids and offers. At major exchanges, prices are electronically recorded and displayed on a large board above the trading floor. Simultaneously, prices are widely disseminated off the trading floor by ticker tape and directly to electronic market quotation services whose subscribers, in turn, further disseminate the data. Within a few seconds at most, even international customers can learn of the prices bid in each pit.

Electronic Wallboard Display

Electronic boards generally display price, volume, and open interest data within view of traders in the pits. For example, Figure 2.5 shows a section of the board at the Chicago Mercantile Exchange. For each contract type, by delivery date, the board shows, from top to bottom:

1. *The opening range*: the lowest price and the highest price at the opening of the market. If only one price was recorded during the open, the space for the opening high is left blank.

2. *The high for the day*: the highest price (trade or bid) recorded during the day up to the current time.

3. *The low for the day*: the lowest price (trade or offer) of the day up to the current time.

4. *Estimated volume*: an estimate of the trading volume, in contracts, during the day up to the current time.

5. *The most recent seven prices recorded before the last recorded price*: a price followed by "B" is a bid price; a price followed by "A" is an offer (ask price); only prices not followed by "A" or "B" correspond to actual trades.

6. *The last recorded price*: trade, bid, or offer.

7. *Net change*: the difference between the last price and the settlement price of the previous trading day.

8. *Settle*: the settlement price of the previous trading day.

9. *Year high*: the highest price (trade or bid) recorded since the beginning of trade in the contract.

10. *Year low*: the lowest price (trade or offer) recorded since the beginning of trade in the contract.

T–Bills		
	March	June
OPEN	9152	9108
RANGE	9140	
HIGH	9158	9115
LOW	9132A	9102
EST VOL	40442	10876
7	9145	9110B
6	44	11
5	45A	12
4	47	13A
3	49B	12
2	46	11
1	42B	10
LAST	9143	9112B
NET	13+	11+
SETTLE	9130	9101
YR. HI	9285	9212
YR. LO	8992	9004

Figure 2.5   A Sample of the CME Wallboard Display

A member of the *pit committee*, that committee of exchange members in charge of pit trading, may call a *fast market* in a situation of unusually heavy trading activity. During a fast market, it is understood that the information collected or displayed on the board may not be complete or accurate. At these times, only the last four (rather than seven) prices are shown; the places of the fifth, sixth, and seventh prices instead show "FAST."

Computerized Time and Sales Inquiry

Throughout the larger futures exchanges, terminals dispense information on trades sorted by time and price according to the user's request. Such systems, which are essentially data base managers, can also respond to requests for other information.

The Ticker

In addition to the prices of futures transactions, a *ticker tape* reports representative bid and offer prices, as well as an array of other futures and spot market information. The ticker service, provided to subscribers by the exchange for a fee, is usually available in two forms: the traditional paper tape or an electronic wall display. Certain subscribers receive, store, manipulate, or retransmit ticker data in machine-readable form. Ticker information is usually reported by contract type according to a symbol. Recent ticker symbols of the Chicago Board of Trade, for example, are shown in Table 2.2.

TABLE 2.2   Some Recent CBOT Ticker Symbols

Contract Type	Ticker Symbol
Wheat	W
Iced Broilers	IB
Corn	C
Silver	AG
Oats	O
Treasury Notes	TN
Soybeans	S
Western Plywood	PW
Kilo Gold	KI
30-Day Commercial Paper	RP
Treasury Bonds	US
Soybean Meal	SM
Soybean Oil	BO
Ten-Year Treasury Notes	TY
Major Market Index	MX

For ticker purposes, the delivery month is appended to the contract symbol, as illustrated in Figure 2.6a, which displays a sample of the CBOT tape showing Treasury bond futures prices for December delivery in the current year (month symbol Z from Table 2.1). The number 84.25 indicates a futures price of 84 and 25/32 percent of the $100,000 face value of the deliverable grade bond. (The deliverable grade bond and substitutions are described in Chapter 9.) The time of the quote is indicated on this sample by the appearance of 1107.00 for 11:07:00 (a.m.). Quantities traded are not reported. Errors in previous quotations are corrected on the tape by symbols indicating revision, as in Figure 2.6b. During periods of heavy trading volume, the ticker may fall behind; this is referred to as a "late tape."

A *spread*, also known as a *straddle*, is the simultaneous, or nearly simultaneous, purchase of one contract and sale of another, and is typically made with the intention of exploiting relative price movements between the two contracts. An *interdelivery spread*, for example, involves two delivery dates for the same contract type; an *intercommodity spread* involves two contract types. Spread transactions are reported on the CBOT ticker using the convention illustrated in Figure 2.6c, where an interdelivery spread of Treasury

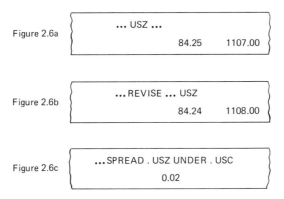

Figure 2.6   Sample Ticker Display

bonds for the current December and following March delivery dates is shown with the indicated price differential; the December contract is shown at a futures price 2/32 under that of the March contract.

Spot market reports are carried on the ticker on a regular schedule, providing such data as prices; deliveries against futures contracts; inventories, receipts, and shipments of commodities at various geographical points; and crop reports of the U.S. Department of Agriculture. Throughout the day, the ticker sporadically carries other news of potential interest to subscribers and traders, such as the timing of upcoming reports and changes in contract specifications or trading rules.

At the end of a trading session the ticker provides a series of reports summarizing the day's trading results in each contract. These include the settlement price, volume of trade, and open interest. The post-session reports also include price limits for the next trading day and errors in previous reports.

Video Monitors

Located throughout the trading floor of large modern exchanges are video monitors showing different selections of information from the ticker and the electronic wallboard display. These monitors are intended to feed traders' needs for fast current information on conditions in related markets.

Newspaper Quotations

Major newspapers carry futures quotations, though they do not list some of the newest or least active contracts. In order to promote trade in unlisted contracts, exchanges often advertise quotations at their own expense. A typical section of futures quotations from a recent issue of *The Wall Street Journal* is shown in Figure 2.7. By contract, the listings show the opening price, daily high, daily low, settlement price, change in settlement price from the previous trading day, highest settlement price to date for the contract, lowest price to date, and open interest of the previous trading day. The estimated volume of trade for each contract type, totaled over all delivery months, is also shown, along with the total volume and open interest for the previous trading day.

3. ORDERS

A *futures order* is an instruction by a customer of a futures commodity merchant (FCM) to a representative of the FCM to buy or sell futures contracts. The representative of the FCM must be licensed as an *associated person* (AP), known in the past as a *registered representative*. We briefly review order placement and the various types of orders.

Order Information and Placement

A typical *market order*, a request to buy or sell a given number of a particular futures contract at the best price available at the time the order reaches the pit, is illustrated in Figure 2.4. As indicated in the figure, the representative of the FCM might place the following information on the multipart order form:

1. The exchange at which the order is to be filled.

2. The *action code*, such as buy (BUY), sell (SL), cancel (CXL), or cancel a former order (CFO), which generally means to cancel only some part of a former order (as opposed to CXL for a complete order cancellation).

3. The *quantity*, an integer number of contracts (or, for certain contract types, a number of units, such as "10,000," or "10M" for 10,000 bushels of wheat).

4. The *contract description*, stating both contract type and delivery date by month, such as "December T-Bills."

5. The *futures price*, or in the case of a market order, "MKT," to indicate "at the market," meaning at the best available price.

6. The *execution instructions* (to be discussed with our classification of order types).

COMMODITY FUTURES PRICES

Tuesday, November 29, 1988

Open Interest Reflects Previous Trading Day.

-GRAINS AND OILSEEDS-

CORN (CBT) 5,000 bu.; cents per bu.

	Open	High	Low	Settle	Change	Lifetime High	Lifetime Low	Open Interest
Dec	257	259	251¾	256¾	- ½	370	184	36,165
Mr89	266½	268¾	262	267	+ ¼	370	193½	112,856
May	271½	273½	267½	272¼	+ ¾	369	207½	36,659
July	273¼	275	270	274¼	+ 1	360	233	21,931
Sept	259½	260¾	256½	258½	- ¼	317¾	245	4,831
Dec	252½	255¾	252	253½	....	295	234	15,606
Mr90	261	261	258	258½	....	270	257½	276

Est vol 55,000; vol Mon 76,016; open int 228,324, -3,324.

FLAXSEED (WPG) 20 metric tons; Can. $ per ton

	Open	High	Low	Settle	Change	Lifetime High	Lifetime Low	Open Interest
Dec	358.50	363.50	354.00	359.90	- 1.10	482.00	242.10	3,936
Mr89	367.50	373.00	363.00	370.50	....	485.00	266.00	4,573
May	....	....	....	371.20	- 3.80	490.00	372.20	1,599
July	377.00	378.00	370.50	372.00	- 4.50	492.00	370.50	301
Oct	351.00	353.50	345.00	353.50	+ 3.50	394.50	345.00	403
Dec	348.00	350.00	342.50	350.00	+ 3.00	434.00	342.50	432

Est vol 1,170; vol Mon 1,002; open int 11,244, +35.

RAPESEED (WPG) 20 metric tons; Can. $ per ton

	Open	High	Low	Settle	Change	Lifetime High	Lifetime Low	Open Interest
Jan	331.00	334.00	323.30	328.90	- 2.20	486.70	291.80	12,170
Mar	338.00	340.50	330.10	336.30	- 2.00	489.50	300.70	9,244
June	349.00	349.50	339.50	346.00	- 1.10	490.00	339.30	2,630
Sept	353.00	354.50	349.00	354.50	- 1.30	390.50	349.00	1,250
Nov	355.00	357.50	352.00	356.30	- 3.70	482.00	261.80	2,366

Est vol 2,260; vol Mon 2,353; open int 27,660, +173.

WHEAT (WPG) 20 metric tons; Can. $ per ton

	Open	High	Low	Settle	Change	Lifetime High	Lifetime Low	Open Interest
Nov	156.80	156.80	154.50	154.50	- 2.70	169.00	94.40	33
Dec	152.50	153.10	149.50	151.10	- 2.20	167.00	94.00	2,899
Mr89	157.50	158.50	156.50	157.00	- .50	170.50	103.50	7,723
May	158.00	158.50	156.70	157.00	- .10	168.50	135.50	3,104
July	156.50	158.00	156.30	156.30	- .20	166.50	144.30	802
Oct	....	....	....	149.50	....	152.00	151.00	342

Est vol 2,860; vol Mon 1,209; open int 19,403, +98.

RYE (WPG) 20 metric tons; Can. $ per ton

	Open	High	Low	Settle	Change	Lifetime High	Lifetime Low	Open Interest
Dec	152.30	152.30	147.30	147.30	- 5.00	194.50	140.00	611
Mr89	157.30	157.30	154.00	154.00	- 3.30	178.00	149.90	1,612
May	157.00	157.00	157.00	157.00	- 3.00	171.50	156.00	424

Est vol 900; vol Mon 159; open int 2,652, -69.

-LIVESTOCK & MEAT-

CATTLE-FEEDER (CME) 44,000 lbs.; cents per lb.

	Open	High	Low	Settle	Change	Lifetime High	Lifetime Low	Open Interest
Jan	82.65	82.75	82.22	82.70	+ .25	85.05	74.00	4,889
Mr89	82.00	82.10	81.32	81.75	+ .07	83.85	74.00	4,527
Apr	81.35	81.35	80.67	80.95	....	82.90	74.40	1,225
May	79.85	79.85	79.37	79.67	+ .05	81.80	76.00	1,097
Aug	78.60	78.62	78.25	78.62	- .02	80.25	77.50	369

Est vol 1,648; vol Mon 1,240; open int 12,142, +22.

CATTLE-LIVE (CME) 40,000 lbs.; cents per lb.

	Open	High	Low	Settle	Change	Lifetime High	Lifetime Low	Open Interest
Dec	73.55	73.62	72.90	73.10	- .17	75.50	60.25	19,033
Fb89	73.75	73.75	72.85	73.10	- .47	75.60	65.10	30,188
Apr	74.50	74.65	74.05	74.17	- .25	76.47	67.20	18,506
June	72.85	72.90	72.35	72.50	- .30	75.20	68.75	5,660
Aug	70.70	70.80	70.30	70.47	- .30	73.20	69.62	4,984
Oct	69.45	69.80	69.35	69.37	- .10	74.00	68.90	1,384

Est vol 19,729; vol Mon 17,743; open int 79,763, -1,910.

-METALS & PETROLEUM-

COPPER-STANDARD (CMX)-25,000 lbs.; cents per lb.

	Open	High	Low	Settle	Change	Lifetime High	Lifetime Low	Open Interest
Dec	151.80	154.50	151.00	153.50	- 1.30	158.50	64.70	11,658
Mr89	131.60	133.50	130.10	133.00	+ .70	133.70	66.50	17,728
May	120.55	123.00	119.00	122.50	+ 1.50	123.00	73.15	2,737
July	114.80	119.00	114.50	119.00	+ 4.00	119.00	76.00	1,469
Sept	112.50	112.50	112.50	116.00	+ 3.30	113.00	76.00	529
Dec	108.70	113.00	108.70	113.00	+ 3.30	113.00	77.45	1,008

Est vol 10,000; vol Mon 12,068; open int 35,256, +49.

GOLD (CMX)-100 troy oz.; $ per troy oz.

	Open	High	Low	Settle	Change	Lifetime High	Lifetime Low	Open Interest
Dec	423.00	424.70	421.20	421.90	- 1.40	546.00	395.50	34,638
Fb89	427.50	429.30	426.50	427.10	- .80	549.50	401.00	37,876
Apr	433.00	434.40	431.40	432.50	- .70	550.00	407.00	13,489
June	439.30	440.20	437.70	438.10	- .70	570.00	412.00	22,385
Aug	443.90	443.90	443.90	444.00	- .70	575.00	419.30	9,425
Oct	....	....	....	449.90	- .60	575.50	423.00	10,340
Dec	456.50	457.50	455.10	455.70	- .50	514.50	428.00	13,153
Fb90	....	....	....	461.50	- .50	516.00	439.70	4,329
Apr	....	....	....	467.40	- .50	525.80	443.00	2,592
June	....	....	....	473.30	- .50	497.00	447.00	2,124
Aug	....	....	....	479.40	- .50	481.50	453.00	1,055

Est vol 75,000; vol Mon 79,514; open int 151,427, -930.

EXCHANGE ABBREVIATIONS
(for commodity futures and futures options)

CBT-Chicago Board of Trade; CME-Chicago Mercantile Exchange; CMX-Commodity Exchange, New York; CRCE-Chicago Rice & Cotton Exchange; CTN-New York Cotton Exchange; CSCE-Coffee, Sugar & Cocoa Exchange, New York; IPEL-International Petroleum Exchange of London; KC-Kansas City Board of Trade; MCE-MidAmerica Commodity Exchange; MPLS-Minneapolis Grain Exchange; NYM-New York Mercantile Exchange; PBOT-Philadelphia Board of Trade; WPG-Winnipeg Commodity Exchange.

Figure 2.7　A Section of the Future's Page of *The Wall Street Journal*

7. The *order duration*, the period of time during which the order may be filled (also to be discussed with order types).

8. The customer's *account number*.

9. The initials of, or some other code for, the AP of the FCM.

An order is generally handled in the following sequence:

1. The customer communicates the order, perhaps by telephone, to the

FCM.

2. A representative of the FCM (usually the associated person) fills out an *order ticket*, containing basically the same information as an order form.

3. The associated person or some other FCM employee *time stamps* the order ticket and transmits (by phone, teletype, or other electronic means) the order information to the desk of the FCM on the trading floor of the relevant exchange (or, if the FCM is not an exchange member, to the desk of a member FCM).

4. A floor representative of the FCM places the order information on an order form, time stamps the order form, and relays the order, often by floor messenger, to a floor broker trading for the FCM in the appropriate pit.

5. The floor broker, or an assigned employee at the edge of the pit, places the order into his or her *order deck* (the batch of orders to be filled) and the floor broker takes the appropriate trading action.

6. At execution, the floor broker records on the order form the price, the quantity (if a partial execution), and the FCM and broker of the opposite side of the trade, and then relays the order form back to the FCM desk.

7. The FCM desk again time stamps the order form and telephones or otherwise transmits the execution information back to the customer's local FCM office, where the information is in turn relayed to the FCM's associated person and the customer.

The entire sequence can take as little as a minute to complete. Despite often hectic conditions and high transactions volumes, errors are uncommon. Discrepancies between the buying and selling traders' execution records are handled by the *out order* procedure at the clearing stage, to be described later in the chapter. Errors in handling an order—for example, failure to execute a market order near the best available price at the time the order is stamped— are corrected if necessary by an exchange regulated procedure. When trades occur in the same contract almost simultaneously, but at different locations in the pit at different prices, this does not necessarily imply a broker error, especially during a period of hectic trading.

Order Types

Futures orders fall into categories according to:

1. Price reservations
2. Execution qualifications
3. Time qualifications

The simplest form of price reservation is, of course, no reservation at all, which characterizes a *market order.* Various forms of price reservations, some of which are not accepted at certain exchanges, are listed below.

> *Limit.*   A limit order is indicated by placing a specific price on the order form without further price qualification. A limit order must be executed at the stated price, or one more favorable (lower for buys, higher for sells), or not executed at all. For example, Figure 2.8 shows a limit order to sell 100,000 bushels of wheat for May delivery at a price of $3.10 per bushel or higher. As with any order having a price reservation, there is no guarantee that the order will be executed even if trades occur at more favorable prices after the order is placed, since the price may quickly move adversely immediately after crossing the limit.

AJAX COMMODITIES—ORDER FORM						
Exchange: CBOT					Order No.: A187057	
CXL	BUY	Quant.	Month	Commodity	Price	Qualification
CXL	SL	Quant.	Month	Commodity	Price	Qualification
	X	100 M	MAY	WHEAT	3.10	

Special Instructions:	Duration:
Account No.: 36254-7 Customer Name: John Poor Associated Person: 15	Execution Price: $3.10\frac{1}{4}$

Figure 2.8   A Sample Limit Order

> *Market-if-touched.*   A market-if-touched price reservation, which is indicated by placing *MIT* on the order form, requests execution at

the best available price after a trade occurs at a price at least as favorable as the price shown on the order. In effect, an MIT order becomes a market order at this time, and may be executed above or below the price reservation. An *MIT order* is sometimes called a *board order*.

Stop.   A stop order, also known as a stop-loss order, is signaled by the letters *STOP* on the order form, and calls for execution at the best available price as soon as a bid or offer occurs at a price at least as unfavorable as the price reservation indicated on the order (above the stop price for a buy, below for a sell). Again, a stop order simply becomes a market order after a price level is hit. As opposed to an MIT order, however, a stop order is activated at a bid or offer, whether or not a trade occurs. As a further distinction, an MIT price reservation to buy is below the prices of current trades (above to sell), while the price reservation for a stop order to buy is above the current market price range (below to sell). Generally speaking, a stop order is often designed to limit the loss that a customer (perhaps already holding a contract position) would incur from unfavorable price movements.

Stop-limit.   A stop-limit order is an order that becomes a limit order (with a given limit price reservation) as soon as a trade, bid, or offer occurs at a price that is equal to or less favorable than the stop price indicated on the order. That is, as with a stop order, the price reservation is above the current market for a buy order, and below current prices for a sell order. For example, a stop-limit order to sell at 108.00 with a stop of 109.00 becomes a limit order to sell at 108.00 once a trade or offer is made at or below 109.00. Such an order is illustrated in Figure 2.9. If the stop and limit prices of a stop-limit order are the same, the order is sometimes called a *stop-and-limit order.*

Discretionary.   A discretionary order, also known as a *market-not-held* or *DRT* (*disregard tape*) order, is treated by the filling broker as a market order, except that the execution of the order may be delayed at the broker's discretion in an attempt to obtain a better price for the customer.

A *contingent order* requests execution contingent on price limits in other

AJAX COMMODITIES—ORDER FORM							
Exchange: **CBOT**					Order No.: **A187088**		
CXL	BUY	Quant.	Month	Commodity	Price	Qualification	
CXL	SL	Quant.	Month	Commodity	Price	Qualification STOP LIMIT
	X	**2**	**DEC**	**T-BOND**	**108.00**	**109.00**	
Special Instructions:					Duration:		
Account No.: **36482-1** Customer Name: **Helen Smith** Associated Person: **12**					Execution Price: **108.03**		

Figure 2.9   A Sample Stop-Limit Order

contracts, on execution of other orders submitted as part of a group, or on other events.

There are several forms of time qualifications. By default, an order is a *day order* unless otherwise specified, which means that the order expires automatically at the end of the trading day. A *time-of-day* order, alternatively, specifies execution at a specific time or interval of time. If a time is entered on the order form under *duration*, the order is effective until that time, and not afterward. Such an order is often called an *off-at-a-specific-time order*. One can also indicate that the order is in effect until the end of the trading week (or month) by entering "week" (or "month") on the order form under duration. An *open order*, also known as a *good-till-canceled (GTC)* order, is in effect until executed, or until the end of trading in the contract. At the other extreme, a *fill-or-kill (FOK)* order (also called an *immediate-or-cancel* or *quick order*) must be executed when received, if at all. A common time qualification is *on-the-open* (or *on-the-close*), which calls for execution at a price in the opening range (or closing range). A limit order can be automatically converted to a *market order on the close*, if not already executed, by adding the qualification *"MOC"* to the order.

In addition to the above-mentioned qualifications for single order execution, there are various ways to submit a *combination order*, a group of orders with mutual qualifications. For example, an *alternative order* is a group of orders coupled with the instruction that execution of any single order in the group automatically cancels the remainder of the group. Alternative orders are also known as *one-cancels-the-others* (OCO). As discussed earlier, a *spread order* is a pair of orders: one to buy, one to sell. A spread can be made as a market order, or with a price limit based on the difference of the two contract prices. For example, "June 4 cents over" on a June–September interdelivery spread order (to buy corn for June delivery and sell for September delivery) indicates execution whenever the September price exceeds the June price by 4 cents per bushel. A *switch order* is a spread order instigated by a previous position. For example, a customer holding a long position in the nearby West German mark contract may wish to replace this position as the contract approaches delivery with a long position in the next contract to deliver, which would call for selling the nearby contract and buying the "next out."

A *scale order* is an order for a series of buys or sells at staggered prices; for example, 50 contracts, made up of 10 contracts at each 4-cent interval from an initial limit price or market order price.

Finally, we recall that a *cancel order*, sometimes called a *straight cancel order* or *CXL*, completely cancels a previously given order. A *CFO* (cancel former order) replaces a previous order with an order that differs in some regard, say the limit price.

4. CLEARING PROCEDURES

Aside from its role in collecting and paying margins, which is described in detail in Chapter 3, a clearinghouse performs a complex array of tasks, some of which are summarized in this section. The clearinghouse is also responsible for organizing the delivery process, which is described in Section 2.5.

Clearing and Out Trades

At the end of each trading session, every exchange member that is not a clearing member must submit trades made during the day to a clearing member for clearing. Clearing members then submit their own trades and those of their clearing customers to the clearinghouse, usually in some machine readable form. To *clear* a trade is merely to make a record of it and to ensure that there is a matching record of an opposite trade. If the trade is cleared, the responsible clearing member is obligated to the clearinghouse for performance of the contract, and must ensure against failure to meet this obligation by submitting margin payments, as was explained briefly in Chapter 1 and will be explained in more detail in Chapter 3. If a trade is not cleared because of a discrepancy, it is termed an *out trade*, and is reported to the appropriate clearing members for *reconciliation*. There are usually several rounds of out trade reconciliation, each round handling any out trades remaining from the previous round. Clearing members resolve most out trades on the first round by reexamining records and interviewing traders, finding perhaps a clerical error or a misunderstanding between traders at the time of execution in the pits. A trader or FCM may voluntarily suffer the cost of an error by accepting the transaction at the price and quantity presumed to be correct. Each exchange has its own judicial procedures, such as arbitration, for settling out trades that are not voluntarily settled in this manner. After a sufficient number of rounds of clearing, the total of all clearing members' contract positions is theoretically zero, although individual clearing members generally have nonzero total positions. In the event that electronic trading is adopted, the clearing procedure is likely to occur simultaneously with order execution, and difficulties arising from out trades should be rare.

Clearing members pay a *clearance fee* to the clearinghouse for each contract cleared. Clearance fees are generally held in a *surplus fund*, which can be applied to cover any defaults by clearing members.

The Guarantee Fund

Once a contract has been cleared, the clearing member is responsible for meeting margin payments due on the position, as explained in Chapter 3. Should the member default on margin obligations, and if all means of obtaining payment from the member eventually fail, the clearinghouse is responsible for covering the default from its own sources of funds.

In addition to the protection against default offered by margins and the surplus fund of clearance fees, a clearinghouse requires its members to post a bond guaranteeing their performance. These bonds are maintained in a *guarantee fund*, which is used only to cover the defaults of members. If a member fails to meet its obligations, the clearinghouse closes out all of that member's positions on the exchange. Any deficit is first covered by the member's margin account, then by the member's guarantee bond, then by the surplus fund, and finally by the guarantee fund of all members according to a contractual assessment formula. Depending on the circumstances, a clearing member can be liable to the extent of its entire net worth. In some cases, large brokerage houses insulate themselves from the default risk associated with their futures operations by incorporating their futures brokerages as separate legal and financial entities. This practice, of course, is frowned upon by those houses that do not follow it, since one member's default can eventually contribute to another's liability.

5. DELIVERY

Although only a small fraction of futures positions are actually delivered upon, the great majority being closed out before delivery, it is only the potential for delivery that gives a specific value to a contract. In Chapter 9 we examine some of the considerations involved in designing a futures contract. It is enough to say here that the delivery provisions should be precise, and the market for the deliverable spot market assets sufficiently large and liquid, to inhibit price *manipulation*. Although manipulation is illegal, it is difficult to detect and prove in a court of law, and perhaps best limited by careful contract design.

Although the clearinghouse is not responsible for guaranteeing that any positions remaining at the delivery date actually meet their delivery obligations, it does handle the distribution of delivery notices, using procedures to be explained shortly.

Delivery Options

A futures contract's delivery provisions specify:

1. The range of deliverable spot market assets, often providing price discounts by grade according to a contractual formula.
2. A range of delivery times, usually within the *delivery month* (the month of the last trading day).
3. A range of delivery locations, again with price discounts according to location.

With some exceptions, the contract generally leaves the selection of the various delivery options up to the seller (the short position holder, or short), since the buyer (the long) could otherwise exploit the "thinness" (that is, lack of suitable quantities or market activity) of certain delivery combinations. Economics often dictate that the seller, on the other hand, will find that the cheapest delivery is made in the "thickest" (or most liquid) spot market, which is thereby less subject to manipulation. Delivery options receive more attention in Chapter 9.

Delivery Notices

From the *first notice day* until the *last notice day*, dates specified in each futures contract, any individual or firm holding a short position in the contract may submit to the clearinghouse a *notice of intention to deliver*, usually via the FCM. This delivery notice states the number of contracts and the various options chosen by the seller: grade, place, and day. The delivery day is usually set contractually as the first or second business day after the submission date of the delivery notice.

If the holder of a long position has not notified the FCM before the first notice day of an intention to accept delivery, the FCM generally reserves the right (since it has guaranteed performance on its customers' positions) to close out the customer's position or to accept delivery for the customer's account. An FCM generally requires those still holding short positions on the day before the last trading day of the contract to communicate their intent: to deliver or to close out the position. The last notice day is typically the last trading day or a business day shortly thereafter. The delivery provisions of the Chicago Board of Trade U.S. Treasury Bond contract are reviewed in Chapter 9 as an extensive example.

Handling Delivery Notices

Each delivery notice received by the clearinghouse is issued to a long FCM (one whose total position, including those of its customers and itself, is long) chosen by a convention that varies by exchange, such as oldest long positions first, or *pro rata* on the basis of size of open positions. An FCM receiving delivery notices from the clearinghouse in turn issues notices to long customers according to its convention, usually oldest positions first. There is no option here; those who receive notices must accept them. A delivery notice is either *transferable* or *nontransferable*, as specified in the futures contract. The receiver of a transferable notice is permitted to sell the deliverable by endorsement and transfer of the notice (which is in effect a claim to the deliverable) to another long within a specified period of time, usually set at one half hour . If the notice is not transferred within the specified time, the notice is *stopped*, that is, considered to be accepted by the long, who then takes delivery. *Taking delivery* merely means accepting a receipt for the goods from the warehouse or agent specified by the short, in return for immediate payment directly to the short (who is informed of the long's identity by the clearinghouse) at a price set by the terms of the contract, such as the previous day's futures settlement price, as adjusted for substitutions, location, and so on.

The receiver of a nontransferable notice cannot transfer the notice immediately (and must thereby pay any warehousing costs until the goods are received or resold). The receiver does have the option, however, to itself issue a delivery notice to the clearinghouse after the trading session ends. The clearinghouse then handles the retendered notice as usual. By *retendering* the notice in this fashion, the receiver maintains a futures position until the retendered notice is stopped.

There are exceptions to these procedures. For example, certain financial futures contracts allow the buyer (the long) to initiate delivery by notifying the clearinghouse, whereupon a seller is selected from the shorts to make delivery.

In summary, a short futures position is generally settled by offset or by issuing a delivery notice and making delivery, tendering a warehouse receipt for the deliverable assets (or tendering the assets themselves) to the buyer designated by the clearinghouse. A long futures position is generally settled only by offset or by accepting a delivery notice and paying the seller for the received goods as specified in the contract. The FCM and (if different) its clearing member are contractually obliged to ensure that all positions they maintain for themselves or their customers are settled as specified above. Finally, the clearinghouse organizes the delivery process.

Cash Settlement

For some contracts, delivery is made "in cash" rather than by delivering any particular commodity or financial instrument. Indeed, for some contracts (for example, a claim to some dollar amount based on an economic index such as a price deflator), there is no deliverable! An example is the U.S. Dollar Index contract of the FINEX division of the New York Cotton Exchange. In some cases, cash settlement has been adopted in order to reduce the potential for manipulation. For *cash delivery* (also known as *cash settlement*), any position that is not offset must be settled by federal funds wire transfer (or in some cases by certified check) in the amount specified by the contract.

EXERCISES

2.1 For this problem, refer to the financial press for actual data, taking "today" to be the first Wednesday after the exercise is assigned.

(a) Fill out a limit order (on an Ajax Commodities order form supplied with the assignment) to sell 10 U.S. Treasury bond futures contracts with nearest delivery possible, with a limit price of yesterday's (Tuesday's) settlement price.

(b) If the above order was submitted today, how far would the price have had to move from today's opening price (and in which direction) for there to have been a chance of filling the order? Would it actually have been filled at all? Assume "perfect" execution.

(c) How many U.S. Treasury bond futures contracts, of any delivery date, were held short on the Chicago Board of Trade between the close on Tuesday and the open on Wednesday? The futures price represents the percentage (in whole numbers and the multiples of $\frac{1}{32}$) of the $100,000 face value of the deliverable U.S. Treasury bond. What is the dollar value of the gain (or loss) for the short side of the nearby contract represented by the change from Tuesday's settlement price to Wednesday's opening price? Is it a gain or loss?

NOTES

Some material for this section was gathered informally from industry sources. The *Commodity Trading Manual* of the Chicago Board of Trade, Feduniak and Fink (1988), and Horn and Farah (1979), were all extremely useful in tying things together. The *INTEX User's Guide* can be consulted for the operating procedures of this electronic exchange. The *Clearing House Manual of the Chicago Mercantile Exchange* was useful as an example of clearinghouse procedures. Trading on Canadian futures markets is reviewed by Hore (1985). A critique of proposals to switch from open outcry to electronic trading is offered by Grossman and Miller (1986b). The institutional arrangements of futures markets are, of course, always subject to change. The mailing addresses of the major exchanges are given in Appendix 9E. Most of the exchanges will provide contract specifications.

The "Report on Exchanges of Futures for Physicals" prepared by the Division of Trading and Markets of the CFTC in October, 1987, was extremely useful in the preparation of Appendix 2A. The workings of the interbank foreign exchange market, reviewed in Appendix 2B, are described in more detail in Tygier (1988). The review of public futures funds given in Appendix 2C draws from Irwin and Brorsen (1985) as well as Elton, Gruber, and Rentzler (1987, 1988).

Appendix 2A: Exchange For Physicals

Section 4c(a) of the Commodity Exchange Act prohibits prearranged or noncompetitive prices in the exchange of futures contracts, but provides for a major exception: an *exchange for physicals (EFP)*. An EFP is also known as an *exchange against actuals (AA)*, *exchange of cash for futures*, *cash commodity for futures*, *versus cash*, *ex-pit*, or, in a variation of the procedure, *on-call*. The term used varies mainly according to the commodity being traded.

The basic EFP involves a spot market trade between two agents who also have previously established futures positions as hedges against their spot commitments. It is not desirable, of course, to leave the futures positions open once the spot trade has eliminated the commitments to be hedged. Rather than offsetting their respective futures positions by a normal trade in the futures pit, the long's position is instead sold to the short by direct negotiation outside of the pit, thereby offsetting both futures positions. The trade is executed merely by notifying the clearinghouse of the quantity and futures price negotiated by the two agents.

Example: The EFP is an especially popular form of effective delivery for the light sweet crude oil contract of the New York Mercantile Exchange (NYMEX). According to the CFTC's *Report on Exchanges of Futures for Physicals* (1987), crude oil EFP volume increased from 5,097 contracts in 1983 to 297,688 contracts in 1986. Although the 1986 figure represented only 3.60 percent of total volume in the contract, the fraction of volume that was settled by the normal delivery provisions of the futures contract in 1986 was merely 0.23 percent.

Suppose, for instance, that Ajax Oil Producers, Inc. (a fictional seller of oil) has stockpiled 100,000 barrels of medium sulfur crude in Galveston, Texas, while Acme Refiners, Inc. (a fictitious oil refinery company) will need to buy 100,000 barrels of this type of oil in June for its refinery at Galveston. Ajax previously hedged its commitment to sell with a short position of 100 NYMEX crude oil futures contracts, each calling for June delivery of 1,000 barrels of West Texas intermediate crude (with substitute grades allowed) in Cushing, Oklahoma. Likewise, Acme is hedged with a long position of 100 in the same contract. Acme and Ajax agree on an EFP of 100,000 barrels. Both report to the NYMEX clearinghouse the quantity and futures price at which Acme sells 100 futures contracts to Ajax. The futures price they negotiate need not be the prevailing futures price in the NYMEX crude oil pit, but must, of course, be within the price limits for the contract. (According to information provided to the CFTC by NYMEX officials, the majority of EFP crude oil futures prices were equal to the settlement price of the day on which the trade is reported.) The clearinghouse processes the trade as usual. The identities of the two traders are not made public, which may be of some strategic advantage. (Indeed, Acme and Ajax may not even have known of one another's identity when the EFP was arranged, since the EFP may have been intermediated by an independent broker.) Simultaneously with the futures trade, Acme buys Ajax's stockpile of 100,000 barrels of crude in Galveston. In some cases, the price for the physical oil might be set in advance at a certain differential (or *basis*) above or below the prevailing futures price, for example the day's settlement futures price for that contract.

It is noteworthy that Acme and Ajax, in effect, were able to obtain or make delivery against their respective futures positions with a different grade of oil than that called for under the terms of their futures contracts, and at a different location. Thus, the EFP effectively extends the flexibility of the contract's delivery provisions. Moreover, both parties could be more confident of the execution of the physical delivery than if the parties to the delivery were chosen by the usual arbitrary manner described in the delivery provisions of the futures contract. The simultaneous nature of the spot and futures transactions of the EFP also allowed Acme and Ajax to avoid the risk that they would otherwise face from changes in the futures price between the time of their spot trade and the time at which they would ultimately execute futures trades offsetting their hedging positions. The advantages of the EFP thus seem reasonably clear.

In some cases, one party to an EFP may not have the exact size of futures position, or indeed any futures position, that offsets the futures position of the other party. In fact, this is especially common in the case of crude oil EFPs, the majority of which involve only one party who originally had a futures position. In such a case, the EFP results in an open futures position for one of the parties. For instance, if Acme's position had been only 90 contracts long, the EFP of 100 contracts could have left Acme with a short futures position of 10 contracts.

EFPs date back at least to 1920, when they were considered an exception to the CBOT rule requiring execution of all futures contracts in the pit. EFPs have been used more recently in markets such as gold and silver as a means of executing arbitrages or obtaining execution of futures trades outside of normal trading hours, especially for transactions involving foreign markets. Since these are not the sorts of transactions that were originally envisioned when the EFP-exception to Section 4c(a) of the Commodity Exchange Act was written, and given the growing popularity of EFPs in many different types of futures markets, EFPs have recently come under more scrutiny by regulators. Since EFPs circumvent the competitive open outcry auction, they are a potential source of market manipulation and may draw some liquidity away from the market. The spot market side of an EFP, moreover, is not required to be verified by the clearinghouse. The study of EFPs undertaken by the CFTC (1987) "did not indicate that widespread abuses of the EFP exception are currently taking place" (p. 257). The report did recommend, however, that the regulations be revised to:

1. Require documentation of the spot market transactions associated with EFPs (p. 261).
2. Establish standards specifying the range of spot market transactions acceptable as the "cash component" of an EFP (p. 262).
3. Establish standards for timely reporting of EFPs (p. 263).
4. Require verification by clearing members of the creditworthiness of customers effecting EFPs (p. 264).

The CFTC report also recommended that the language of the Commodity Exchange Act should be interpreted so as not to allow EFPs on options.

Appendix 2B: The Interbank Market

Although futures contracts are the predominant form of forward agreement for most commodities and financial assets, one of the major exceptions is the market for foreign currencies. The *interbank market*, a network of institutions dominated by commercial banks and linked by brokers and telecommunications networks, is the dominant market for foreign exchange. The interbank market handles both spot and forward transactions in currencies and interest rate instruments.

The interbank market, while it has major geographical centers such as New York, London, and Tokyo, is in reality a global market operating essentially 24 hours per day, mainly via telephone and telex links. The network has an informal hierarchy, with a select group of giant commercial banks forming its backbone. These major banks are linked to each other and to a large group of international banks, which are in turn linked to smaller institutions.

The three major types of traders in the interbank market are:

1. Market makers.
2. Brokers.
3. Clients.

The most active banks act as market makers, willing to quote prices and buy or sell on demand. Market makers deal with one another directly or via brokerage houses, which earn commissions and depend largely on market makers (banks) for price quotes. Clients, the customers of the interbank market, are corporations (including some banks) who call on the banks for quotes but do not reciprocate themselves. Some corporations that are heavily involved in international business operate their own currency trading operations, acting much as other (bank) market makers.

Trading operations in the interbank market take place in the *trading rooms*, also known as *dealing rooms*, of the major participants. A dealing room may have trading desks dedicated to spot, forward, and options trading, usually under the direction of a chief dealer. Individual dealers in each group have responsibility for certain currencies, and generally must maintain positions within designated limits. A back office handles a wide variety of support operations involved with processing trades and maintaining accounts.

Prices are quoted on a *bid-ask* basis. For example, if the Deutsche mark is currently trading at around 1.8140 Deutsche marks per U.S. dollar, a quote of "36–46" means that the dealer is willing to buy at 1.8136 and sell at 1.8146. In providing price quotes, if there is no mention of quantities, the quote is assumed to apply to "normal" amounts, say \$3 million. A quote of "36–46 on 10" would mean that the bid-ask applies for either buying or selling \$10 million worth of marks. A quote of "36–46, 5 by 10" by a broker would mean that the broker is willing to buy \$5 million worth of marks at 1.8136 on behalf of one client and sell \$10 million worth of marks at 1.8146 on behalf of another. A dealer may not wish to quote prices on both sides of the market. For example, "46 I sell 10" would mean that the dealer is willing to sell \$10 million worth of marks at 1.8146. The terminology varies. A bid or offer is accepted by various means. For example, a response to the offer "46 I sell 10" of "mine," or "mine at 46," would imply that the deal is done.

Forward prices are normally quoted for delivery in 1, 2, 3, 6, or 12 months from the current spot date, as opposed to the regular delivery months (March, June, September, and December) of the futures markets. Only special customers can obtain forward interbank quotes at irregular dates. Forward prices are often quoted at differentials from spot quotes. For example, if the quoted spot bid-ask on Deutsche marks is 36-46 (that is, 1.8136 bid, 1.8146 ask) and the six month forward quote is 560-555, the outright bid-ask on 6-month forward Deutsche marks is $1.8136 - 0.0560 = 1.7576$ (bid) and $1.8146 - 0.0555 = 1.7591$ (ask). In this example, it is implicit from previous trades that the forward rate is below the spot rate; if there is any ambiguity, a plus or minus sign is used.

According to a survey conducted every three years by the Federal Reserve Bank of New York and cited by Tygier (1988), total transactions in the United States foreign exchange market by 123 banks in March 1986 averaged approximately \$50 billion per day. Of this, 63 percent was spot trading. Based on very rough calculations using the figures in Table 1.5, that puts the interbank forward foreign exchange market in the U.S. at approximately triple the total size of the U.S. futures markets for foreign currencies. Of course, it is difficult to oblain a precise comparision, especially considering the dramatic changes in activity in both markets over the last few years.

Appendix 2C: Public Futures Funds

As an alternative to taking a futures position directly, one can invest in a *publicly traded futures fund*. Futures funds, also known as *commodity pools* or *commodity funds*, have typically been set up in the United States as limited partnerships, mainly for tax reasons. Subject to SEC approval, however, shares in such a partnership can be publicly offered. According to Irwin and Brorsen (1985), public futures funds have been traded in the U.S. since 1948. Only since 1975, however, have the number and size of active futures funds grown to significant levels. According to Elton, Gruber, and Rentzler (1987), the number of funds for which data are available has grown from only one before 1979 to 94 by 1985. These 94 funds included over \$600 million under management.

Publicly traded futures funds, like other registered mutual funds, are offered by prospectus. The *commodity pool operator* and *commodity trading adviser* (a registered advisor to a futures fund), who are both under the supervision and registration requirements of the CFTC and National Futures

Association, must provide potential investors with at least the three most recent years of performance history in the prospectus. Details regarding the nature and quality of this information are reported by Elton, Gruber, and Rentzler (1988), who find that, based on their extensive sample, the prospectuses of public futures funds are "grossly misleading." The typical prospectus fails to state the performance of the fund had futures commission charges and other transactions costs been included. There is also the problem of selection bias: Those privately held funds which have had unusually good performance, perhaps by random coincidence, are also those that are more likely to go public. Once having gone public, of course, past luck is no advantage.

Elton, Gruber, and Rentzler (1987) report: "Yearly management fees and transactions costs of commodity funds have been estimated to average over 19.2% of assets under management." Based on a statistical analysis of returns, they find it "doubtful that public commodity funds should be included in an investor's portfolio." While the principle of public futures funds may be sound, the record seems to show that they have typically not served public investors well.

3

FUTURES ACCOUNTS

This chapter continues our overview of the institutional structure of futures markets, with the main goal of tracing the cash flows generated by a futures position through the various customer, FCM, and clearing accounts. We also review the standards for journal accounting of futures transactions. By far the most important concept of the chapter is variation margin, the series of resettlement payments that mark futures positions to the most recent settlement price.

1. INTRODUCTION

We proceed first with an informal picture of the cash flows generated by a futures position, elaborating on the brief review given in Section 1.5. Our first pass is merely suggestive of the concepts involved, and is not strictly accurate. Later we correct some false impressions that may have been created concerning actual accounts and transactions.

Forward Contracts versus Futures Contracts

Figure 3.1 illustrates the basic cash flow generated by a forward contract made on December 12, 1988, between agent A and agent B, a contract that obligates A to purchase 1,000 ounces of gold from B on a particular future date, say December 15, 1988, at a particular forward price, say $500 per ounce.

Figure 3.2 shows what the role of the clearinghouse and daily resettlement payments would be if the agreement between agents A and B on December 12 were made instead in the form of a futures contract with delivery on December 15. The clearinghouse (labeled CH) acts as though it is the buyer toward the seller (agent A), and as the seller toward the buyer (agent B). This is known

---

Chapter Outline

---

as the *principle of interposition*, or sometimes as the *principle of substitution*. Rather than paying agent B the full amount due on the delivery date, as in the forward contract shown in Figure 3.1, agent A pays the clearinghouse daily the difference between the previous price to which the account was marked and the new price to which the account is marked. The first price to which the account is marked is the original execution price, $500 per ounce in this example. The next price to which the account is marked is the first new settlement price, in this case the settlement price on December 12, $495 per ounce. The difference, $500 − $495 = $5 per ounce, is due the day after the account is marked to the new price. Thus, on December 13, agent A must pay the clearinghouse 1,000 ounces multiplied by $5 per ounce, or $5,000. After this payment, there is essentially no further distinction between agent A's position and any other long position of the same size. Since all positions established by the end of trading on December 12 have been marked to the

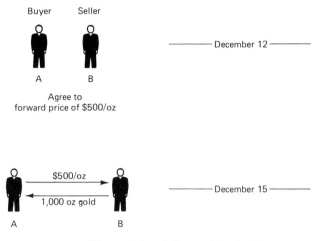

Figure 3.1   A Forward Contract

December 12 settlement price, it is as though all positions were executed at this price, $495. With this idea in mind, one says that all futures positions are *marked to market*.

Likewise, the resettlement payment due to the clearinghouse from agent A on December 14 is the drop from $495 per ounce to the December 13 settlement price of $491 per ounce, or $4 per ounce. Such a payment from an agent to the clearinghouse is known as a *pay*. On December 15, however, agent A should receive the $6 increase in settlement price from $491 to $497 per ounce on December 14. This amount due from the clearinghouse is a *collect*. Finally, on the delivery date of the contract, December 15, the futures price settles at $498, which generates two new transactions involving agent A. First, the clearinghouse must make a final resettlement payment on December 16 to agent A of $1 per ounce, the last increase in settlement price. Second, agent A must accept delivery of 1,000 ounces of gold from agent B at the final settlement price of $498 per ounce. All of these transactions, the resettlement pays and collects as well as the delivery, are depicted in Figure 3.2, where the corresponding (opposite) transactions involving agent B are also shown. The resettlement payments described here are a simplified version of *variation margin*, one part of a complex system of margins described in the following section.

Since any agent could buy or sell gold on both the futures and spot markets on December 15 for delivery on the same day, the December 15 futures

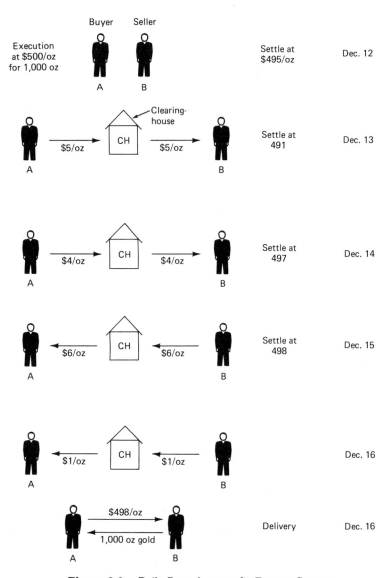

Figure 3.2   Daily Resettlement of a Futures Contract

and spot prices must coincide (neglecting intra-day price movements). If they did not—for example, if the spot price on December 15 were $496 and the futures price were $498— then any agent could buy gold on the spot market on December 15 and sell it immediately on the futures market for an instant risk-free profit of $2 per ounce, contrary to our general assumption that markets cannot clear when arbitrage is possible. We thus have the following general proposition.

Fact: Spot and futures prices coincide at the delivery of the futures contract.

Using this fact, it may appear that the forward agreement shown in Figure 3.1 and the futures contract shown in Figure 3.2 are effectively the same. For both the futures and forward, the net accumulated loss for agent A is the drop of $2 from the original execution price of $500 per ounce to the final spot price of $498 per ounce on December 15. The futures contract and forward contract do not have the same financial effect, however, since the accumulated loss of $2 per ounce on the forward contract is paid all at once on December 15, while the accumulated loss of $2 per ounce on agent A's futures position is collected (or paid) in several daily installments. In Chapter 5 we look more deeply into this distinction between futures and forwards.

Positions: Long and Short

Reviewing the definitions given in Section 1.5, the *position* of any agent in a given futures contract is the cumulative total of contracts purchased minus contracts sold. If the difference is positive (more purchases than sales), the position is said to be *long*; if negative, the position is said to be *short*. In the previous example, agent A held a long position of 1,000 ounces. At 100 ounces per futures contract, this is a long position of 10 contracts. Agent B held a position of −10 contracts, which is also said to be a "short position of 10 contracts." In the industry jargon, agent A is "a long," is "long 10," or "longed 10 contracts"; the word "long" is used as a noun, an adjective, and a verb. Likewise, agent B is a "short," is "short 10," and "shorted ten contracts." Because every contract purchased by one agent must be sold by another, the sum of all positions is always zero, or as it is often expressed, the total of all long positions is equal to the total of all short positions. Recall from Chapter 2 that the total of all long positions in the market is the *open interest*.

Settlement by Offset

To *offset* a futures position is to make a futures trade that eliminates the position. There are only two ways to settle a futures contract, by delivery and by offset. In practice, the vast majority of futures contracts are settled by offset.

In the example illustrated in Figure 3.2, agents A and B settled their futures contracts by holding their positions until the delivery date of the contract, accepting and making delivery, respectively. Either agent could also have settled the contract by offsetting the position at any time before delivery. For example, agent A could have sold 10 futures contracts to agent C on December 13 at a futures price of $494 per ounce. Agent A's account is then marked to this execution price (rather than the December 13 settlement price), causing a final resettlement payment by agent A to the clearinghouse of $1 per ounce on December 14 (the drop from the previous day's settlement price of $495). Agents B and C could have offset their positions on December 14 at a futures price of, say, $495 per ounce, leaving an open interest of zero at delivery time. Exercise 3.1 calls for the complete schedule of daily futures positions and resettlement payments for all three agents in this example.

Even though no deliveries occur in this example, the futures trades may have served a useful role. For example, agent A may have hedged the cost of a commitment to purchase gold on the spot market on December 13. Likewise, agents B and C could have hedged the values of commitments to buy or sell spot gold on December 14.

Because the total market position—total longs less total shorts—is always zero, the total of resettlement pays is always equal to the total of resettlement collects. The clearinghouse therefore always has a net cash flow of zero (unless some agent defaults).

Rather than being offset in its entirety, a futures position can be partially offset, or can even be moved from long to short (or vice versa). If we continue to neglect some of the finer points of resettlement, it should be obvious to the reader that the stream of resettlement cash flows generated by a series of futures transactions on a single account is the same as the total cash flow generated by setting up a separate futures account for each transaction and maintaining all the accounts until they are settled by delivery.

In fact, daily resettlement and delivery procedures are somewhat more complicated than suggested so far, but we shall soon have a more complete story.

2. MARGINS

At the heart of futures market procedures is the system of collateral margins that has evolved as a means to reduce default risks. As opposed to margins on stock accounts, a futures margin payment is not a form of down payment on the balance due. This will be clear if we keep in mind the fact that a futures transaction is not an investment of initial capital in return for a later payoff, but rather, in its purest form, is an agreement made at no initial investment. Margin payments are used as a means of gradually settling the losses and gains on the contract and also as collateral against default. Margin payments are made frequently (usually daily) in small amounts relative to the size of the contract, rather than in one large initial lump sum, so as to preserve the basic character of a futures contract as a forward agreement: deferred payment for deferred delivery. This allows individual agents to take a large market position without committing a large amount of capital. For this reason, futures contracts are considered an extremely highly leveraged instrument relative to most other financial securities. Although high leverage is often associated with financial instability and high default risk, futures markets have a history of financial integrity and low default risk. No U.S. clearinghouse has ever defaulted on its obligations, and there are relatively few defaults by individual traders. This unusual combination of high leverage with low default risk is largely a property of the intricate, multi-tiered, continually adjusting margining system, which we will now look at in more detail.

The Margin Tree

As illustrated in Figure 3.3, the margin system of a futures market is set up like a tree, beginning at the bottom with clearing margins, and extending up through outside customer margins. The system is intended to be fault-tolerant, in the sense that default of required margins on one branch of the tree should not normally affect the other branches. For example, if an outside customer defaults on its margin payments to its FCM, the FCM must still meet its other margin obligations. Figure 3.3 reflects the possibility that one futures account may include positions in several different futures contracts that may be cleared at different clearinghouses.

The futures exchange itself does not appear in the margin tree; the exchange is responsible for providing a marketplace, that is, the facilities for executing trades. In most cases, the clearinghouse is separately incorporated as a means of insulating the exchange from the financial and legal liabilities involved in clearing. The Chicago Mercantile Exchange and the New York Mercantile Exchange, however, currently operate their own clearinghouses as divisions of their exchanges. In addition to the collection and payment of margin to and from its members, the clearinghouse is responsible for several functions described in Chapter 2.

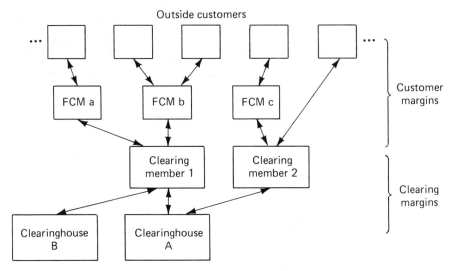

Figure 3.3   The Margin Tree

Clearing Margin Requirements

The performance of a clearing member's obligation to the clearinghouse is ensured mainly by *clearing margin*, deposits held in escrow at approved banks. Clearing margin can typically be deposited in several forms, depending on the rules of the clearinghouse. These include:

1. Cash.
2. Direct obligations of the United States government, such as U.S. Treasury bills, bonds, or notes.
3. Letters of credit from an approved bank.
4. Shares of the clearing corporation.

Clearing margins are of two types:

1. *Original margin*, also called *initial margin*: the initial deposit required whenever a position is opened or increased.
2. *Variation margin*: the daily resettlement payments calculated as in the example given in the previous section.

At the end of each trading day, the clearinghouse reports in a *trade register*, for each contract, the settlement price and the position of each clearing member. Each clearing member must deposit original margin based on its trades during the day, and variation margin to cover adverse price movements on all positions. Generally, variation margin must be deposited in cash on the following morning. The determination of these margins varies by exchange. A simple example seems the easiest way to explain.

Example: Suppose Ajax Commodities, Inc., a (fictional) clearing member, had at the end of a trading session a long position of 150 of a particular contract whose settlement price is $10,000 per contract. At the following trading session, Ajax cleared a long trade of 50 contracts at a futures price of $10,500 per contract. The settlement price was established that day at $10,200 per contract. Suppose also that the original margin for this contract is set at $2,000 per contract. Then Ajax's margin pay at the end of this new trading session is calculated at $50 \times \$2,000 = \$100,000$ in original margin on the newly executed contracts, less $150 \times \$500 = \$75,000$ in variation margin marking the old position to the execution price of $10,500, plus $200 \times \$300 = \$60,000$ in variation marking the new position to the day's settlement price of $10,200, for a total pay of $85,000.

The general recipe is:

$$\text{Net pay} = \text{position size increase} \times \text{original margin per contract}$$

$$+ \text{ Variation on old position to execution price}$$

$$+ \text{ Variation on new position to new settlement price,}$$

where

$$\text{Variation} = \text{contract position} \times (\text{old price} - \text{new price}).$$

Filling in the corresponding numbers from the last example, Ajax Commodities must deposit the net pay:

$$\$85,000 = 50 \times \$2,000$$

$$+ 150 \times (\$10,000 - \$10,500)$$

$$+ 200 \times (\$10,500 - \$10,200).$$

The pay must generally be deposited at the beginning of the following business day. A negative net pay, on the other hand, is called a *collect*, and may be withdrawn by the clearing member. Changing the last example, suppose the trade cleared by Ajax was short 50 contracts instead of long 50 contracts. Because Ajax already had a long position of 150, the new position will be long 100 contracts, which allows a reduction in original margin for 50 contracts. The new calculation, following the same general recipe, yields

$$\text{Net pay} = -50 \times \$2,000 + 150 \times (\$10,000 - \$10,500)$$
$$+ 100 \times (\$10,500 - \$10,200)$$
$$= -\$145,000.$$

In this case, the collect of $145,000 is payable to the clearing member on the following day.

It must be noted that clearing a short trade can also increase the original margin required. For example, had Ajax's previous position in this example been short 150 contracts rather than long, an additional 50 contracts short would bring the position to 200 contracts short, requiring an additional $100,000 in original margin. The size of the position, whether short or long, determines the required original margin.

Example: As of this writing, the Chicago Mercantile Exchange requires margin payments by cash only (via the federal funds wire service) 10 minutes prior to the opening of the first CME market. Margin deposits in excess of $25,000, however, can be replaced (at the discretion of the CME) by U.S. Treasury bills with one year or less to maturity, in multiples of $5,000. If the T-bills are deposited by the clearing member at its settlement bank by 9:00 a.m., the CME instructs the bank to release cash to the clearing member to the extent of the market value of the T-bills, as published in the previous day's *Wall Street Journal*. (The cash is not released until the following morning at 7:00 a.m.) Likewise, for clearing members meeting certain capital requirements, the CME allows clearing margin in excess of $50,000 to be replaced with letters of credit from a CME-approved bank. Like most clearinghouses, the clearing division of the CME handles collects (margin payments due to the clearing member) by transferring cash (usually by the federal funds wire service) to the settlement bank of the clearing member. Each clearinghouse has its own special procedures, which change periodically, but this example of the clearing margin procedures of the CME is typical of the larger exchanges.

During periods of rapid price changes, a clearinghouse may make *variation calls* during the trading session, usually based on members' positions at the end of the previous trading session. At a variation call, a member can be required to pay variation margin within an hour. Original margin can also be changed on short notice, for long positions only, for short only, or for both.

If an individual customer of the clearing member fails to provide the required customer margins set by the clearing member, the clearing member is nevertheless itself obligated to deposit the corresponding clearing margin as set by the clearinghouse. Since it is generally more difficult for a clearing member to receive pays from its customers as quickly as the clearinghouse requires its own pays, the clearing member must have reserve sources of capital, especially during emergencies such as large variation calls.

How is the required original margin deposit per contract determined? The amount is usually specified in dollars per contract, and may be changed on short notice. In principle, the amount is designed to safely cover the potential daily resettlement payments due on one contract. In practice, clearinghouses often use statistical theory to choose an amount that is estimated to be exceeded by price changes over a period of a few days with a specified low probability. Of course, this amount varies widely by contract. The issue is discussed in Chapter 9. The New York Mercantile Exchange, at the time of this writing, set initial clearing margin deposits for its propane gas contract at $550, while the Chicago Mercantile Exchange's most recent margin requirement for the S&P 500 Stock Index contract was set at $15,000, the latter margin level having increased dramatically since the October 19, 1987, stock market crash (described in Appendix 5A). Spread positions are generally allowed lower initial margins since the price risks on the two sides of the spread typically offset one another to some extent.

Gross versus Net Clearing Margin

Clearing margin may be required on either a *gross* or a *net* basis. Gross margining, required by certain clearinghouses, calls for deposits based on the total of all long positions of the clearing member plus the total of all short positions. Net margining, on the other hand, requires deposits based only on the net position of the clearing member. Suppose, for example, that at the end of a given trading day, Ajax Commodities has two clearing customers for a particular futures contract with respective positions of $+100$ and -150. Gross margining would call for margin of 250 contracts multiplied by the margin required per contract. Net margining, on the other hand, would call for deposits based on the clearing member's net (short) position of 50 contracts.

Futures exchanges and the CFTC have rules requiring that a clearing member's own accounts be segregated from customer accounts. In particular, positions on a clearing member's own account must be separately margined. With net margining, for example, if Ajax Commodities also has a long position of 50 contracts on its own account, it must make its margin payments on two separate accounts, a customer account with a net of 50 contracts (short) and a house account with a position of 50 contracts (long). These two accounts cannot be netted to zero for margin purposes.

Although most exchanges use the net margining convention, the Chicago Mercantile Exchange and the New York Mercantile Exchange currently use gross margining. If the required margin per contract were the same whether gross or net margining, the clearing member would obviously prefer to use net margining, since the opportunity cost of the capital committed to margining would be smaller. Of course, the net margin per contract would typically be more than the gross margin per contract, other things being equal.

Customer Margins

Just as a clearing member must maintain margin with the clearinghouse, customers of the member must maintain margin with the clearing member. Here we restrict our attention to the case of margins for an outside customer of an FCM.

As with clearing margin, customer margins are in two forms, original (also called *initial*) margin and variation margin. With few exceptions, variation margin pays may only be made in cash. Original margin can be deposited by the customer in cash or, for large or preferred customers and by negotiation with the FCM, in U.S. Treasury bills or shares of certain corporations (for example, shares traded on the New York Stock Exchange). T-bills are usually accepted in lieu of cash at some fixed fraction of their face value such as 90 percent, while stocks are generally accepted at a smaller fraction of their market value, such as 50 percent.

Although each exchange sets minimum customer margin requirements by contract, an FCM generally sets higher-than-minimum margin requirements for its customers. Based on individual credit ratings, an FCM may then reduce required margins (but not below the exchange minimum) for certain customers. The exchange and FCM may vary required margins according to the nature of the account and the nature of trades, as we shall see.

Maintenance Margin

When a futures position is established, the original margin is placed with the FCM or a designated bank in the name of the customer, in an account regulated by the CFTC and subject to the terms of agreements with the FCM signed by the customer, as discussed in the following section. At the end of each trading session, each customer's positions are marked to the new settlement prices. As with clearing variation margin, each account is in effect credited with favorable price changes and debited with unfavorable price changes. The formula determining customer variation margin, however, is not usually the same simple rule used for clearing margin. Instead, the exchange sets a *maintenance margin* level per contract. Whenever the variation in settlement price brings the margin account below the maintenance level, the customer must pay (in cash) at least the amount necessary to bring the margin account back up to the original margin level per contract. The maintenance margin level is often set at a fixed percentage of the original margin; 75 percent is popular. Thus we can think of clearing margin as determined by the same formula with 100 percent maintenance margins. Even if the deposit made to meet original margin is well in excess of the required original margin, but is not in cash, any variation margin payment must be made in cash. For large customers, cash payments are usually made by the federal funds wire service. Original margin may be required in advance of the establishment of the position, or the day after, depending on the relationship between the FCM and the customer. The FCM must, however, ensure that margins are paid in the timely fashion required to meet CFTC and exchange regulations.

When a margin account drops below the maintenance level, a *variation call* is made by the FCM to the customer, both orally (usually by phone) and in writing. The amount required to bring the position up to the level of original margin is usually due within 24 hours. If, on the other hand, the variation in settlement price is to the favor of the customer position and brings the value of a position above the required original margin, any excess over the original margin may be withdrawn by the customer or used to meet variation pays on other positions.

Example: Suppose a 5,000-ounce silver contract has an initial margin of $2,000 and a maintenance margin of $1,500 per contract. On a given trading day, 10 contracts long are executed for a customer at a price of 500.00 (cents per ounce, or $25,000 per contract). The day's settlement price is 495.00, representing a loss of $2,500 on the position. The initial margin of $20,000 is deposited the next day. The value credited to the margin account is then $20,000 less the $2,500 loss for a net margin level of $17,500, still above the maintenance level of $15,000. Suppose the next day's settlement price is 485.00. If the position is not offset, the margin account is debited $5,000, bringing it to $12,500, which is below the maintenance level. A variation call for $7,500 is then issued. When deposited, the $7,500 returns the margin account to the original level of $2,000 per contract.

Figure 3.4 is a graphical representation of the principles of customer margins explained in the last example. To summarize, these basic principles are:

1. If there is any margin in excess of the required original margin per contract, that excess may be collected by the customer.

2. Whenever the margin account falls below the required maintenance margin per contract, sufficient cash funds to bring the account to the required original margin per contract must be deposited.

3. Each trading day, or even more frequently in some cases, the margin account is credited with the variation (or debited, if the variation is negative).

4. The variation is the contract position multiplied by the change in futures price (new price minus old price), where

   a. the "old" price is the previous settlement price (or execution price, if the position is new), and

   b. the "new" price is the new settlement price (or closeout execution price, if the position is closed out).

Liquidating Margin Calls

Original margin must be paid within the time stipulated by the customer agreement (which cannot, by CFTC regulation, be more than 48 hours from the time the trade is executed). The amount must be deposited even if the position is offset before the original margin is due. Variation calls, on the other hand, need not be paid at all. Instead, a customer can liquidate the relevant position by issuing an offsetting order, which must be executed within 24 hours of the call. Extending the previous margin example, the variation call for $7,500 on the silver position could have been met by a sale the next day of 5 contracts, provided the execution price of the sale was sufficiently high to leave

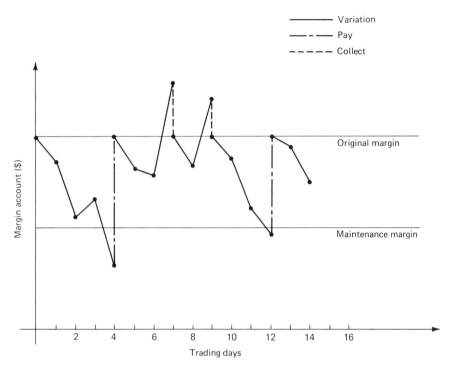

Figure 3.4   Resettlement and Margin Variation

a balance of at least $10,000, the new original margin requirements for the remaining 5-contract position, plus any required margin on other positions.

Sellouts

If a margin call is not met by the required time, the FCM is still responsible to cover the position, and has the right to *sell out* the customer's position by submitting orders in the customer's name, as stated in the customer agreement. The customer must be given *due notification*, and is credited with the proceeds of the liquidated contracts.

Margin Adjustments

There are at least three cases in which margin requirements are typically reduced:

1. Positions for trade accounts
2. Day trades
3. Spread positions

For *trade accounts*, also known as *hedge accounts*, the customer presumably has reduced default risk because of offsetting spot market commitments. An exchange, as well as an FCM, may therefore place lower margin requirements on trade accounts. *Day trades*, those offset on the day executed, often have lower margin requirements. Because a *spread position* in closely related contracts generally represents less than twice the risk of the positions on each side of the spread, lower margin requirements are generally set by exchanges and FCMs on spreads.

Since futures prices for a given contract often become more volatile as the delivery date of the contract approaches, many FCMs increase margin requirements for the nearby contract, or during the delivery month of a contract. Those holding positions prior to the increase in margin requirements are sometimes excused by the FCM from such increases.

3. CUSTOMER ACCOUNTS

Procedures for opening and handling futures accounts for the customers of a futures commission merchant (FCM) are rich with institutional detail and regulatory restriction. We shall review only the basics.

FCMs and Their Associated Persons

The basic function of an FCM, known also as a *commission house, wire house, brokerage house,* or *commodity commission merchant,* is to provide futures transactions services to those without exchange memberships. The FCM places orders, collects and maintains funds, and provides accounting and consulting services, all in return for fees. Each FCM is licensed and regulated by the Commodity Futures Trading Commission (CFTC), as is any *associated person* (AP) (formerly known as a *registered representative*) of an FCM. The AP deals with customers on an individual basis. The CFTC, exchanges, and FCMs all place controls on the relationship between AP and customer, and all stipulate special accounting procedures and documentation. The AP is paid by the FCM according to some combination of salary and commissions, and is not permitted to conduct futures business for any other employer.

Opening an Account

Among the documents designed to protect and inform the FCM, AP, and customers are:

1. The *new account report*, which identifies the customer, credit references, the AP, and account handling details.

2. The *risk disclosure statement*, which the customer signs to acknowledge the risks involved.

3. The *customer agreement*, which gives the customer's authorization for the manner in which the account will be handled; for example, allowing the FCM to make trades so as to maintain proper margin.

4. The *supplemental commodity customer's agreement*, empowering the FCM to transfer between the futures account and other accounts such funds as are needed to maintain margin.

One customer may have several accounts, provided they are mutually guaranteed in writing. The FCM must meet regulations pertaining to customer accounts according to the total positions of each customer. Conversely, one joint account may be set up for several customers, although additional agreements must then be signed indicating the authority of the different customers to initiate trades and providing for disbursements in case of death or incapacity.

A *discretionary account*, also known as a *controlled* or *managed* account, is an account with authorization for trading decisions given to a party other than the customer, for example, the AP. In order to manage a discretionary account, the AP is normally required to obtain the customer's power of attorney. Many exchanges require security deposits, in addition to margin, for discretionary accounts.

A customer, by filing the appropriate documentation, can obtain a *numbered account* for reasons of confidentiality.

Customers may be individuals or corporations. For *corporation accounts*, exchanges generally require a *corporate resolution* authorizing particular employees of the corporation to initiate trades or otherwise act on its behalf.

One FCM may establish an account with another FCM that combines the positions of various customers of the first FCM. Such an *omnibus account* could be opened because an FCM does not hold a membership on a futures exchange listing contracts of interest to a customer. Again, the individual customers must provide written authorization. The identities of the individual accounts making up an omnibus account are not disclosed to the FCM providing the transaction service.

A *guaranteed account* is one set up with procedures for transferring funds from a secondary account in order to meet margin requirements. In some cases, subject to limitations, the margin requirements for the guaranteed account are considered to be met by surplus funds in the guarantor's account. A guaranteed account form must be signed, and additional records must be kept indicating the current amount of the guarantor's account serving as margin for the guaranteed account.

Accounts are often categorized as either *speculative* or *trade*. As mentioned previously, trade accounts, sometimes called hedge accounts, are those maintained by customers holding futures contracts as a financial business tool, for example as a substitute for forward buying or selling. A processor of wheat, for instance, may purchase wheat futures in order to limit the risk of spot price changes before the time at which wheat inputs are needed. *Speculative accounts*, which are more closely scrutinized, are those maintained by customers without hedging intent, who presumably hope to profit by futures price changes. Of course, the distinction is not always so clear in practice.

Commissions

Commissions are the brokerage fees charged to customers for futures transactions. Most FCMs set commissions on a *round trip* per contract basis. That is, the fee is charged per contract bought and sold, and often may be paid at the time a position is offset. In most cases, the fee is fixed, subject to occasional revision. For certain contracts, however, the per contract fee may depend on the prices of the trades. Exchanges sometimes establish minimum commission levels that are generally well below the fees actually charged by FCMs.

As with margin requirements, commissions are generally reduced for day trades and spreads. An FCM usually sets commissions for exchange members at a level much lower than that charged to outside customers. (Each exchange member is also charged a fee per contract traded by the exchange; the fee varies according to the class of trader, with the lowest fees generally charged to scalpers.)

Customer Statements

Whenever a customer's order is executed, the FCM must send the customer a *written confirmation*, typically stating (as shown in Figure 3.5):

- The contract type and delivery date
- The quantity traded, under "bought" (B) or "sold" (S)
- The date of execution

- The execution price

- The exchange on which the trade was made

- The account number to which the trade is credited

- The identity of the FCM and associated person

- The identity of the opposite party to the trade, or words to the effect that this identity can be supplied at the customer's request

---

AJAX COMMODITIES INCORPORATED
100 Main Street, Tradeton IL

Date	Account Number
3/18/87	ABC123654

COMMODITY STATEMENT—CONFIRMATION

Customer: John Poor	Associated Person: 15

Date	Quant. B	Quant. S	Description	Price	Amount (U.S. $) Debit	Amount (U.S. $) Credit
3/17/87	2		SEP 87 B-POUND (IMM)	1.5755		
3/17/87		2	SEP 87 D-MARK (IMM)	.5636		

Name of Other Party Furnished on Request.

Subject to All Applicable Clearinghouse and Exchange Rules and Bylaws.

Subject to All Applicable State and Federal Laws.

Figure 3.5   A Sample Written Confirmation

By CFTC regulation, unless an account is a trade account, it cannot simultaneously have long and short positions in the same contract. That is, if the position in a particular contract is long, any sale is taken to *offset* the long position. Conversely, a purchase offsets any short position. Such a trade is a *closeout*, and triggers a *statement of purchase and sale* for the customer, as illustrated in Figure 3.6, which shows all the information (listed above)

that is given on the written confirmations of the trades opening and closing
the position, as well as:

- The gross dollar amount of profit (as a credit) or loss (as a debit) to
  the customer's account
- The fees and commissions debited
- The net credit or debit accruing from the closeout

AJAX COMMODITIES INCORPORATED

100 Main Street, Tradeton IL

Date   Account Number

3/24/87   ABC123654

STATEMENT OF PURCHASE AND SALE   (CLOSEOUT)

Customer: John Poor   Associated Person: 15

Date	Quant. B	Quant. S	Description	Price	Amount (U.S. $) Debit	Amount (U.S. $) Credit
3/17/87	2		SEP 87 B-POUND (IMM)	1.5755		
3/24/87		2	SEP 87 B-POUND (IMM)	1.5540		
3/24/87			PROFIT/LOSS		1075.00	
3/24/87			FEES/COMMISSION		50.00	
3/17/87		2	SEP 87 D-MARK (IMM)	.5636		
3/24/87	2		SEP 87 D-MARK (IMM)	.5586		
3/24/87			PROFIT/LOSS			1250.00
3/24/87			FEES/COMMISSION		50.00	
			TOTAL PROFIT/LOSS			75.00

Figure 3.6   A Sample Statement of Purchase and Sale

For the closeout illustrated in Figure 3.6, the figures can be checked
by assuming round trip commissions of $25 per contract, and by assuming
that the Chicago Mercantile Exchange (IMM) British Pound Contract is for
delivery of[1] 25,000 pounds, while the West German Mark (Deutsche mark)

---

[1] The size of this contract has recently been increased to £62,500.

contract is for delivery of 125,000 marks.

If an offsetting trade does not exactly match the size of the open position, the customer may specify which position-opening trades are being offset, for purposes of determining close-out profits or losses. Regulations require the FCM to close out trades in chronological order (earliest first) unless the customer specifies otherwise.

Each month, a customer receives a *monthly statement*, as shown in Figure 3.7, chronologically summarizing the data for each trade with credits and debits from closeouts. The monthly statement generally includes the beginning and end-of-month account balances and the value of open positions, known as *unrealized equity* or *open trade equity*, calculated at the month-ending settlement price. The value shown in Figure 3.7 for the open Swiss franc contract is based on the IMM contract delivering 125,000 Swiss francs.

Regulated and Nonregulated Accounts

The monthly statement also shows funds transferred to and from the futures account by the customer, for example, to meet margin requirements. Regulations strictly govern any such transfers out of a (CFTC-regulated) futures account, often called a *regulated account*. Margin funds and funds for other purposes such as stock trading are generally held in a *nonregulated account*, one that is not regulated by the CFTC. Transferring funds in excess of margin requirements from a non-regulated account is relatively straightforward. In order for an FCM to transfer regulated account funds to a non-regulated account to meet margin requirements or other specific non-regulated debit balances, however, the FCM generally must have a signed *supplemental customer agreement* to this effect on file. Each transfer from a regulated account for other reasons requires a separate written request from the customer.

4. FUTURES ACCOUNTING STANDARDS

How are gains or losses generated by futures positions to be reported for accounting purposes? Ideally, accounts should accurately reflect income as it occurs, as well as the current market values of assets and liabilities. Definitions of "income," "asset," and "liability," however, are subject to debate. In practice, one relies on standard accounting procedures. This section reviews current practices for accounting treatments of futures transactions, but the reader should note that these procedures are always subject to change. This short survey is insufficient as a practical guide, and is only intended to convey certain basic notions.

AJAX COMMODITIES INCORPORATED

100 Main Street, Tradeton IL

Date   Account Number

3/24/87   ABC123654

MONTHLY COMMODITY STATEMENT:

ACTIVITY AND OPEN POSITIONS

Customer: John Poor   Associated Person: 15

Date	Quant. B	Quant. S	Description	Price	Amount (U.S. $) Debit	Amount (U.S. $) Credit
2/27/87			BALANCE FORWARDED			6550.00
3/17/87	2		SEP 87 B-POUND (IMM)	1.5755		
3/17/87		2	SEP 87 D-MARK (IMM)	.5636		
3/24/87		2	SEP 87 B-POUND (IMM)	1.5540		
			SEP 87 B-POUND (IMM)	P & S	1125.00	
3/24/87	2		SEP 87 D-MARK (IMM)	.5586		
3/24/87			SEP 87 D-MARK (IMM)	P & S		1200.00
3/26/87			CHECK DEPOSITED			1500.00
			NET PROFIT/LOSS			75.00
3/31/87			ACCOUNT BALANCE			8125.00
			OPEN POSITIONS			
2/18/87	1		SEP 87 SW. FRANC (IMM)	.6650		
3/31/87	1		SETTLE PRICE	.6763		
			UNREALIZED EQUITY			1412.50
			ACCT. VALUE AT MARKET			9537.50

Figure 3.7 Sample Monthly Statement

FASB 80

The *Financial Accounting Standards Board (FASB)* is a recognized source of accounting standards in the United States. After studying the issues involved in accounting for futures transactions, issuing an Exposure Draft of a proposed statement on this topic, and reviewing a large number of responses to the Exposure Draft, in December 1984 the FASB released its *Statement of Financial Accounting Standards Number 80—Accounting for Futures Con-*

tracts, commonly referred to as *FASB 80*. FASB 80 can be obtained by writing to the Futures Accounting Standards Board (whose address is given in the Notes at the end of this chapter). This statement establishes standards of financial accounting and reporting for all futures contracts with the exception of foreign currency futures, which were earlier dealt with in *FASB 52—Foreign Currency Translation*. The principle underlying FASB 80 is that gains or losses generated by futures positions are to be reported in income for the period in which the gains or losses occurred. There are a number of exceptions, however, for futures hedges against changes in the value of assets, liabilities, or future commitments. Provided a number of conditions (which we will review shortly) are satisfied, hedging gains or losses are recognized in income whenever changes in value of the corresponding asset, liability, or commitment are recognized.

Nonhedge Transactions

If a futures position is not taken as a hedge, gains or losses are treated as income in the manner of any other investment gains or losses.

Example: Suppose Company A takes a short futures position of 10 Comex contracts for September 1987 delivery of copper. The position is taken on April 1, 1987, at a futures price of 67.40 cents per pound; each contract is for delivery of 25,000 pounds of copper. The initial margin is $2,500 per contract. The corresponding journal entry is:

April 1, 1987	Due from Broker	25,000	
	Cash		25,000

If initial margin had been deposited in Treasury bills, the margin would not be shown as due from the broker. By June 30, 1987, we suppose that the futures price for this contract had dropped in various stages to 62.20 cents per pound, for a net gain of

$$10 \times 25,000 \times (\$0.6740 - \$0.6220) = \$13,000.$$

Assuming that the cash deposited by the FCM to Company A's margin account in daily resettlement payments was withdrawn by Company A whenever possible, the end-of-quarter entry aggregating this income would be:

Various Dates	Cash	13,000	
	Gain on Investment		13,000

Assuming the position was closed out on September 21, 1987, at a futures price of 51.20 cents per pound (for a further gain of $27,500), and that the resettlement gains since June 30 had been left in the margin account, the following entry would recognize the closeout of the futures position:

Sept. 21, 1987	Cash	52,500	
	Due from Broker		25,000
	Gain on Investment		27,500

Hedge Accounting

According to FASB 80, in order to be considered a hedge for accounting purposes, a futures position must satisfy two basic criteria:

1. The item to be hedged exposes the enterprise to price (or interest rate) risk.
2. The futures contract reduces that exposure and is designated as a hedge.

In order to meet the first criterion, the enterprise must not already be hedged against the indicated exposure by some other means. There are two parts to the second criterion. *First*, "high correlation" "shall be probable" (in the words of the FASB) between the futures gains (or losses) and the "fair value" of (or income or expense associated with) the item being hedged. Indeed, if the high correlation should disappear at some point, the futures position would then cease to be considered a hedge for accounting purposes. *Second*, by "designated," the FASB implies that the intention to hedge is to be documented in advance.

Accounting for futures under the hedging designation does not necessarily imply that futures gains or losses are to be deferred. The notion of hedge accounting is that hedging gains or losses are an integral part of the value of the corresponding asset, liability, or commitment; the item hedged and the associated futures position are treated as a package. Futures gains or losses are recognized whenever changes in the value of the item being hedged are recognized. Some items, such as certain pension funds, are "reported at fair value," meaning that changes in the item's value are marked to market.

Example: Suppose, in the scenario presented above for Company A's copper futures transactions, that the short position was taken to hedge the value to be received for the sale of 250,000 pounds of copper held in inventory and was documented as such. Verifying that hedging criteria 1 and 2 apply should be straightforward. In that case, the journal entries shown above would be modified by replacing the *gain on investment* entries with entries showing *deferred gains on futures contracts*; the deferred gains are recognized at the time the copper inventory is actually sold. (This assumes that the physical copper is not carried at "fair value," in which case the futures profits would be recognized whenever the copper's value is marked to market.)

To continue the example, suppose that the copper inventories are actually deliverable against Comex futures contracts and that it is probable that the inventories and futures position will both be maintained until the futures delivery date. In that case, the difference between the spot price of copper when the hedge was put on and the futures price at that time could be amortized as income over the life of the contract. That is, if the spot price of copper on April 1 is 57.40 cents per pound, the excess of 10 cents per pound in the futures price over the spot price represents income of $25,000 on the sale of the copper that can be reported in two quarterly entries of $12,500 each.

Hedges of Anticipated Transactions

Hedge accounting for futures positions is also called for when the futures position is taken to hedge an anticipated transaction, such as the future purchase or sale of an asset, provided the following two FASB 80 criteria are met, in addition to the earlier stated criteria 1 and 2:

3. The significant characteristics and expected terms of the anticipated transaction are identified.

4. It is probable that the anticipated transaction will occur.

The "significant characteristics," such as the expected date, the commodity or financial instrument, and the quantity, should be documented at the time the hedge is placed. The futures gains or losses from an anticipatory hedge would be reflected appropriately as part of the anticipated transaction.

Foreign Currency Translation

Accounting procedures for foreign currency transactions are prescribed in FASB 52, *Foreign Currency Translation*. These procedures, covering forward, futures, and swap contracts, are based on the following main guidelines (quoting from the Financial Accounting Standards Board):

1. The economic effects of an exchange rate change on an operation that is relatively self-contained and integrated within a foreign country relate to the net investment in that operation. Translation adjustments that arise from consolidating that foreign operation do not impact cash flows and are not included in net income.

2. The economic effects of an exchange rate change on a foreign operation that is an extension of the parent's domestic operations relate to individual assets and liabilities and impact the parent's cash flows directly. Accordingly, the foreign exchange gains and losses in such an operation are included in net income.

3. Contracts, transactions, or balances that are, in fact, effective hedges of foreign exchange risk will be accounted for as hedges without regard to their form.

Although the wording of the hedge accounting criteria in FASB 52 is different from that of FASB 80, the spirit of these two standards with regard to hedge accounting is quite similar. One should consult the statements themselves as well as the sources cited in the Notes for analysis and explanation of these standards. The key distinction is that accounts are kept in the *functional currency* (FASB terminology) of the transaction, whether foreign, as in the first guideline above, or domestic, as in the second guideline.

EXERCISES

3.1 In Section 3.1, in the discussion of settlement by offset, the following scenario was given for the trades of agents A, B, and C in the 100 ounce gold contract for December 15 delivery:

(Dec. 12) Agent A purchases 10 contracts at $500 per ounce; agent B sells 10 contracts at $500 per ounce; and the contract settles at $495 per ounce.

(Dec. 13) Agent A sells 10 contracts at \$494 per ounce; agents C buys 10 contracts at \$494 per ounce; and the contract settles at \$491 per ounce.

(Dec. 14) Agent B buys 10 contracts at \$495 per ounce; agent C sells 10 contracts at \$495 per ounce; and the contract settles at \$497 per ounce.

(Dec. 15) The contracts settle at the final delivery price of \$498 per ounce.

Prepare a daily schedule for December 12 through 15 of the position and collect or pay of each agent. Here, we are following the simple clearing margin rules of 100 percent variation margin, and we are ignoring original margin.

3.2 It is 10:00 a.m. Monday morning. You have just executed 3 contracts, long, of the U.S. Treasury bond futures contract at $90\frac{16}{32}$. (The futures price is expressed as a percentage of the face value of \$100,000 per contract.) Today's settlement price is $89\frac{8}{32}$. Original customer margin is \$2,000 per contract; maintenance margin is \$1,500 per contract.

(a) Assuming you paid exactly the required original margin before making the trade, is there a pay or collect tomorrow morning on your margin account? If any, how much?

(b) The contract settles on Tuesday at 91 and any pays or collects due Tuesday morning were made. What is the pay or collect on Wednesday morning, if any?

(c) What is the maximum and minimum for Wednesday's settlement price that would avoid any further resettlement payments on Thursday morning?

3.3 The "second out," or "second nearby," contract for a particular type of futures contract is the contract whose delivery date follows the nearby (or first possible) delivery date. Consider the following scenario for trades in the second out New York Mercantile Exchange Crude Oil Contract, for delivery of 1,000 barrels of light sweet crude oil. Take "today" to be the day this exercise is assigned, or (if not a business day) the first business day thereafter. Assume that Ajax Commodities requires the NYME minimum margins, \$2,000 initial and \$1,500 maintenance.

Today Summit Oil Producers, Inc. took a short position of 200 contracts at the opening price in order to hedge the price it will receive for an oil shipment due to reach the spot market at a time close to the delivery date of the second nearby contract. Summit's FCM for its oil futures trades is

Ajax Commodities. The first business day after today, Summit increased its position to 350 contracts (short) to hedge new delivery commitments. The additional contracts were executed at the opening price of the day.

Give a complete schedule of Summit's margin payments for the next three business days (on which the futures market is open), assuming it uses cash for margins and always withdraws any excess cash from its margin account. Show the required calculations, referring to the financial press for futures prices.

NOTES

The details in this chapter are always subject to change; reader beware. Institutional details are based on personal interviews, an array of exchange literature including the *Clearing House Manual of the Chicago Mercantile Exchange*, as well as the monographs by Feduniak and Fink (1988) and Horn and Farah (1979). The paper "Accounting for Interest Rate Futures Contracts" by Beaver (1981) is a useful guide to the conceptual problems of futures and hedge accounting. FASB 80 is published in the *Journal of Accountancy*, December 1984. For a short synopsis of FASB 80, one may consult Munter, Clancy, and Moores (1985). FASB 80 can be obtained by writing to *Order Department, Financial Accounting Standards Board, High Ridge Park, P.O. Box 3821, Stamford Connecticut 06905-0821*. This document, as well as FASB 52 (the standard for foreign currency translation), are covered as well in FASB (1987), Sections F80 and F60, respectively. Explanation and analysis of these standards are given by Jarnigan and Booker (1986).

EQUILIBRIUM
IN FUTURES MARKETS

A standard model of the determination of futures prices is the *competitive equilibrium*. In this theoretical model, each agent determines an optimal futures position at the given futures price. The futures price and futures positions of the various agents form an equilibrium if the total of all short positions is equal to the total of all long positions. In a more general setting, spot market prices, futures prices, and all other security prices jointly determine demands and supplies in all markets simultaneously. There are still major open questions about the competitive equilibrium story, how well it corresponds to reality, and how one models it. Still, the concept of competitive equilibrium is simple, provides a useful intuitive perspective, and in some cases allows one to estimate prices or quantities of interest in practical decisions.

In this chapter we view the behavior of a futures market through the window of a simple competitive equilibrium model. We will eventually add some essential details, but of course we can never reproduce the richness of real markets in a theoretical model.

1. SUPPLY AND DEMAND IN A FUTURES MARKET

An *equilibrium futures price* is a futures price at which demand is equal to supply. Since there is no initial supply of futures contracts, and since they cannot be produced like commodities, the total supply of futures contracts to the economy is always zero. Thus an equilibrium futures price is one at which the total demand is equal to zero. Of course, individual demands could be positive (long) or negative (short), but they must sum to zero in equilibrium.

Figure 4.1 represents the determination of an equilibrium in a competitive futures market populated by two agents, A and B. According to the

Chapter Outline

competitive equilibrium story, any futures price f_0 could be announced. For each futures price f_0, agent A announces a demand $D_A(f_0)$. If f_0 is an extremely low price, $D_A(f_0)$ is likely to be positive, indicating a demand for a long position; if f_0 is extremely high, $D_A(f_0)$ is more likely to be negative, indicating a short position. Adding up the demands of the two agents, we have the total demand $D(f_0) = D_A(f_0) + D_B(f_0)$. If $D(f_0) = 0$, then f_0 is an equilibrium futures price. In some (difficult to describe) situations, there could be more than one equilibrium futures price, but we shall stick to the usual case in which the total demand function D is downward sloping, as shown in Figure 4.1, implying at most one equilibrium futures price. At the equilibrium futures price, agent A takes a long position that is exactly offset by agent B's short position. In the general case of m agents with demand functions $D_1, D_2, \ldots, D_m$, the total demand $D(f_0) = D_1(f_0) + \cdots + D(f_0)$ is zero if and only if f_0 is an equilibrium futures price.

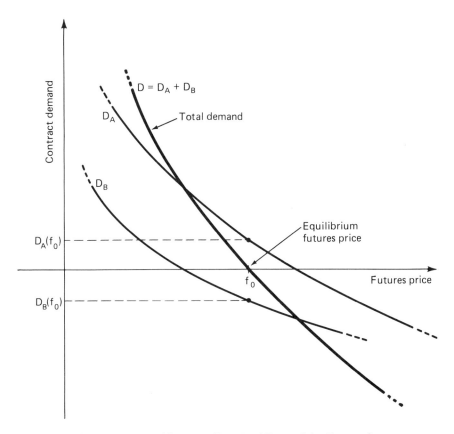

Figure 4.1   Equilibrium at Zero Total Demand for Futures Contracts

The remainder of this section is devoted to several possible scenarios explaining the positions taken by agents A and B shown in Figure 4.1.

Scenario 1: A Long Hedger and a Short Speculator

Suppose that the futures contract delivers crude oil, that agent A will be a spot market consumer of crude oil close to the time at which the futures contract delivers, and that agent B has no stake in the spot market for crude oil. In this simple scenario, each agent holds a futures position until delivery, when the determination of a futures delivery price f_1 leads to a resettlement payment of $f_1 - f_0$ per contract to long positions, and $f_0 - f_1$ per contract to short positions. It is easy to see that agent A might take a long futures position in order to hedge against the cost of crude oil purchases, since unanticipated increases in the purchase cost of the oil would be offset by profits on the long futures position. Of course, any savings resulting from an unanticipated decline in spot oil prices could be wiped out by the corresponding losses on a long futures position. Nevertheless, the price risks in the spot and futures markets are offsetting, allowing agent A to insure herself against oil price risk.

Why should agent B participate in the futures market, given no spot commitment? There could be no other reason than agent B's expectation of profits on his short futures position. Agent B must therefore feel that the futures price is more likely to decline than to rise. Of course, there is always the chance of an increase in the futures price, but agent B is willing to shoulder this risk given the expected rewards. This situation is illustrated in Figure 4.2, where the probabilities of the various possible outcomes of the futures price f_1 at delivery are plotted in a bar chart. Also shown is the current futures price $f_0 = \$20$ per barrel and the expected value $\overline{f}_1 = \$18$ per barrel of the delivery futures price (the probability-weighted sum of the outcomes). As suggested in this scenario, a short position has an expected profit of $2 per barrel, but there are some states of the world in which a short position loses, those states in which f_1 is greater than $20 per barrel.

Even if agent A concurs with the expected futures price decline illustrated in Figure 4.2, it may still be in her interest to suffer the corresponding expected loss on a long futures position in order to benefit from the reduction in price risk. In this scenario, we can think of the expected loss of $f_0 - \overline{f}_1$ per barrel as an insurance premium paid by agent A to agent B in return for agent B's agreement to bear some of agent A's price risk. In general, in a futures market whose hedgers all take long futures positions, there is reason to believe that the futures price f_0 is above the expected delivery price $\overline{f}_1$, and that all speculators will be on the short side of the market. The *futures price bias* $f_0 - \overline{f}_1$ in this case is positive.

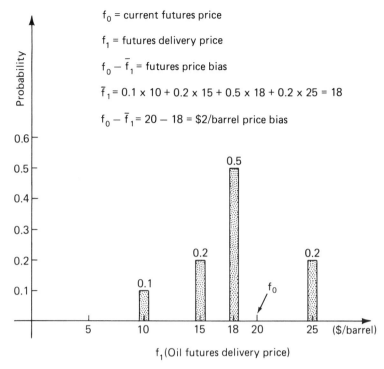

f_0 = current futures price

f_1 = futures delivery price

$f_0 - \bar{f}_1$ = futures price bias

$\bar{f}_1$ = 0.1 x 10 + 0.2 x 15 + 0.5 x 18 + 0.2 x 25 = 18

$f_0 - \bar{f}_1$ = 20 − 18 = $2/barrel price bias

f_1(Oil futures delivery price)

Figure 4.2   The Distribution of Possible Delivery Prices

Scenario 2: A Short Hedger and a Long Speculator

The mirror image of Scenario 1 is one in which agent B is hedging against the cost of a commitment to sell crude oil, while agent A has no spot market position. This explains agent B's short futures position (shown in Figure 4.1), taken in order to hedge against the price to be received for oil on the spot market. If agent A is to take a long position with nothing to hedge, it is likely that she expects profit, so we can guess that $\bar{f}_1 > f_0$. The negative price bias, $f_0 - \bar{f}_1 < 0$, is in this case to be thought of as an insurance premium paid by agent B to agent A in return for agent A's willingness to bear some of agent B's price risk.

Scenario 3: A Short Hedger and a Long Hedger

Our third scenario involves an extremely convenient situation for agents A and B. While A has committed to buy spot oil, and hedges accordingly with a long futures position, agent B has committed to sell spot oil, and hedges with a short futures position. By taking offsetting futures positions, A and B offset each other's risk. Without more information, it is difficult to say whether the futures price shows positive or negative bias. This would depend on the relative sizes of the spot commitments of A and B, among other things such as their risk attitudes. If A's commitment to buy is much larger in quantity than B's commitment to sell, we might expect the equilibrium futures price to show some positive bias, other things being equal, and vice versa. Under special assumptions concerning risk attitudes that are explored later in this chapter, we could come to a definite answer.

Scenario 4: A Long Speculator and a Short Speculator

Although this scenario cannot be ruled out, it is somewhat unusual and difficult to deal with. Suppose that neither agent A nor agent B has any commitment to hedge. In order to explain A's long futures position, it must be the case that A expects the futures price to increase at delivery. Likewise, to explain B's short position, it must be that B expects the futures price to decline. How could both be right? The only explanation is that A and B do not assign the same probabilities to the different possible futures prices. Somehow agent A calculates an expected delivery price $\overline{f}_1^A$ greater than f_0, while B's expected delivery price $\overline{f}_1^B$ is lower than f_0. Perhaps A knows something that B doesn't know, or vice versa. Perhaps both know something the other doesn't know!

Asymmetric Information

The situation described in Scenario 4 has presented deep theoretical difficulties for economic theorists. A scenario of *asymmetric information*, as this is called, is difficult to analyze because the announced futures price reveals some of the information known by one or more of the agents. For example, suppose it is agent A that has superior information concerning the delivery price of the oil contract. (Perhaps A is a party to private OPEC negotiations; we will ignore any legal restrictions against trade based on private information.) Agent A knows whether spot supplies of oil at delivery will be normal or low. If A knows that spot supplies will be low, then she expects the futures price to rise, and would presumably take a long futures position in order to profit on her inside information. In order for the futures market to clear, the futures price must therefore be higher than it would be if future spot conditions were known by A to be normal. The higher futures price would then be a signal to agent B that spot oil supplies will be low. Thus agent B will be as well informed as A, and neither agent will trade.

The story is more interesting if the futures price reveals only part of the privately held information, but we do not yet have a convenient competitive equilibrium model for this case. Kyle (1985) recently devised a model (which is not, however, a competitive equilibrium model) indicating that a well-informed speculator will extract some advantage from private information by taking a futures position whose size reflects the amount of private information the futures price will reveal to the rest of the market. In some sense, the informed agent "holds back" in order to balance the costs of revealing information against the expected profits from exploiting it.

If the various agents in a market are asymmetrically informed and consider the effects of their trades on prices, not to mention the reactions of other agents in the market, the simple competitive equilibrium story is inappropriate, and must be replaced with a more complicated model. This is currently a major area of research in financial economic theory. Some of the literature is cited in the Notes.

Scenario 5: A Likely Hedger Who Doesn't Hedge

One possibility that we haven't mentioned is that agents A and B may both have commitments to buy crude oil on the spot market. How can both agents be long futures hedgers if the futures market is to clear? They cannot! If agent A hedges long, then in order for the market to clear, agent B must take a short position. Agent B must have found the futures price bias $f_0 - \overline{f}_1$ sufficiently positive that it is to his advantage to add to (rather than reduce) his spot market risk by taking a short futures position. In other words, despite his spot market position, agent B behaves like a short speculator. This scenario is unusual, but far from impossible. Of course, we could describe a parallel Scenario 6 in which both agents have spot commitments to sell oil, but one of them nevertheless takes a long speculative position.

Other Scenarios

We have seen most of the possible scenarios involving market equilibrium between two agents. Of course, there are more than two agents in most futures markets, but the situations facing individual agents can usually be reduced to one of those presented in the five scenarios we have covered. Likewise, market equilibrium generally involves four classes of traders: short hedgers, short speculators, long hedgers, and long speculators. How a particular agent is classified, however, may depend on the equilibrium futures price. For example, agent B turned out to be a short speculator in Scenario 5 only because the equilibrium futures price was so high that it induced him to ignore his "natural" role as a long hedger. The equilibrium futures price is that which equates the sum of short positions and the sum of long positions.

2. MEAN-VARIANCE DEMAND AND EQUILIBRIUM

This section lays out a simple theory of individual demand for futures contracts and futures market equilibrium in a two-period competitive equilibrium model with mean-variance preferences. Although this is an extremely restrictive setting, it is an easy place to begin building one's intuition for more general problems. Furthermore, the mean-variance preference assumption is popular because it allows the use of simple (albeit naive) statistical methods for estimating futures prices and individual demands.

Mean and Variance

Appendix 4A outlines the basic theory of random variables, their expected values, and their covariances. Most readers will be able to proceed without reviewing this appendix. As explained in the previous section, the *expected value* of a random variable such as the delivery futures price f_1 is the probability-weighted sum of its possible outcomes, denoted $\overline{f}_1$. Likewise, we denote the expectation of any random variable x by $\overline{x}$, or sometimes by $E(x)$. The expected value of a random variable is also known as its *mean*.

In order to determine the attractiveness of receiving an uncertain amount of wealth defined by a random variable x, one must be concerned not only with the expected amount to be received, $\overline{x}$, but also with the associated "risk" represented by x. Although it is difficult to quantify risk with a single measure, we nevertheless often do so for the sake of convenience or simplicity. One common measure of the risk represented by a random variable x is the *variance* of x, denoted var(x), which is the expected squared deviation of x from its mean. Specifically, var$(x) = E[(x - \overline{x})^2]$.

Example: Consider a payment x of \$100 if a coin lands "heads" and zero if "tails," using a fair $(0.50/0.50)$ coin. The mean of x is

$$\overline{x} = .50 \times \$100 + .50 \times \$0 = \$50.$$

The variance of x is thus

$$\text{var}(x) = 0.50 \times (\$100 - \$50)^2 + 0.50 \times (\$0 - \$50)^2$$
$$= 0.50 \times 2500 + 0.50 \times 2500 = 2500.$$

The units of var(x) are "dollars squared," which is sometimes difficult intuitively. Another convenient measure of the risk of x is thus the square root of var(x), known as the *standard deviation* of x, and denoted sdev(x). In this example, sdev(x) = $\sqrt{\text{var}(x)}$ = $\sqrt{2500}$ = 50 (dollars). As measures of risk, variance and standard deviation are equivalent, in the sense that, for any two random variables x and y, var(x) > var(y) if and only if sdev(x) > sdev(y).

Covariance and Correlation

To most readers, a claim that two random variables x and y are "highly correlated" conveys some sense that, on average, when x is higher than anticipated, y is also higher than anticipated (and when x is lower than anticipated, so is y). That is, x and y "move together." This vague definition is made precise via the *covariance* of x and y, denoted cov(x, y), given by the formula

$$\text{cov}(x, y) = E[(x - \overline{x})(y - \overline{y})].$$

The correlation between x and y, denoted corr(x, y), is defined by the formula

$$\text{corr}(x, y) = \frac{\text{cov}(x, y)}{\text{sdev}(x) \times \text{sdev}(y)}.$$

(If either sdev(x) or sdev(y) is zero, we define corr(x, y) to be zero even though the above formula is not well defined.) Since cov(x, x) = var(x), we know that corr(x, x) = 1. A correlation of 1 is the highest possible, and if corr(x, y) = 1, then x and y are said to be perfectly positively correlated. Likewise, corr($x, -x$) = -1, as is easily checked. If corr(x, y) = -1, we say x and y are perfectly negatively correlated.

Example: One would expect the spot prices of corn in Chicago and corn in Iowa on the same future date to be highly (positively) correlated random variables. In order for an Iowa farmer to hedge the spot price to be received for delivering her corn to the Iowa corn market, it may therefore be appropriate for her to take a short position on a Chicago corn futures contract delivering on the same date, since the profits on a short (negative) futures position are correspondingly negatively correlated with Iowa spot prices. An unanticipated low spot price for the farmer's corn crop, on average, is likely to be offset by profits on her short futures position.

The Total Payoff to a Hedger

Our first step in calculating the demand of a given agent for futures is to calculate the random variable x corresponding to the agent's total payoff at the delivery date of the futures contract. The payoff is made up of two parts, the value of the agent's committed endowment, denoted e, and the gains or losses generated by the futures position. A typical case is an endowment determined by a quantity Q of an asset whose spot price at the delivery date of the futures contract is denoted s_1. In this case, the endowment value is $e = Qs_1$. The quantity Q may be a random variable (such as the size of a farmer's crop when determined by unknown weather conditions), or it may be a fixed constant. In some cases, Q may be a number chosen by the agent, such as the amount of copper that a metals dealer commits to deliver. In some cases, the endowment e is not the market value Qs_1 of some specific spot market commitment, but rather some cash flow determined by a more complicated formula, such as an executive's bonus that is tied to individual and corporate performance measures.

Example: Suppose that there is only one futures contract available for trade, that the agent can execute any size of trade at a given futures price f_0 per contract, and that the contract has a delivery price of f_1 (a random variable). For example, if the contract is for 10 ounces of gold and the spot price (in dollars) of gold at delivery is given by a random variable g, then $f_1 = 10g$. To be even more concrete, if there are three possible states of the economy, labeled 1, 2, and 3, and the gold spot price g has the three corresponding outcomes ($300, $350, $400), representing a gold spot price of $300 per ounce in State 1, $350 per ounce in State 2, and $400 per ounce in State 3, then a 10-ounce futures contract for this delivery date has a delivery futures price of f_1 with the respective outcomes ($3,000, $3,500, $4,000), as shown in Figure 4.3.

Ignoring commissions and margin, if the agent takes a position of y contracts at the futures price f_0, then the futures resettlement profit (or loss, if negative) is $y(f_1 - f_0)$. Adding in the endowment e, the total amount to be

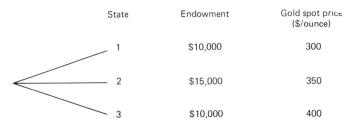

State	Endowment	Gold spot price ($/ounce)
1	$10,000	300
2	$15,000	350
3	$10,000	400

Figure 4.3   A Three–State Payoff

received by the agent is $x = e + y(f_1 - f_0)$. In our last numerical example, if the futures price per 10-ounce gold contract is $3,500 and if the agent's endowment e has the outcomes: $(\$10,000, \$15,000, \$10,000)$ in the three states of the economy, then a futures position of $y = -2$ contracts (that is, a short position of two contracts) yields the net random payoff $x = e + y(f_1 - f_0)$ with outcomes

$$\$10,000 - 2 \times (\$3,000 - \$3,500) = \$11,000 \qquad \text{(State 1)}$$
$$\$15,000 - 2 \times (\$3,500 - \$3,500) = \$15,000 \qquad \text{(State 2)}$$
$$\$10,000 - 2 \times (\$4,000 - \$3,500) = \ \ \$9,000 \qquad \text{(State 3)}$$

In State 3, for instance, the agent has an endowment of $10,000 and a close-out loss on two short contracts at a price change of $500 per contract, for a total payoff of $9,000.

Mean-Variance Demand

Our main concern now is determining the agent's *demand* for the futures contract. The modern theory of demand is based on *utility maximization*, as follows. The agent has a *utility function* U that assigns a *utility* (number) $U(x)$ to each random payoff x. The utility $U(x)$ is an index of the "happiness" of the agent with the payoff x. It is always assumed that any agent makes decisions so as to achieve the highest possible utility. A frequently used utility function is the *mean-variance* function U defined by $U(x) = E(x) - r \operatorname{var}(x)$, for some number $r > 0$. This is a crude model for utility with the properties:

1. *Mean-preference*: $U(x)$ is higher when the mean $\overline{x}$ is higher, holding $\operatorname{var}(x)$ constant.

2. *variance-aversion:* $U(x)$ is higher when the variance var(x) is lower, holding the mean $\overline{x}$ constant.

Variance-aversion is one form of risk aversion since variance is one measure of risk, albeit an overly simple measure for many purposes. The coefficient r appearing in a mean-variance utility function is known as its *risk-aversion coefficient.* The reciprocal $1/r$ is the *risk tolerance* of this utility function. Despite the crudeness of mean-variance utility, it offers simple and sometimes natural solutions to the problem of optimal choice of a futures position, so we shall proceed, and later return to consider other utility functions.

The agent's demand $D(f_0)$ for futures contracts at the futures price f_0 is the solution to the *maximization problem*

$$\text{Maximize}_y \qquad V(y) \equiv U[e + y(f_1 - f_0)], \tag{1}$$

the notation suggesting that $D(f_0)$ is that futures position y yielding the highest possible utility $V(y) = U[e + y(f_1 - f_0)]$, taking e, f_1, and f_0 as given. For any given position y, a series of calculations shown at the end of this section leads to the equation

$$\begin{aligned} V(y) &= U[e + y(f_1 - f_0)] \\ &= \overline{e} + y(\overline{f}_1 - f_0) - r[\text{var}(e) + y^2\,\text{var}(f_1) + 2y\,\text{cov}(e, f_1)] \\ &= C + By - Ay^2, \end{aligned} \tag{2}$$

where

$$C = \overline{e} - r\,\text{var}(e),$$

$$B = \overline{f}_1 - f_0 - 2r\,\text{cov}(e, f_1), \qquad \text{and}$$

$$A = r\,\text{var}(f_1).$$

Of course, $C + By - Ay^2$ is a simple quadratic expression in y. Figure 4.4 shows a plot of this function, with the maximum point indicated by the futures position $\widehat{y}$. Freshman calculus reminds us that the maximum occurs at the position $\widehat{y}$ where the first derivative $V'(\widehat{y})$ is equal to zero. The derivative of a quadratic function of the form $V(y) = C + By - Ay^2$ is $V'(y) = B - 2Ay$. Thus $V'(\widehat{y}) = 0$ implies that $\widehat{y} = B/(2A)$. Thus we have the demand solution

$$D(f_0) = \widehat{y} = \frac{\overline{f}_1 - f_0 - 2r\,\text{cov}(e, f_1)}{2r\,\text{var}(f_1)}. \tag{3}$$

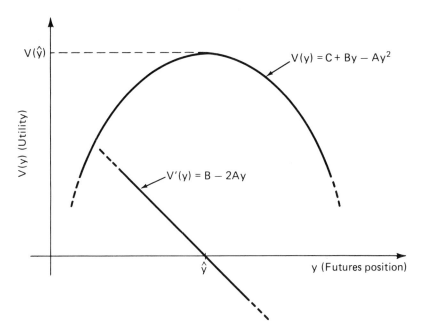

Figure 4.4   The Maximum of a Quadratic Function

(This assumes that $\text{var}(f_1)$ is not zero, but we shall always make that assumption.)

We can represent the demand $D(f_0)$ shown in equation (3) as the sum $D(f_0) = z + h$ of two components:

1. The *pure speculative demand*: $z = (\overline{f}_1 - f_0)/[2r\,\text{var}(f)]$, which is increasing in the expected change in the futures price and decreasing in risk aversion and in the variance of the contract.

2. The *pure hedging demand*: $h = -\text{cov}(e, f_1)/\text{var}(f_1)$, which is negative when e and f_1 are positively correlated and positive otherwise.

Example: To illustrate, consider a farmer whose endowment is a commitment to sell $Q = 500{,}000$ bushels of corn at a spot price of s_1 per bushel on the delivery date of the corn futures contract. The farmer's endowment is therefore $e = Qs_1 = 500{,}000s_1$. The spot price of corn s_1 and the futures delivery price f_1 (per bushel) are assumed to be the same. The pure hedging demand for this agent is therefore

$$h = -\frac{\text{cov}[(500{,}000s_1), s_1]}{\text{var}(s_1)} = -500{,}000\,\frac{\text{cov}(s_1, s_1)}{\text{var}(s_1)} = -500{,}000 \text{ bushels.}$$

We have used the fact that, for any two random variables x and y and any constant k, $\text{cov}(kx, y) = k\,\text{cov}(x, y)$. If each contract delivers 5,000 bushels, the hedging demand is therefore a short position of 100 contracts, an equal and opposite position to the spot commitment. These calculations are easy because $f_1 = s_1$, implying perfect correlation. The futures price is not typically perfectly correlated with the hedger's spot price, so the "equal and opposite" rule is not usually correct. We will look at hedging in more detail in Chapter 7. Had the agent's spot commitment been to buy 500,000 bushels rather than to sell (that is, $Q = -500{,}000$), the endowment would be $e = -500{,}000s_1$, and the optimal hedge would therefore be a long (rather than a short) position of 100 contracts. When hedging a spot market commitment of a fixed number of units of some asset with a futures contract delivering the same asset, the general rule is: When buying spot, hedge futures long; when selling spot, hedge futures short.

In order to calculate the speculative portion of this agent's demand, suppose the futures price bias is $f_0 - \overline{f}_1 = -10$ cents per bushel, the standard deviation of f_1 is 20 cents per bushel, and the agent's risk aversion coefficient is $r = 0.00005$. The purely speculative portion of the agent's demand is therefore

$$z = \frac{\overline{f}_1 - f_0}{2r\,\text{var}(f_1)} = \frac{0.10}{2 \times 0.00005 \times 0.20^2} = 25{,}000 \text{ bushels,}$$

or 5 contracts (long). The optimal total position for the agent is thus

$$y = z + h = 5 - 100 = -95 \text{ contracts,}$$

or 95 contracts short.

In practice, it is difficult to calculate the purely speculative component z of demand, and most of our attention in the remaining chapters will be directed toward hedging. This is not to say that speculation is unimportant, but rather that, as a practical matter, it is currently difficult to give a good textbook model of the rational determination of speculative futures positions that could be taken seriously for practical purposes.

In the exercises, the reader is asked to show that the pure hedging demand is the optimal position for an agent with the (infinitely risk-averse) utility function $U(x) = -\text{var}(x)$. That is, $h = -\text{cov}(e, f_1)/\text{var}(f_1)$ is the *variance-minimizing position.* The total position is equal to the pure spec-ulative demand $z = (\overline{f}_1 - f_0)/[2r\operatorname{var}(f_1)]$ whenever the contract f_1 and en-dowment e are uncorrelated. This corresponds to our vague notion of a pure *speculator*, one who trades with no insurance motive.

We will eventually cover some practical examples of hedging demand, but our next task is to characterize market clearing futures prices.

Mean-Variance Equilibrium

We now suppose that all of the agents 1 through m in the futures market have a mean-variance utility function. Agent i has the risk aversion coefficient r_i and endowment e^i, and therefore has the demand $D_i(f_0)$ at a given futures price f_0 given by equation (3) as

$$D_i(f_0) = \frac{\overline{f}_1 - f_0}{2r_i \operatorname{var}(f_1)} - \frac{\operatorname{cov}(e^i, f_1)}{\operatorname{var}(f_1)}.$$

Let $\tau = \frac{1}{r_1} + \cdots + \frac{1}{r_m}$ denote the *market risk tolerance*, the total of individual risk tolerances. (The symbol τ is the Greek letter *tau*.) Let $e = e^1 + \cdots + e^m$ be the *total endowment*. For any random variables v, w, and x, the sum of the covariances $\operatorname{cov}(w, v) + \operatorname{cov}(x, v)$ is equal to $\operatorname{cov}(w + x, v)$. Thus

$$\operatorname{cov}(e^1, f_1) + \cdots + \operatorname{cov}(e^m, f_1) = \operatorname{cov}(e^1 + \cdots + e^m, f_1) = \operatorname{cov}(e, f_1).$$

The *total demand* at f_0 is therefore

$$D(f_0) = D_1(f_0) + \cdots + D_m(f_0) = \frac{(\overline{f}_1 - f_0)\tau}{2\operatorname{var}(f_1)} - \frac{\operatorname{cov}(e, f_1)}{\operatorname{var}(f_1)}. \tag{4}$$

The equilibrium futures price f_0 must satisfy $D(f_0) = 0$. Solving from (4),

$$f_0 = \overline{f}_1 - \frac{2\operatorname{cov}(e, f_1)}{\tau}. \tag{5}$$

The price bias, $f_0 - \overline{f}_1 = -2\operatorname{cov}(e, f_1)/\tau$, can be positive or negative, and is increasing in the risk aversion of each agent. The futures price bias $f_0 - \overline{f}_1$ is positive if and only if the futures delivery price f_1 is negatively correlated with the aggregate endowment e (indicating, in some sense, a net hedging demand on the long side of the futures market, as in Scenario 1 of Section 4.1).

Unfinished Calculations

There is one piece of unfinished business: the calculations leading to equation (2). First, if $x = e + y(f_1 - f_0)$, then

$$\bar{x} = \bar{e} + y(\bar{f}_1 - f_0),$$

as can easily be checked. In order to calculate the variance of x, we use the following three simple rules: For any random variables v and w, and any number k,

$$\text{var}(v + w) = \text{var}(v) + \text{var}(w) + 2\,\text{cov}(v, w), \tag{6}$$

$$\text{var}(v + k) = \text{var}(v), \tag{7}$$

and

$$\text{cov}(kv, w) = k\,\text{cov}(v, w). \tag{8}$$

Taking $w = kv$, relation (8) implies that

$$\text{var}(kv) = k^2\,\text{var}(v). \tag{9}$$

Finally,

$$\text{cov}(v + k, w) = \text{cov}(v, w). \tag{10}$$

Thus, for $x = e + y(f_1 - f_0)$, we have

$$\text{var}(x) = \text{var}(e) + y^2\,\text{var}(f_1 - f_0) + 2y\,\text{cov}(e, f_1 - f_0)$$
$$= \text{var}(e) + y^2\,\text{var}(f_1) + 2y\,\text{cov}(e, f_1).$$

We then have

$$V(y) = U[x + y(f_1 - f_0)]$$
$$= \bar{e} + y(\bar{f}_1 - f_0) - r[\text{var}(e) + y^2\,\text{var}(f_1) + 2y\,\text{cov}(e, f_1)],$$

which is equation (2), as desired.

3. STORAGE, BACKWARDATION, AND CONTANGO

There are many assets, whether oil, grain, silver, or Treasury bonds, that can either be purchased for later delivery on a futures market or physically stored for later delivery. When there are alternative methods for obtaining future supplies, economics dictate that the cheaper of the two will be used. This simple principle can sometimes be used to obtain a good estimate of the market-clearing futures price in terms of the cost of the storable asset on the spot market plus the cost of storage. In fact, this is the main subject matter of the next chapter, but we will review the basic ideas here and now.

Futures Prices with Storage

The delivered cost of a unit of the asset by way of a futures contract is f_0, the futures price. The delivered cost of a unit of the asset by way of storage is the spot cost, say s_0; plus the interest payable on borrowing the spot cost until delivery, say $I s_0$, where I is the simple rate of interest over this period; plus the cost of storage until delivery, say C (payable at delivery). Thus the total cost is $s_0 + I s_0 + C$.

In order to analyze the relationship between the futures price f_0 and the stored delivery cost $s_0 + I s_0 + C$, let us think first in terms of a grain, say wheat, and consider the storage decision faced by the operator of a grain elevator. How much wheat should be purchased and stored for later sale? Suppose the futures price f_0 is less than the total delivered cost $s_0 + I s_0 + C$ of purchasing and storing the wheat. The operator of the grain elevator would then be foolish to store any wheat at all, since the future wheat can be obtained more economically by taking a long futures position. Likewise, if there is already some wheat in storage, rather than continuing to store the wheat for later delivery, it would be cheaper to:

1. Take a long futures position.

2. Remove the wheat from storage immediately and sell it on the current spot market.

3. Invest the proceeds until delivery.

Step 1 creates the equivalent amount of delivered wheat at a unit cost of f_0; steps 2 and 3 reduce the operator's expenses by $s_0 + I s_0 + C$. Since $s_0 + I s_0 + C$ exceeds the futures price f_0, the elevator operator would be wise to adopt this strategy and continually reduce storage until there is no remaining storage or until the actions of all agents in like situations eliminate the excess of the *stored delivery cost* $s_0 + I s_0 + C$ over the futures price. Note that we are neglecting transactions costs throughout this discussion.

We have the following basic principle of storage in futures markets.

Principle 1: *The futures price f_0 must be at least as large as the stored delivery cost $s_0 + I s_0 + C$ if there is some amount of the deliverable asset in storage.*

Now, suppose f_0 is strictly larger than the stored delivery cost $s_0 + I s_0 + C$. In this case, it is economical for the grain elevator operator to purchase spot wheat and store it, rather than purchase futures contracts. Likewise, it is not economical for anyone to take a long futures position, since the same effect can be accomplished more cheaply by storage (if necessary, by hiring storage capacity from a grain elevator operator). Indeed, it would be profitable to take a short futures position and make delivery by storing grain; the net profit is the futures price f_0 received from the long side of the futures contract, net of the stored delivery cost, $s_0 + I s_0 + C$. Moreover, this involves no risk or initial investment; that is, this is an *arbitrage*. Presumably, this situtation would be exploited until the excess demand for spot wheat and for storage space (not to mention for borrowing) drives the cost of stored delivery up to the price f_0 of future delivery. We thus have our next basic principle.

Principle 2:   *The futures price f_0 can not exceed the cost $s_0 + I s_0 + C$ of stored delivery.*

The careful reader will see that Principle 2 is essentially a restatement of the arbitrage arguments at the end of Chapter 1, where the notation $s_0 B_{0,1}$ was used in place of $s_0 + I s_0$, with $B_{0,1}$ denoting the amount due at time 1 on a riskless loan of \$1 borrowed at time 0. Of course, $B_{0,1} = 1 + I$, since I is the interest due on a loan of \$1, so $s_0 B_{0,1} = s_0 (1 + I) = s_0 + I s_0$. In Chapter 1 we were also ignoring storage costs ($c = 0$).

Putting Principles 1 and 2 together, we have:

Principle 3:   *The futures price f_0 is equal to the cost $s_0 + I s_0 + C$ of stored delivery if there is some of the deliverable asset in storage. If there is none of the deliverable asset in storage, the futures price is less than or equal to the stored delivery cost.*

Now, being a little more realistic, there are few assets that adhere exactly to Principle 3, since storage and interest costs until delivery are sometimes uncertain, since the asset may pay uncertain dividends, and since transactions costs may be important. Nevertheless, Principle 3 is a useful basis for discussion in most futures markets and, when applied carefully, works quite well for a selection of markets.

Backwardation and John Maynard Keynes

Given the amount of confusion that has arisen over the term *backwardation*, it may be best to quote directly from the source of its usage for futures markets, John Maynard Keynes. The following passage is from Volume II, Chapter 29, part *(v)*, "The Theory of the 'Forward Market'" of Keynes's *Treatise on Money*, originally published in 1930.

In the case of organized markets for staple raw materials there exist at any time two price-quotations—the one for immediate delivery, the other for delivery at some future date, say six months hence.... Now if the period of production is of the order of six months, the latter price is the one which matters to a producer considering whether he shall extend or curtail the scope of his operations; for this is the price at which he can at once sell his goods forward for delivery on the date they will be ready. If this price shows a profit on his costs of production, then he can go full steam ahead, selling his product forward and running no risk. If, on other hand, this price does not cover his costs (even after allowing for what he loses by temporarily laying up his plant), then it cannot pay him to produce at all.

> If there are no redundant liquid stocks, the spot price may exceed the forward price (*i.e.* in the language of the market there is a "backwardation"). If there is a shortage of supply capable of being remedied in six months but not at once, then the spot price can rise above the forward price to an extent which is only limited by the unwillingness of the buyer to pay the higher spot price rather than postpone the date of his purchase.

Aside from giving a definite sense of the term "backwardation"— the excess of the spot price over the futures price—Keynes has also provided us with an unusually clear explanation of the basic theory of storage and production with forward markets. Skipping ahead two sentences, however, we find Keynes erring when he states:

> But it is not necessary that there should be an abnormal shortage of supply in order that a backwardation should be established. If supply and demand are balanced, the spot price must exceed the forward price by the amount which the producer is ready to sacrifice in order to "hedge" himself, *i.e.* to avoid the risk of price fluctuations during his production period. Thus in normal conditions the spot price exceeds the forward price, *i.e.* there is a backwardation.

Keynes correctly suggests that the producer may be willing to pay an insurance premium to reduce the spot price risk he faces at delivery. The premium, however, is the excess of the expected spot price at delivery over the forward price, and not the excess of the current spot price over the forward price. (For our purposes here, the futures and forward prices may be treated as equal.) The arguments made in our earlier discussion of the grain elevator operator are no less valid because of any arguments about risk premiums. In fact, if the spot price s_0 exceeds the futures price f_0, then the stored delivery cost $s_0 + Is_0 + C$ certainly exceeds the futures price by even more, and it is optimal to reduce storage and take a longer futures position until storage can be no further reduced or the price backwardation is eliminated.

Finally, even Keynes's presumption of a risk premium $\bar{s}_1 - f_0 > 0$, an excess of the expected delivery price over the current futures price, may be questioned. Even though a risk-averse producer is *willing* to pay a risk premium, he may not be required to do so. For example, Scenario 5 at the beginning of this chapter indicates that there could be another hedger on the other side of the market who is willing to pay an even greater risk premium to buy, rather than sell. In this unusual scenario, the producer discussed by Keynes might have his cake (risk protection) and eat it too (obtain expected profits). Thus the willingness to pay a risk premium does not necessarily imply that one will exist, once all the forces of supply and demand come into play in a general equilibrium. Keynes may be excused to some extent by his proviso "if supply and demand are balanced," but this does not make his analysis correct. If by "balanced," Keynes means that stocks are equal to zero, but there are no incentives to reduce or increase stocks, then the same analysis shows that there can be no backwardation.

How is it, then, that there are often exceptions to Principle 3, cases in which the spot price exceeds the futures price even though there are supplies available? Our analysis has so far been in the framework of a one-period model. If there are intermediate rounds of trade, then current stockpiles could dwindle before delivery. By Principle 1, if stocks approach zero, spot prices may exceed futures prices, and the option to exploit this possibility during the interim before delivery is valuable to those holding stocks. The current spot price may therefore be higher (relative to the futures price) than our analysis so far has suggested, and backwardation can indeed occur. Of course, backwardation could also occur because of factors discussed earlier, such as transactions costs and uncertainty over storage costs or dividends.

Keynes on Contango

Later in his chapter Keynes gets back on the right track with the following definition of *contango*, using essentially the arguments we made earlier for

Principle 2: $f_0 = s_0 + I s_0 + C$ whenever there exist excess stocks.

What is the position in the case important to the argument of this chapter, namely where there exist redundant liquid stocks? In this case there cannot exist a backwardation; for if there was one, it would always pay to sell the stocks spot and buy them back forward rather than incur the warehousing and interest charges for carrying them during the intervening period. Indeed, the existence of surplus stocks must cause the forward price to rise *above* the spot price, *i.e.* to establish, in the language of the market, a "contango"; and this contango must be equal to the cost of the warehouse, depreciation and interest charges of carrying the stocks.

Normal Backwardation

Finally, Keynes suggests that, with the "existence of stocks," by which one may presume he means greater than normal stocks, the current futures price f_0 should be below the expected spot price at delivery, $\bar{s}_1$. Since the futures and spot prices coincide at delivery, that is $f_1 = s_1$, this means that the current futures price is below the expected futures price at delivery, or a negative price bias, $f_0 - \bar{f}_1 < 0$.

But the existence of a contango does not mean that a producer can hedge himself without paying the usual insurance against price changes. On the contrary, the additional element of uncertainty introduced by the existence of stocks and the additional supply of risk-bearing which they require mean that he must pay more than usual. In other words, the quoted forward price, though above the present spot price, must fall below the anticipated future spot price by at least the amount of the normal backwardation.

The same criticism of Keynes' analysis mentioned earlier also applies here. The willingness of the producer to pay insurance costs does not imply that he will in face be forced to do so in equilibrium. The term *normal backwardation*, probably coined in this passsage from Keynes, has come into usuage as the amount $\bar{f}_1 - f_0$ by which the expected futures price at a later date exceeds the current futures price, as illustrated in Figure 4.5. In an unfortunate confusion, the term backwardation can thus refer to either of two usages:

1. The excess $s_0 - f_0$ of the current spot price over the current futures price (Keynes's usage, and that predominating in England before

Keynes[1]).

2. The extent of the negative price bias; that is, backwardation is equal to $\overline{f}_1 - f_0$ (the usage that is now popular in economics).

In his 1938 classic *Value and Capital*, Sir John Hicks followed and developed Keynes's usage (1), whereas Houthakker (1957) began the latter, more modern usage (2). In its daily reporting on futures markets, *The Wall Street Journal* still occasionally uses "backwardation" in Keynes's original sense.

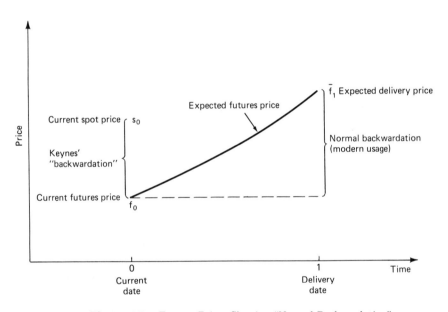

Figure 4.5   Futures Prices Showing "Normal Backwardation"

In Chapter 6 we return to examine the statistical evidence on whether futures prices are greater than, less than, or indistinguishable from their expected value at later dates. From a theoretical point of view, however, any

---

[1] The *Shorter Oxford English Dictionary* provides the following definition, stemming from usage of the term *backwardation* on stock markets in 1850: the "percentage paid by a seller of stock for the privilege of postponing delivery till the next account or to any other future day." Again, this is the excess of the current stock price over the price received for later delivery.

of these three cases is possible, depending on the assumptions of one's model. Realistically, futures price biases are positive at some times, negative at other times, and rarely exactly equal to zero. Appendix 4F explains how the *Capital Asset Pricing Model (CAPM)* predicts futures price biases within the mean-variance setting of the previous section.

EXERCISES

4.1 *(Theoretical Mean-Variance Futures Positions)* You are an agent with mean-variance utility and risk aversion coefficient $r = 0.001$. There are three states of the world (in your model), with the respective probabilities shown in Table 4.1. Your endowment e in the three states is also indicated, as is the futures delivery price f_1 of a given futures contract. The current futures price is $f_0 = \$9,000$.

TABLE 4.1   A Three-State Example

State	Probability (p)	Endowment (e)	Futures Price (f_1)
1	0.50	$25,000	$10,000
2	0.20	30,000	15,000
3	0.30	20,000	8,000

(a) Calculate:

(i) the expected delivery price of the futures contract, $\overline{f}_1$,

(ii) the variance of the delivery price, $\operatorname{var}(f_1)$,

(iii) the covariance of f_1 with your endowment, $\operatorname{cov}(e, f_1)$, and

(iv) the correlation of f_1 with your endowment, $\operatorname{corr}(e, f_1)$.

(b) What futures position maximizes your utility?

(c) What is the variance-minimizing futures position (the pure hedge)?

4.2 Verify equations (4) and (5) by showing the necessary calculations.

4.3 Suppose v and w are random variables with finite-variance and k is a number. Demonstrate relations (6), (7), (8), (9), and (10).

4.4 Show that the problem $Minimize_y \quad \text{var}[e + y(f_1 - f_0)]$, for given (finite variance) random variables e and f and a given futures price f_0, is solved by the pure hedging demand $y = -\text{cov}(e, f_1)/\text{var}(f_1)$.

4.5 Show that a mean-variance utility function is not strictly increasing in the sense defined in Appendix 4D.

NOTES

The material in this chapter is extremely standard. Standard references include Anderson and Danthine (1983a) and Rolfo (1980). Monographs on the economic theory of futures markets include Stein (1986), Williams (1986), and Newberry and Stiglitz (1981). On the theoretical implications of asymmetric information, an issue raised in Section 4.1, further reading can be found in Grossman (1977), Danthine (1978), and Kyle (1984, 1985). Theoretical models of equilibrium futures prices are found in Grauer and Litzenberger (1979) and Richard and Sundaresan (1981).

There is a longstanding debate on backwardation in futures prices. Early notable works are those of Keynes (1930), Hicks (1939), and Kaldor (1940). Well known later articles include Cootner (1960), Houthakker (1957, 1961, 1968, 1974), and Telser (1957, 1960). Some of the later statistical literature is reviewed in Chapter 6.

For the basic notions of probability used here and extensions to the infinite-state case, see Chung (1974), for example. The given conditions for a maximum of a differentiable function are extended, for example, in Luenberger (1984). The CAPM (Appendix 4F) was developed by Sharpe (1964) and Lintner (1965), and extended to a multi-period setting by Rubinstein (1974) and Breeden (1979). The consumption-based CAPM of Breeden (1979) has been tested by Breeden, Gibbons, and Litzenberger (1986) and applied to futures markets by Breeden (1982).

Appendix 4A: Mean and Covariance of Random Variables

An essential aspect of futures markets is uncertainty. This section reviews the standard model of uncertainty and the key statistical measures: mean, variance, covariance, and correlation.

Mean and Variance

To take a simple case, let $\{1, 2, \ldots, S\}$ denote a set of possible "states," one of which is to be chosen at random. (One could imagine the $S = 6$ faces of a die.) The respective likelihoods with which they are chosen can be modeled as *probabilities* $p_1, \ldots, p_S$, positive numbers summing to 1. We can organize any such list of numbers into an *S-vector* $p = (p_1, \ldots, p_S)$. Likewise, we can think of a random variable as an S-vector $x = (x_1, \ldots, x_S)$, where x_1 is the outcome of x in State 1, x_2 is the outcome in State 2, and so on. For two such random variables, say $x = (x_1, \ldots, x_S)$ and $y = (y_1, \ldots, y_S)$, let $x^\top y = x_1 y_1 + x_2 y_2 + \cdots + x_S y_S$ denote their *inner product*. Now, if one were to receive x_1 dollars in state 1, x_2 dollars in state 2, and so on, the inner product $p^\top x$ is the (probability-weighted) average amount to be received, which we can call the *expected value* (or *mean*) of x, denoted $E(x)$ or $\bar{x}$. In this context, x represents a *random variable*.

For notation, if x and y are random variables, then $x + y$ is the S-vector $(x_1 + y_1, \ldots, x_S + y_S)$, and xy is the S-vector $(x_1 y_1, \ldots, x_S y_S)$. If k is a number, then kx is the vector $(kx_1, \ldots, kx_S)$ and (abusing the notation) $x + k$ is the vector $(x_1 + k, \ldots, x_S + k)$.

The variance of a random variable x is $\operatorname{var}(x) = E[(x - \bar{x})(x - \bar{x})]$, the expected squared deviation of x from its mean. If x describes a random amount of goods or wealth to be received, $\operatorname{var}(x)$ is sometimes used as a measure of the risk involved for the receiving individual. The *standard deviation* of a random variable x is the square root of its variance, denoted $\operatorname{sdev}(x) = \sqrt{\operatorname{var}(x)}$. Standard deviation is in some cases a more easily interpreted measure of volatility or risk, since it can be thought of in the same units as those of the underlying random variables, rather than the square of those units.

Extensions

In many interesting examples the set of possible states is not finite, and one must make a natural extension of the notions of a vector, probabilities, and expected value. In fact, the variance of some random values could then be infinite, but we shall always restrict ourselves to the subset of random variables with finite variance. As it turns out, whenever a random variable x has a finite variance, it also has a well-defined and finite expected value $E(x)$. Of course, two different individuals may have differing probability assessments for the various states, but we generally avoid this complication. Whenever we discuss uncertainty in this book, we always speak in terms of some particular states and probabilities, whether explicitly described or not.

Covariance and Correlation

Two random variables x and y have the *covariance*

$$\text{cov}(x, y) = E[(x - \overline{x})(y - \overline{y})].$$

We note that $\text{cov}(x, x) = \text{var}(x)$. The covariance of two random variables is considered a measure of the degree to which they move in tandem, or fluctuate up and down together over the various states. If $\text{cov}(x, y)$ is positive, then the fluctuations x and y above and below their means are, on average, occurring in tandem. If, on the other hand, $\text{cov}(x, y)$ is negative, then x moves above its mean, on average, when y moves below its own mean, and likewise for movements in the oppposite directions. Of course, this is only a loose verbal interpretation; the mathematical definition is unambiguous. We can normalize the covariance of x and y by the product of their standard deviations (provided neither of the standard deviations is zero) to obtain their *correlation*:

$$\text{corr}(x, y) = \frac{\text{cov}(x, y)}{\text{sdev}(x)\,\text{sdev}(y)}.$$

Example: Let $S = 3$ states, $p = (1/3, 1/3, 1/3)$ denote their probabilities, and let $x = (3, -3, 3)$ and $y = (-6, 6, -6)$. Then $E(x) = 1$, $E(y) = -2$, $\text{var}(x) = 24/3$, $\text{var}(y) = 32$, $\text{cov}(x, y) = -16$, and $\text{corr}(x, y) = -1$.

The correlation between any two random variables (of non-zero variance) must be between -1 and $+1$, corresponding, respectively, to *perfect negative correlation* and *perfect positive correlation*, the two polar cases of interest. If two random variables have zero covariance, they are said to be *uncorrelated*.

Appendix 4B: Some Linear Algebra

The following principles of linear algebra are useful for finding solutions to systems of linear equations. We say that any given vectors or random variables $f_1^1, \ldots, f_1^n$ are *linearly independent* if there is no (non-zero) n-vector $y = (y_1, \ldots, y_n)$ such that $y^\top f = y_1 f_1^1 + \cdots + y_n f_1^n = 0$. In economic terms, this implies that none of the n futures contracts represented by the uncertain delivery prices $f_1^1, \ldots, f_1^n$ are *redundant*. For example, suppose $y^\top f = 0$ and $y_1 \neq 0$. Then $y_1 f_1^1 = -(y_2 f_1^2 + \cdots + y_n f_1^n)$, implying that

$$f_1^1 = (-y_2/y_1) f_1^2 + \cdots + (-y_n/y_1) f_1^n,$$

which shows that the first contract is redundant; the payoff f_1^1 can be duplicated by a portfolio of positions in the other contracts.

An (n, m)-*matrix* is a collection of nm numbers tabulated as n rows and m columns, as illustrated below. The j-th element of the i-th row of a matrix A is the (i, j)-*element* of A, denoted A_{ij}, or in standard notation,

$$A = \begin{pmatrix} A_{11} & A_{12} & \cdots & A_{1m} \\ A_{21} & A_{22} & \cdots & A_{2m} \\ \vdots & \vdots & \ddots & \vdots \\ A_{n1} & A_{n2} & \cdots & A_{nm} \end{pmatrix}$$

The i-th *row* of A is the vector $A_i = (A_{i1}, A_{i2}, \ldots, A_{im})$. The j-th *column* is the vector $A^j = (A_{1j}, A_{2j}, \ldots, A_{nj})$.

The product of any (n, m)-matrix A and any m-vector $y = (y_1, \ldots, y_m)$ is the n-vector Ay whose i-th element is $A_i^\top y$. For example, if

$$A = \begin{pmatrix} 1 & 2 & 3 \\ 4 & 5 & 6 \end{pmatrix}$$

and $y = (2, 3, 4)$, then Ay is the 2-vector $(20, 47)$. Other notational conventions for writing matrices, vectors, and their products are in common use.

The product of an (n, m)-matrix A and an (m, k)-matrix B is the (n, k)-matrix $C = AB$ whose (i, j)-element is $A_i^\top B^j$. The (n, n)-matrix whose diagonal elements are 1 and whose off- diagonal elements are zero is the n-*dimensional identity matrix* I. That is,

$$I = \begin{pmatrix} 1 & 0 & 0 & \cdots & 0 \\ 0 & 1 & 0 & \cdots & 0 \\ 0 & 0 & 1 & \cdots & 0 \\ \vdots & \vdots & \vdots & \ddots & \vdots \\ 0 & 0 & 0 & \cdots & 1 \end{pmatrix}$$

It follows that, for any (n, m)-matrix A, we have $IA = A$.

In many situations one wishes to find an m-vector y solving the equation $Ay = x$ for a given (n, m)-matrix A and a given n-vector x. For our purposes, it suffices to consider the case in which $n = m$, meaning that A is a *square matrix*. We will use the next well-known result.

Proposition 4B: *The following properties of an (n,n)-matrix A are equivalent:*

1. *There exists a unique (n,n)-matrix, called the inverse of A and denoted A^{-1}, such that $AA^{-1} = A^{-1}A = I$.*

2. *For any n-vector x, there exists a unique n-vector y solving the equation $Ay = x$.*

3. *The rows of A are linearly independent vectors.*

4. *The columns of A are linearly independent vectors.*

Furthermore, if any of properties 1–4 are true, then for any given n-vector x the unique n-vector y solving the equation $Ay = x$ is $y = A^{-1}x$.

Example: Consider the $(2,2)$-matrix

$$A = \begin{pmatrix} 4 & 2 \\ 2 & 4 \end{pmatrix}.$$

The rows A_1 and A_2 are linearly independent. In order to see this, suppose that they are not linearly independent, which implies $y_1 A_1 + y_2 A_2 = (0,0)$ for some numbers y_1 and y_2. Then $4y_1 + 2y_2 = 0$, or $y_2 = 2y_1$. Likewise, $2y_1 + 4y_2 = 0$, or $y_2 = y_1/2$. This can only be true if $y_1 = y_2 = 0$, proving that A_1 and A_2 are linearly independent. By Proposition 4B, A has an inverse. The inverse of A is easily calculated as

$$A^{-1} = \begin{pmatrix} \frac{1}{3} & -\frac{1}{6} \\ -\frac{1}{6} & \frac{1}{3} \end{pmatrix}.$$

If $x = (12, -36)$, the equation $Ay = x$ is solved by $y = A^{-1}x$, which is the vector $y = (10, -14)$.

The following fact is used implicitly in the calculations leading to demand in the multiple-contract mean-variance case examined in Appendix 4E. The result below applies to the finite-state case, but has an extension to the general case.

Fact 4B: *Suppose the probabilities $p_1, \ldots, p_S$ of the S states are all nonzero. Then the random variables $f_1^1, \ldots, f_1^n$ are linearly independent if and only if $\operatorname{cov}(f_1)$ has a well-defined inverse.*

Appendix 4C: Normal and Log-Normal Distributions

The *distribution function* of a random variable x is the function G which assigns to each number t the probability $G(t)$ that the realization of x is less than or equal to t. The *density* of this random variable x (when it exists) is the first derivative $g = G'$ of G. For example, a random variable x with non-zero standard deviation q is *normally distributed* if it has the density function $g(t) = \exp[(t - \bar{x})^2/q]$, where $\exp(z)$ is the *exponential* of z, also denoted e^z, the well-known scientific constant e raised to the power z. A random variable v is *log-normally* distributed if the logarithm of v, denoted $\log(v)$, is normally distributed. Of course, it then follows that $v = \exp(x)$ for some normally distributed random variable x. In this case, if $\mathrm{sdev}(x) = q$, a calculation shows that

$$E(v) = E[\exp(x)] = \exp(\bar{x} + q^2/2).$$

The densities of a normally distributed random variable x and of a log-normally distributed random variable v are shown in Figures 4.6 and 4.7, respectively. The probability $G(t)$ that the realization of x is less than t can also be treated as the area between the horizontal axis and the graph of the density function g, to the left of t. A normally distributed random variable has a realization less than any number t with strictly positive probability. A log-normally distributed random variable, however, cannot have a negative realization, and is thought to be a more reasonable model for the random prices of certain securities, such as some futures contracts. (This is a topic for consideration in Chapter 6.) A collection $x^1, \ldots, x^n$ of random variables is *jointly normally distributed* if any linear combination $A_1 x^1 + \cdots + A_n x^n$ is normally distributed.

Appendix 4D: General Demand and Equilibrium Conditions

This appendix, which is more advanced mathematically and could be skipped on a first reading or considered to be optional, generalizes the mean-variance example of equilibrium given in Section 4.2 to the case of general utility functions. First we review the classical first order conditions for a maximum, then we turn to conditions for an equilibrium.

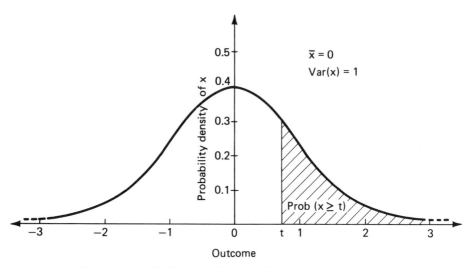

Figure 4.6   The Density of a Normally Distributed Random Variable

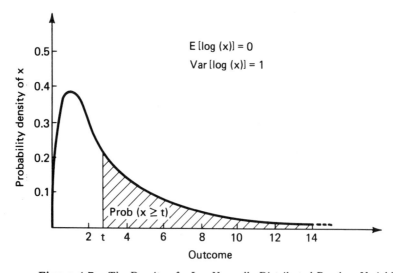

Figure 4.7   The Density of a Log-Normally Distributed Random Variable

Conditions for a Maximum

Suppose V is a function assigning to each number y some number $V(y)$. The

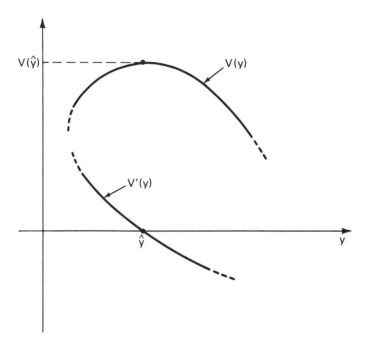

Figure 4.8   A Differentiable Concave Function V and its Derivative V'

reader is understood to be familiar with the notions of the first derivative $V'(y)$ and the second derivative $V''(y)$, when they exist. We say that V is *concave* if, for any two distinct numbers y and y' and any number a with $0 < a < 1$, we have

$$V[ay + (1 - a)y'] \geq aV(y) + (1 - a)V(y'),$$

meaning that the value of the weighted average is always at least as large as the weighted average of the values. Further, V is *strictly concave* if, under the same circumstances, we have the strict inequality

$$V[ay + (1 - a)y'] > aV(y) + (1 - a)V(y').$$

Lemma 1: *If V is twice differentiable (has a first and second derivative), then V is concave if and only if $V''(y) \leq 0$ for all y; and strictly concave if and only if $V''(y) < 0$ for all y.*

A differentiable concave function V is illustrated in Figure 4.8. From the figure, it is clear that any differentiable function attains its maximum only at a point y where $V'(y) = 0$. We can state this as a formal result.

Proposition 1: *Suppose V is a differentiable function.*

(a.) If $\widehat{y}$ maximizes V, then $V'(\widehat{y}) = 0$.

(b.) Conversely, if V is concave and $V'(\widehat{y}) = 0$, then $\widehat{y}$ maximizes V.

(c.) If V is a strictly concave function, then it has at most a single max-imizer.

Futures Demand

From our diversion into the theory of optimization, we see that an agent with a differentiable concave value function V for futures contracts will demand any number $\widehat{y}$ of contracts for which $V'(\widehat{y}) = 0$, just as in the mean-variance case. Concavity in this context is a natural symptom of risk aversion.

Futures Market Equilibrium

We now suppose the entire market is made up of m individual agents, with respective endowments $e^1, \ldots, e^m$ and utility functions $U_1, \ldots, U_m$.

The *demand* of any agent i for futures contracts, given a futures price f_0, is any number y_i solving the maximization problem (2), which we restate as:

$$\text{Maximize}_y \qquad V_i(y) \equiv U_i[e^i + y(f_1 - f_0)]. \tag{11}$$

An *equilibrium* for the given *futures market* $[(e^1, U_1), \ldots (e^m, U_m), f_1]$ is a futures price f_0 and with the two properties:

1. *Individual utility maximization*: for any agent i, y_i solves the de-mand problem (11).

2. *Market clearing*: $y_1 + \cdots + y_m = 0$, meaning the total of longs is equal to (minus) the total of shorts.

Expected Utility

An equilibrium can often be succinctly characterized when the utility func-tions of agents are of the *expected utility* form $U(x) = E[u(x)]$, where u is a function assigning a utility index $u(w)$ to any number w representing the wealth received in a given state. The expected utility function is defined as follows. For a random variable x whose possible outcomes $(x_1, \ldots, x_S)$ have respective probabilities $(p_1, \ldots, p_S)$, let

$$U(x) = E[u(x)] = p_1 u(x_1) + \cdots + p_S u(x_S),$$

which is termed the *expected utility* of x. As an exercise, if u is differentiable, the optimality condition $V'(y) = 0$ can be written in the form

$$E[u'(x)f_1] - f_0 E[u'(x)] = 0,$$

letting $u'(x)$ denote the random variable with outcomes $(u'(x_1), \ldots, u'(x_S))$. Assuming that $u'(z) > 0$ for all z, and thus that $E[u'(x)]$ is not zero, we can rearrange to see that

$$f_0 = \frac{E[u'(x)f_1]}{E[u'(x)]}, \tag{12}$$

which can finally be re-written using the definition of covariance as

$$f_0 = \frac{E[u'(x)]E(f_1)}{E[u'(x)]} + \frac{\text{cov}[u'(x), f_1]}{E[u'(x)]}$$

$$= \overline{f}_1 + \frac{\text{cov}[u'(x), f_1]}{E[u'(x)]}. \tag{13}$$

Unfortunately, the random variable $u'(x)$ is not directly observable, for we would otherwise have a convenient measure of the price bias

$$f_0 - \overline{f}_1 = \frac{\text{cov}[u'(x), f_1]}{E[u'(x)]}. \tag{14}$$

Under special assumptions, such as in the following example, we can calculate this price bias.

Example: We consider a simple example in which equilibrium futures prices can be calculated in closed form. The example depends, however, on many special assumptions. In particular, we will have only one agent, and allow an infinite number of outcomes. Suppose that utility function U is the expected *power function* $U(x) = E[u(x)]$, where $u(x) = x^a/a$ for some exponent a with $0 < a < 1$ or $a < 0$. Suppose also that $w = \log(e)$ and $z = \log(f_1)$ are jointly normally distributed. (The properties of normal distributions used in this example are reviewed in Appendix 4C.) We have the derivative $u'(x) = x^{a-1}$. In order for $y = 0$ to be the (market clearing) demand for the single agent, relation (12) implies that

$$f_0 = \frac{E[u'(e)f_1]}{E[u'(e)]}$$

$$= \frac{E\big[[\exp(w)]^{a-1}\exp(z)\big]}{E\big[[\exp(w)]^{a-1}\big]}$$

$$= \frac{E\left[\exp[(a-1)w+z]\right]}{E\left[\exp[(a-1)w]\right]}$$

$$= \frac{\exp\left[(a-1)\overline{w}+\overline{z}+\frac{1}{2}\operatorname{var}[(a-1)w+z]\right]}{\exp\left[(a-1)\overline{w}+\frac{1}{2}\operatorname{var}[(a-1)w]\right]}$$

$$= \exp[\overline{z}+\tfrac{1}{2}\operatorname{var}(z)+(a-1)\operatorname{cov}(w,z)]$$

$$= E(f_1)\exp[(a-1)\operatorname{cov}(w,z)]. \tag{15}$$

The price bias is thus $f_0 - \overline{f}_1 = B\overline{f}_1$, where

$$B = \exp\left[(a-1)\operatorname{cov}[\log(e),\log(f_1)]\right] - 1. \tag{16}$$

If $\log(e)$ (the logarithm of the endowment e) and $\log(f_1)$ (the logarithm of the futures delivery price) are uncorrelated, we have $B = \exp(0) - 1 = 0$, or no price bias, which is somewhat intuitive. If $\log(e)$ and $\log(f_1)$ are positively correlated, then (since $a < 1$) we know that $B < 0$, so the futures price bias $f_0 - f_1$ is negative, which is also intuitive. On the other hand, this is an extremely special example.

Simple Equilibrium Conditions

For any two random variables v and w, we write $v \geq w$ if every outcome of v is larger than the corresponding outcome of w. If $v \geq w$ and some outcome of v is strictly larger than the corresponding outcome of w, we write $v > w$, or equivalently $v - w > 0$.

Now suppose $f_1 - f_0 > 0$, meaning that purchasing one futures contract yields positive closeout profits in every state, and strictly positive profits in at least some states. We then say that f_0 is an *arbitrage price* for the obvious reason. The larger the position taken, the larger will be the closeout profits, with no risk of closeout losses. Similarly, if $f_0 - f_1 > 0$, any short position yields arbitrage profits, and f_0 is again an arbitrage price. If f_0 is not an arbitrage price (that is, neither $f_0 - f_1 > 0$ nor $f_1 - f_0 > 0$), we say f_0 is *arbitrage-free*. A utility function U is *strictly increasing* if $U(v) > U(w)$ whenever $v > w$, which is a natural assumption: More in every state and strictly more in some states is strictly better. We note, however, that a mean-variance utility function is *not* strictly increasing, another exercise for the reader.

Fact 1: *If f_0 is an arbitrage price and U is strictly increasing, then there is no demand y solving the demand problem (1).*

This fact is trivial, for if $f_1 - f_0 > 0$ and y is a demand for U given e, f_1, and f_0, then we have the contradiction $V(k) > V(y)$ for any number $k > y$, since $e + k(f_1 - f_0) > e + y(f_1 - f_0)$. Similarly, if $f_0 - f_1 > 0$, then $V(k) > V(y)$ for any $k < y$. Thus, in most cases, we only look for demands at arbitrage-free prices. If, at each given arbitrage-free futures price f_0, there exists a demand $D_i(f_0)$ for futures contracts solving (1), then we call D_i the *arbitrage-free demand function* for agent i. We recall that a function such as D_i is *continuous* if its graph is connected, or roughly speaking, if it can be plotted without breaking the plot, as shown in Figure 4.9(a). Figure 4.9(b) illustrates a *discontinuous* demand function.

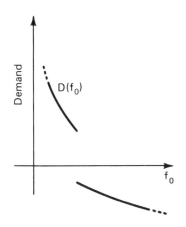 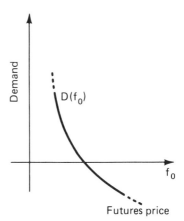

Figure 4.9a Continuous Demand   **Figure 4.9b** Discontinuous Demand

Figure 4.9   Demand Functions

An arbitrage-free demand function D_i is *normal* if there is some futures price f_0^L so low that $D_i(f_0) \geq 0$ whenever f_0 is less than f_0^L, and there is also some arbitrage-free price f_0^H so high that $D_i(f_0) \leq 0$ whenever f_0 is a price greater than f_0^H.

Proposition 2:   *Suppose the futures market $[(e^1, U_1), \ldots, (e^m, U_m), f_1]$ has the property that each agent has a normal and continuous arbitrage-free demand function. Then there exists an equilibrium.*

The proposition is easily proved as follows. Let D be the *total demand function*, defined at any arbitrage-free price f_0 by $D(f_0) = D_1(f_0) + \cdots + D_m(f_0)$.

The reader can also check that D is normal and continuous. If there is a price f_0^H at which $D(f_0^H) \leq 0$ and a price f_0^L at which $D(f_0^L) \geq 0$, then the continuity of D implies an intermediate price $\widehat{f_0}$ at which $D(\widehat{f_0}) = 0$. Let $y_1 = D_1(\widehat{f_0}), y_2 = D_2(\widehat{f_0})$, and so on, be the demands of the various agents at the futures price $\widehat{f_0}$. Then $(y_1, \ldots, y_m, \widehat{f_0})$ is an equilibrium since $y_1 + \cdots + y_m = 0$. As to the conditions of the theorem, we leave the following as a simple justification of demand continuity.

Fact 2: *If U_i is strictly concave and has an arbitrage-free demand function D_i, then D_i is continuous.*

Equilibrium in the case of mean-variance utility can easily occur at an arbitrage price f_0 for a sufficiently small market risk tolerance τ. We should not place much faith in the mean-variance example except with sufficiently small coefficients of risk aversion.

Appendix 4E: Multiple Futures Contracts

Like the last, this appendix is mathematically advanced, and may be regarded as optional.

Equilibrium in Several Contracts

Suppose a futures market is characterized by m agents defined by utility functions and endowments $\big((U_1, e^1), \ldots, (U_m, e^m)\big)$ as before, and by n futures contracts represented by the random delivery prices $f_1^1, f_1^2, \ldots, f_1^n$. For any vector $y = (y_1, \ldots, y_n)$ of futures positions, let $y^\top f_1$ denote the total $y_1 f_1^1 + \cdots + y_n f_1^n$. (The principles of linear algebra used here are reviewed in Appendix 4B.) If the current futures prices of the n contracts are given by the vector $f_0 = (f_0^1, \ldots, f_0^n)$, the total closeout profits of a position made up of y_1 of the first contract, y_2 of the second contract, and so on are represented by the random payoff $y^\top f_1 - y^\top f_0$. The demand problem of agent i is then

$$\text{Maximize}_y \quad V_i(y) \equiv U_i(e^i + y^\top f_1 - y^\top f_0),$$

much as before, except that the value function V is expressed over a vector $y = (y_1, \ldots, y_n)$ of futures positions, rather than merely a single position. A vector position y is a *demand* for agent i given the futures price vector f_0

if there is no other demand y' such that $V_i(y') > V_i(y)$. An *equilibrium* for $((U_1, e^1), \ldots, (U_m, e^m), (f^1, \ldots, f^n))$ is a collection $(y^1, \ldots, y^m, f_0)$ such that for each agent i, y^i is a demand vector given the futures price vector f_0, and such that all markets clear: $y^1 + \cdots + y^m = 0$.

The Multi-contract Mean-Variance Case

In order to calcuate the variance of a position in all n contracts, we introduce the *covariance matrix*. The covariance matrix, denoted $\mathrm{cov}(f_1)$, of $f_1 = (f_1^1, \ldots, f_1^n)$ is the (n, n)-matrix whose (i, j)-element is $\mathrm{cov}(f_1^i, f_1^j)$. That is,

$$\mathrm{cov}(f_1) = \begin{pmatrix} \mathrm{cov}(f_1^1, f_1^1) & \mathrm{cov}(f_1^1, f_1^2) & \cdots & \mathrm{cov}(f_1^1, f_1^n) \\ \mathrm{cov}(f_1^2, f_1^1) & \mathrm{cov}(f_1^2, f_1^2) & \cdots & \mathrm{cov}(f_1^2, f_1^n) \\ \vdots & \vdots & \ddots & \vdots \\ \mathrm{cov}(f_1^n, f_1^1) & \mathrm{cov}(f_1^n, f_1^2) & \cdots & \mathrm{cov}(f_1^n, f_1^n) \end{pmatrix}$$

The following fact will be useful.

Fact 3:   For any n-vector y, the variance of $y^\top f_1$ is $y^\top [\mathrm{cov}(f_1)y]$.

The covariance of $y^\top f_1$ with any other random variable x can be calcuated as

$$\begin{aligned} \mathrm{cov}(x, y^\top f_1) &= \mathrm{cov}(x, y_1 f_1^1) + \cdots + \mathrm{cov}(x, y_n f_1^n) \\ &= y_1 \mathrm{cov}(x, f_1^1) + \cdots + y_n \mathrm{cov}(x, f_1^n) \\ &= y^\top \mathrm{cov}(x, f_1), \end{aligned}$$

where $\mathrm{cov}(x, f_1)$ denotes the vector whose j-element is $\mathrm{cov}(x, f_1^j)$. Then the total variance of a position y for agent i is

$$\begin{aligned} \mathrm{var}(e^i + y^\top f_1 + y^\top f_0) &= \mathrm{var}(e^i + y^\top f_1) \\ &= \mathrm{var}(e^i) + \mathrm{var}(y^\top f_1) + 2\,\mathrm{cov}(e^i, y^\top f_1) \\ &= \mathrm{var}(e^i) + y^\top [\mathrm{cov}(f_1)y] + 2y^\top \mathrm{cov}(e^i, f_1). \end{aligned}$$

Let $\overline{f}_1 = (\overline{f}_1^1, \ldots, \overline{f}_1^n)$ denote the vector of expected delivery prices. If U_i is mean-variance with risk-aversion coefficient r_i, then the utility value $V_i(y)$ of a futures position vector y is given by

$$\begin{aligned} V(y) &= U_i(e^i + y^\top f_1 - y^\top f_0) \\ &= E(e^i + y^\top f_1 - y^\top f_0) - r_i \,\mathrm{var}(e^i + y^\top f_1 - y^\top f_0) \\ &= \overline{e}^i + y^\top \overline{f}_1 - y^\top f_0 - r_i \left(\mathrm{var}(e^i) + y^\top [\mathrm{cov}(f_1)y] + 2y^\top \mathrm{cov}(e^i, f_1) \right). \end{aligned}$$

The vector $\nabla V(y)$ of partial derivatives of V at y is given by

$$\nabla V(y) = \overline{f}_1 - f_0 - 2r_i \, \text{cov}(e^i, f_1) - 2r_i \, \text{cov}(f_1)y.$$

The reader can show that V is concave as an exercise. Thus, using an extension of earlier calculations to the multi-contract case, the demand for agent i is any vector y solving the equation $\nabla V(y) = 0$, implying that

$$\text{cov}(f_1)y = \frac{(\overline{f}_1 - f_0)}{2r_i} - \text{cov}(e^i, f_1).$$

If $\text{cov}(f_1)$ has an inverse, then the unique demand of agent i is given by Proposition 4B (Appendix 4B) as

$$y^i = [\text{cov}(f_1)]^{-1} \frac{(\overline{f}_1 - f_0)}{2r_i} - [\text{cov}(f_1)]^{-1} \text{cov}(e^i, f_1). \tag{17}$$

Again, we have written the total demand of a mean-variance agent as the sum of a pure speculative demand $z = [\text{cov}(f_1)]^{-1}(\overline{f}_1 - f_0)/2r_i$ and a pure hedging demand $h = -[\text{cov}(f_1)]^{-1}\text{cov}(e^i, f_1)$. Some readers may recognize the hedging demand h as (minus) the regression coefficients of the random variable e^i regressed on the random variables $f_1^1, \ldots, f_1^n$, in the form

$$e^i = A_1 f_1^1 + \cdots + A_2 f_1^n + \epsilon,$$

explaining e^i as a linear combination of $f_1^1, \ldots, f_1^n$ and a residual term ϵ. That is, the vector $A = (A_1, \ldots, A_n)$ of regression coefficients minimizing the variance of the residual term ϵ is given by $A = -h$. (A review of multiple linear regression appears in Appendix 6B.)

For equilibrium in the mean-variance case, we must find a futures price vector f_0 at which the sum of the m individual demand vectors $y^1, \ldots, y^m$ from (17) is zero. As in the one-dimensional case, let τ denote the market risk tolerance and $e = e^1 + \cdots + e^m$ denote the total endowment. Then equilibrium implies that

$$y^1 + \cdots + y^m = [\text{cov}(f_1)]^{-1} [(f_1 - f_0)\tau/2 - \text{cov}(e, f_1)] = 0. \tag{18}$$

Multiplying (18) throughout by $\text{cov}(f_1)$, we have

$$\frac{(f_1 - f_0)\tau}{2} - \text{cov}(e, f_1) = 0,$$

or

$$f_0 = \overline{f}_1 - \frac{2\operatorname{cov}(e, f_1)}{\tau}, \tag{19}$$

in exact parallel with the one-dimensional case.

Appendix 4F: The CAPM for Futures Markets

This appendix reviews the CAPM for futures markets. Originally due to Sharpe (1964) and Lintner (1965), the *Capital Asset Pricing Model* (*CAPM*) is a formula relating individual asset returns to the return on a special asset, called the *market portfolio*, which pays off the aggregate consumption of the economy. The CAPM formula is a useful source of intuition and is sometimes employed in practical business decisions.

The Single Period CAPM

We can easily derive a form of the CAPM that applies in futures markets, as follows. With mean-variance utility for all agents, equation (19) states that the expected change $\overline{f}_1 - f_0$ in any futures price is equal to $2\operatorname{cov}(e, f_1)/\tau$, where τ is the market risk tolerance. (Those readers who have not reviewed the derivation of equation (19) in Appendix 4E may rely on the fact that it is the same as the formula (5) specifying the equilibrium futures price in the case of trading in a single futures contract.) Unfortunately, τ is not directly observable. Suppose, however, that there is a futures contract delivering e, the total endowment of the economy. We call this special futures contract the *market contract*. For practical purposes, the S&P 500 contract is sometimes used as a proxy for the market contract, since the S&P 500 is thought to represent a large component of the total endowment of all agents. (This is true if one limits one's perspective to U.S. equities, but that is a limited perspective.) If we let f^e denote the initial futures price of the market contract, equation (19) implies that

$$f^e - \overline{e} = \frac{2\operatorname{cov}(e, e)}{\tau} = \frac{2\operatorname{var}(e)}{\tau}, \tag{20}$$

which tells us that the market risk tolerance is therefore given by the expression

$$\tau = \frac{2\operatorname{var}(e)}{f^e - \overline{e}}. \tag{21}$$

Substituting (21) into (19) tells us that the expected change $\overline{f}_1 - f_0$ in an arbitrarily chosen futures contract is given by the equation

$$\overline{f}_1 - f_0 = \frac{\text{cov}(f_1, e)}{\text{var}(e)}(\overline{e} - f^c). \tag{22}$$

The coefficient

$$\beta_f = \frac{\text{cov}(f_1, e)}{\text{var}(e)} = \text{corr}(f_1, e) \times \frac{\text{sdev}(f_1)}{\text{sdev}(e)} \tag{23}$$

is known as the *beta* of the futures contract of interest with respect to the market futures contract. As will be explained in Chapters 6 and 7, β_f can be estimated statistically (under assumptions). Finally, rearranging (22), we have the CAPM formula for futures prices:

$$f_0 = \overline{f}_1 + \beta_f(f^e - \overline{e}). \tag{24}$$

By equation (20), $f^e - \overline{e}$ is positive since τ and $\text{var}(e)$ are both positive. The formula states that the futures price bias $f_0 - \overline{f}_1 = \beta_f(f^e - \overline{e})$ may be thought of as a *risk premium* that is:

- Positive if the delivery futures price f_1 is positively correlated with the total endowment e of the economy.

- Negative if the delivery price f_1 is negatively correlated with the total endowment of the economy.

- Zero if f_1 is uncorrelated with e.

In other words, the risk premium in futures prices is based only on that portion of the risk that is correlated with the market. The traditional CAPM for general securities is essentially the same relationship as equation (24), except that it is conventional to write it in terms of the return of the asset rather than the payoff of the asset. Of course, a futures contract does not have a well-defined return since no initial investment (neglecting margin) is required to adopt a futures position.

Example: It is well-known that gold prices tend to be negatively correlated with the S&P 500 Index. For this reason, investment in gold has often been treated as a "safe haven" during times when investors lack confidence in the value of the entire market. Indeed, gold prices tend to hold up better than the average investment during broad market declines, though they tend to rise more slowly or even drop when the market is generally improving. The CAPM therefore predicts that gold futures should have a negative price bias. That is, if f_1 indicates the delivery futures price of gold and e indicates the S&P 500 Index at delivery (assumed to be a suitable substitute for the total endowment of the economy), then the fact that $\text{corr}(e, f_1)$ is negative implies that

$$\beta_f = \text{corr}(e, f_1) \times \frac{\text{sdev}(f_1)}{\text{sdev}(e)} < 0.$$

The CAPM tell us that

$$f_0 - \overline{f}_1 = \beta_f (f^e - \overline{e}).$$

According to this formula, since $\beta_f < 0$ and $f^e - \overline{e} > 0$, we should have $f_0 - \overline{f}_1 < 0$. Although it is difficult to demonstrate a significantly negative bias in gold futures prices using standard statistical tests on the available data, it is also difficult to reject this CAPM conclusion.

The Multi-period CAPM

Suppose futures trades occur at periods 0, 1, 2, and so on, rather than merely stopping at period 1. The CAPM formula

$$f_0 = \overline{f}_1 + \beta_f (f^e - \overline{e}) \tag{25}$$

remains correct in principle (in a setting with continuous–time trading), but its interpretation must change. Rather than treating e as the aggregate wealth of the economy at period 1, we must treat e as the aggregate *consumption* of the economy at period 1, measured approximately, for example, by national accounting measures of gross consumption. Unfortunately, it is difficult to find a futures contract that delivers even a rough proxy for aggregate market consumption. Nevertheless, some calculations show that the formula works in theory if we treat f^e instead as the total futures price of some combination of futures positions whose total payoff has the maximum possible correlation with the aggregate market consumption e.

The multi-period form of the CAPM, developed by Rubinstein (1976) and Breeden (1979), is now known as the *Consumption-Based CAPM*. When Breeden, Gibbons, and Litzenberger (1988) subjected the Consumption-Based CAPM to statistical tests; the results were "mixed." Perhaps the assumptions underlying the model are inappropriate; perhaps it is too difficult to measure aggregate consumption accurately; perhaps there is too much noise to obtain accurate results. The Consumption-Based CAPM is a mainstay of modern asset-pricing theory. Breeden (1980) has studied the implications of the Consumption-Based CAPM for futures markets.

5

ARBITRAGE
IN FUTURES MARKETS

This chapter states a strict relationship that must hold between certain futures, forwards, bond, and spot prices in order to rule out arbitrage. Of course, these restrictions do not apply exactly in imperfect capital markets, and arbitrage rents can accrue to those with sufficiently low transactions costs. Of particular interest are restrictions on futures and forward prices implied by storage opportunities, as well as the role of arbitrageurs in enforcing these restrictions. Stock index arbitrage is included as a motivating example. The role of program trading in the Stock Crash of 1987 is highlighted in Appendix 5B. We begin with a review of interest rates, which figure heavily in determining arbitrage price restrictions on futures markets.

1. INTEREST RATES

Table 5.1 shows a sample of interest rate quotations from the financial press. Notably, there are different rates quoted for the same loan period. Rate differences occur mainly because:

- Borrowers are segregated according to their size and credit risk, with larger and more secure borrowers (such as the U.S. government) obtaining money at lower interest rates.
- Tax, legal, and other institutional factors favor particular borrowers to particular lenders.

In order to characterize a link between futures prices and interest rates, a major objective of this chapter, we will often refer to "the" interest rate, which the reader should treat as the lowest borrowing rate or the highest lending rate available for the purpose considered. The gap between these two rates is a transactions cost that limits the precision of some of the results in this chapter.

Chapter Outline

What Is an Interest Rate?

What does an annual interest rate of "10 percent" mean? The answer depends on the frequency of compounding. With annual compounding, an interest rate r of 10 percent (that is, $r = 0.10$) means that $1.00 invested today yields $1.10 in one year. With semi-annual compounding at 10 percent, an investment of $1.00 today yields $1.05 in six months, and finally $1.05 \times \$1.05 = \$1.1025$ in one year. The *effective annual interest rate* R is thus 10.25 percent, or $R = 0.1025$. The general formula for the effective annual rate R given a semi-annual compounding rate of r is $R = (1 + r/2)^2 - 1$. With quarterly

TABLE 5.1   Commonly Published Short-Term Rates

Money
TUESDAY, DEC. 6, 1988

Broker Call Loans 9½-9¾%
Federal Funds:
High: 8⅝ Low: 8⁹/₁₆ Close: 8⁹/₁₆
*Dealer Placed Commercial Paper:
30 day 9.25
*Financial Co. Commercial Paper:
15 day 8.56
30 day 9.08
60 day 8.61
*Bankers Acceptances:
30 day 9.22
90 day 8.95
180 day 8.80
Certificates of Deposit
Secondary Market Offerings:
30 day 9.28
90 day 9.20
180 day 9.20
Primary Offerings by N.Y.C. Banks:
30 day 8.55
90 day 8.35
180 day 8.50
Eurodollar Time Deposits:
Overnight.............................. 8.56
30 day 9.56
90 day 9.31
180 day 9.31
London Interbank Offered Rate:
90 day 9.37
180 day 9.37
*Discount rate. *Source: Telerate Systems Inc.*
Source: *The New York Times.*

compounding, $R = (1 + r/4)^4 - 1$, and so on.

Example: The 90-day *London Interbank Offered Rate* (or 90-day *LIBOR*) shown in Table 5.1 refers to a representative quote for U.S. dollar 90-day borrowing through London intermediaries. A 90-day LIBOR quote of 10 percent actually means an interest rate of $\frac{10}{4}$ percent = 2.5 percent per quarter, for an effective annual rate of $(1.025)^4 - 1 = 10.25$ percent. (In the LIBOR market, a "quarter" is 90 days and a "year" is 360 days.)

As the number n of compounding periods per year increases without limit, the total payback $(1 + r/n)^n$ to a \$1 investment gradually increases to the limit e^r, where e is the famous scientific constant. (Rounding to the first five places, e is approximately 2.71828.) For example, $e^{0.10} = 1.1052$, so the effective annual interest rate for continuous compounding at 10 percent interest is $e^{0.10} - 1 = 0.1052$, or 10.52 percent. The expression e^r is called "the *exponential* of r," and is sometimes written as $\exp(r)$.

The Continuously Compounding Interest Rate

Suppose the payback in one year on a loan of \$1.00 is \$1.20. What is the continuously compounding rate r for the loan? We know that $e^r = 1.20$, so we can solve for r by taking logarithms and using the general fact that $\log(e^r) = r$. The solution is $r = \log(1.20) = 0.1823 = 18.23$ percent. We can easily calculate the continuously compounding interest rate implicit in a Treasury bill paying \$10,000 in one year. If the current price of the T-bill is \$8,000, then the payback per dollar invested is \$10,000/\$8000 = 1.25, so the continuously compounding rate r is $\log(1.25) = 0.2231 = 22.31$ percent. Let's compare with the continuously compounding rate on a six-month T-bill whose price is \$9,200. Each dollar invested today yields \$10,000/\$9,200 = \$1.087 in six months. Reinvestment at the same return for an additional six months yields a total payback of $1.087 \times \$1.087 = \$1.182$ in one year. The continuously compounding rate is thus $r = \log(1.182) = 0.1669 = 16.69$ percent. More directly, $r = \log[(10,000/9,200)^2] = 0.1669$. The continuously compounding rate of interest over a period of T years on a security (such as a T-bill) whose initial price is p_t and whose final value (at time $t + T$) is p_{t+T} is given by the general formula

$$r = \log\left[(p_{t+T}/p_t)^{1/T}\right]. \tag{1}$$

In the above T-bill example, $T = 0.5$ years, $p_t = \$9,200$, and $p_{t+T} = \$10,000$. Using the rules of logarithms, equation (1) simplifies to

$$r = \frac{\log(p_{t+T}) - \log(p_t)}{T}, \tag{2}$$

an expression that will crop up frequently.

Bank Discounts

Consider again the \$10,000 T-bill maturing in one year that currently sells for \$8,000. The effective annual interest rate is 25 percent; the continuously compounding rate, as we saw, is $\log(1.25) = 0.2231 = 22.31$ percent. Complicating matters, banks and other financial institutions sometimes refer to this

T-bill's "discount" of 20 percent, meaning that it sells at 20 percent off its face value. Similarly, a T-bill with six months to maturity selling for $9,200 might be said (by some) to have a "discount" of 16 percent (a six-month discount of 8 percent multiplied by two for the "annual discount"). While sometimes misleading, this convention reflects a natural desire for quick and easy calculations.

Another source of confusion is the common practice in the bond market of treating a "month" as 30 days and a "year" as 360 days. For example, a "three-month T-bill" actually refers to a 90-day T-bill, while the "annual" interest rate is actually the interest rate per 360-day period.

The Term Structure

The *term structure* is the schedule of interest rates paid on riskless bonds of various maturities. In the United States, the term structure is usually shown in terms of U.S. Treasury bond yields. Figure 5.1 shows a sample *yield curve*, the graph of the term structure, showing interest rates on the vertical axis and time to maturity on the horizontal axis.

Treasury issues of less than two years to maturity are referred to as "T-bills," those with more than 10 years to maturity are "T-bonds," while those in between are "T-notes."

Each interest rate shown in Figure 5.1 is in the form of a *bond-equivalent yield*, the interest rate at which the present discounted value of the coupon payments and principal is equal to the current market value of the bond. Consider, for example, a 10-year $100,000 bond with annual 8-percent coupons that currently sells for $101,000. The yield on this bond is the simple interest rate r satisfying the equation

$$\$101,000 = \frac{\$8,000}{1+r} + \frac{\$8,000}{(1+r)^2} + \cdots + \frac{\$8,000}{(1+r)^{10}} + \frac{\$100,000}{(1+r)^{10}}.$$

The right-hand side of the equation is the discounted value of the annual coupon payments (each of which is 8 percent of the $100,000 face value) plus the discounted value of the principal at maturity. The solution to this equation is $r = 0.0785$, so the bond has a *yield to maturity* of 7.85 percent. If the bond currently sells at par ($100,000), then the yield to maturity is automatically equal to the coupon rate, 8 percent in this case. An adjustment must be made, however, if the first coupon payment occurs in some fraction of a year. More detailed calculations are shown in the discussion in Chapter 9 of the design of the Chicago Board of Trade U.S. Treasury bond futures contract.

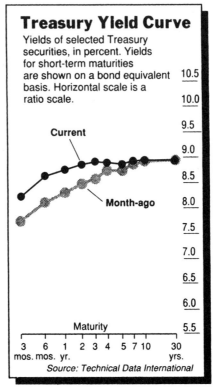

The New York Times/Dec. 7, 1988

Source: *The New York Times.*

Figure 5.1   The Term Structure of Interest Rates

The Treasury yield curve is a popular benchmark for interest rates since the U.S. Treasury Department usually receives the lowest available rates, given its miniscule default risk and the liquid secondary market for U.S. Treasury securities. There are also active forward and futures markets for Treasury securities. An exercise at the end of the chapter calls on the reader to establish relationships between spot and forward Treasury prices that are implied by an absence of arbitrage opportunities.

Continuous Compounding Revisited

What is the payback in T years on an investment of p_t dollars at a continuously compounding interest rate of r? We can use equation (2) to solve for the payback p_{t+T}. The properties of logarithms and exponentials applied to (2) give the solution

$$p_{t+T} = p_t \, e^{rT}. \tag{3}$$

Example: An investment of $10 (that is $p_t = 10$) for 150 days ($T = 0.041$ years) at a continuously compounding annual rate of 10 percent yields the payback $p_{t+T} = p_t e^{rT} = \$10 \exp(0.10 \times 0.41) = \$10.42$.

---

2. ARBITRAGE-FREE FORWARD PRICES

Forwards versus Futures

A *forward contract*, like a futures contract, is a commitment between two agents to make a particular exchange at a particular future date. Among its other differences with a futures contract, a conventional forward contract is not typically resettled daily through margin transactions. Depending on the behavior of interest rates, this distinction may not be negligible, and is brought up for consideration in Appendix 5A.

Suppose g_t is the forward price at time t for delivery of one unit of a particular asset at a given time T. This means that the buyer of such a forward contract agrees at time t to receive one unit of the asset at time T from the seller of the contract, in exchange for g_t dollars paid at time T.

Storage and Arbitrage

As an alternative to obtaining the future delivery of an asset by taking a long forward or futures position, one could instead buy the asset on the spot market and store it until the future delivery date. Storage is impossible, of course, for *perishable* commodities such as labor hours. Although all physical commodities are somewhat costly to store, or physically depreciate somewhat in storage, or both, we begin with the ideal case of a *perfectly storable* commodity. Some financial instruments (as opposed to commodities) are almost perfectly storable, and also fit into the following framework for pricing forwards. The remainder of this section repeats, with more precision, the arguments of Section 4.3.

An Upper Bound on Forward Prices

At date t, let s_t denote the spot price of a given asset, and let g_t denote the forward price for delivery of one unit of the same asset at a future date T.

Let $B_{t,T}$ denote the amount due at time T on a loan of $1 borrowed from time t until time T, assuming such a loan is possible. The *theoretical forward price*, which is merely a concept to be compared to the actual forward price, is defined as $g_t^* = B_{t,T} s_t$. In order to make a succinct comparison, we will work for the moment under the (rather unrealistic) *perfect forward and storage assumptions:*

1. Costless transactions

2. Riskless borrowing

3. Costless and perfect storage

As always, we presume as well that arbitrage—any trading strategy that generates profits without risk or investment—is impossible. If arbitrage were possible, the forces of supply and demand could not be in equilibrium, and the corresponding prices could not be market clearing.

Under the three assumptions made above, the current forward price g_t could be no greater than the theoretical forward price g_t^*. The proof of this is almost trivial. Suppose, in order to generate a contradiction, that $g_t > g_t^*$. An arbitrageur could adopt the strategy:

1. At time t, take a short position of one forward contract.

2. At time t, borrow s_t dollars risklessly for repayment at time T.

3. At time t, buy one unit of the deliverable asset on the spot market.

4. Store the asset from time t until the delivery time T.

5. Deliver the stored asset against the forward contract, collecting g_t from the other side of the contract.

6. Repay $g_t^* = B_{t,T} s_t$ due on the loan.

The net cash flow from this strategy is a profit of $g_t - g_t^* > 0$ at time T, requiring no risk, initial investment, or intermediate payments. Such an opportunity is an arbitrage, and the arbitrage profits can be scaled up arbitrarily by shorting any number, say k, forward contracts, buying and storing k units of the asset, and borrowing ks_t dollars. Theoretically speaking, markets cannot clear if such an arbitrage opportunity is available. We can summarize as follows.

Fact: *Under the perfect forward and storage assumptions 1–3, if there is no arbitrage, then the (actual) forward price g_t is less than or equal to the theoretical forward price $g_t^* = B_{t,T} s_t$.*

A Lower Bound on Forward Prices

Can we reverse the above arbitrage argument to show that $g_t^* = B_{t,T} s_t$ is also a lower bound on the forward price g_t? The answer is "yes," with one extra important assumption: The asset can be short sold at its spot price s_t. Physical commodities cannot always be short sold, but it is enough to assume that there exists at least one agent in the economy that has definite plans to store the asset from time t until time T, and would therefore be willing to lend the asset during this period for a small fee; we call this agent the *asset lender*.

Suppose, in order to make an arbitrage argument, that the current forward price g_t is lower than its theoretical level, $g_t^* = s_t B_{t,T}$. Consider another agent, whom we may as well call an arbitrageur, who takes a long position of one forward contract at time t and makes the following arrangement with the asset lender. The lender gives one unit of the asset to the arbitrageur at time t. The arbitrageur sells this unit on the current spot market for s_t and invests this amount in riskless bonds maturing at time T, when the bonds are worth $g_t^* = B_{t,T} s_t$. At the delivery date T, the arbitrageur settles the forward contract by accepting delivery of one unit of the asset in return for g_t dollars. The arbitrageur transfers this unit of the asset directly to the asset lender, along with a payment of some small asset lending fee, say half of the excess value of the bonds g_t^* over the forward price g_t. The other half of the excess value is kept by the arbitrageur as a pure profit. The arbitrageur risked nothing and invested nothing, in net. The asset lender has the same effective storage plans; one unit of planned storage has merely been replaced with the arrangement proposed by the arbitrageur. The lender also receives an additional riskless profit. The arbitrageur would scale up the proposed transactions until all storage between t and T is eliminated by spot sales, or until the forward price g_t goes up to at least the theoretical forward price $g_t^* = B_{t,T} s_t$.

If the asset is not a physical commodity, but instead a financial security that can be freely short sold, the argument does not depend on the requirement that some particular agent store the asset in positive quantities. Even if no particular agent stores the asset for the entire period from time t until time T, there may still be two storers, one storing from time t until at least some intermediate time t', and another storing from time t' until at least time T. The arbitrageur could accomplish the same effective cash flows by contracting with each storer individually, and splitting the arbitrage profits three ways. The argument extends indefinitely, so long as there exists storage at all dates between t and T.

Our arguments have established, under stated assumptions, that $g_t^* = B_{t,T} s_t$ is a lower bound on the forward price g_t. Since we argued earlier that g_t^* is also an upper bound, we have the following conclusion:

The Theoretical Forward Price: *Suppose the perfect forward and storage assumptions 1–3 apply and that the deliverable asset can be short sold at its spot price s_t. Then, unless arbitrage is possible, the forward price g_t and the theoretical forward price $g_t^* = B_{t,T} s_t$ are the same.*

In order to argue that an asset can be short sold at its spot market price, it is generally necessary for storage to occur with certainty. If the asset lender merely intends to store from t until T, but may decide to sell the stored commodity at some intermediate date if spot prices turn out to be sufficiently attractive, then the arbitrageur would have to compensate the asset lender for giving up this option. *Ex post* observed storage and *ex ante* certain storage are not the same; only the latter is a basis for our arguments. In particular, the term *theoretical forward price* is misleading; there is rarely a sound theoretical basis for certain storage of physical commodities. With financial assets such as common stocks, of course, there are good reasons to believe that the shares will be stored with certainty, since someone must own them at all times; they are not consumed.

We will extend the above arguments shortly to cover such details as storage costs, dividends, and coupon payments. For physical commodities, however, the greater the likelihood that current stocks of the commodity will become tight during the period before delivery of the forward contract, the less well does the theoretical forward price approximate the market forward price.

The Theoretical Futures Price

The term *theoretical futures price* is widely used in place of the term theoretical forward price. Of course, with the daily resettlement feature of futures contracts, the above arbitrage arguments would not generally apply. We can, however, appeal to the Futures-Forwards Equivalence Principle shown in Appendix 5A, provided changes in bond prices are not statistically correlated with changes in forward prices. A special case of this condition is *deterministic interest rates*, which means that interest rates at future dates are known with certainty. With deterministic interest rates, the Futures-Forwards Equivalence Principle implies that futures prices and forward prices are always the same.

The Theoretical Futures Price: *Suppose interest rates are deterministic, the perfect storage and forward assumptions apply, the deliverable asset can be short sold at its market price s_t, and there is no arbitrage. Then the futures price f_t is equal to the theoretical forward price $g_t^* = B_{t,T} s_t$.*

The term *theoretical futures price* is therefore also legitimate under special circumstances.

Costs of Carry

Let us relax the perfect storage assumptions and suppose the deliverable asset is subject to a continual storage cost of c dollars per unit per year. Gold is a useful example, taking c to be the cost of vault space and insurance per ounce per year. Let $A_{t,T}$ denote the amount one would have pay back at date T if one borrows \$1 at the riskless rate from date t until date T, \$1 more at the riskless rate from date $t + 1$ until date T, and so on until date T. This payback $A_{t,T}$ is called the *future value of an annuity factor*. (We will always measure time in years.) It follows that

$$A_{t,T} = B_{t,T} + B_{t+1,T} + \cdots + B_{T-1,T}. \tag{4}$$

Example: As a simple case, if interest rates are constant at an annual (continuously compounding) rate of r, and the dollar is borrowed continuously through time, a bit of calculus shows that

$$A_{t,T} = \frac{\exp[r(T - t)] - 1}{r}.$$

If $r = 0.10$ (10 percent), for example, and $T - t = 0.50$ years, then $A_{t,T} = 0.5127$. In other words, one would have to pay back \$0.5127 in six months if one continuously borrowed at the rate of \$1 per year (\$1/356.25 per day) for six months. Likewise, one would have to pay back \$51.27 in six months if the rate of borrowing were scaled up to \$100 per year.

One could finance the costs of storage of one unit of the asset in question from time t until time T by borrowing the storage costs continually as they are incurred and making a payment of $cA_{t,T}$ at time T, where c is the annual storage cost (paid continuously). Provided $A_{t,T}$ is known in advance, one can extend the earlier arbitrage arguments to obtain a theoretical formula for forward prices in the presence of storage costs. This is known as the *cost-of-carry* formula.

Cost-of-Carry Formula: *Suppose the underlying commodity is stored at a constant continuous cost of c dollars per year from time t until time T and that the future value of an annuity factor $A_{t,T}$ is known at time t. Assume also that transactions are costless and that the deliverable asset can be short sold at its market price s_t. Then, barring arbitrage, the forward price of the commodity at time t for delivery at time T is the theoretical forward price*

$$g_t^* = A_{t,T}c + B_{t,T}s_t. \tag{5}$$

The reader is expected to be able to prove this proposition as an exercise by making an appropriate arbitrage argument. Figure 5.2 graphs the theoretical forward price and quoted futures price of gold against time to delivery, assuming a particular constant interest rate. The actual data and assumed parameters are shown in Table 5.2. In this case, the cost-of-carry formula fits rather well, although at a surprisingly low storage cost. This low assumed cost of storage might be related to the so-called *convenience yield*, the value of the option to sell out of storage, which is not accounted for under our assumption of certain storage. Likewise, one could also correct for the upward sloping yield curve instead of assuming that r is independent of maturity.

As the current stockpile of a storable asset becomes larger, one can generally short sell the asset at a price closer to its spot market price, since the value of the option to sell out of storage before the end of the short sale period becomes smaller and smaller with increasing stockpiles. Gold is a good example for demonstrating the theoretical forward price formula since world stockpiles of gold are greatly in excess of anticipated consumption far into the future.

The exercises for this chapter explore various extensions of the cost-of-carry formula for handling a series of storage costs that changes through time, dividends (which can be treated as negative storage costs), and uncertain interest rates. The formula can be extended to the case of uncertain interest rates provided there exists a sufficiently rich set of forward interest rate contracts.

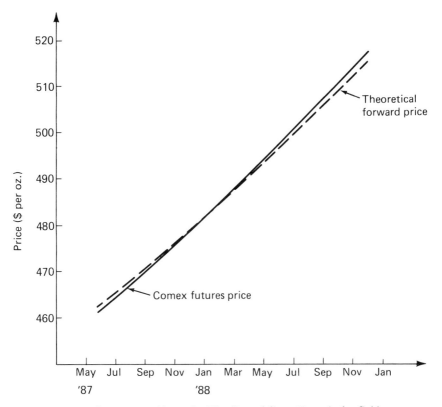

Figure 5.2   Example: The Cost-of-Carry Formula for Gold

The Implied Repo Rate

Ignoring storage costs and assuming that the theoretical and actual futures prices coincide, we can use the cost-of-carry formula $f_t = B_{t,T} s_t$ to calculate the continuously compounding riskless interest rate r implied by the current spot and futures prices. Since $B_{t,T} = \exp[r(T - t)]$, our formula $f_t = B_{t,T} s_t$ implies that

$$\exp\left[r(T - t)\right] = \frac{f_t}{s_t},$$

and taking the logarithm of each side leaves

$$r(T - t) = \log\left(\frac{f_t}{s_t}\right),$$

which gives us the *implied repo rate*

$$r = \frac{\log(f_t) - \log(s_t)}{T - t}. \tag{6}$$

TABLE 5.2   Futures Price and Theoretical Forward Price: Gold

May 12, 1987, Spot Comex Price: $s_t = \$459.7$ per ounce

Assumed Constant Interest Rate: $r = 7$ percent per year

Assumed Carrying Cost: $c = \$1$ per ounce per year

Theoretical Forward Price: $g^*_{t,T} = A_{t,T}c + B_{t,T}s_t$

May 12 Futures Price for Delivery at T: $f_{t,T}$

Delivery Month	$T-t$ (Years)	$A_{t,T}$	$B_{t,T}$	$g^*_{t,T}$	$f_{t,T}$
Jun 87	0.082	0.082	1.005	462.1	461.5
Jul 87	0.164	0.165	1.011	465.0	464.3
Aug 87	0.247	0.249	1.017	467.7	467.0
Oct 87	0.411	0.417	1.029	473.4	472.6
Dec 87	0.575	0.586	1.041	479.1	478.3
Feb 88	0.740	0.759	1.053	484.9	484.4
Apr 88	0.904	0.933	1.065	490.5	490.4
Jun 88	1.068	1.109	1.078	496.7	496.6
Aug 88	1.233	1.287	1.090	502.4	503.1
Oct 88	1.397	1.467	1.103	508.5	509.9
Dec 88	1.562	1.649	1.115	514.3	516.7

The implied repo rate, in other words, is the interest rate implicit in the forward price, that interest rate which would preclude arbitrage via the strategy of selling the spot asset and repurchasing it for later delivery in the forward market.

Example: Assuming zero storage costs, the repurchase rate r implicit in the futures price of 484.4 shown in Table 5.2 for February 1988 delivery of gold is

$$r = \frac{\log(484.4) - \log(459.7)}{0.740} = 0.0708 = 7.08 \text{ percent.}$$

In order to create arbitrage profits by purchasing gold and shorting the futures, one must therefore be able to borrow the purchase cost of the gold at an interest rate (continuously compounding) less than 7.08 percent. In order to profit by the reverse arbitrage (lending money generated by sales of gold), one must be able to obtain at least 7.08 percent interest on 270-day loans. Since the interest rates available to borrowers are somewhat higher than those available to lenders because of transactions costs, it is most often the case that the implied repo rate lies above the best interest rate available to lenders who

are in a position to short sell the deliverable asset, and below the best rates
available to borrowers who are in a position to buy the deliverable asset.

With non-zero storage costs or dividends, one must generally use a computer to solve for the interest rate r implicit in the theoretical equation $f_t = B_{t,T} s_t + A_{t,T} c$, or in the more general cost-of-carry formula shown in Exercise 5.3. A mixture of positive and negative storage costs through time, perhaps caused by fluctuating dividends, may yield several different implied repo rates consistent with the cost-of-carry formula. In such cases, implied repo rates are not generally valid measures of arbitrage potential.

3. STOCK INDEX ARBITRAGE

Although the term *program trading* has come to mean different things to different people, in a broad sense, it means the trading of futures contracts, the underlying deliverable assets, and related assets in a "programmable" manner, that is, following a mechanistic trading recipe. The proportions in which the assets are held are usually dictated by the construction of a particular stock index. We will limit ourselves to treatments of two particular program trading activities: stock index arbitrage and portfolio insurance. *Index arbitrage* exploits differences between stock index futures prices and the corresponding theoretical futures prices suggested by the cost-of-carry formula from the previous section. *Portfolio insurance* is a dynamic futures trading strategy that, at a cost, provides an approximate floor under the value of a stock portfolio, net of futures profits. Portfolio insurance will be explained in Chapter 8. Appendix 5B reviews the role of program trading in the Stock Crash of 1987.

Stock Indices

A *stock index* is a formula converting the current prices $S_t^{(1)}, S_t^{(2)}, \ldots, S_t^{(N)}$ of N selected common stocks to an index $I(S_t^{(1)}, S_t^{(2)}, \ldots, S_t^{(N)})$. For example, a commonly cited stock index is the Dow Jones Industrial Average (DJIA), the sum of the prices of 30 selected industrial stocks divided by a constant of normalization. That is,

$$\text{DJIA}_t = \frac{S_t^{(1)} + S_t^{(2)} + \cdots + S_t^{(30)}}{A}. \tag{7}$$

The normalizing constant A corrects for stock splits and occasional changes in the selection of stocks.

Another commonly cited stock index is the Value-Line Composite Average (VLA). Without going into details, the Value-Line Average is the *geometric mean* of a selection of stock prices $S_t^{(1)}, S_t^{(2)}, \ldots, S_t^{(N)}$. That is,

$$\text{VLA}_t = \frac{\left(S_t^{(1)} \times S_t^{(2)} \times \cdots \times S_t^{(N)} \right)^{1/N}}{A}, \tag{8}$$

where A is a constant of normalization. While the Value-Line Average is, for some purposes, a useful summary of the performance of the underlying stocks, it is not easily exploited for index arbitrage. Why? Even though there is currently a futures contract with cash settlement on the VLA traded on the Kansas City Board of Trade, there is no fixed portfolio of stocks whose market value tracks the Value Line Average. (There is, however, a dynamic trading strategy that could be designed to track the VLA under some assumptions.)

The S&P 500 Index is, with minor exceptions, the total market value of all outstanding common shares of approximately 500 selected major corporations. That is, if $S_t^{(n)}$ is the price of the n-th of those 500 stocks at time t, and $K_t^{(n)}$ is the number of shares outstanding of the n-th stock, then the S&P 500 Index at time t is

$$S_t = \frac{K_t^{(1)} S_t^{(1)} + K_t^{(2)} S_t^{(2)} + \cdots + K_t^{(500)} S_t^{(500)}}{A}, \tag{9}$$

where A is a constant of normalization. The *S&P 500 portfolio* is the portfolio $K_t^{(1)}, \ldots, K_t^{(500)}$ of all outstanding shares of the 500 selected corporations. Contrary to popular belief, the stocks included are not the 500 with the largest total market values, but rather a selection designed to represent the largest stocks in a cross-section of sectors of the economy. In order to remain representative and to take into account mergers and takeovers, the selection of stocks gradually changes over the years. In fact, there need not be exactly 500 firms included in the index. For simplicity, we will proceed as though equation (9) gives the exact definition of the S&P 500 Index during the period of any possible arbitrage strategy.

The S&P 500 Tracking Portfolio

The S&P 500 is a popular index because it represents such a large fraction of the total market value of publicly traded U.S. stocks, and also because it is feasible to form a portfolio of stocks whose total market value tracks that of the S&P 500 Index almost exactly. In addition, there is some theoretical

support for the popularity of the S&P 500 contract. A basic theory of security
market equilibrium, the Capital Asset Pricing Model (CAPM), suggests that
investors optimally choose to hold all of their investments to just two funds,
riskless bonds and the *market portfolio*, the portfolio made up of all outstanding shares of all securities. In practice, the S&P 500 portfolio of stocks is often
taken to be a proxy for the market portfolio. (Of course, even if it forms a
large fraction of U.S. stocks, the S&P 500 portfolio represents a relatively
small fraction of the value of all investments in the world.) Although the
CAPM is a simplified version of more detailed theories in which this form of
investor behavior is not necessarily optimal, the idea of splitting investments
into two funds—riskless assets and the market portfolio—has made the S&P
500 portfolio especially popular for investors. A strategy known as *asset allocation*, for example, is designed to quickly adjust the fraction of a portfolio's
return that is tied to the stock market by varying the portfolio's position in
S&P 500 futures and the underlying stocks. Moreover, the return on the S&P
500 portfolio is used as a performance benchmark for many mutual funds and
stock analysts. To "beat the market" has often come to mean constructing a
trading strategy that consistently outperforms the S&P 500 portfolio.

In order to construct a portfolio at time t having a dollar value equal to
500 times the current S&P 500 Index, one would purchase $500K_t^{(1)}/A$ shares
of the first stock, $500K_t^{(2)}/A$ shares of the second stock, and so on. Indeed,
the total market value V_t of this *S&P 500 tracking portfolio* when purchased
at time t is

$$V_t = \frac{500K_t^{(1)}}{A}S_t^{(1)} + \frac{500K_t^{(2)}}{A}S_t^{(2)} + \cdots + \frac{500K_t^{(500)}}{A}S_t^{(500)} = 500 \times S_t.$$

At time $t+1$, assuming no dividends or stock splits, the new market value V_{t+1}
of this tracking portfolio is obviously still equal to 500 times the new index,
S_{t+1}. Even if the n-th stock splits two-for-one, the holder of the tracking
portfolio receives one new share for each of the $500K_t^{(n)}/A$ originally purchased
shares, for a total holding of $500 \times 2K_t^{(n)}/A$ shares of the split stock. Since
$K_{t+1}^{(n)} = 2K_t^{(n)}$, we still have $V_{t+1} = 500 \times S_{t+1}$. Thus, ignoring what one does
with dividends, the market value of the tracking portfolio stays at 500 times
the S&P 500 Index without additional purchases or sales of stock.

There are indeed mutual funds that attempt to track the S&P 500 portfolio as closely as possible. One of the largest of these is currently managed
by Wells Fargo Investment Advisers (WFIA). Because this S&P 500 fund is
so large (recently on the order of $50 billion), WFIA is able to smoothly apply

the proceeds from new fund purchases (net of withdrawals) and stock dividends to the purchase and sale of the individual stocks making up the S&P 500 portfolio, so as to track the S&P 500 Index with a small tolerance for error. The availability of such mutual funds that track the S&P 500 portfolio is another reason for popular interest in the S&P 500 futures contract.

S&P 500 Futures

The S&P 500 Index futures contract of the Chicago Mercantile Exchange has cash settlement at the S&P 500 Index. This means that the futures settlement price f_T on the delivery date of the contract is mandated to be the S&P 500 index S_T on that date. A single contract actually settles at 500 times the futures price. That is, a long position of 10 contracts is credited with the resettlement variation $10 \times 500 \times (f_{t+1} - f_t)$ on day $t+1$. Neglecting transactions costs, one could just as well have physical delivery of the S&P 500 tracking portfolio described above, since the market value of this tracking portfolio at delivery is $V_T = 500 \times S_T$.

Although previously traded without price limits, since the Stock Crash of 1987 the CME has imposed a system of price limits known as *shock absorbers*; details are outlined in Appendix 5B. Although volume in the S&P 500 contract is, at this writing, approximately half its pre-crash level, current daily volumes are nevertheless large, on the order of 50,000 contracts. At a futures price (or "index," as it is more properly known) of 250, this represents the effective risk transfer of approximately

$$50{,}000 \times 500 \times \$250 = \$6{,}250{,}000{,}000$$

worth of common stocks on an average trading day. Typical daily volumes on the New York Stock Exchange (NYSE) are currently on the order of 150 million shares at an average share price of roughly $40, which generally represents about $6 billion in market value. Of course, these figures fluctuate daily, but the total dollar impacts of the two markets, spot and futures, are similar.

The NYSE is currently considering the introduction of spot trading in preassembled S&P 500 tracking portfolios. Since some of the current futures trades are intended as a way of approximating the effect of trading tracking portfolios without incurring the transactions costs of 500 separate trades, NYSE-packaged S&P 500 spot trading might draw some volume away from the futures market. Although the S&P 500 futures contract is the world's

largest stock index contract (in volume) at this writing, its position of dominance is threatened by the advent of trading in Japanese stock index futures
contracts. A number of European countries also have emergent stock index
futures contracts.

The Theoretical S&P 500 Futures Price

The cost-of-carry formula developed earlier in this chapter can be applied to
S&P 500 futures under the following approximating assumptions:

Deterministic interest rates

Deterministic stock dividends

No transactions costs

All three assumptions are typically violated, but only to an extent that leaves
the theoretical futures price tied closely to the actual futures price, excluding
periods such as the Stock Crash of 1987. Adapting the cost-of-carry formula
given by equation (5),

$$f_t^* = B_{t,T} s_t + A_{t,T} c,$$

to the case at hand, the theoretical futures index f_t^* for the S&P 500 Index
contract is given by the formula

$$f_t^* = B_{t,T} S_t - A_{t,T} D, \tag{10}$$

where S_t is the current spot S&P 500 Index, D is the constant dividend rate
(in dollars per day) assumed to apply between the current date t and the
contract's delivery date T, while the future value factors $B_{t,T}$ and $A_{t,T}$ are
described in the previous section. The *fractional dividend rate* $d = D/S_t$
is the assumed constant rate at which the S&P 500 tracking portfolio pays
dividends between times t and T, as a fraction of its initial value. Rearranging
equation (10) leaves the theoretical futures index

$$f_t^* = (B_{t,T} - dA_{t,T})S_t. \tag{11}$$

Example: The 180-day LIBOR on May 12, 1987, was 7.43 percent. The 180-
day rate on bankers' acceptance on that day was 6.90 percent. For simplicity,
we will assume a constant annual continuously compounding interest rate of
7 percent, or $r = 0.07$. The assumed time until delivery of the December 1987

futures contract is 210 days, or $T - t = 0.575$ years. We also assume that transactions and storage costs are negligible, and that the S&P 500 tracking portfolio pays dividends continuously at an annual rate of 3.5 percent of its market value on May 12, or $d = 0.035$. We have

$$B_{t,T} = \exp[r(T - t)] = \exp(0.07 \times 0.575) = 1.041,$$

and

$$A_{t,T} = \frac{\exp[r(T - t)] - 1}{r} = \frac{\exp(0.07 \times 0.575) - 1}{0.07} = 0.586.$$

Substituting into equation (11) the closing May 12, 1987, S&P 500 Index of 293.30, we have the theoretical futures index

$$f_t^* = (1.041 - 0.035 \times 0.586)\,293.3 = 299.3.$$

The actual S&P 500 futures closing index for May 12, 1987, was 299.00. The *futures-to-cash spread*, or *basis*, as is it is often called, is

$$f_t - s_t = 299.0 - 293.3 = 5.7.$$

In this example, the actual basis is approximately equal to the theoretical basis

$$f_t^* - s_t = 299.3 - 293.3 = 6.0.$$

Typically, the estimated discrepancy between f_t and f_t^* is small indeed, less than 1 percent. During the Stock Crash of 1987, however, the measured discrepancy was large, as discussed in Appendix 5B and shown in Figure 5.3.

Other Arbitrage Indicators

Rather than using an assumed constant rate D of dividend payments, it is also common to account for dividend payments in the form of a continuously compounding rate of dividend return, in the same sense as an interest rate. (This only makes theoretical sense under special assumptions about price behavior.) The implied repo rate formula (6) is then commonly reinterpreted by stock index arbitrageurs as a formula for the implied repo rate r net of the dividend yield y, or

$$r - y = \frac{\log(f_t) - \log(s_t)}{T - t}. \tag{12}$$

There are several ways to apply equation (12). We can treat it as a definition of the *implied dividend yield* y by substituting measured values for r, f_t, and

S&P 500 Cash-to-Futures Spread
In points, at 15 minute intervals

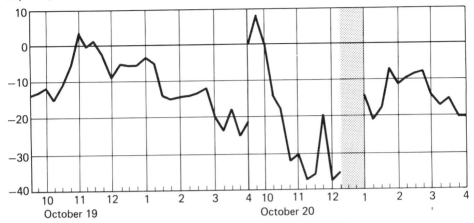

Note: Trading in futures contracts halted between 12:15 and 1:05

Major Market Index Cash-to-Futures Spread
In points, at 15 minute intervals

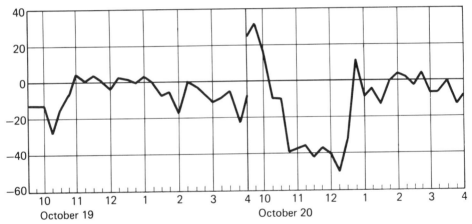

Source: *The Wall Street Journal*

Figure 5.3   S&P 500 Futures-to-Cash Spread During the Crash of 1987

s_t into the equation and solving for y. The more common alternative is to substitute some conventional value for the dividend yield y and solve for the implied repo rate r. In the previous example, an assumed dividend yield of $y = 4.0$ percent leaves an implied repo rate of

$$r = 4.0 + \frac{\log(299.0) - \log(293.3)}{0.575} = 0.0685 = 6.8 \text{ percent.}$$

One can alternatively substitute observed values of r, s_t, and y into equation (12) and solve for the theoretical futures price

$$f_t^* = B_{t,T}^* s_t, \tag{13}$$

where

$$B_{t,T}^* = \exp\left[(r - y)(T - t)\right] \tag{14}$$

is the value at delivery of \$1 invested on day t at the net continuously compounding riskless rate of $r - y$. For example, at $r = 0.07$ and $y = 0.04$, the net yield of $r - y = 0.03$ implies a theoretical futures index in our last example of

$$f_t^* = 293.3 \times \exp(0.03 \times 0.575) = 298.4,$$

as opposed to the actual futures index of $f_t = 299.0$. Equation (13) reinforces the view that, for markets in which the arbitrage arguments of this chapter apply, the ratio of the futures to spot price, $f_t/s_t = B_{t,T}^*$, theoretically follows a smooth path through time until the futures and spot prices coincide at delivery, as shown in Figure 5.4.

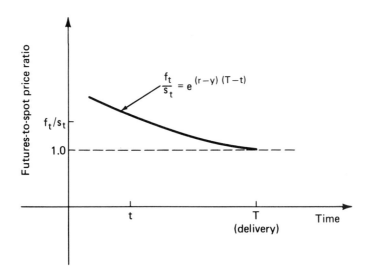

Figure 5.4   Theoretical Futures-to-Cash Ratio

Transactions Costs

Actual stock index arbitrage is somewhat different than suggested by our theoretical model, largely because of transactions costs.

Example: Suppose, in the context of our last example, that the current S&P 500 futures index is 301.0, while the spot index is 293.3. This 7.7-point basis exceeds the 6-point theoretical basis suggested by our assumptions on dividends and interest rates. Neglecting transactions costs, an arbitrage strategy would call for shorting S&P 500 futures contracts and buying multiples of the S&P 500 tracking portfolio, financing the cost of the stocks by borrowing. (In practice, the borrowing component of the arbitrage strategy is often ignored.)

For a $100 million arbitrage position, rough estimates of the transactions costs are shown in Table 5.3. These estimates would change dramatically with changes in market liquidity, and should not be taken seriously except for purposes of illustration. A significant portion of these transactions costs are not formal brokerage fees, but rather reflect the impact of the proposed order on the market price. A small sell order has minimal impact on the market. Other things being equal, however, in order to execute a sell order that is large relative to the typical order flow, other traders will only accommodate the contracts in their position "inventory" at a discount that reflects the risk they will carry until their increased inventories can be reduced by future buy orders. (The same principle applies to large buy orders.) This expected discount on sell orders or premium on buy orders is referred to as a *market impact cost*. In this sense, scalpers act as brokers who are willing to buy and sell so as to accommodate order imbalances; their unofficial brokerage fees for this service are the profits they realize in the form of market impact costs.

TABLE 5.3   Estimated S&P 500 Arbitrage Transactions Costs, $100m.

	Commissions	Market Impact	Total
Futures	27,280	17,050	44,330
Spot	200,000	340,950	540,950
Total	227,280	358,000	$585,280

In order to calculate the required spot and futures positions for an arbitrage of $100 million, we need to know the number of tracking portfolios that can be purchased with $100 million. At a spot index of 293.3, one can

purchase
$$\frac{\$100,000,000}{500 \times \$293.3} = 682 \quad \text{tracking portfolios.}$$

The arbitrage strategy therefore requires shorting 682 futures contracts. At round-turn commission fees of $40 per contract, this involves a total of $27,280 in commissions. Market impact costs can only be estimated roughly as the difference between the bid and offer futures prices one might be quoted for a position of this size. In the relatively liquid S&P 500 futures market, the market impact might only be 0.05 index points, for a total of $682 \times 500 \times 0.05 = \$17,050$. (As mentioned, these figures change with changes in liquidity.) For the stocks themselves, assuming an average price per share of $50 (or more precisely, an average of 1 share per $50) and an average commission per share of 5 cents (buying or selling), the total commission costs for the $100 million worth of tracking portfolio would be approximately

$$\frac{\$100,000,000}{\$50} \times (\$0.05 + \$0.05) = \$200,000.$$

Market impact costs for the 500 individual stock transactions could be on the order of 1 S&P 500 index point, for a total of

$$\$100,000,000 \times \frac{1.0}{293.3} = \$340,950.$$

The total transactions costs, as shown in Table 5.3, are roughly estimated at $585,000. In terms of the futures part of the arbitrage, these costs are approximately

$$\frac{44,330 \times 301}{100,000,000} = 0.13 \quad \text{S\&P 500 points.}$$

For the stocks themselves, the costs are approximately

$$\frac{540,950 \times 293.3}{100,000,000} = 1.6 \quad \text{S\&P 500 points.}$$

The effective spot index purchase cost is therefore approximately $293.3 + 1.6 = 294.9$, while the effective futures index (offer) is apparently $301.0 - 0.13 = 300.87$. The effective futures-to-cash spread, after transactions costs, is $300.87 - 294.9 = 6.0$ points. At a 4 percent dividend yield, the effective repo rate (continuously compounding, after total transactions costs) implied by equation (12) is

$$r = 4.0 + \frac{\log(300.87) - \log(294.9)}{0.575} = 0.040 + 0.015 = 0.055 = 5.5 \quad \text{percent.}$$

In effect, one would have to be able to borrow at no more than 5.5 percent interest in order to create profitable arbitrage. Given current interest rates of about 7 percent, what may have appeared to be a potential arbitrage turns out to be an unattractive opportunity once transactions costs are counted in. Of course, as already mentioned, our crude estimates are merely for purposes of illustration.

For the reverse arbitrage strategy (sell spot, buy futures, and lend), competitive lending rates should exceed the effective implied repo rate—the opposite relationship. The reverse strategy involves selling the tracking portfolio of stocks. If the stocks are not already owned, the transactions costs for their short sale and repurchase far exceed the transactions costs previously estimated for puchase and sale. The reverse (long futures, short spot) arbitrage therefore tends to be more easily carried out by those investors already holding the 500 stocks in large quantities. An obvious candidate is an S&P 500 index fund, such as the S&P 500 fund managed by Wells Fargo Investment Advisers.

Having reviewed the effects of transactions costs on stock index arbitrage, we can see that the futures-to-cash spread is free to roam within a band in which arbitrage is not possible. Once the spread moves outside this band, arbitrageurs tend to take positions that collectively move the spread back into line, increasing demand on the relatively underpriced market, while increasing supply on the relatively overpriced market. This equilibrating mechanism does not always work perfectly, at least not from appearances. Factors limiting the equilibrating properties of arbitrage include:

- Limited arbitrage capital
- Imperfect execution
- Uncertain dividends and interest

To repeat, an arbitrage is only possible when the difference between the theoretical futures price and the actual futures price is larger in magnitude than the arbitrageur's costs for making the corresponding arbitrage transactions. Those arbitrageurs with lowest transactions costs are therefore typically the first to exploit any price difference, and may in fact reduce the difference to the point where it cannot be exploited by others. The costs of purchasing or selling a portfolio of 500 stocks are not negligible. Furthermore, the prices quoted when arbitrage orders are placed are not the execution prices obtained for the orders. Speed is essential in obtaining a strategy that even

approximates an arbitrage. It becomes clear that the practical effect of the
word "arbitrage" and the theoretical usage (non-zero profits at zero investment and zero risk) are quite different. An arbitrageur earns economic rents
on trading skills, energy, the capital and labor costs of an efficient high-volume
order placement system, and the willingness to bear the risks of price changes
over small time intervals.

Differences between actual and theoretical futures prices are typically
smaller in magnitude than suggested by the gap defined by transactions costs.
For example, if the futures price exceeds the theoretical futures price, but not
by an amount large enough to allow arbitrage, those who would have taken
long futures positions for reasons other than arbitrage are free to take advantage of the price discrepancy by purchasing instead the underlying asset and
borrowing the purchase cost. The increased demand for the underlying asset
will tend to reduce the relative "mispricing" of futures and spot. Likewise,
those planning to sell the underlying asset can postpone the sale by adopting
a short futures position. If the futures price is below its theoretical value, the
forces of supply and demand again tend to eliminate discrepancies between
the actual and theoretical futures prices, even when arbitrage is not effective
because of transactions costs.

Triple Witching Hours

At times in the past, the usually frenetic trading behavior just prior to delivery
of the S&P 500 futures contract has been called the *triple witching hour*, the
hour before simultaneous expiry of the S&P 500 futures contract, options on
the S&P 500 futures contract, and options on individual stocks included in
this index. This period had been characterized by extremes of trading volume
and price volatility. Some of this volatility may be ascribed to simultaneous
attempts at arbitrage by various agents, causing occasional "overcorrections"
in prices. This is not necessarily a sound explanation, but no theoretical model
has yet been offered to explain market behavior during the triple witching
hour. Recently, various exchanges have adjusted the delivery times of these
instruments so that they do not exactly coincide, in an attempt to reduce
"unstable" market conditions.

Portfolio insurers and other hedgers typically roll their positions in the
nearby futures contract into the next nearby contract several weeks before the
nearby delivery date in order to avoid the turbulent execution conditions just
prior to delivery. The "rolling" procedure offsets the nearby position, substituting positions in the following contract. This is often done gradually, over a

period of days, in order to mitigate the market-impact portion of transactions costs.

EXERCISES

5.1 Show that the cost-of-carry formula $g_t = g_t^* = A_{t,T}c + B_{t,T}s_t$ must be true by first assuming that it is false, and then demonstrating an arbitrage strategy. Show the arbitrage strategy in both cases: $g_t > g_t^*$ (forward price "too high") and $g_t < g_t^*$ (forward price too low).

5.2 (Forward Bond Prices from the Yield Curve) On June 30, 1988, the price of a 1-year $10,000 Treasury bill is $9,000, that of a six-month T-bill is $9,500, and there is a forward contract delivering a six-month Treasury bill on December 30, 1988. The forward price is $9,430.

(a) Describe an arbitrage strategy that captures a current profit of approximately $20 million and involves no future cash flow or risk. (Neglect transactions costs.)

(b) Assuming the given spot T-bill prices are correct, what must the forward price be in order to preclude arbitrage?

(c) Let p_n be the fraction of face value at which an n-year Treasury bond is currently priced, for any n. Let $g_{n,m}$ denote the forward price per dollar of face value of an m-year Treasury bond delivered in n years. (Both n and m could be fractions.) Demonstrate an arbitrage opportunity if, for any n and m, the forward price $g_{n,m}$ is not equal to p_{n+m}/p_n.

5.3 The simple cost-of-carry model is easily extended to the case of an underlying asset that requires payment of a general (non-random) cash flow process $c_1, c_2, \ldots$. The cash flow c_t is the sum of all storage costs, net of any income generated by the asset, such as rental payments, dividends, or coupons that occur at date t. (Thus c_t could be negative.) Show that, unless arbitrage is possible, the forward price at time t for delivery of the asset at time T is

$$g_t^* = G_{t,T}(s_t + c_t) + G_{t+1,T}\, c_{t+1} + \cdots + G_{T-1,T}\, c_{T-1} + c_T, \qquad (15)$$

where $G_{t+k,T} = B_{t,T}/B_{t,t+k}$.

5.4 *(Bond Arbitrage)* Suppose "today" is a business day in early 1989. Markets for the following instruments are assumed to be currently open:

(i) A forward contract delivering one year Treasury bills at the end of 1989. The current forward price is g_t; the contract delivers a U.S. Treasury bill paying \$10,000 to the bearer at the end of 1990.

(ii) A forward contract delivering U.S. Treasury bonds at the end of 1990. The current forward price is G_t; the contract delivers a U.S. Treasury bond paying the face value of \$100,000 to the bearer at the end of year 2009. This bond, issued in 1979, pays annual coupons of 11.75 percent of face value at the end of each year. Assume that the coupon for 1990 is paid just milliseconds before the forward contract's delivery time. That is, the forward contract delivers the bond with the coupon for 1990 already clipped.

(iii) The 11.75 percent U.S. Treasury bond of 2009 described under (ii) is currently available for sale at the price s_t.

(iv) The 2-year U.S. Treasury note maturing at the end of 1990 is currently selling for p_t. This note pays the face value of \$100,000 to the bearer at the end of 1990. Assume it pays no coupons. (Coupons are included in part [d] of the exercise.)

(a) Assuming no transactions costs, state a formula for the unique bond forward price G_t that precludes arbitrage, based only on the variables s_t, g_t, and p_t.

(b) Assume the following bid and ask prices in these markets. The December 1990 T-note p_t, bid: 89.00 percent of face value; ask: 89.04 percent of face value. The $11\frac{3}{4}$ bond of 2009, s_t: bid 123.16 percent of face value, ask: 123.20 percent of face value. Assume all other transactions are costless, with the forward price g_t for December 1989 delivery of 1-year T-bills currently at 91.22 percent of face value. Give the highest value of G_t that precludes arbitrage and the lowest value of G_t that precludes arbitrage.

(c) Assuming the same price data given in part (b), suppose the bond forward price is $G_t = \$113,000$ (or 113 percent of face value). Outline a particular arbitrage strategy. Consider solely those strategies that require current input of transactions costs only, and generate cash flows only at the end of 1990.

(d) Suppose the 2-year Treasury note of December 1990 pays a coupon of 7 percent of face value at the end of 1989. Under the conditions of part (a), is there still a unique arbitrage-free bond forward price G_t? If so, state the formula for G_t in terms of the other available data.

5.5 *(Silver Arbitrage)*   The following assumptions for this problem are obviously not realistic.

(i) Silver is perfectly stored at a cost of 20 cents per troy ounce per year, on a continual-payment basis.

(ii) Interest rates are at the fixed deterministic continuously compounding annual rate represented by the current LIBOR rate for 180-day borrowing, as published in the financial press on the first Wednesday after this problem is assigned.

(iii) Today is the first Wednesday after this problem is assigned, and today's silver spot price is as quoted by Handy and Harmon. (This quotation is published daily in *The New York Times* and *The Wall Street Journal*. Take the average of bid and ask if ignoring transactions costs.)

(iv) Transactions costs are negligible.

(a) Calculate the theoretical forward prices for silver at the futures delivery dates available on the Comex silver futures market. In particular, fill out a table analogous to Table 5.2, showing also the actual futures prices for "today." You may assume, as in Table 5.2, that the contracts deliver in multiples of 30 days from today.

(b) Find the delivery month for which the futures price differs from the theoretical forward price by the greatest amount. State precisely the strategy you would perform in order to obtain "arbitrage" profits of $1 million at this delivery date. Scale your strategy to the nearest whole number of contracts.

NOTES

Cox, Ingersoll, and Ross (1985) have developed a well known equilibrium model of the term structure of interest rates. Cox, Ingersoll, and Ross (1981) is the basis for most of Appendix 5A. See Duffie and Stanton (1988) for an extension of these results, as well as Jarrow and Oldfield (1981) for related work. The case of riskless interest rates was earlier analyzed by Black (1976). Differences between futures and forward prices for foreign currencies were examined by Cornell and Reinganum (1981). French (1983) compares futures and forward prices for copper and silver. Park and Chen (1985) examine six commodities and four foreign currencies. Miller (1986) reviews the forward contracting market for cotton.

The discussion of theoretical forward prices in Section 5.2 is fairly standard. The relationship between spot and futures prices is examined in a theoretical framework by Turnovsky (1983) (for storable commodities) and by Kawai (1983) (for non-storable commodities). Brennan (1986) analyzes the convenience yield, a concept mentioned in Section 5.2. Brennan and Schwartz (1987) examine the optimal behavior of arbitrageurs when the cost-of-carry formula does not apply. A special case is solved by Duffie (1987); McKinlay and Ramaswamy (1987) investigate more of the empirical implications. Richard and Sundaresan (1981) develop a continuous-time equilibrium model of forward and futures prices.

There is a large literature connecting the behavior of producers with their ability to take futures positions, and demonstrating the resulting effect on futures prices. Storage is, of course, one special case. Recent examples include Hirshleifer (1985, 1986) as well as Anderson and Danthine (1983).

Appendix 5B, The Stock Crash of 1987, is based mainly on newspaper reports, the Report of the Presidential Task Force on Market Mechanisms (The Brady Report), as well as Miller, Malkiel, Scholes, and Hawke (1988). Other sources referred to include Kleidon (1988) and Harris (1987). In addition to the Brady Report, the public agencies which have issued reports include the CFTC and the SEC. Numerous references on portfolio insurance, including its role in the crash, are cited in the Notes to Chapter 8.

Appendix 5A: The Futures-Forwards Equivalence Principle

A conventional forward contract is distinct from a futures contract in that forward positions are not regularly marked-to-market. This appendix, summarizing the work of Black (1976) and (especially) Cox, Ingersoll, and Ross (1981), explores the distinction between futures and forwards, and shows special conditions under which futures and forward contracts have the same prices. In general, however, these prices are not the same because of the difference between long-term borrowing and rolling over short-term loans.

Rolling over the Short Rate

As an alternative to investing \$1 on day t in bonds maturing at day T, one could invest \$1 on day t at the one-day (or "overnight") riskless rate for that day. The proceeds, $B_{t,t+1}$, could again be invested for one day at the new one-day rate, yielding a compounded value of $B_{t,t+1}B_{t+1,t+2}$ after two days, and so on. By day T, the value of this strategy of rolling over the proceeds daily at the one-day riskless rate would be

$$R_{t,T} = B_{t,t+1}B_{t+1,t+2}\cdots B_{T-1,T}.$$

Generally speaking, the payoffs $R_{t,T}$, from investing "short" and rolling over, and $B_{t,T}$, from investing "long," are not the same. The former is typically random, while the latter is known at time t. Suppose, however, that we can neglect transactions costs and assume that interest rates are *deterministic*, meaning that $B_{t+1,t+2}, B_{t+2,t+3}$, and so on are all known with certainty at time t. Then $B_{t,T} = R_{t,T}$, barring arbitrage. This can be shown by the following typical arbitrage argument. Suppose, in order to generate a contradiction, that $B_{t,T} < R_{t,T}$. Consider an agent, whom we will call an arbitrageur, who "borrows long" by selling at time t \$1's worth of bonds maturing at time T. The arbitrageur must pay back $B_{t,T}$ at time T. At time t the arbitrageur also lends \$1 short and rolls over the loans daily, generating a payback of $R_{t,T}$ at time T. The net effect is no cash flow until time T, when the arbitrageur nets a profit of $R_{t,T} - B_{t,T}$. If this amount is indeed strictly positive, the arbitrageur could magnify the profit without limit by increasing the scale of borrowing and lending. If $R_{t,T} < B_{t,T}$, then the reverse strategy is an arbitrage. We summarize as follows.

Fact 1:   *Suppose there are no transactions costs and arbitrage is impossible. If interest rates are deterministic then, for any times t and $T \geq t$, the value $B_{t,T}$ received from \$1 invested risklessly long-term (from t until T) is equal to the value $R_{t,T}$ received from \$1 invested risklessly short-term and rolled over short until time T.*

Two Additional Useful Facts

We wish to characterize the forward and futures prices for delivery at time T of an asset whose current spot price is s_t. We will not need to make any assumptions about storage of the asset.

Like a futures price, a forward price is not itself the price of an asset, but we do have the following characterization of what one can receive by investing the forward price g_t at time t.

Fact 2: *One can invest g_t at time t in such a way as to receive $B_{t,T} s_T$ at time T.*

In order to see why this is true, consider the following investment plan. Invest g_t at time t in bonds maturing at time T. The bonds will pay off $g_t B_{t,T}$ at time T. Take a long position of $B_{t,T}$ forward contracts. The forward position is a commitment to pay $g_t B_{t,T}$ dollars at time T in exchange for $B_{t,T}$ units of the asset, whose total value will be $B_{t,T} s_T$ at delivery. The net cash flows generated by the combined strategy is thus as stated by Fact 2, and as illustrated in Figure 5.5(a).

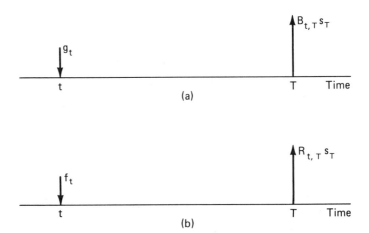

Figure 5.5   Feasible Cash Flows

For comparison, we can also view the futures price f_t for delivery at time T as the cost of a particular investment strategy.

Fact 3: *One can invest f_t at time t in such a way as to receive $R_{t,T} s_T$ at time T.*

Again, we can prove the result by adding up the cash flows generated by a combination of investments, as follows:

Day t Take a long position of $B_{t,t+1}$ futures contracts. Offset the position after one day, and invest the profits $B_{t,t+1}(f_{t+1} - f_t)$ in short-term lending on day $t + 1$, rolling over the proceeds daily until time T, yielding final proceeds of

$$B_{t,t+1}(f_{t+1} - f_t)[B_{t+1,t+2}B_{t+2,t+3} \cdots B_{T-1,T}] = R_{t,T}(f_{t+1} - f_t).$$

Day $t + 1$ Take a long position of $B_{t,t+1}B_{t+1,t+2}$ futures contracts. Offset the position after one day, and invest $B_{t,t+1}B_{t+1,t+2}(f_{t+2} - f_{t+1})$, the closeout profits, in short-term lending on day $t + 2$, rolling over the proceeds daily until time T, finally yielding

$$B_{t,t+1}B_{t+1,t+2}(f_{t+2}-f_{t+1})[B_{t+2,t+3} \cdots B_{T-1,T}] = R_{t,T}(f_{t+2}-f_{t+1}).$$

On each succesive day, one continues with the following general recipe.

Day $t + k$ Take a long position of $R_{t,t+k+1}$ futures contracts. Offset the position after one day and invest the profits $R_{t,t+k+1}(f_{t+k+1} - f_{t+k})$ risklessly for one day, rolling the proceeds over each day, generating the delivery date payoff

$$R_{t,t+k+1}(f_{t+k+1} - f_{t+k})R_{t+k+1,T} = R_{t,T}(f_{t+k+1} - f_{t+k}).$$

Continuing in this way until day T, the total proceeds for the futures transactions combined are

$$R_{t,T}[(f_{t+1} - f_t) + (f_{t+2} - f_{t+1}) + \cdots + (f_T - f_{T-1})] = R_{t,T}(f_T - f_t).$$

One combines these futures transactions with the following riskless lending strategy:

Day t Invest f_t in short-term lending, rolling over daily until time T, yielding $R_{t,T}f_t$ at time T.

The total proceeds from futures trades, $R_{t,T}(f_T - f_t)$, added to the payoff $R_{t,T}f_t$ from lending risklessly, make for a grand total payoff of $R_{t,T}f_T$. Since $f_T = s_T$ (ruling out arbitrage at delivery), the total effect of all of these cash flows is thus as stated by Fact 3, and as illustrated in Figure 5.5(b).

Are Futures and Forward Prices the Same?

Combining Facts 1, 2, and 3 leads to the following equivalence between futures and forward prices with deterministic interest rates.

The Futures-Forwards Equivalence Principle: *Suppose there are no transactions costs and interest rates are deterministic. Then, barring arbitrage, at any time* t *the futures price* f_t *and the forward price* g_t *are the same.*

Again, a proof can be given by arbitrage arguments. Suppose that at some time t it happens that $g_t > f_t$. An arbitrageur could adopt the strategy described in the demonstration of Fact 3 at an initial cost of f_t, and reverse the strategy supporting Fact 2, for an initial payoff of g_t. The terminal payoff is $s_T(R_{t,T} - B_{t,T})$, which is zero by Fact 1. The grand net effect of this strategy is a riskless payoff of $g_t - f_t$ at time t. The combination of these strategies is shown in Figure 5.6. But this is an arbitrage! If $g_t < f_t$, the reverse strategy is an arbitrage. We have therefore verified the Futures-Forwards Equivalence Principle.

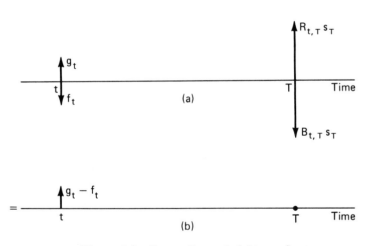

Figure 5.6   Futures-Forwards Arbitrage Strategy

Futures-Forwards Equivalence with Uncertain Interest Rates

Of course, one cannot realistically assume, as we have so far, that interest rates are deterministic. An article by Cox, Ingersoll, and Ross (1981) cited in the Notes shows that if bond returns and futures price increments are always positively correlated in a sense that can be made precise, then an absence of arbitrage implies that the forward price always exceeds the futures price. If the stated variables are always negatively correlated, then the futures price always exceeds the forward price. With zero correlation at all times, the futures and forward prices are always the same. A special case of zero correlation is deterministic interest rates, consistent with the Futures-Forwards Equivalence Principle. Of course, none of these cases need apply. Statistical tests of this model, cited in the Notes, tend to support the Futures-Forwards Equivalence Principle, but differences between forward and futures prices are small enough to give inconclusive test results for some markets. A study of the foreign currency market by Cornell and Reinganum (1981) shows that, for futures and forward contracts on the same currency with the same delivery date, it is typical that the futures and forward prices differ by an amount less than the bid-ask spread in the forward market.

Appendix 5B: The Stock Crash of 1987

The Crash

On October 19, 1987, American and foreign stock markets crashed. Almost any broadly based measure indicated a one-day drop of 20 to 30 percent in the market value of U.S. equities, significantly more than the percentage loss recorded in the famous Crash of 1929. Wilshire Associates reported that the total market value of 6,000 publicly traded U.S. firms fell from a record-high level of $3.3 trillion on August 25, 1987, to $2.3 trillion at the close of trading on Monday, October 19. Approximately half of this trillion-dollar loss occurred on that Monday itself. The most commonly quoted single measure of the crash was a fall in the Dow Jones Industrial Average of 508 points from the close on Friday the 16th to Monday's close of 1739, this following on Friday's loss of 108 points (itself a record at that time). Trading volume on the NYSE on both Monday the 19th and Tuesday the 20th exceeded 600 million shares, nearly doubling the previous daily volume record of 338 million shares established only the Friday before.

Without question, the Stock Crash of 1987 was unprecedented in magnitude. It is difficult to sort out the causes. Among those cited are a falling U.S. dollar, rising interest rates, panic, and insufficient capitalization of stock specialists and other market makers. Other commonly mentioned causes are program trading, including both portfolio insurance and index arbitrage.

We will briefly focus here on the role of, and effects on, program trading in the crash. A simplistic story that lays the magnitude of the crash at least partly at the feet of program trading goes roughly as follows. Based on some important pieces of fundamental news, perhaps combined with Friday's forboding stock performance, many investors anticipated sharply lower stock prices at Monday's open. Large orders to sell, not counterbalanced by buy orders, had arrived at brokerage houses prior to the opening. As will be explained in Chapter 8, portfolio insurance calls for selling S&P 500 futures in a falling stock market (and buying in a rising market). Stock index arbitrage would quickly transfer some of the futures selling (whatever its motive) to the stock markets themselves, since a drop of the S&P 500 futures index relative to the spot index signals the profitability of an arbitrage that buys futures and sells the S&P 500 portfolio. This sort of arbitrage can be quickly accomplished by those already holding the stocks, using the DOT (Direct Order Turnaround) "list function," which allows simultaneous electronic execution of 500 different stock trades. Even if the DOT system breaks down, as it did during the crash, or even if there is insufficient arbitrage capacity, some of those sending sell orders for stock index futures can substitute with orders to the New York Stock Exchange to sell the stocks themselves. In any case, even if such a wave of selling was not to be triggered by portfolio insurance, many investors would naturally expect it to be, since portfolio insurance is designed to respond mechanically, selling in quantities dictated by well-known formulas, without recourse. Thus there was cause for concern among those with long equity positions. Furthermore, sophisticated equity holders such as large institutional fund managers knew not only to expect a wave of selling, but knew as well that other investors like themselves were also expecting such a selling wave, and would perhaps attempt to pre-empt losses by selling in advance of others. (This is sometimes called *front-running*.) In other words, there was ample latitude for "fear of fear itself." If one carries this thinking one step further (and many perhaps did), a wave of selling triggered in part by portfolio insurance would itself induce further price declines, and therefore a second round of selling, and so on.

Ironically, the form of apparent "panic" that this scenario describes could be treated as completely rational: each individual could be acting optimally in the face of the expected behavior of prices and other individuals. And what about "fundamentals"? Would there not be a pool of capital waiting to exploit prices below their fundamental levels (that is, the competitive equilibrium prices dictated by information, technologies, and preferences)? Would not the application of such capital tend to cushion the fall? At least two lines of response to these questions are worth considering. First, it could indeed be the case that prices reached their appropriate new fundamental levels. Certainly, most asset-pricing models in use allow that such dramatic events will occur occasionally. How are we to know? Economists have not isolated a single, unambiguous, easily calculated, and correct model for asset price behavior. This leads to a second line of response: If we do not have a single correct model for fundamental value, how can investors know whether a large drop in prices represents fundamental effects or not? Recent work in economic theory indeed indicates that there may be more uncertainty in equilibrium prices than represented by fundamentals alone. Instead of uniquely determined market-clearing prices for each set of fundamentals, there may be a wide band of candidate prices from which market-clearing prices are chosen at random (or chosen on the basis of the institutional structure of the market). Faced with this sort of uncertainty, it is dfficult to say what magnitude of stock price declines represents a bargain.

Ultimately, it is difficult to apportion blame for the crash between fundamental factors on one hand (such as international and national economic news) and technical factors on the other (such as the market's trading technology, front running, as well as trading rules that are programmed to stock price movements themselves). Obviously, as the magnitude of the crash became apparent, the response of fundamental expectations of economic performance to declining market indices may have contributed to further declines. It is difficult, however, to believe that index arbitrage itself could be a major source of net downward pressure on the market. Since the futures market tends to be an easier market in which to quickly change one's exposure to general market shifts, it is not surprising that futures price declines may have led the general market decline, and that index arbitrage would have transferred some of the selling pressure to the stock markets themselves. Rather than "shooting the messenger," perhaps we can credit index arbitrage for expanding the effective amount of available market-making capital and for lowering transactions costs. There seems to be little available statistical support for the hypothesis index arbitrage is associated with increasing volatility or reduced price levels.

Turning from conjecture to fact, the nearby S&P 500 futures index settled on Monday the 19th at 201.5, an unprecedented 81 points below its previous settlement. Since trading in the underlying stocks was illiquid because of the breakdown of the DOT computerized execution system and sporadic trading stoppages in some of the largest stocks, arbitrage may have become difficult. As shown in Figure 5.3, the reported futures-to-cash spread in the S&P 500 Index dipped to unheard of negative levels of around -20 on Monday to -40 on Tuesday, just prior to a mid-day halt in S&P 500 futures trading at the Chicago Mercantile Exchange. Faltering liquidity in both stocks and futures stemmed in some part from inadequate market making. There was not enough capacity on the part of stock specialists and futures traders to completely absorb order imbalances by taking positions on their own accounts, considering the risks involved in doing so. By most accounts, illiquidity was more serious for stocks than for futures. For example, the USX specialist Tompane was taken over by Merrill Lynch as an alternative to failure. The superior liquidity of futures over stocks is indeed consistent with the negative S&P 500 basis shown in Figure 5.3 during a period in which the outside order flow contained an imbalance on the selling side. On the other hand, as pointed out by Harris (1987) and Kleidon (1988), a major source of explanation of the apparently large negative basis may have been the reporting of stale prices for the individual stocks making up the S&P 500 (especially, of course, those stocks whose trading had halted). On October 19, the NYSE trading system had a backlog of unprocessed orders of as much as 45 minutes. Naturally, if futures prices are reported in a more up-to-date manner than stock prices, it will appear that arbitrage opportunities exist when they do not. These two factors, illiquidity in stock trading and stale reporting of stock prices, could account for most of the large negative basis seen during the crash.

According to reporting in *The Wall Street Journal* by James Stewart and Daniel Hertzberg, the situation at mid-day on Tuesday, October 20, 1987, was at a crisis. Illiquidity on the NYSE was threatening to force a shutdown of the exchange, and with that a possible destabilization of the entire financial system. The Chicago Mercantile Exchange, as already mentioned, had halted trading in the S&P 500 pit at mid-day, as had most index options markets. A strange event then occurred in the *Major Market Index* (MMI) futures pit of the Chicago Board of Trade. The MMI contract has cash settlement on the value of 20 blue chip stocks, 17 of which are included in the closely watched Dow Jones Industrial Average of 30 stocks. As with the S&P 500 contract, the reported MMI futures-to-cash spread had moved to large negative values, contrary to the positive basis that precludes arbitrage during periods of greater liquidity. As illustrated in Figure 5.3, the MMI basis suddenly shifted from −60 to +12. One theory discussed in the article by Stewart and Hertzberg is that concerted and perhaps coordinated buying of MMI futures during this period of relative thinness in the MMI futures pit was sufficient to boost the index. To be blunt, this suggests manipulation, which is illegal. Whether or not manipulation of the MMI contract occurred, the sudden correction in its basis may have triggered active buying of several of the high-

profile DJIA stocks, and a general return to liquidity at the NYSE and the
S&P 500 pit at the CME. According to Miller, Malkiel, Scholes, and Hawke
(1988), "the recovery is more plausibly linked to the commencement of large
corporate buyback programs and the promise of Federal Reserve support of
bank liquidity."

Prior to the crash, an estimated $60 billion worth of stock was "protected"
by portfolio insurance, a program trading technique explained in Chapter
8. Developed by Hayne Leland and Mark Rubinstein in the early 1980s on
the basis of the Black-Scholes model of option pricing, portfolio insurance
was widely practiced by portfolio managers such as Wells Fargo Investment
Advisers, Aetna Life, and Leland O'Brien Rubinstein (LOR), to name a few
of the biggest users. Of the record 162,000 S&P 500 futures contracts traded
on October 19, portfolio insurance accounted for 12 to 24 percent according to
the Commodity Futures Trading Commission. The corresponding estimate for
October 20 was 19 to 26 percent. (These figures are as published in *The New
York Times*). Index arbitrage, however, accounted for only 9 percent of this
trade on the 19th and less than 2 percent on the 20th, according to the same
source. (Different sources quote different estimates.) Because the version of
portfolio insurance employed by LOR calls for delaying futures trades when
the futures-to-cash spread appears to be unfavorable, and apparently because
of confusion during the crash, some of LOR's clients did not receive the full
theoretical protection of portfolio insurance during the crash. Wells Fargo
Investment Advisers apparently executed its portfolio insurance-motivated
futures sales despite the extremely unattractive (apparent) futures-to-cash
spread, and achieved most of the full theoretical protection.

The Aftermath

According to reporting by Anise Wallace of *The New York Times*, brokers
estimated that the value of stock portfolios that were covered by portfolio
insurance had shrunk to between $30 billion and $45 billion by the end of
November 1987. After the crash, LOR changed its portfolio insurance strategy by extending the insurance horizon—the effective expiry date of the syn-
thetically created put option—from less than one year to more than three
years. It was estimated that this would reduce the required futures trades by
about 50 percent. According to *The Wall Street Journal* (October 17, 1988),
Aetna Life has reduced its portfolio insurance accounts from $19 billion just
prior to the Crash to only $1.5 billion a year later. The daily contract volume
in S&P 500 futures fell from close to 100,000 in the period preceding the crash

to approximately 40,000 during the following month. Some of the reduction in volume is likely related to severe increases in margin requirements imposed by the Chicago Mercantile Exchange and member FCMs. At this writing, S&P 500 futures volume is roughly half its pre-crash level, and the S&P 500 index futures contract has been overtaken by Eurodollar futures as the highest volume contract traded on the CME.

As for stock index arbitrage, the practice was halted by the New York Stock Exchange for over a week after the crash. Manual arbitrage by NYSE member firms for their own accounts was permitted after November 3, but use of the DOT system for index arbitrage was not permitted until November 9, well after the DOT system was repaired. In the meantime, arbitrage was also possible via a new trading system set up off the NYSE by Jeffries and Company. During the year following the crash many of the largest investment banks stated that they would not practice index arbitrage for their own accounts, although some have reversed their decisions. According to *The Wall Street Journal* (October 21, 1988), program trading in September, 1988 (of which 54 percent was index arbitrage) accounted for 12.1 percent of NYSE average daily volume. The five largest program traders of that month were: Morgan Stanley, Susquehanna Investment Group, Merrill Lynch, Bear Stearns, and Kidder Peabody.

In addition to severe increases in required margin and new limits on the size of trades during any half hour period, the Chicago Mercantile Exchange imposed a daily price limit on the S&P 500 futures index that has been revised several times. In addition, the CME has imposed a 5-point opening price limit, precluding trades at prices more than 5 points above or below the previous day's settlement price until 10 minutes after the open or until the contract trades within the 5 point limit, whichever comes first. Daily price limits were also imposed on the stock index contracts of the New York Futures Exchange, the Kansas City Board of Trade, and the Chicago Board of Trade. The CME and the NYSE have instituted a system of coordinated trading halts and price limits that have become known as *circuit breakers* or *shock absorbers*. As approved by the CFTC and SEC on October 18, 1988, this system is triggered by intra-day declines of the Dow Jones Industrial Average (DJIA) or S&P 500 nearby futures index as follows:

- DJIA down 25:   program traders lose priority on the DOT computerized trading system.
- S&P 500 down 12:   S&P 500 futures trades may only occur at a higher futures index for the following half-hour.

- DJIA down 96:   NYSE computers divert program trades to a separate queue which is delayed so long as the order imbalance is more than 50,000 shares.
- DJIA down 250:   a one-hour halt in NYSE trading.
- S&P 500 down 30:   a one-hour halt in S&P 500 futures trading.
- DJIA down 400:   a two-hour halt in NYSE trading.
- S&P 500 down 50:   a halt in CME stock-index related futures and options trading for the remainder of the day.

These measures coordinate the behavior of the CME and NYSE in that the declines in the DJIA and S&P 500 are designed to be approximately equal (S&P 500 down 12 is approximately equal to DJIA down 96, S&P 500 down 30 is approximately equal to DJIA down 250, and so on). The *National Association of Securities Dealers* (NASD) has reluctantly agreed to follow suit on these circuit breakers, and other exchanges are likely to follow. Regulatory review of the system is slated for October, 1989.

Circuit breakers represent the only measure adopted from the Report of the *Presidential Task Force on Market Mechanisms*, commonly known as the *Brady Report*. The major proposals which have not (by the time of this writing) been adopted are:

1. A role for the Federal Reserve Board as an inter-market regulator.
2. Coordination of margin requirements for stocks, options, and futures.
3. Disclosure of the names of ultimate buyers and sellers of securities.
4. Improvements in the clearing system.

In addition to the adoption of circuit breakers (including its 5-point opening price limit) and general increases in stock index margins, the CME has changed its variation margin procedures to allow large profits to be paid out during the day so as to improve market liquidity. According to *The Wall Street Journal* (October 17, 1988), Goldman, Sachs and Company and Kidder, Peabody were owed a combined total of $1.5 billion in resettlement profits on October 20, 1987, but did not receive it until after the trading day. In another liquidity-motivated move, the CME and the Options Clearing Corporation have proposed to jointly reduce margins for positions on the two markets with offsetting risks. The NYSE has increased its trade-handling capacity to over 800 million shares per day, even though average daily volume of trade on the NYSE has shrunk markedly since the crash.

The CFTC has written letters to the Chicago Mercantile Exchange, the Chicago Board of Trade, and the Coffee, Sugar, and Cocoa Exchange advising them to consider further safeguards in the designs of 11 proposed new stock index futures contracts. Many of these contracts propose to offer cash settlement on foreign stock indices, such as the Nikkei 225. The crash caused a postponement of approval of these new contracts. One, the CBOE 250 stock index futures contract at the Chicago Board of Trade, has been approved by the time of this writing. As will be explained in Chapter 9, the Securities and Exchange Commission (SEC) can exercise an effective veto over approval of these new stock index contracts, and may also delay or prevent approval.

Further information on the Stock Crash of 1987 can be gleaned from various sources listed in the Notes.

6

STATISTICAL BEHAVIOR
OF FUTURES PRICES

Statistical properties of futures prices are essential ingredients in many applications, such as the choice of a hedging position or the decision by an exchange to introduce a new futures contract. In this chapter we review the most basic statistical methods and issues, along with some of the recent empirical evidence. We offer a caution: One cannot give a blanket characterization of futures price behavior. There is no reason to believe, for example, that Japanese yen futures prices and cotton futures prices will have similar statistical properties.

1. LEAST SQUARES ESTIMATORS

A *stochastic process* is a sequence $X = (X_1, X_2, \ldots)$ of random variables. As a motivating example, we can think of X_t as the change in a futures price from time $t - 1$ to time t. Given the theoretical formulas developed in Chapter 4, we would clearly like to be able to estimate the mean and variance of X_t, as well as the covariance of X_t with other market variables. At time t, suppose an econometrician (one who estimates properties of stochastic processes) observes a number, say x_t, as the *realization* of X_t. (One must distinguish clearly between the random variable X_t with unknown outcome and the actual outcome x_t.) Generally speaking, an econometrician does not have a complete description of X_t, but may estimate certain properties of X_t such as its mean or variance by analyzing the available observations $x_1, x_2, \ldots$, perhaps in addition to observations of other random variables.

Estimating Expected Values

For example, suppose the random variables $X_1, X_2, \ldots$ have the same expected values, the same variances, and are uncorrelated. A stochastic process

Chapter Outline

that is uncorrelated in this sense is said to have no *serial correlation*. These three properties (equal means, equal variances, and no serial correlation) are called the *ordinary least squares* or *OLS conditions*. Under the OLS conditions, a natural estimate of $E(X_1)$ (or the expectation of X_t for any t, since they have equal means), using the observations $x_1, \ldots, x_T$, is the *simple average* $\bar{x} = (x_1 + \cdots + x_T)/T$. Of course, the outcome $\bar{x}$ is itself a realization of the random variable

$$\overline{X} = \frac{X_1 + \cdots + X_T}{T}. \tag{1}$$

At time zero we do not know the outcome of the *estimator* $\overline{X}$, but we would like to know that, on average, $\overline{X}$ is a "good" estimator for $E(X_1)$. For example, it would be good to know that $\overline{X}$ is *unbiased*, in the sense that $E\left(\overline{X}\right) = E(X_1)$ under the OLS conditions. This is true, and left to be shown as an exercise.

Example: Suppose the consecutive daily settlement prices for the World Sugar Contract (nearby delivery) on the Cotton, Sugar, and Cocoa Exchange, for Friday of one week through Friday of the next, are 13.27, 13.75, 14.01, 13.50, 13.95, and 14.22, in cents per pound. (Each contract is for delivery of 112,000 pounds.) The outcomes of the daily changes in the sugar futures prices are:

$$x_1 = 13.75 - 13.27 = 0.48$$
$$x_2 = 14.01 - 13.75 = 0.26$$
$$x_3 = 13.50 - 14.01 = -0.51$$
$$x_4 = 13.95 - 13.50 = 0.45$$
$$x_5 = 14.22 - 13.95 = 0.27$$

The outcome $\overline{x}$ of the estimator $\overline{X}$ for the expected value of daily price changes is the simple average

$$\overline{x} = \frac{0.48 + 0.26 - 0.51 + 0.45 + 0.27}{5} = 0.19 \quad \text{cents per pound.}$$

As with most commodity futures price changes, it seems unlikely that the process $X_1, X_2, \ldots$ of daily sugar futures price changes would satisfy the OLS conditions. Thus, despite its simple construction and popularity, $\overline{X}$ may be a biased estimator.

Estimator Efficiency

We will generally be concerned with estimators for such statistical properties as the expected value, variance, and covariance of futures price changes. It is desirable that these estimators be unbiased, in the above sense, but other properties are also desirable. For instance, with observations of $X_1, \ldots, X_5$ of the daily sugar futures price changes in the above example, the estimator $(X_1 + X_2)/2$ is also unbiased for $E(X_1)$ under the OLS conditions, but seems to be inefficient in that it neglects the information contained in the observations of X_3, X_4, and X_5.

In order to consider a formal notion of efficiency of estimators, suppose we limit our attention to a *linear estimator*, that is, an estimator of the form $X^a = a_1 X_1 + \cdots + a_T X_T$, for some coefficients $a = (a_1, \ldots, a_T)$. Consider the problem

$$Minimize_a \ \text{var}[E(X_1) - X^a] \quad subject \ to \quad E(X^a) = E(X_1). \quad (2)$$

That is, choose the coefficients $a_1, \ldots, a_T$ so as to minimize the variance of the estimation error $E(X_1) - X^a$, subject to zero estimation bias. As an exercise, one can show that, under the OLS conditions, problem (2) is solved only by choosing $a_1 = a_2 = \cdots = a_T = \frac{1}{T}$. The estimator $\overline{X}$ is thus *efficient* in the sense that it solves problem (2). Since the variance of the error is the expected square of the error, $\overline{X}$ is called the *least squares*, or *ordinary least squares (OLS)* estimator for $E(X_1)$. Sources cited in the Notes show $\overline{X}$ to have other efficiency properties.

Variance Estimators

For T periods of data, a natural estimator of the variance $\text{var}(X_1)$ using observations of $X_1, \ldots, X_T$ is the *sample variance estimator*

$$\overline{V} = \frac{\left(X_1 - \overline{X}\right)^2 + \cdots + \left(X_T - \overline{X}\right)^2}{T}, \quad (3)$$

the simple average of squared deviations from the mean estimator $\overline{X}$. In fact, $\overline{V}$ is biased in that

$$E\left(\overline{V}\right) = \frac{T-1}{T} \text{var}(X_1), \quad (4)$$

which can be shown as an exercise. The unbiased estimator $\widehat{V} = \overline{V}T/(T-1)$ is often used instead of $\overline{V}$. The estimator $\widehat{V}$ is usually called the *least squares variance estimator*. The variance estimators $\overline{V}$ and $\widehat{V}$ have certain efficiency properties that we do not delve into here.

Example: We will continue the previous example of sugar futures prices by calculating the sample variance for the daily nearby futures price changes given above. The data, for Monday through Friday consecutively, are the price changes 0.48, 0.26, −0.51, 0.45, and 0.27 cents per pound. The sample mean was calculated at 0.19. The deviations from the sample mean are thus 0.29, 0.07, -0.70, 0.26, and 0.08. The sample variance is therefore

$$\frac{0.29^2 + 0.07^2 + (-0.70)^2 + 0.26^2 + 0.08^2}{5}$$

$$= \frac{0.0841 + 0.0049 + 0.4900 + 0.1820 + 0.0064}{5} = \frac{0.7674}{5} = 0.1538.$$

The least squares variance estimate is obtained by replacing the denominator 5 with 4, one less than the number of observations; this gives the least-squares variance estimate 0.19185. The *least squares estimator of standard deviation* is the square root of the least squares variance estimator. The least squares estimate of the standard deviation of daily nearby sugar futures price changes for the given data is therefore $\sqrt{0.19185} = 0.438$ cents per pound.

Covariance Estimators

Suppose $Y = (Y_1, Y_2, \ldots)$ is another stochastic process that may be related somehow to X. We say that the pair of processes (X, Y) satisfies the OLS conditions if:

- X and Y individually satisfy the OLS conditions: equal means, equal variances, and no serial correlation.
- X_s and Y_t are uncorrelated whenever $s \neq t$.
- $\mathrm{cov}(X_t, Y_t) = \mathrm{cov}(X_s, Y_s)$ for all times s and t.

We are interested in an estimator for $\mathrm{cov}(X_1, Y_1)$. For T periods of data, a natural choice is the *sample covariance estimator*

$$C(X, Y) = \frac{\left(X_1 - \overline{X}\right)\left(Y_1 - \overline{Y}\right) + \cdots + \left(X_T - \overline{X}\right)\left(Y_T - \overline{Y}\right)}{T}. \qquad (5)$$

Example: Suppose Y_1, Y_2, Y_3, Y_4, and Y_5 are the daily changes in spot sugar prices for the same period of the previous example. We are interested in an estimate of $\mathrm{cov}(X_t, Y_t)$, the covariance between futures and spot price increments. Suppose the outcomes of Y are $y_1 = 0.45$, $y_2 = 0.30$, $y_3 = -0.40$, $y_4 = 0.55$, and $y_5 = 0.30$, in cents per pound. The outcome of the sample mean of spot price increments is

$$\overline{y} = \frac{0.45 + 0.30 - 0.40 + 0.55 + 0.30}{5} = 0.24.$$

The deviations from the sample mean are $y_1 - \bar{y} = 0.21$ on Monday, and likewise 0.06, −0.64, 0.31, and 0.06 for the remaining four days of the week. We recall that the corresponding deviations from the sample mean of the futures price changes are 0.29, 0.07, −0.70, 0.26, and 0.08. The outcome of the sample covariance estimator $C(X, Y)$ is therefore

$$\frac{0.21 \times 0.29 + 0.06 \times 0.07 + (-0.64) \times (-0.70) + 0.31 \times 0.26 + 0.06 \times 0.08}{5}$$

$$= \frac{0.5985}{5} = 0.1197.$$

Like the sample variance estimator, the sample covariance estimator is biased. The *least squares covariance estimator* $\frac{T}{T-1}C(X, Y)$ is unbiased. In the last example, the least squares covariance estimate is $0.5985/4 = 0.1496$.

Although more sophisticated estimators are superior under many circumstances, the *least squares estimators* are a simple starting point. Moreover, under the the OLS conditions plus the assumption that the random variables are normally distributed (as defined in Appendix 4C), it turns out that the least squares estimators are the best estimators in the strongest sense used by statisticians. Later in this chapter we question whether the assumption of normal distributions is appropriate for futures price processes.

2. AN EXAMPLE: T-BILL FUTURES PRICES

Appendix 6A shows weekly U.S. Treasury bill futures and spot price data for the period July 11, 1979 to December 31, 1980. The futures data are the International Monetary Market (IMM) Indices for 90-Day T-bill futures. The spot data are 90-day T-bill daily cash market discounts (bid).

T-Bills: From Index to Yield to Price

The IMM Index is not itself the futures price; rather, one must first convert the index, I_t at time t, to the (so-called) *T-bill yield*, Y_t at time t, using the formula

$$Y_t = \frac{100.00 - I_t}{100.00}.$$

Here, "yield" actually means the bank discount on 90-day loans, taking 360 days as a "year" for calculation purposes. Once the yield is obtained, one can calculate the price. The price of a $1,000,000 Treasury bill with 90 days to maturity, quoted at a bank discount of 0.1398 (or 13.98 percent), is

$$\$1,000,000 \left(1 - 0.1398 \times \frac{90}{360} \right) = \$965,000.$$

Thus an IMM 90-Day T-Bill Index of 86.02 represents a discount of 13.98 percent, and therefore a futures price of $965,000. The general conversion formula from index to futures price is

$$\text{Futures price} = \$1,000,000 \left(1 - \frac{\text{days to maturity}}{360} \times \frac{100 - \text{IMM Index}}{100} \right).$$

The IMM T-bill contracts actually call for delivery of $1,000,000 (face value) worth of 90-day U.S. Treasury bills, with substitution of bills having 89, 91, or 92 days to maturity based on the above valuation formula. Spot market prices are obtained from spot discounts by the same yield-to-price calculation.

From Prices to Log-Price Increments

For week t, let $f_t^{(0)}$ denote the 90-Day Treasury bill spot price and let $f_t^{(i)}$ denote the corresponding futures price for the contract i-th nearest to delivery. (That is, the contract whose delivery date is the i-th earliest.) For most securities, it is widely believed that weekly price changes do not meet the OLS conditions. The OLS conditions are sometimes felt to be more appropriate, however, for the continuously compounding percentage rates of growth of prices. As explained in Section 5.1, these are equivalent to the changes in the logarithms of prices, that is, the *log-price increments*:

$$X_t^{(i)} = \log \left(f_t^{(i)} \right) - \log \left(f_{t-1}^{(i)} \right). \tag{6}$$

As also explained in Section 5.1, $X_t^{(0)}$ is the weekly return (continuously compounding) at week t on spot Treasury bills. The continuously compounding annual return at week t is therefore $52X_t^{(0)}$. If $X_t^{(i)}$ is a futures log-price increment, it cannot be directly interpreted as a return since one does not invest the futures price $f_{t-1}^{(i)}$ at time $t-1$ and obtain $f_t^{(i)}$ at time t. Instead, one commits only the required margin at time $t-1$ and collects the resettlement payment $f_t^{(i)} - f_{t-1}^{(i)}$ plus margin (if offsetting) at time t. Estimates of the means and covariances of $X_t^{(0)}, X_t^{(1)}, \ldots, X_t^{(5)}$ are nevertheless useful, as we shall see.

Splicing Price Data for the n-th Nearest Contract to Delivery

Appendix 6A periodically shows an extra row of futures price data at the delivery week of the nearby contract. At these "splice" points, the previously second nearest contract becomes the nearby, the third nearest becomes the second nearest, and so on. The futures prices at the splice points are translated accordingly so as to obtain a contiguous time series for the nearby futures prices $f^{(1)}$, for the second nearby prices $f^{(2)}$, and so on. Increments across these splice points are not included in the statistical calculations.

Sample Covariance and Correlation Matrices

The *sample covariance matrix* $C\left(X^{(0)}, \ldots, X^{(5)}\right)$ shown in Table 6.1 is a table with six rows and six columns. The entry in the i-th row and j-th column is the sample covariance between $X_t^{(i)}$ and $X_t^{(j)}$. The diagonal elements of this matrix are therefore the sample estimates of the variances of $X_t^{(0)}$, $X_t^{(1)}$, ..., and $X_t^{(5)}$. These estimates seem to indicate that the contracts nearer to delivery displayed more volatile prices during the sample period. This is another hypothesis to be considered later in the chapter.

TABLE 6.1   Sample Covariance Matrix: U.S. Treasury Bills

Spot and Futures Prices for 1979–1980:   1-Week Log-Price Increments

$$
C\left(X^{(0)}, \ldots, X^{(5)}\right) = 10^{-6} \times
\begin{pmatrix}
3.8 & 3.4 & 3.0 & 2.6 & 2.1 & 1.7 \\
3.4 & 3.8 & 3.4 & 2.9 & 2.4 & 1.9 \\
3.0 & 3.4 & 3.4 & 3.0 & 2.5 & 2.1 \\
2.6 & 2.9 & 3.0 & 2.8 & 2.4 & 2.1 \\
2.1 & 2.4 & 2.5 & 2.4 & 2.3 & 2.0 \\
1.7 & 1.9 & 2.1 & 2.1 & 2.0 & 1.8
\end{pmatrix}
$$

The *sample correlation matrix* R, shown in Table 6.2, is an estimate of the correlations among $X_t^{(0)}, \ldots, X_t^{(5)}$. The (i, j)-element of R is the outcome of the *sample correlation estimator*

$$
R_{ij} = \frac{C\left(X^{(i)}, X^{(j)}\right)}{\sqrt{C\left(X^{(i)}, X^{(i)}\right) C(X^{(j)}, X^{(j)})}},
$$

an estimate of corr $\left(X_t^{(i)}, X_t^{(j)}\right)$. As one might suspect, the nearer the two futures delivery dates, the greater is the estimated correlation.

It is worth noting that the sample correlation estimator is unaffected by replacing the sample covariance estimators $C(X^{(i)}, X^{(j)})$ with the least squares covariance estimators $C(X^{(i)}, X^{(j)})T/(T-1)$, since this amounts to multiplying and dividing by the same constant, $T/(T-1)$.

TABLE 6.2   Sample Correlation Matrix: U.S. Treasury Bills

Spot and Futures Prices for 1979–1980:   1-Week Log-Price Increments

$$R = \begin{pmatrix} 1.00 & .91 & .85 & .79 & .72 & .64 \\ .91 & 1.00 & .95 & .90 & .82 & .74 \\ .85 & .95 & 1.00 & .98 & .92 & .85 \\ .79 & .90 & .98 & 1.00 & .97 & .92 \\ .72 & .82 & .92 & .97 & 1.00 & .98 \\ .64 & .74 & .85 & .92 & .98 & 1.00 \end{pmatrix}$$

One-Week versus Two-Week Time Intervals

Table 6.3 shows the outcome of the sample covariance matrix for the stochastic processes $Y^{(0)}, Y^{(1)}, \ldots, Y^{(5)}$, where

$$Y_k^{(i)} = X_{2k}^{(i)} + X_{2k-1}^{(i)}.$$

In other words, $Y^{(i)}$ is the process of two-week log-price increments. If $X^{(i)}$ is truly free of serial correlation, we know that

$$\operatorname{var}\left(Y_k^{(i)}\right) = \operatorname{var}\left(X_{2k}^{(i)}\right) + \operatorname{var}\left(X_{2k-1}^{(i)}\right).$$

Thus a simple check for serial correlation is a comparison of Tables 6.3 and 6.1. The OLS conditions, in particular the absence of serial correlation, would lead the entries of the former to be about twice the corresponding entries of the latter, given a "typical" large sample. Later in the chapter we will be reviewing evidence of this sort on the issue of zero serial correlation of futures price increments. Incidentally, the serial correlation of price increments and of log-price increments are distinct issues; neither implies the other.

TABLE 6.3   Sample Covariance Matrix: U.S. Treasury Bills

Spot and Futures Prices for 1979–1980:   2-Week Log-Price Increments

$$
C\left(Y^{(0)}, \ldots, Y^{(5)}\right) = 10^{-6} \times
\begin{pmatrix}
8.5 & 7.5 & 6.3 & 5.0 & 4.0 & 3.2 \\
7.5 & 7.9 & 6.9 & 5.8 & 4.7 & 3.8 \\
6.3 & 6.9 & 6.7 & 5.9 & 5.1 & 4.3 \\
5.0 & 5.8 & 5.9 & 5.5 & 4.9 & 4.4 \\
4.0 & 4.7 & 5.1 & 4.9 & 4.7 & 4.2 \\
3.2 & 3.8 & 4.3 & 4.4 & 4.2 & 4.0
\end{pmatrix}
$$

3. HETEROSKEDASTICITY: VARIANCES CHANGE

It has often been proposed that the variance of futures price increments increases as the delivery date approaches. Our observations on Treasury bill futures prices during 1979–1980 are consistent with this notion. It is also widely believed that certain futures price increments show seasonal effects in variance. For example, the variance of price increments may be a function of the day of the week or of the month of the year. Various such hypotheses of nonconstant variance, or *heteroskedasticity*, have been statistically examined in a number of studies. The answer to our basic question seems to be: "Yes, the volatility of futures price increments for most contract types generally depends on time." We briefly review some of the evidence on this violation of the OLS conditions.

The Samuelson Hypothesis

The *Samuelson hypothesis*, proposed by Paul Samuelson, states that futures price increments show higher variance closer to delivery. In fact, this is just one of several possibilities suggested by Samuelson.

Variance (or any statistical property) ought to be measured given all available information. Probability assessments can change as time progresses and more information is received. The estimate of variance of the price increment from time t to time $t + 1$ should be made on the basis of information available at time t. This is called the *conditional variance* estimate. The notion underlying the Samuelson hypothesis is that the current futures price reflects current information about the spot price at delivery time. If information on the deliverable market is received more quickly as the delivery date approaches, one might expect futures prices to show correspondingly higher volatility as delivery approaches. One can actually build special theoretical models in which this effect occurs; one can also build special models in which the opposite occurs: price volatility decreases as delivery approaches. In any case, recent empirical evidence largely supports the Samuelson hypothesis for many contracts.

Milonas (1986) studied 11 contract types for Samuelson effects over periods ranging from 6 to 11 years: 5 agricultural commodities, 3 metals, and 3 financial instruments. For a particular contract type (say, wheat) and during a particular month t (say, January 1980), futures contracts for N different delivery dates were available for trade. This leads to N variance estimates:

$$V_1(t), V_2(t), \ldots, V_N(t),$$

with $V_n(t)$ denoting the least squares estimate of the variance of the daily log-price increments of the n-th nearest contract, for the daily price observations during month t. The *geometric average* of these estimates is

$$A_t = [V_1(t)V_2(t) \cdots V_N(t)]^{1/N},$$

the N-th root of their product. If the n-th nearest contract delivers at month $t+k$, let $V(t,k) = V_n(t)/A_t$ denote the *normalized-variance* estimate for wheat k months to delivery during month t. Finally, let

$$\overline{V}_k = \frac{V(1,k) + V(2,k) + \cdots + V(T,k)}{T}$$

be the *average normalized variance* estimate over the T months of data for wheat k months to delivery. For wheat, there were actually $N = 5$ contracts and approximately $T = 133$ months of observations over the period January 1972 to January 1983. The average normalized variance estimates for $k = 1$ to $k = 15$ months are plotted in Figure 6.1 for corn, wheat, and soybeans. Similar results for selected financials and metals are plotted in Figures 6.2 and 6.3, respectively. These results seem to be consistent with a Samuelson effect. Statistically, the effect is significant (with respect to a particular test explained in Milonas' study) for 10 of the 11 contracts tested. Other studies cited in the Notes do not so clearly support the Samuelson effect (and have occasionally rejected it), but the evidence seems to lean in its favor.

Of course, the Samuelson effect, when present, may be only a symptom of more relevant properties, such as *seasonality* in agricultural commodity price volatility. As we shall see, futures price volatility is also related to the extent

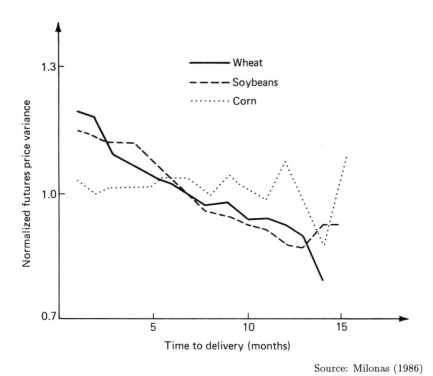

Source: Milonas (1986)

Figure 6.1   The Samuelson Effect for Corn, Wheat, and Soybeans

of market participation (for example, the volume of trade), which tends to be greater as delivery approaches. This might be an effect or a cause (or both) of the Samuelson effect.

Seasonality in Price Volatility

It is hardly surprising that grain futures prices are generally most volatile during the summer months. The harvest size of grain crops is strongly affected by summer weather, and spot prices are inversely related to stocks of grain (which is storable). Summer weather information becomes available, largely, in the summer.

Kenyon, Kling, Jordan, Seale, and McCabe (1987) studied the relationship between futures price volatility and the month of the year. Volatility is measured as an annualized estimate of the standard deviation of the daily futures log-price increments. That is, if f_i is the futures price on day i, let

$$X_i = \log(f_i) - \log(f_{i-1}),$$

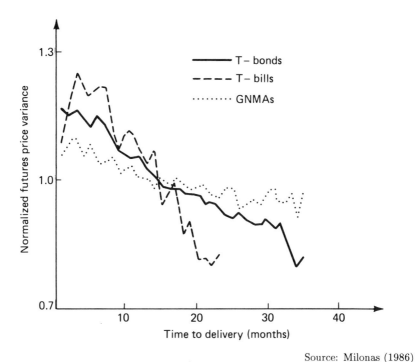

Source: Milonas (1986)

Figure 6.2   The Samuelson Effect for GNMA, T-Bonds, and T-Bills

and let V_t denote the least-squares estimator of $\text{var}(X_i)$ based on observations of X_i only for i in month t (of any year). For example, June is $t = 6$. A "year" is taken to be 250 trading days of observations, so the annualized version of V_t, denoted V_t^a, is $250 V_t$. Figure 6.4 plots the outcomes of $\sqrt{V_t^a}$, the least squares standard deviation estimator, for corn and wheat contracts during 1974–1983, after correcting for other determinants of volatility such as the loan rate on government grain price support programs. (The reader should consult the study for the actual estimation procedure.) Seasonality is clearly observed.

Anderson (1985) showed that seasonality in fact offers a better explanation of futures price volatility than does time-to-delivery, at least from extensive data on nine commodities during 1966–1980. This study also shows that volatility, again measured by least-squares estimates of log-price increments, changes significantly from year to year.

One would not necessarily expect such a marked seasonality effect for financial futures, although monthly seasonality studies of financial futures

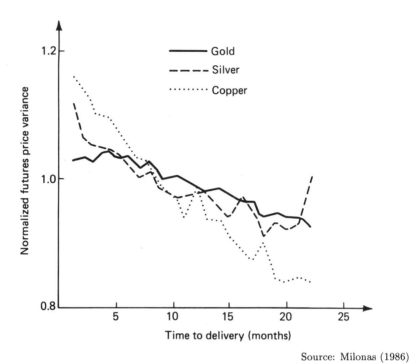

Source: Milonas (1986)

Figure 6.3   The Samuelson Effect for Copper, Gold, and Silver

price volatility are not yet available. There is, however, a study by Dyl and Maberly (1986) of the day-of-the-week effect for the volatility of the Standard and Poor's 500 Futures Index contract of the Chicago Mercantile Exchange for June 1982 through May 1985. Although the results, shown in Table 6.4, do not include a test of significant difference in variance across the days of the week, the tabulated estimates do vary considerably. Notably, this study estimates the variance of price changes themselves, rather than the changes of log-prices. Also shown in Table 6.4 are similar results by Chang and Kim (1988) on the day-of-the week effect for the volatility of commodity futures prices. In this study Chang and Kim also report the results of statistical tests indicating significantly higher variance of percentage growth rates of the Dow Jones Commodity Futures Index on Monday versus the other days of the week. The reader should see their article and another by Gay and Kim (1987) for more details.

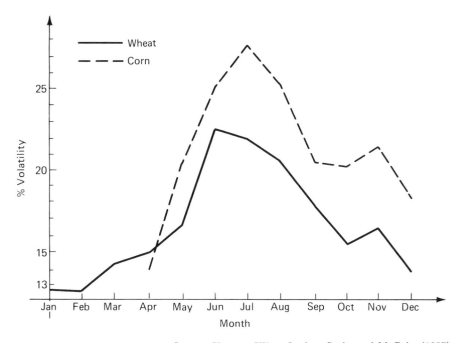

Source: Kenyon, Kling, Jordan, Seale, and McCabe (1987)

Figure 6.4   Seasonality in Futures Price Volatility—Test Results

Price Volatility and Volume of Trade

Following a seminal study by Clark (1973) connecting the volume of trade with the price volatility of cotton futures, Cornell (1981) related daily volume of trade to variance estimates of daily log-price increments for 21 different futures contract types during 1968–1979. The results show a consistently significant relationship, according to standard statistical tests. Although Cornell seemed most interested in the causal effect of price volatility on the volume-of-trade, perhaps each of these two variables affects the other. Although we do not yet have general equilibrium models of market behavior in cases for which traders possess diverse information, the results of Admati and Pfleiderer (1988) indicate that traders prefer to exploit their private information during times when other traders are also active. At such times, threshold levels of volume-of-trade and price volatility may breed even greater levels of volume-of-trade and price volatility.

TABLE 6.4   Day-of-the Week Effect on Futures Price Volatility

| Estimates of The Variance of Daily Changes | | | | | |
	Mon.	Tue.	Wed.	Thu.	Fri.	All
S&P 500 Futures[a] (close to open)	.49	.24	.19	.31	.31	.31
S&P 500 Futures[a] (open to close)	2.49	2.80	2.83	2.10	1.86	2.41
Commodity Futures[b] (Dow Jones Index)	2.19	1.42	1.48	1.62	1.36	n.a.

[a] Dyl and Maberly (1986), Table III, Daily Index Change.
[b] 365× Chang and Kim (1988), Table IV, Daily Log–Price Increment (%).

4. ARE FUTURES PRICES MARTINGALES?

Risk Premia

Let $E_t(X)$ denote the expectation of a random variable X for a particular agent at time t. One sometimes calls $E_t(X)$ "the *conditional expectation* of X given information available at time t," begging the question: "Whose information is relevant?" Some theoretical attention has been paid to the notion that the stochastic process $f_1, f_2, f_3, \ldots$ for a futures price should display a *risk premium*, meaning that

$$E_t(f_s) \geq f_t \quad \text{whenever} \quad s \geq t. \tag{7}$$

The risk premium $E_t(f_s) - f_t$ is thought of as the expected payment to a speculator buying at time t one contract from a hedger who is "insuring" a commitment to sell later on the spot market. "Risk premium" is thus used in the sense of an insurance premium. As seen in our theoretical mean-variance model of equilibrium futures prices in Chapter 4, risk premiums could apply if most hedging is done in the form of short futures positions as insurance against long spot positions. For assets stockpiled in positive total supply, there is some support for the notion of positive risk premia, but there is no theoretical guarantee of this. The term *normal backwardation*, as explained in Chapter 4, is sometimes used to describe the risk premium. *Contango* is sometimes used to describe the opposite relationship: $E_t(f_s) \leq f_t$ when $s \geq t$. Unfortunately, both of these terms have other meanings as well, as pointed out in Chapter 4.

The futures price process $f_1, f_2, \ldots$ is a *martingale* if

$$E_t(f_s) = f_t \quad \text{whenever} \quad t \leq s, \tag{8}$$

or zero risk premia.

For further insight, suppose the futures contract under consideration delivers at some time T and that s_t is the spot price of the underlying deliverable at time t. The futures price at delivery, f_T, and the spot price at delivery, s_T, must coincide in order to preclude arbitrage. That is, as pointed out in Chapter 3,

$$s_T = f_T. \tag{9}$$

The martingale hypothesis (8) is therefore equivalent to

$$E_t(s_T) = f_t \quad \text{whenever} \quad t \leq T. \tag{10}$$

If the futures price process is a martingale, any agent can therefore obtain an unbiased estimate of the spot price at a delivery date merely by observing the price of the corresponding futures contract. It is in this sense that the presence of a futures market is often asserted to be of social benefit in amalgamating information on the behavior of spot markets.

The martingale hypothesis (8) (or [10]) has also been called the *efficient markets hypothesis*, or *market rationality hypothesis*, although much confusion has been caused by these terms. As we know from many different models in which all agents act rationally and markets clear (such as the simple mean-variance model of Chapter 4), there is no particular reason that futures prices should be martingales. Roughly speaking, there is a negligible likelihood that agents' preferences, their endowments, and production conditions will coincide in exactly the manner required for unbiased futures prices.

Martingale Tests

Notions connecting the proper functioning of markets and the unbiasedness of futures prices have nevertheless persisted. Tests have sometimes failed to reject the martingale hypothesis in a statistically significant manner, leading to further interest in the hypothesis. Many of the tests that fail to reject unbiasedness are weak tests. In estimating the expected value of the futures price at a later date, some tests do not account for all available information pertinent to future market conditions. For example, the martingale hypothesis (8) implies, but is not implied by, the hypothesis

$$E[f_s \mid f_1, f_2, \ldots, f_t] = f_t \quad \text{whenever} \quad s \geq t, \tag{11}$$

where $E[X \mid Y]$ denotes the expectation of a random variable X given only the information obtained by observing a random variable Y, sometimes called "the expectation of X given Y" or "the expectation of X conditional on Y." The left-hand side of (11), the expectation of f_s given past futures prices, is not generally the same as $E_t(f_s)$, the expectation of f_s given *all* information available at time t. For example, suppose the demand for corn depends on agents' disposable incomes from sales of many different goods and services. One could hardly expect all information pertinent to corn prices in the future to be revealed by past corn prices alone. Thus (11) is a weak test of the martingale hypothesis: it is necessary but not sufficient for the martingale property, and one could fail to statistically reject (11) even if there is a strong bias in futures prices. The hypothesis

$$E\left[f_s \mid (s_1, f_1), (s_2, f_2), \ldots, (s_t, f_t)\right] = f_t \quad \text{whenever} \quad s \geq t, \qquad (12)$$

conditioning on both spot and futures prices, is stronger than (11), but still much weaker than the martingale hypothesis.

Statistical conclusions are often clouded by the limitations of statistical methods. Although it is difficult to test (11) directly, more specific models for prices can be tested. For example, let $L_t = \log(f_t) - \log(f_{t-1})$ denote the log-price increment at time t. A popular model is the *autoregressive* equation

$$L_{t+1} = A_0 + A_1 L_{t-1} + \cdots + A_n L_{t-n} + \epsilon_{t+1}, \qquad (13)$$

for some *time lag* n, where $\epsilon_1, \epsilon_2, \ldots$ is *white noise*: a process of uncorrelated normally distributed random variables with zero mean and constant non-zero variance. If $\log(f_1), \log(f_2), \ldots$ is a martingale, then

$$A_0 = A_1 = A_2 = \cdots = A_n = 0, \qquad (14)$$

which is left as another exercise. Of course, the assumption that the logarithm of futures prices is a martingale does not imply that f is itself a martingale. Nevertheless, the hypothesis that the logarithm of futures prices forms a martingale is also widely tested.

If futures prices do not conform to (13), then statistical rejection of (13)–(14) obviously says little about whether or not $\log(f_t)$ forms a martingale. Statistics is a useful but limited tool. Based on monthly gold price data for 1975–1983, a study by Jackson (1986) was unable to obtain a statistically significant rejection of (13)–(14) (according to a standard test) for $n = 2$

lags. The data are thus consistent with the following *random walk* martingale hypothesis for log-price behavior:

$$\log(f_{t+1}) = \log(f_t) + \epsilon_{t+1}. \tag{15}$$

One could instead directly test the specification:

$$\log(f_{t+1}) = A_0 + A_1\log(f_t) + \epsilon_{t+1}, \tag{16}$$

where $\epsilon_1, \epsilon_2, \ldots$ is white noise. The log-price martingale hypothesis and (16) together imply that $A_0 = 0$ and $A_1 = 1$. Rajaraman (1986) recently tested (16) and the hypothesis that $A_0 = 0$ and $A_1 = 1$ for coffee (New York and London exchanges), cocoa (New York and London exchanges), and rubber (London exchange) futures prices data during 1973–1982. Except for the New York coffee contract, the martingale hypothesis was rejected with typical confidence levels.

Many of the published martingale tests specify a model similar to the more general equation

$$\log\left(f_{t+1}^{(j)}\right) - \log\left(f_t^{(j)}\right) = A_0 + A_1 X_t^{(1)} + A_2 X_t^{(2)} + \cdots + A_n X^{(n)} + \epsilon_{t+1}, \tag{17}$$

where $f_t^{(j)}$ is the futures price of contract j at time t; $X_t^{(1)}, X_t^{(2)}, \ldots, X_t^{(n)}$ is a collection of n random variables observable at time t; and $\epsilon_1, \epsilon_2, \ldots$ is white noise. The process $X = (X^{(1)}, \ldots, X^{(n)})$ is sometimes referred to as a *state-variable process*. For example, (13) is a special case with

$$X_t^{(i)} = \log\left(f_{t-i}^{(j)}\right) - \log\left(f_{t-i-1}^{(j)}\right). \tag{18}$$

Raynauld and Tessier (1984) questioned whether the logarithms of wheat, corn, and oats futures prices form martingales. Their specification is similar to (17), with state variables for interest rates, gross national product, current U.S. inventories of wheat, corn, and oats, as well as one lagged observation of price increments. The exact specification is found in their paper. If the specification they chose is correct (a major qualification), then their inclusion of more state variables than merely lagged prices makes for a more discriminating test. If only lagged prices are relevant, however, then adding other state variables reduces the discriminatory power of the test in a statistical sense that we won't explain here. Individual tests of wheat, corn, and oats futures prices allowed Raynauld and Tessier to reject the log-price martingale hypothesis only for oats. When (18) was tested simultaneously for $j = 1$ (wheat), $j = 2$ (corn), and $j = 3$ (oats), however, the martingale hypothesis was rejected for all three contract types (in a statistical sense reported in the cited paper). Generally speaking, more discriminatory power can be obtained by using all of the available data simultaneously.

5. AUTOCORRELATION

The presence of autocorrelation (also known as serial correlation) in futures price increments has often been mistakenly thought to indicate some special opportunity for profit making, or even arbitrage. Autocorrelation is basically the hypothesis that past price increments are useful predictors of future price increments. Autocorrelation may imply non-zero expected price changes and therefore non-zero expected profits. We are already aware, however, of a trade-off between risk and expected profit. Serial correlation does not itself imply that the associated expected profit justifies the risk involved in exploiting it, for a given investor. Just as with the martingale hypothesis, the presence or absence of serial correlation in futures prices does not in any way imply irrationality or inefficiency in futures markets. Indeed, one would be surprised, on the basis of current economic theory, if one were to learn that futures price increments are serially uncorrelated. A standard test for autocorrelation, the *Durbin-Watson statistic*, is mentioned in Appendix 6B.

Autocorrelation of futures prices is more than a theoretical nicety. We know that the least squares estimators are biased in the presence of auto-correlation. Although that bias can be corrected to some extent, one must examine the nature of the autocorrelation in order to make the appropriate adjustments. This can be important, for example, in hedging. Furthermore, for some investors, autocorrelation may indicate an attractive profit opportunity, relative to the risks involved.

If a futures price process $f_1, f_2, \ldots$ is a martingale, its price increments $f_t - f_{t-1}$ are uncorrelated. This is shown in Appendix 6C. The converse, however, is not true. For example, if $X_1, X_2, \ldots$ is a martingale and $f_t = X_t + At$ for a non-zero constant A, then $f_1, f_2, \ldots$ is not a martingale, but has uncorrelated increments (another exercise).

Evidence on Serial Correlation in Futures Price Increments

By and large, futures prices exhibit non-trivial serial correlation, perhaps with some exceptions. The Notes cite a collection of papers that apply a battery of different statistical tests to futures price data on many different contracts during different time periods. A test tells whether one can reject the hypothesis of zero correlation between successive price increments with a statistical level of confidence. Although there are many different ways to conduct such a test, the zero autocorrelation hypothesis was rejected in most of the cited studies. We should repeat the caution that serially uncorrelated price increments and serially uncorrelated log-price increments are independent properties: neither implies the other. Some of the papers cited actually test for correlation in log-price increments.

One of the tests for serial correlation was mentioned in the discussion of Treasury bill data in Section 6.2. We pointed out there that if the log-price increments are indeed serially uncorrelated, then the variance of the sum of increments over successive periods is the sum of the variances of the increments over each of the periods. In particular, under the assumption of equal variances over each time period and no serial correlation, the variance of increments over k periods is precisely k times the variance over a single period. The covariance estimates in Table 6.3 for two-week increments are indeed roughly double those of Table 6.1 for one-week increments. This is not a test, of course; one needs to establish how much different from 2 the ratio of these variance estimates would have to be in order to confidently reject zero autocorrelation. For example, let

$$\text{ITVR}_k = \frac{\text{var}(f_t - f_{t-k})}{k \times \text{var}(f_t - f_{t-1})}$$

denote the *intertemporal variance ratio* at k time periods. The appearance of k in the denominator normalizes ITVR_k to 1.0 under the OLS conditions. Estimates of ITVR_k for corn futures prices during 1960–1969 are plotted in Figure 6.5 from a study by Petzel (1980). Also shown is the 95 percent confidence band; divergence of the plot outside this confidence band indicates rejection (with 95 percent confidence) of the zero autocorrelation hypothesis.

6. NORMALITY AND LOG-NORMALITY

Normality Is a Useful Property

From an econometric point of view, it would be an ideal situation if futures price increments for a contract of interest are normally distributed, uncorrelated, and have equal means and variances. In that case, the least squares estimates would be efficient and unbiased. Many theoretical and practical

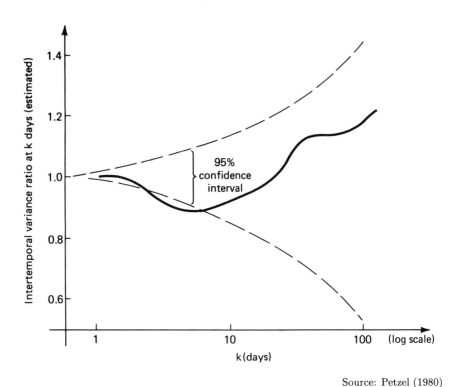

Source: Petzel (1980)

Figure 6.5   Intertemporal Variance Ratio Estimates for Corn Futures Prices

calculations would be much simplified under the normality assumption. Unfortunately, we can be confident from many tests, some cited in the Notes, that futures price increments are not normally distributed and, in particular, do not have equal means and variances. Moreover, the variance of price increments for many types of futures tends to be larger during periods of larger prices, contradicting the OLS conditions.

Log-Normal Price Processes

Let us concede that our ideal wish for normality of price increments satisfying the OLS conditions is unrealistic. We will consider, instead, whether a futures price process $f_1, f_2, \ldots$ satisfies an equation of the form

$$f_{t+1} = f_t \exp(A + \epsilon_{t+1}), \tag{19}$$

where A is a constant and $\epsilon_1, \epsilon_2, \ldots$ is white noise (normally distributed random variables with zero means satisfying the OLS conditions). Such a futures price process f is said to be a *log-normal process* since the logarithm $Y_t = \log(f_t)$ has increments $Y_{t+1} - Y_t = A + \epsilon_{t+1}$ that are normally distributed with constant mean A and variance $v = \text{var}(\epsilon_t)$. The log-normal futures price process has the following desirable properties:

1. provided f_0 is positive, f_t is always positive.
2. The variance of the price increment $f_{t+1} - f_t$ increases with the current price f_t.
3. The continuously compounding rate of price growth, $\log(f_{t+1}) - \log(f_t)$, satisfies the OLS conditions.

Figure 6.6 shows a simulated comparison of the behavior of a log-normal process and the logarithm of that process. The two simulated processes are normalized to have the same starting point and the same total annual standard deviation, 75. Noticeably, the log-normal process is more volatile at higher levels and less volatile at lower levels. Otherwise, however, the two processes behave much alike, even though the log-normal process was simulated so as to have a standard deviation of 50 percent in its continuously compounding rate of annual growth, which would be considered relatively volatile in many financial markets. It might indeed be difficult to distinguish between the normal and log-normal hypotheses concerning futures price processes.

If one believed the log-normal model (19), then one could obtain efficient and unbiased estimates of A and $v = \text{var}(\epsilon_t)$ by applying the least squares estimators to observations of the log-price increment process $(X_1, X_2, \ldots)$ generated by the equation

$$X_t = \log(f_{t+1}) - \log(f_t) = A + \epsilon_{t+1}. \tag{20}$$

If (19) is true and one applied the least squares estimators instead directly to the price increments $f_{t+1} - f_t$, the resulting estimates of means and variances of these price increments would be biased. For example, if $A = 0$ and $\text{var}(\epsilon_{t+1}) = 2 \log(1.25)$, then $E_t(f_{t+1}) = 1.25 f_t$, or an expected growth rate of 25 percent (left to be shown as an exercise). Clearly the price increments could not have constant means, and it is easy to show that they do not have constant variances. In particular, the larger is f_t, the greater is the variance of the price increment $f_{t+1} - f_t$.

A mean-variance investor is concerned with the variance of price increments, not with the variance of log-price increments. The hedging position, we recall, involves both covariances and variances of price increments. In

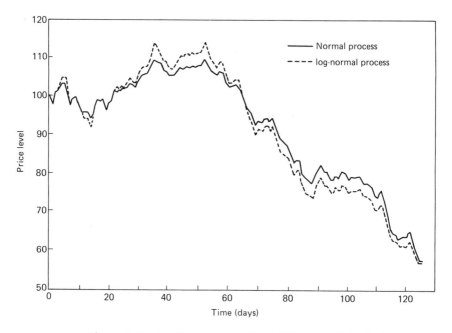

Figure 6.6   Log-Normal versus Normal Simulated Price Paths

Chapter 7 we will examine a method of estimating optimal hedging positions when futures and spot prices follow a log-normal model such as that described by (19).

There are, of course, many other competing statistical models for futures price behavior (some of them cited in the Notes), and each futures contract type will have its own characteristic price behavior.

Test Results on Normality

The normality and log-normality assumptions have been tested over and over again, and fairly consistently rejected on the basis of a wide variety of different tests cited in the Notes. Many of the studies find that the empirical distribution of futures log-price increments is too *leptokurtic* to be normal, meaning essentially that too many observations are located in "tails" of the empirical distributions, as illustrated in Figure 6.7. This finding of *fat tails* has been questioned, however, in a recent study by Helms and Martell (1985).

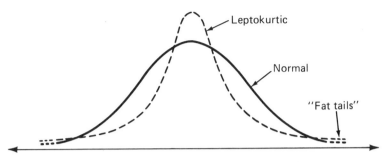

Figure 6.7   Normality versus "Fat Tails"

EXERCISES

6.1 Suppose the stochastic process $X_1, X_2, \ldots$ has equal means and variances, and is serially uncorrelated. Show that the estimator $\overline{X}$ for $E(X_t)$ is unbiased.

6.2 Let $X_1, X_2, \ldots$ be as in Exercise 1. Show that problem (2) of Section 6.1, minimize the variance of the estimation error among unbiased linear estimators, is solved by $X^a = \overline{X}$.

6.3 Show that equation (4) is true and that $\widehat{V}$ is therefore an unbiased variance estimator under the OLS conditions.

6.4 *(Statistical Covariance and Variance Estimates)*   Statistical software should be used for this problem, as available. The data set includes three columns of data: (i) S&P 500 Futures Indices, (ii) U.S. Treasury Bond Futures Indices, and (iii) prices of General Electric 8.5 percent bonds maturing in 2004. In each case, there are 52 observations of Wednesday closing data for 1986. The first 10 observations are shown as a sample in Table 6.5; the remaining observations are found in Appendix 6D. The GE bond data are spot market quotations (as in *The Wall Street Journal*, New York Exchange Bond Table). The futures data are, for each Wednesday, the settlement index of the nearby contract. The GE bond spot price, denoted s_t for week t, is the price per $100 of face value. The S&P 500 futures index is denoted f_t at week t. Finally, the T-bond futures price per $100 face value of the deliverable bond is denoted g_t at week t.

(a) Using any computing method you prefer, obtain estimates of the following statistics. You should assume that the OLS conditions

TABLE 6.5   First 10 Weeks of Sample Price Data

Week No.	S&P 500 Futures	T-Bond Futures	GE Bonds 8.5's of '04
1	208.25	84.313	91.500
2	208.95	83.250	89.375
3	202.80	83.313	78.750
4	211.45	84.875	90.250
5	214.00	85.875	90.125
6	216.85	86.219	90.375
7	220.90	88.063	91.125
8	224.65	92.281	94.375
9	228.00	93.625	96.625
10	235.65	97.063	98.125

apply, as necessary, and use the least-squares estimators (but state your precise assumptions explicitly).

(i) $\text{cov}(f_{t+1} - f_t, s_{t+1} - s_t)$, the covariance of the price increments.

(ii) $\text{corr}(f_{t+1} - f_t, s_{t+1} - s_t)$, the correlation of the price increments.

(iii) $\text{cov}(g_{t+1} - g_t, s_{t+1} - s_t)$, the covariance of the price increments.

(iv) $\text{corr}(g_{t+1} - g_t, s_{t+1} - s_t)$, the correlation of the price increments.

(v) $\text{var}(f_{t+1} - f_t)$, the variance of the price increments.

(vi) $\text{var}(g_{t+1} - g_t)$, the variance of the price increments.

(vii) $\text{sdev}(f_{t+1} - f_t)$, the standard deviation of the price increments.

(b) Which of the two futures contracts would you say is the better for purposes of hedging the GE bonds? Why? Assuming your estimates from part (a) of the exercise are in fact the true values of these statistics and that you are to sell \$10,000,000 (face value) of the GE bonds in one week, what futures position would you take in your preferred hedging instrument in order to minimize your risk (variance of bond sale value plus futures losses or gains)?

6.5 *(Simple Futures Demand Problem)* Suppose you are obligated to purchase 10 million Danish kroner in 10 days. You have decided to hedge the purchase cost by taking a position in West German mark futures. You are willing to assume that spot and futures price increments satisfy the OLS conditions, and that least squares estimates of covariances of price increments based on the last five days of closing prices are accurate measures of covariances. (This is not a realistic problem, but rather designed so that any necessary calculations can easily be done manually.) Suppose the last five days of data (closing prices) are as follows:

U.S. dollars per Danish krone (spot exchange market):

0.1488, 0.1492, 0.1501, 0.1498, 0.1490

U.S. dollars per West German mark (nearby futures price):

0.5614, 0.5626, 0.5650, 0.5643, 0.5610

(a) State the variance-minimizing futures hedge, ignoring the integer constraint on futures contracts.

(b) State the variance-minimizing futures position in a whole-number of contracts. You should not assume that rounding will work. Show that you have chosen the correct whole number.

(c) Suppose, for you, that the expected change in the futures price over the next 10 days is 0.01 U.S. dollars per mark. Also suppose that you have a mean-variance utility function with a risk-aversion coefficient of $r = 0.001$. Your only endowment is the above requirement to purchase 10 million kroner. State your utility- maximizing futures position. (Refer to Chapter 4.)

6.6 Suppose $X_1, X_2, \ldots$ is a martingale and $Y_t = X_t - X_{t-1}$. Show that $E(Y_t) = 0$, as claimed in the proof of Appendix 6C, Lemma 2.

6.7 Suppose $X_1, X_2, \ldots$ is a martingale, and also suppose that $f_t = X_t + At$ for all t, where A is some fixed constant. Show that $f_1, f_2, \ldots$ has serially uncorrelated increments, as claimed in Section 6.5.

6.8 Suppose that a futures price process $f_1, f_2, \ldots$ satisfies equation (19), where $A = 0$ and $v = \mathrm{var}(\epsilon_t) = 2\log(1.25)$. Show that $E_t(f_{t+1}) = 1.25 f_t$. (See Appendix 4C.)

NOTES

Johnston (1968) and Morrison (1976) give standard treatments of least squares estimation. Amemiya (1985) has a more advanced treatment. Taylor (1985) surveys the statistical properties of futures prices. For statistical data on futures and related spot prices, one may consult the annually published data of the various exchanges, for example, the *Year Book* of the Chicago Mercantile Exchange (including the International Monetary Market) and the *Statistical Annual* of the Chicago Board of Trade.

We referred in Section 6.3 to the *Samuelson hypothesis*; this is actually only one possible hypothesis in the model proposed by Samuelson (1965). Rutledge (1976) shows that the opposite effect is theoretically possible. On heteroskedasticity of futures price increments, we referred to the work of Milonas (1986), Kenyon, Kling, Jordan, Seale, and McCabe (1987), Anderson (1985), Dyl and Maberly (1986), Chang and Kim (1988), Gay and Kim (1987), and Cornell (1981). Clark (1973) is a precursor to Cornell's study of the connection between volatility and volume of trade. See also Cheng (1982) for evidence on the seasonality of the volatility of futures prices for soybeans from 1968 through 1981. We also cited Admati and Pfleiderer (1988) on volume concentrations for markets with traders having private information. The literature on the martingale hypothesis for futures prices is too extensive to cite in detail. In Section 6.4 we referred to the results of Jackson (1986) on gold; Rajaraman (1986) on coffee, cocoa, and rubber; and Raynauld and Tessier (1984) on wheat, corn, and oats. We merely mention some published results on other contracts: live cattle: Palme and Graham (1981) and Helmuth (1981); iced broilers: Goodwin and Sheffrin (1982); soybeans: Rausser and Carter (1983); Treasury bills: Fama (1976), Friedman (1979), and Maness (1979); and foreign exchange: Cornell (1977), Hansen and Hodrick (1980), Hodrick and Srivastava (1984), and Korajczyk (1985). The foreign exchange papers well represent new advances and modern econometric methods. Carter, Rausser, and Schmitz (1983) study a variety of commodity types. This is but a small sample of the literature.

The autocorrelation studies referred to in Section 6.5 include Houthakker (1961), Smidt (1965), Larson (1960), Brinegar (1970), Rocca (1969), Stevenson and Bear (1972), Cargill and Rausser (1972), Mann and Heifner (1976), Dusak (1973), Petzel (1980), and Helms, Kaen, and Rosenman (1984). Praetz (1976) gives a critique of some of these tests. Among the papers that do not reject the hypothesis of zero autocorrelation in futures price increments for certain commodities are Praetz (1975) and Labys and Granger (1970). The tests include sample correlation, intertemporal variance ratios, runs tests, turning point tests (Mann and Heifner [1976]), filter tests, spectral analysis (Labys and Granger [1970]), and rescaled range analysis (Helms, Kaen, and Rosenman [1984]). Also, as pointed out in Appendix 6C, inability to reject the martingale hypothesis implies inability to reject the hypothesis of serially uncorrelated increments, so martingale tests are also relevant. Lo and MacKinlay (1987) examine the statistical properties of the intertemporal variance ratio.

Section 6.6 refers to tests of normality and log-normality of futures price increments by Grauer (1977), Rocca (1970), Mann and Heifner (1976), Clark (1973), Dusak (1973), So (1987), and Helms and Martell (1985). Most of the results support the finding of excess kurtosis, meaning "fat tails." Clark (1973) suggests that this leptokurtosis may be due to the relationship between volume and volatility; heteroskedasticity of this form can lead to fat tails unless time intervals are adjusted for volume of trade. Dusak (1973) and So (1987) suggest instead that the fat tails displayed by certain types of futures price increments may be from the non-normal stable Paretian family of Mandelbrot (1963, 1967), with infinite variance. Helms and Martell (1985) test and reject this hypothesis. These various papers should be examined for the data and tests used, and for more careful statements of their results.

Appendix 6A: Example Treasury Bill Data

TABLE 6.6   90-Day U.S. Treasury Bill Price Data

Spot Discounts and Futures Indices

Date			Spot Disc't.	Index of n-th Nearby Futures Contract				
				$n = 1$	$n = 2$	$n = 3$	$n = 4$	$n = 5$
79	7	11	9.30	91.08	91.52	92.02	92.29	92.33
79	7	18	9.22	90.95	91.32	91.71	91.94	92.06
79	7	25	9.18	90.77	91.04	91.44	91.73	91.92
79	8	1	9.15	90.81	91.17	91.64	91.91	92.12
79	8	8	9.40	90.73	91.10	91.66	92.01	92.21
79	8	15	9.54	90.46	90.68	91.18	91.63	91.87
79	8	22	9.53	90.40	90.51	90.93	91.39	91.81
79	8	29	9.80	90.19	90.27	90.70	91.07	91.40
79	9	5	10.06	89.93	89.97	90.26	90.54	90.85
79	9	12	10.47	89.66	89.83	90.31	90.83	91.15
79	9	19	10.21	89.58	90.31	90.94	91.43	91.60
79	9	19	10.21	90.31	90.94	91.43	91.60	91.64
79	9	26	10.21	90.13	90.67	91.26	91.62	91.79
79	10	3	10.40	89.80	90.37	91.03	91.39	91.57
79	10	10	11.70	88.15	88.68	89.55	90.16	90.67
79	10	17	11.66	88.50	89.15	89.97	90.55	91.11
79	10	24	12.75	87.50	88.04	88.82	89.58	90.11
79	10	31	12.15	87.94	88.49	89.30	89.92	90.42
79	11	7	12.50	87.56	88.06	88.90	89.52	89.94
79	11	14	12.20	88.70	89.37	90.07	90.46	90.66
79	11	21	11.68	88.66	89.32	90.04	90.53	90.73
79	11	28	11.40	89.06	89.91	90.61	91.00	91.06
79	12	5	11.65	88.52	89.77	90.69	91.13	91.17
79	12	12	12.55	87.49	88.45	89.44	90.04	90.50
79	12	19	12.00	87.93	89.06	90.11	90.70	90.87
79	12	19	12.00	89.06	90.11	90.70	90.87	90.90
79	12	26	12.02	88.69	89.76	90.39	90.65	90.71
80	1	2	12.20	88.65	89.68	90.37	90.65	90.74
80	1	9	11.74	89.03	90.08	90.65	90.90	91.00
80	1	16	11.82	89.05	90.17	90.82	91.03	91.13
80	1	23	12.00	88.78	89.83	90.43	90.73	90.94
80	1	30	12.12	88.10	88.75	89.37	89.85	90.17
80	2	6	12.05	88.10	88.70	89.32	89.80	90.00
80	2	13	12.15	87.68	87.85	88.51	88.90	89.17
80	2	20	13.26	86.40	86.67	87.09	87.52	87.75
80	2	27	13.85	86.13	86.58	87.11	87.55	87.87
80	3	5	15.30	84.65	85.50	86.33	87.10	87.73
80	3	12	15.60	84.33	85.00	85.90	86.65	87.24
80	3	19	14.20	85.90	85.62	86.45	87.28	87.73
80	3	19	14.20	85.62	86.45	87.28	87.73	88.03
80	3	26	15.92	84.67	85.56	86.28	86.73	87.15
80	4	2	14.94	85.95	86.75	87.42	87.84	87.99

Source: International Monetary Market Yearbook, 1979–1980,
Chicago Mercantile Exchange.

TABLE 6.6   (Continued) 90-Day U.S. Treasury Bill Price Data

Spot Discounts and Futures IMM Indices

Date			Spot Disc't.	Index of n-th Nearby Futures Contract				
				$n = 1$	$n = 2$	$n = 3$	$n = 4$	$n = 5$
80	4	9	14.42	86.66	87.73	88.57	89.08	89.31
80	4	16	13.48	88.10	89.07	89.75	90.09	90.18
80	4	23	12.07	88.85	89.51	89.95	90.15	90.18
80	4	30	10.20	89.88	90.47	90.74	90.86	90.79
80	5	7	8.80	90.95	91.36	91.55	91.67	91.61
80	5	14	8.12	91.91	91.88	91.72	91.43	91.28
80	5	21	8.08	92.24	92.18	92.00	91.91	91.73
80	5	28	7.68	92.43	92.34	92.22	92.04	91.81
80	6	4	7.29	92.84	92.55	92.34	92.12	91.87
80	6	11	6.18	93.32	93.26	92.88	92.54	92.34
80	6	18	6.90	93.11	93.04	92.79	92.40	92.20
80	6	18	6.90	93.04	92.79	92.40	92.20	91.98
80	6	25	7.38	92.53	92.24	91.89	91.66	91.43
80	7	2	7.96	92.05	91.83	91.59	91.40	91.16
80	7	9	7.94	92.04	91.92	91.69	91.46	91.22
80	7	16	7.74	92.40	92.24	92.08	91.90	91.68
80	7	23	7.83	92.20	92.00	91.86	91.67	91.45
80	7	30	8.37	91.46	91.35	91.18	90.98	90.78
80	8	6	8.52	91.37	91.22	91.12	90.96	90.80
80	8	13	8.37	91.31	91.05	90.87	90.64	90.43
80	8	20	9.26	90.46	90.25	90.10	89.94	89.80
80	8	27	10.06	89.57	89.27	89.17	89.06	89.00
80	9	3	9.72	90.13	89.82	89.64	89.54	89.44
80	9	10	10.00	90.08	89.74	89.54	89.40	89.32
80	9	17	10.40	89.72	88.91	88.61	88.46	88.40
80	9	17	10.40	88.91	88.61	88.46	88.40	88.37
80	9	24	10.17	88.86	88.57	88.46	88.38	88.33
80	10	1	11.49	88.12	88.02	88.15	88.30	88.39
80	10	8	11.38	88.97	89.16	89.24	89.21	89.14
80	10	15	10.82	89.56	89.65	89.65	89.65	89.64
80	10	22	11.78	88.53	88.55	88.66	88.70	88.73
80	10	29	12.55	87.40	87.53	87.75	87.95	88.06
80	11	5	13.46	86.58	86.89	87.25	87.58	87.72
80	11	12	13.16	87.23	87.86	88.25	88.36	88.42
80	11	19	13.70	86.63	87.48	88.00	88.14	88.23
80	11	26	14.16	86.23	87.09	87.50	87.65	87.78
80	12	3	14.62	85.75	86.75	87.46	87.78	87.98
80	12	10	16.98	83.41	85.03	86.33	87.43	88.02
80	12	17	16.50	83.49	85.62	86.65	87.33	87.64
80	12	17	16.50	85.62	86.65	87.33	87.64	87.79
80	12	24	14.60	87.85	88.50	88.77	88.81	88.66
80	12	31	14.32	87.31	88.20	88.64	88.84	88.88

Appendix 6B: Linear Regression

This appendix reviews least squares linear regression, and could be avoided on a first reading. For brevity, we begin directly with multiple linear regression. Some readers might be advised to first review the simple linear regression model outlined in Section 7.4.

Least Squares Regression Estimators

Consider random variables W and $Z^1, Z^2, \ldots, Z^n$ with known means, variances, and covariances. What coefficients $b = (b_1, b_2, \ldots, b_n)$ will minimize the variance of the *regression residual* $\epsilon = W - (b_1 Z^1 + b_2 Z^2 + \cdots + b_n Z^n)$? This is a basic form of the *linear regression* problem: Get as "close as possible" to W by forming some weighted sum of $Z^1, Z^2, \ldots, Z^n$, with the distance between two random variables measured as the variance of their difference. We can also work in terms of coefficients $h = -b$ in order to simplify the calculations, leaving the problem:

$$\text{Minimize}_h \quad V(h) = \text{var}\left(W + h^\top Z\right),\tag{21}$$

where $h^\top Z$ denotes $h_1 Z^1 + \cdots + h_n Z^n$. (Our notation here is from Appendices 4B and 4E.) By our rule for the variance of a sum,

$$V(h) = \text{var}\left(W + h^\top Z\right) = \text{var}(W) + \text{var}\left(h^\top Z\right) + 2\,\text{cov}\left(W, h^\top Z\right).$$

Let $\text{cov}(Z)$ denote the covariance matrix for $(Z^1, Z^2, \ldots, Z^n)$, the (n, n)-matrix whose (i, j)-element is $\text{cov}(Z^i, Z^j)$. From Appendix 4E, Fact 3, we know that $\text{var}\left(h^\top Z\right) = h^\top[\text{cov}(Z)h]$. If we let $\text{cov}(W, Z)$ denote the n-vector whose i-element is $\text{cov}(W, Z^i)$, we can also write $\text{cov}\left(W, h^\top Z\right)$ as $h^\top \text{cov}(Z, W)$. Then

$$V(h) = \text{var}(W) + h^\top[\text{cov}(Z)h] + 2h^\top \text{cov}(W, Z).$$

The vector of partial derivatives of $V(h)$ with respect to h is

$$\nabla V(h) = 2\,\text{cov}(Z)h + 2\,\text{cov}(W, Z).$$

Just as with maximization, minimization occurs only at a vector h where $\nabla V(h) = 0$, or $\text{cov}(Z)h = -\text{cov}(W, Z)$. Assuming that $\text{cov}(Z)$ has an inverse, Proposition 4B implies that this equation is solved uniquely by $h = -\beta$, where

$$\beta = [\text{cov}(Z)]^{-1}\text{cov}(W, Z).\tag{22}$$

This vector β is known as the *beta* vector of *regression coefficients*. This substantiates a claim made in Appendix 4E interpreting the optimal hedge h as (minus) the regression coefficients β of the endowment e regressed on the futures contracts $f = (f^1, \ldots, f^n)$.

In some cases, we would like to solve the slightly more complicated problem: Find a number a and an n-vector $b = (b_1, \ldots, b_n)$ solving

$$\text{Minimize}_{a,b} \quad \text{var}\left[W - \left(a + b^\top Z\right)\right] \quad \text{subject to} \quad E\left(a + b^\top Z\right) = E(W). \tag{23}$$

The main difference between this and the previous problem is that we are allowed one extra coefficient a to explain W in a minimum-variance way, but our "explanation" must be unbiased. To see how simply this problem is solved, let $\overline{Z} = (\overline{Z}_1, \ldots, \overline{Z}_N)$ denote the n-vector of expected values of $Z_1, \ldots, Z_n$, respectively, and let $\alpha = E(W) - \beta^\top \overline{Z}$, where β is the same beta vector given by equation (22). Problem (23) is solved by $a = \alpha$ and $b = \beta$, which can be checked by observing two simple facts. First, adding a constant a does not change the variance. Thus the best one can do to minimize the stated variance, regardless of the choice of a, is to choose $b = \beta$, since that solves the previous problem. Second, if we choose $a = \alpha$, the explanation $\alpha + \beta^\top Z$ is unbiased, since $E(\alpha + \beta^\top Z) = E(W)$ by our choice of α. Thus (α, β) solves the problem.

Regression of Stochastic Processes

Now, to consider a problem more likely to be encountered by futures hedgers, suppose that there are $n + 1$ stochastic processes, whose values at any time t are denoted W_t and $Z_t^1, Z_t^2, \ldots, Z_t^n$, respectively. After T periods of observations, we can construct the least squares estimators for the covariance matrix $\text{cov}(Z_t)$ and the covariance vector $\text{cov}(W_t, Z_t)$; call these estimators $C(Z)$ and $C(W, Z)$, respectively. At time T, given our T periods of observations, we again face the problem: Choose an n-vector b minimizing the variance of $W_{T+1} - b^\top Z_{T+1}$. By "variance," of course, we mean variance based on all available information. The available information does not often include $\text{cov}(Z_t)$ or $\text{cov}(W_t, Z_t)$. A rather important issue is whether $\widehat{\beta} = [C(Z)]^{-1} C(W, Z)$, an estimator for β, is in fact the solution to this problem. In order for this to be the case, stringent conditions must be satisfied, going well beyond the OLS conditions described in Section 6.1. We refer readers to the Notes for a reference on the required additional conditions.

Regression Diagnostics

Most statistical software packages for linear regression report the coefficients $\widehat{\beta}$ and $\widehat{\alpha} = \overline{W} - \widehat{\beta}^\top \overline{Z}$, where $\overline{W}$ and $\overline{Z}$ are the least squares estimators for W_t and Z_t, respectively. Most regression packages also report the least squares estimate of the standard deviation of $\widehat{\beta}_i$ for each explanatory variable i. This number, sometimes called the *standard error* of the regression coefficient $\widehat{\beta}_i$, can be used to estimate the probability that β_i differs significantly from zero, based on statistical assumptions. The actual test can be reviewed in sources cited in the Notes.

Let $\widehat{W}_t = \widehat{\alpha} + \widehat{\beta}^\top Z_t$ denote the estimated "explanation" of W_t. A measure of the quality of the regression is the square of the estimated sample correlation between $\widehat{W}_t$ and W_t based on the observations for $W_1, W_2, \ldots, W_T$ and $\widehat{W}_1, \widehat{W}_2, \ldots, \widehat{W}_T$. This measure is usually denoted R^2 and reported along with the regression coefficients. Let $\hat{\epsilon}_t = W_t - \widehat{W}_t$ denote the observed *regression residual*. The least squares estimate of the standard deviation of the regression residual based on the observations $\hat{\epsilon}_1, \hat{\epsilon}_2, \ldots, \hat{\epsilon}_T$, is the *standard error of the regression*, and is also reported by most statistical packages.

Many regression packages also report the *Durbin-Watson statistic*

$$d = \frac{(\hat{\epsilon}_2 - \hat{\epsilon}_1)^2 + (\hat{\epsilon}_3 - \hat{\epsilon}_2)^2 + \cdots + (\hat{\epsilon}_T - \hat{\epsilon}_{T-1})^2}{\hat{\epsilon}_1^2 + \hat{\epsilon}_2^2 + \cdots + \hat{\epsilon}_T^2}.$$

For a large number of observations, large deviations of d from 2 decrease the likelihood of zero autocorrelation. For example, with $n = 2$ explanatory variables and $T = 100$ observations, a reported value of d less than 1.522 or greater than 2.478 allows one to correctly reject the hypothesis of zero autocorrelation with 99 percent confidence, under additional conditions and according to research cited in the Notes.

Appendix 6C: Martingales and Zero Autocorrelation

We will show that a martingale has no autocorrelation in its increments. We start with a useful rule of probability theory, the *law of iterated expectations*. If X is a random variable with finite variance, the conditional expectation $E_s(X)$ at time s depends on information that becomes available at time s. Thus at any time t before s, $E_s(X)$ is itself a random variable.

Lemma 1: (The Law of Iterated Expectations). *If X is a random variable with finite variance and $t \leq s$, then $E_t[E_s(X)] = E_t(X)$.*

Now we can show that the martingale price hypothesis implies the hypothesis of no serial correlation in price increments.

Lemma 2: *Suppose $X_1, X_2, \ldots$ is a martingale of (finite-variance) random variables. For any time t, let $Y_t = X_t - X_{t-1}$. Then the increment process $Y_1, Y_2, \ldots$ has no serial correlation.*

To prove the lemma, we must show, for any times t and $s \neq t$, that Y_t and Y_s are uncorrelated, or

$$E_0\big[\big(Y_t - E_0(Y_t)\big)\big(Y_s - E_0(Y_s)\big)\big] = 0, \tag{24}$$

where E_0 denotes expectation at time 0. As an easy exercise, the reader can show that the martingale property implies that $E_t(Y_s) = 0$ whenever $t < s$. Since $X_1, X_2, \ldots$ is a martingale, $E_0(Y_t) = E_0(Y_s) = 0$, so (24) is equivalent to

$$E_0[Y_t Y_s] = 0. \tag{25}$$

By Lemma 1, equation (25) is equivalent to

$$E_0[E_t(Y_t Y_s)] = 0.$$

At time t, the observation of Y_t is a known constant, implying that $E_t(Y_t Y_s) = Y_t E_t(Y_s) = 0$, using the martingale property (that is, $E_t(Y_s) = 0$). Thus (24) follows, and Lemma 2 is proven.

Appendix 6D: Example Bond and Stock Index Data

TABLE 6.7   Data: T-Bond Futures, GE Bonds, and S&P 500 Futures

Week[a] No.	S&P 500[b] Futures	T-Bond[c] Futures	GE Bonds[d] 8.5's of '04
11	238.50	96.250	98.500
12	241.50	98.438	99.000
13	237.45	102.031	99.250
14	235.35	103.063	99.875
15	244.20	104.844	99.375
16	243.30	100.156	97.875
17	234.80	100.781	98.750
18	236.95	100.063	99.125
19	237.15	97.906	99.500
20	236.40	95.938	97.125
21	247.85	95.469	98.750
22	246.55	90.625	95.750
23	242.40	93.031	95.875
24	247.25	96.719	96.375
25	249.60	98.094	97.250
26	254.50	99.313	98.500
27	242.85	99.750	99.000
28	235.10	100.188	99.000
29	237.95	97.719	98.750
30	237.70	97.031	97.750
31	237.30	96.188	97.000
32	246.45	101.000	96.875
33	250.75	102.469	98.500
34	253.85	101.000	99.500
35	252.35	98.219	98.250
36	248.65	96.719	99.875
37	230.35	95.344	98.500
38	235.90	95.594	97.000
39	233.60	96.625	98.000
40	236.70	96.563	97.875
41	239.70	95.250	97.500
42	235.15	95.625	97.375
43	240.70	97.094	97.625
44	247.20	98.625	99.000
45	246.95	96.875	97.625
46	238.10	99.875	98.625
47	249.55	99.594	100.000
48	255.25	100.094	100.875
49	252.15	100.000	100.625
50	248.50	99.281	100.625
51	248.80	100.063	100.625
52	243.45	98.531	100.000

[a]Weeks 1 through 10 are shown in Table 6.5.
[b]Futures Index, nearby contract. Source: *IMM Yearbook*, Chicago Mercantile Exchange.
[c]Futures Discount, nearby contract. Source: *Statistical Annual*, Chicago Board of Trade.
[d]Discount. Source: *The Wall Street Journal*, New York Exchange Bonds.

7

HEDGING WITH FUTURES

This chapter discusses some practical aspects of hedging with futures contracts. We apply the theoretical determination of optimal futures positions explained in Chapter 4, and the statistical estimation principles covered in Chapter 6, as well as some of the institutional details behind several hedging scenarios. A key technique is the estimation of risk-minimal hedges using linear regression and historical price data.

1. INTRODUCTION

By *futures hedging*, we mean taking a position in futures contracts that offsets some of the risk associated with some given market commitment. The essence of hedging is the adoption of a futures position that, on average, generates profits when the market value of the given commitment is lower than expected, and generates losses when the market value of the commitment is higher than expected. The notion of designing a futures strategy to generate losses under certain circumstances may seem quixotic to some. One must keep in mind the well-repeated adage: "There are no free lunches." One cannot expect trading profits as well as risk reduction (although that sometimes happens). The key is to coordinate losses in futures with gains elsewhere, and vice versa. How does one achieve that kind of coordination? That is the topic of this chapter.

A Simple Scenario: Hedging Foreign Exchange Risk

We begin our explanation of hedging with a simple scenario that involves a commitment by a firm to sell 25,000,000 West German marks on November 15, 1989, by taking a position in the IMM West German mark futures contract for December 1989 delivery. (This contract delivers 125,000 marks and is traded

Chapter Outline

on the Chicago Mercantile Exchange.) The spot market commitment could arise, for example, from an account receivable on foreign sales. The 25 million marks receivable will be sold immediately (on November 15) for U.S. dollars on the spot foreign exchange market. We will assume for simplicity that the value of a U.S. dollar is riskless; that is, we will ignore inflation risk. The hedger must make three basic decisions:

1. Whether to hedge short or long.
2. The size of position.
3. The timing of the hedge.

In this simple scenario, these three decisions are rather straightforward.

Short or Long? Generally, but not always, an increase in the spot exchange rate is accompanied by an increase in the nearby futures price. In statistical terms, spot price increments and futures price increments are positively correlated. Thus a short futures position, on average, generate profits if the dollar value of the marks receivable is lower than expected, and vice versa. The obvious hedging strategy is a short futures position.

Size of Position? How many contracts? If the spot commitment date were, instead, precisely the futures delivery date, the risk-minimizing futures position would be an equal and opposite position, or in this case, a short position of 200 contracts (25 million marks divided by 125,000 marks per contract). Since the futures and spot prices at the delivery date would be the same, every dollar lost on the futures position would be recouped by a corresponding dollar gain in the value of the committed marks receivable, and vice versa.

Because of the actual mismatch in spot commitment date and futures delivery date, however, there is no way to completely eliminate the spot risk. The risk due to the mismatch in dates is called *delivery basis risk.* Generally speaking, the delivery basis risk is smaller with smaller differences in time between the spot commitment date and the delivery date of the futures contract. This risk is minimized by choosing the futures position

$$h = -\text{size of spot commitment} \times \beta, \qquad (1)$$

where β (beta), the *hedging coefficient*, is defined by the formula

$$\beta = \frac{\text{covariance of futures price change with spot price change}}{\text{variance of futures price change}}.$$

That is, h is the futures position that minimizes the variance of the dollar value of the total position value at the commitment date, which is made up of the spot commitment value plus the profits or losses on futures.

The key unknown is the hedging coefficient β. It is useful to interpret the optimal hedge by using the definition of correlation to rewrite the hedging coefficient β in the form

$$\beta = \text{corr(futures, spot)} \times \frac{\text{sdev(spot)}}{\text{sdev(futures)}}, \qquad (2)$$

where "futures" and "spot" are of course shorthand for "futures price change" and "spot price change." The magnitude of the optimal futures hedging position is therefore increasing in the correlation between futures and spot, increasing in the standard deviation of the spot, and decreasing in the standard deviation of the futures.

The formula (1) for the risk-minimizing futures position h is justified in Chapter 4. Based on calculations to be explained later in this chapter, we will estimate β to be 0.935. The quantity commitment Q is 25,000,000 marks. We therefore estimate the risk-minimizing hedge $h = -Q\beta$ to be $-0.935 \times 25 = -23.37$ million marks. At 125,000 marks per contract, this is approximately -187 contracts, meaning a short position of 187 contracts. This is somewhat less than an equal and opposite (short) position of 25 million marks, or 200 contracts short. A short position of 200 contracts is in fact "over-hedged," and involves more risk than the minimum-variance hedge h.

Timing of Hedge? Normally, one would "put on the hedge," as is commonly said, as soon as the risk is perceived, and remove it (that is, offset the futures position) at the spot commitment date. A more sophisticated approach is *dynamic hedging*—continually adjusting the size of the hedge as the spot commitment date approaches. Dynamic hedges can compensate for changing volatility in the futures or spot markets, or for new information. Calculating an optimal dynamic hedging strategy is, in some cases, quite complicated.

This chapter reviews several methods for estimating h, the size of the optimal hedge, using simple principles and linear regression. We will also cover techniques for choosing the best futures contract for hedging purposes, for offsetting the effects of interest on margin accounts, for the simultaneous use of several different futures contracts, for hedging several different commitments at the same time, for obtaining dynamic hedging strategies, and for checking the quality of the hedge.

Alternate Meanings of "Hedging"

Among economists, the meaning of "to hedge" is not universally accepted as "to adopt a strategy designed to reduce risk," although that is the accepted English definition of the word. For some economists, to hedge with futures contracts may also mean to trade in order to profit from futures price changes. While there are certainly profit motives for trading futures, as discussed in Chapter 4, in this book we always prefer to treat the expression "futures hedging" as futures trading motivated solely by risk reduction. The same economic agent may take a futures position that is partly motivated by risk reduction (the hedge portion) and partly motivated by expected profits.

In a broad context, hedging also encompasses *synthetic insurance*, the adoption of a dynamic trading strategy that puts a lower bound on the value of a position at a given time in the future. We limit the discussion in this chapter to the selection of a minimum-variance futures position. Chapter 8 deals with synthetic insurance.

Alternate Hedging Markets

We cannot assert that the best hedge for a given commitment is always made with a futures position. There are alternatives. For instance, in order to hedge the commitment to sell 25 million marks on November 15, one could instead use the three-step strategy:

1. Borrow marks now from a German bank through the firm's German subsidiary, enough so that the amount to be repaid on November 15 is approximately 25 million marks.

2. Exchange the borrowed marks immediately for U.S. dollars and deposit the dollars in a U.S. bank.

3. On November 15, repay the 25 million marks due on the German bank loan with the German account receivable of 25 million marks.

This strategy essentially eliminates the spot commitment risk and, in some situations, may be more attractive than futures hedging. On the other hand, the transactions costs generated by the strategy may (or may not) be large relative to the futures transactions costs. In general, the main advantages of hedging in futures markets are the relatively low transactions costs, low default risk, and ease of execution relative to more customized hedging arrangements.

For protection against exchange rate risk, one can also turn to the interbank market for forward foreign exchange, outlined in Appendix 2B. In contrast with many forward markets, the interbank foreign exchange markets compare quite favorably with futures contracts in terms of their volume of trade and liquidity. In fact, forward foreign exchange markets are especially well suited to large trades, relative to the typical size of trades in currency futures. The principles of hedging in forward markets are quite similar to those of hedging in futures markets, and most of the techniques explained in this chapter apply to forwards with minor changes.

The options and futures options markets are also quite popular arenas for hedging. The idea of options hedging, however, is not to reduce the volatility of one's position, as it is with a futures hedge, but rather to obtain a floor under one's position value in return for the option premium. The distinction between these two approaches is illustrated in Chapter 8, along with a general review of options and futures options.

2. BASIS

Many situations call for hedging a fixed quantity of a spot market asset with a futures contract delivering the same or a related asset. The *basis* is the difference between the futures and spot prices at the spot commitment date. In general, the basis is random, and represents a risk that cannot be eliminated. In some cases, however, there is a formula for the futures price in terms of the spot price that, in principle, eliminates basis risk and makes the optimal hedge simple to choose and extremely effective. We will look at the two cases: zero basis and a random basis. (An exercise examines the case of a non-zero non-random basis.)

Hedging with Zero Basis

If the spot commitment date is the delivery date of the futures contract, the basis is zero! We illustrate the case of zero basis with the following example.

Example: Suppose Acme Mint, Inc. (a fictional firm), has commitments to buy 20,000 ounces of gold on December 14, 1989, in order to meet its production needs for a large order of gold coins. Assuming the Comex futures contract for December 1989 delivery also delivers on December 14, there is little question about basis risk. We know that, for any futures contract, the threat of arbitrage equates the futures price with the spot price on the contract's delivery date. Thus the cost of the gold can be effectively "locked in" by taking a long position of 200 contracts at 100 ounces each. The spot gold will cost Acme

Mint $20,000 \times s_T$, where s_T is the gold spot price per ounce at the delivery date T. The cumulative futures resettlement profit (or loss) from today's date t to the delivery date T is $200\,\text{contracts} \times 100\,\text{ounces}$ per contract $\times (f_T - f_t)$, where f_t denotes the futures price per ounce at date t. Neglecting interest on margin, the cost of the gold, net of futures resettlement profits, is

$$\text{Net cost} = 20,000 \times s_T - 200 \times 100 \times (f_T - f_t)$$

$$= 20,000 \times s_T - 20,000 \times (s_T - f_t)$$

$$= 20,000 \times f_t,$$

using the fact that $s_T = f_T$. The net cost of the gold is therefore the cost at the current (known) futures price f_t, say $500 per ounce, or $10 million. (Of course, we are ignoring interest costs on margin payments, transactions costs, and so on.) Even though s_T and f_T are unknown, the fact that they are the same implies that an equal and opposite futures position of 20,000 ounces eliminates the risk of the hedged position.

Let's check our results against the "beta" hedging formula (1) given in the introduction. In order to calculate β, we divide $\text{cov}(f_T - f_t, s_T - s_t)$ by $\text{var}(f_T - f_t)$. Since f_t and s_t are known at time the hedge is calculated,

$$\text{cov}(f_T - f_t, s_T - s_t) = \text{cov}(f_T, s_T).$$

Since $s_T = f_T$, we know that $\text{cov}(f_T, s_T) = \text{var}(f_T)$, implying that

$$\beta = \frac{\text{cov}(f_T, s_T)}{\text{var}(f_T)} = \frac{\text{var}(f_T)}{\text{var}(f_T)} = 1.$$

The risk-minimizing futures position is $h = -Q\beta$, where Q is the size of the spot market commitment. In this case, $Q = -20,000$ ounces since Acme Mint has a commitment to buy 20,000 ounces of gold. (This is a short spot market position; had Acme committed instead to sell 20,000 ounces, Q would be $+20,000$ ounces.) Thus

$$h = -Q\beta = -(-20,000) \times 1 = 20,000 \text{ ounces},$$

or 200 contracts of 100 ounces each, confirming the "equal and opposite" rule of thumb for hedging with zero basis.

Hedging with a Random Basis

In general, the basis is random: a risk minimizing futures position exists, but does not reduce the total risk to zero.

Example: Consider a hedge for a spot market commitment to receive 10 million Dutch gulden, the currency of Holland, by USCX, Inc., a small U.S. exporter of computer equipment.[1] The payment is due to be deposited in USCX's account in one month and converted immediately into U.S. dollars, in return for a shipment of computers due to arrive in Amsterdam at the same time. Since there is currently no Dutch guilder futures contract, USCX must hedge in a different currency futures contract, say West German marks. Clearly, the basis in this case is random unless the German-Dutch exchange rate is fixed for the entire period of the hedge, and there is no evidence of fixed exchange rates. In fact, the monthly exchange rate data for 1984–1986 shown in Appendix 7A indicate that, although movements in the spot guilder exchange rate and the nearby futures price for marks are related, they are not perfectly correlated. (The OLS estimate of their correlation during this period is in fact 0.78.)

We have a formula, $h = -Q\beta$, for the risk-minimizing futures position h in deutsche marks, but before we estimate the hedging coefficient β, it may help USCX managers to better understand the hedging situation if we can show them the plot in Figure 7.1 of the estimated risk as a function of their futures position y in the nearby deutsche mark contract. There are two easy ways to produce this plot with a computer, as follows.

1. The first method requires one to calculate the value of the hedged position had the hedge been placed at some month t in the past for which data are available. Appendix 7A has data for 36 months during 1984–1986. The calculation is made separately for each month t from 1 to 36 as follows. For each futures position y, using the data in Appendix 7A, calculate the total dollar value, denoted $P_t(y)$, that USCX would receive at month $t + 1$ if it were to be credited the change from month t to month $t + 1$ in the cash market value of 10 million gulden plus the resettlement profits or losses on a futures position of y million deutsche marks established at month t and offset

---

[1] This example uses information provided by a former student, Joshua Sommer, and is based on his response to Exercise 7.2. Gulden is the plural of guilder.

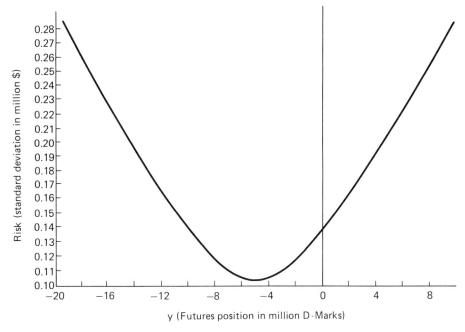

y (Futures position in million D-Marks)

Figure 7.1   The Estimated Risk as a Function of the Futures Position

at month $t + 1$. This total, in millions of U.S. dollars, is

$$P_t(y) = 10(s_{t+1} - s_t) + y(f_{t+1} - f_t),$$

where s_t is the spot guilder exchange rate at month t (U.S. dollars per Dutch guilder), f_t is the deutsche mark futures price at month t (U.S. dollars per deutsche mark), and y is the futures position (in millions of marks). If USCX had faced its current hedging situation at month t and adopted the futures position y, $P_t(y)$ would have been the change in market value of its hedged position. For example, with $t = 1$ and a futures position of $y = 10$ contracts (10 short), the change in position value is

$$P_1(y) = 10 \times (0.3397 - 0.3155) - 10 \times (0.3975 - 0.3670)$$

$$= 0.063 \text{ million dollars.}$$

Based on the 36 available monthly price observations for 1984–1986, this new series $P_1(y), P_2(y), \ldots, P_{35}(y)$ of monthly observations is put into a new column of data in the computer. At this stage, one can calculate the OLS estimate $SD(y)$ of the standard deviation of $P_t(y)$. The OLS estimate of standard deviation is the square root of the OLS estimate of variance, which is explained in Chapter 6. Figure 7.1 shows a plot of $SD(y)$ for a range of possible values for the futures position y.

2. Those who prefer to use less time on the computer can instead use the formula

$$\text{var}[P_t(y)] = \text{var}[10(s_{t+1} - s_t) + y(f_{t+1} - f_t)]$$

$$= \text{var}[10(s_{t+1} - s_t)] + \text{var}[y(f_{t+1} - f_t)]$$

$$+ 2\,\text{cov}[10(s_{t+1} - s_t), y(f_{t+1} - f_t)]$$

$$= 100\,\text{var}(s_{t+1} - s_t) + y^2\,\text{var}(f_{t+1} - f_t)$$

$$+ 20y\,\text{cov}(s_{t+1} - s_t, f_{t+1} - f_t).$$

The computer can be used to calculate the OLS estimates V_s, V_f, and C_{sf} of the respective unknown statistics $\text{var}(s_{t+1} - s_t)$, $\text{var}(f_{t+1} - f_t)$, and $\text{cov}(s_{t+1} - s_t, f_{t+1} - f_t)$, using the data in Appendix 7A. It turns out that $V_f = 0.0003376$, $V_s = 0.000189$, and $C_{sf} = 0.000167$. We then have an alternative derivation of the risk (standard deviation) estimate $SD(y)$ via the equation

$$SD(y) = \sqrt{100V_s + 20y\,C_{sf} + y^2 V_f}$$

$$= \sqrt{0.0189 + 0.00335\,y + 0.0003376\,y^2}.$$

Using either method 1 or method 2, a plot of the estimated risk $SD(y)$ for different values of y is shown in Figure 7.1. The managers of USCX may find this information quite useful in deciding whether to hedge, and if so, how much. From the plot, we can see that the minimum estimated risk is obtained at a short futures position of 5 million deutsche marks, or short 40 contracts of 125,000 deutsche marks each. The formula $h = -Q\beta$ produces the same result (as it must) if we substitute the OLS estimate for β, which is

$$\widehat{\beta} = \frac{C_{sf}}{V_f} = \frac{0.000167}{0.0003376} = 0.496.$$

Since the quantity to be hedged is $Q = 10$ million gulden, the futures position minimizing the estimated risk is

$$\widehat{h} = -Q\widehat{\beta} = -10 \times 0.496 = -4.96 \quad \text{(million deutsche marks)},$$

or about 40 contracts short, confirming the graphical solution.

To check the performance of the recommended hedge over the historical period, USCX management may also appreciate the plots of the change in value $P_t(y)$ of the hedged position shown in Figure 7.2 for the risk-minimizing futures position of $y = -5$ million deutsche marks, as well as for the zero hedging choice, $y = 0$. The plot of $P_t(0)$ clearly shows greater volatility than that of $P_t(-5)$.

At this writing, the spot exchange rates are 0.5319 U.S. dollars per guilder and 0.5968 U.S. dollars per deutsche mark. The mark-guilder exchange rate is therefore $0.5319/0.5968 = 0.8913$ deutsche marks per guilder. An "equal and opposite" strategy in deutsche mark futures would therefore call for a futures position of -10 million gulden $\times$ 0.8913 deutsche marks per guilder $= -8.9$ million deutsche marks, or 71 contracts (short). Comparing the performance of the equal-and-opposite strategy with the risk-minimizing strategy leaves no doubt as to the relative efficacy of the risk-minimizing strategy in controlling the volatility of the hedged position change during the three-year historical period. This can be verified graphically in both Figures 7.1 and 7.3. The equal-and-opposite strategy over-hedges by not accounting for the basis risk.

Exercise 7.3 supplies an additional 12 months of exchange rate data for the period following the initial 36-month historical period. This exercise asks for a check of the performance during the latter 12-month period of the hedge chosen using the first 36 months of data. Since there is no guarantee that exchange rate data come even close to satisfying the OLS conditions, this is a prudent check to make when using old data for statistical estimation of β.

3. PRINCIPLES OF STATISTICAL HEDGING

This section reviews several basic principles of the statistical approach to hedging illustrated in the previous two sections.

The Minimum-Variance Criterion

One should immediately question the minimum-variance criterion. Reusing the notation of Chapter 4, for example, suppose the commitment of a given

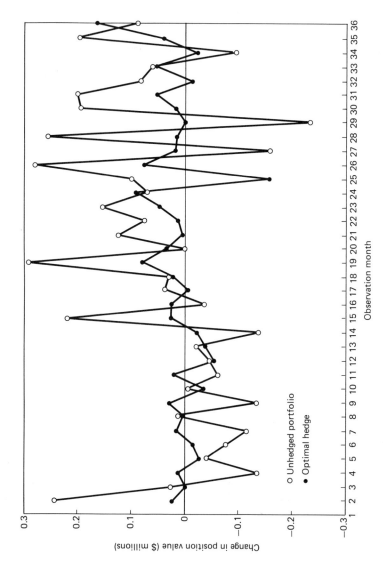

Figure 7.2 Historical Performance of Risk-Minimizing Hedge

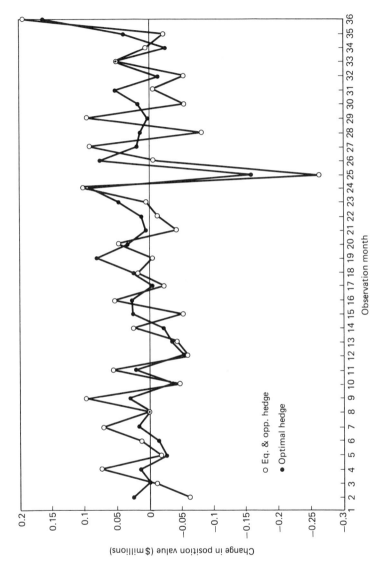

Figure 7.3 Risk-Minimizing and Equal-and-Opposite Hedging Performance

213

agent has an uncertain market value e (the *endowment*), while f_1 is the futures price at the date the endowment is received. The current futures price is f_0. If the given agent has mean-variance utility with risk-aversion coefficient r, we saw in Chapter 4 that the agent's optimal futures position is

$$y = \frac{\overline{f}_1 - f_0}{2r \operatorname{var}(f_1)} - \frac{\operatorname{cov}(e, f_1)}{\operatorname{var}(f_1)}.$$

The minimum-variance futures position is the second term of this expression, the *pure hedge*

$$h = -\frac{\operatorname{cov}(e, f_1)}{\operatorname{var}(f_1)}.$$

The remainder, we recall, is the purely speculative demand

$$z = \frac{\overline{f}_1 - f_0}{2r \operatorname{var}(f_1)}.$$

Why, then, would a hedger choose only the pure hedge h and ignore the speculative portion z of the optimal position? Of course the hedger should *not* ignore the speculative portion; that is the point of the calculations showing the total position $y = z + h$ to be optimal. Nevertheless, there are at least two good reasons for focusing special attention on the pure hedging term h:

1. It is much easier to estimate covariances and variances of futures and spot price changes than it is to estimate their expected values. The pure hedge h is thus easier to estimate than is the speculative demand z. Furthermore, there may be substantial risk involved from estimating $\overline{f}_1$ inaccurately. Our model does not account for estimation risk, but rather assumes that the agent's actual means, covariances, and variances are available. Some agents, especially those involved in particular business risks, do not specialize in projecting futures prices, having their expertise in other pursuits. Always making the martingale estimate $\overline{f}_1 = f_0$ is a simple estimation model. It may not be in certain agents' economic interests to pay the costs of more accurate estimates of $\overline{f}_1$. If that is true, the optimal futures position is h, since $\overline{f}_1 = f_0$ implies a speculative demand of $z = 0$.

2. The pure hedge (per unit of spot market position) is common to all mean-variance agents with commitments in the same spot market, while the speculative portion of a futures position is specific to

the individual agent, since the risk-aversion coefficient r depends on the agent. Furthermore, there are reasons to believe that, although different agents may estimate $\bar{f}_1$ quite differently on the basis of private information, their estimates of covariances and variances will not differ as much. Thus calculating the pure hedge (per unit of spot market commitment) can be a useful service to many different agents, who can individually multiply by the size of their spot market commitments and then add on their own speculative demands.

As far as the first reason is concerned, one could, in principle, extend the mean-variance model to account for estimation risk based on restrictive assumptions, but there are few available guidelines. For most of this chapter we focus on the "pure hedge," and naively proceed as though the least squares estimates of covariances are the agent's covariances. Possible corrections for estimation risk are suggested in sources cited in the Notes.

Data Intervals

For practical purposes, one often takes the length of a time interval to be one day. This is convenient because positions are resettled daily and because the shortest time periods for which price observations are easily available is one day. For example, many data services provide daily settlement prices for futures contracts and closing prices for related spot assets. This is not to say that one should estimate covariances based on daily observations, and says nothing about how far into the past one should go. These two basic decisions, the size of a time interval between observations (the *sampling interval*) and the number of time intervals to include in the sample, are illustrated in Figure 7.4. This figure illustrates a hedging decision made at day t for a spot commitment at day $t + K$.

Figure 7.4   Data and Hedging Intervals

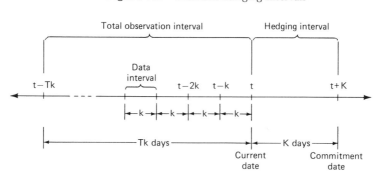

For example, let $f_1, f_2, \ldots$ denote the stochastic process of the daily futures settlement prices of a given futures contract, and let $s_1, s_2, \ldots$ denote the stochastic process of daily closing spot prices for a related spot asset. For each day t, let $F_t = f_t - f_{t-1}$ and $S_t = s_t - s_{t-1}$ denote the corresponding price increments. Under the joint OLS conditions on F and S, we know that, for a time interval of k days,

$$\text{var}(f_{t+k} - f_t) = \text{var}\,(F_{t+1} + F_{t+2} + \cdots + F_{t+k}) = k\,\text{var}(F_{t+1}), \qquad (3)$$

and likewise that

$$
\begin{aligned}
\text{cov}&(f_{t+k} - f_t, s_{t+k} - s_t) \\
&= \text{cov}\,[(F_{t+1} + F_{t+2} \cdots + F_{t+k}), (S_{t+1} + S_{t+2} + \cdots + S_{t+k})] \\
&= k\,\text{cov}(F_{t+1}, S_{t+1}). \qquad (4)
\end{aligned}
$$

Based on equations (3) and (4), one could use daily variance and covariance estimates to obtain, say, weekly ($k = 7$) covariance and variance estimates for hedging purposes. Furthermore, under the OLS conditions, better estimates of covariances can be obtained by more frequent observations. In this case, no matter how long the interval between the day t at which the hedge is "put on" (the time at which the futures position is first taken) and the day $t + K$ at which the hedge is "taken off" (the closeout date), one would be better off using daily observations than, say, weekly observations. Indeed, pushing this to the extreme, one might want to estimate covariances on the basis of observations taken as frequently as possible, say hour by hour or minute by minute. Furthermore, under these ideal conditions, one would always obtain more accurate estimates by including the earliest available price observations.

Of course, the OLS conditions do not actually apply. For instance, in Chapter 6 we cited a number of studies indicating the presence of autocorrelation and heteroskedasticity in futures price increments. Moreover, because of a changing economic environment, older data simply become less relevant. There are several basic strategies to consider here:

1. *Statistical Correction:* One could attempt to correct for failure of the OLS conditions. For example, if the OLS conditions apply with the exception of the zero autocorrelation assumption, one could estimate the autocorrelation structure, and correct for it, using methods explained in sources cited in the Notes. If this can be done properly, one would still be better off sampling as frequently as possible (ignoring data and computational costs). Similarly, one can correct for

heteroskedasticity problems such as the Samuelson effect or seasonality effects described in Chapter 6.

2. *Adjustment of Sampling Interval:*   One could choose a sampling interval that accounts for the length of time the futures position is fixed. This is a vague prescription, and will be left mainly to the reader to sort out. There is still a trade-off between the number of observations and estimation bias. With only a year of relevant data and a proposed three-month hedging interval, for instance, one might be inclined to resort to weekly rather than quarterly observations if the data do not show severe autocorrelation. (Most statistical estimation packages include tests of significant autocorrelation.) In order to use all of the available data, one can also choose overlapping time intervals, for example, take monthly sampling intervals with weekly data, so that one month's interval includes three weeks from the previous month's interval. If the weekly data satisfies the OLS conditions, this procedure clearly generates a violation of the OLS conditions. As explained by Hansen and Hodrick (1980), however, by properly accounting for the induced autocorrelation, one can improve the quality of the estimates over those obtained by monthly non-overlapping sampling intervals, under certain conditions.

3. *Dynamic Hedging:*   One can adjust the hedge as time transpires. For example, if the OLS conditions do not apply because of heteroskedasticity (along the lines, say, of the Samuelson effect or seasonality in variances), the appropriate hedge may change through time. If price increments are serially uncorrelated, for example, then the optimal hedge can be adjusted through time as though the hedge is to be taken off at the next opportunity, even if the spot commitment is far into the future. We will see a particular example of an optimal dynamic hedging strategy later in the chapter.

Strategies 1–3 can be combined when appropriate.

The Least Squares Hedge Estimator

Suppose it is currently day number t, and that one is committed to Q units of the spot asset at day $t+K$. (A commitment to buy the spot asset corresponds to a negative value for Q.) We have shown earlier that the risk-minimizing futures position is $h = -Q\beta$, where

$$\beta = \frac{\text{cov}(s_{t+K} - s_t, f_{t+K} - f_t)}{\text{var}(f_{t+K} - f_t)}.$$

Under the OLS conditions, equations (3) and (4) tell us that the hedging coefficient β is independent of the time interval over which the price change occurs. For example, we know that

$$\beta = \frac{\text{cov}(s_{t+1} - s_t, f_{t+1} - f_t)}{\text{var}(f_{t+1} - f_t)} = \frac{\text{cov}(S_{t+1}, F_{t+1})}{\text{var}(F_{t+1})}. \tag{5}$$

In fact, if we have price data at k-day intervals, the OLS conditions allow us to treat β as the ratio of covariance to variance over this sampling interval, or

$$\beta = \frac{\text{cov}(s_{t+k} - s_t, f_{t+k} - f_t)}{\text{var}(f_{t+k} - f_t)}. \tag{6}$$

How does one estimate β ? The obvious procedure is to calculate the sample covariance $C(S, F)$ for $\text{cov}(s_{t+k} - s_t, f_{t+k} - f_t)$ and sample variance $V(F)$ for var $(f_{t+k} - f_t)$, and then to construct the *least squares beta estimator*

$$\widehat{\beta} = \frac{C(S, F)}{V(F)}. \tag{7}$$

(A more convenient way to estimate β is explained in Section 7.4.) The least squares estimator (7) is based on the observations:

$$[(f_k - f_0, s_k - s_0), (f_{2k} - f_k, s_{2k} - s_k), \ldots, (f_{kT} - f_{k(T-1)}, s_{kT} - s_{k(T-1)})],$$

or T observations over Tk days, as illustrated in Figure 7.4. Taking successive Wednesday settlement prices for T weeks, for example, would correspond to $k = 7$ days.

If the OLS conditions apply jointly to the spot and futures price increments, then the *least squares hedge estimator*

$$H = -Q\widehat{\beta} \tag{8}$$

is a reasonable estimator for the pure hedge $h = -Q\beta$. These qualifications, however, are rather large and important, and adjustments are often appropriate, as we have discussed. The least squares hedge estimator is widely used in practice.

Hedging Based on Percentage Price Changes

For many futures contracts, it is more palatable to assume that *percentage price changes* satisfy the OLS conditions than it is to assume that price changes themselves satisfy the OLS conditions. As pointed out in Chapter 6, there is an important distinction. For example, suppose the percentage price change from f_t to f_{t+1} is $+50$ percent or -50 percent, with equal probabilities, at any time t. If $f_t = 100$, then at time t, $\mathrm{sdev}(f_{t+1} - f_t) = 50$. Suppose the futures price goes up from $f_t = 100$ to $f_{t+1} = 150$. Then at time $t + 1$ an increase or decrease of 50 percent represents a price change of 75, and the standard deviation of $f_{t+2} - f_{t+1}$ at time $t + 1$ goes up to 75, whereas the standard deviation of the percentage price change from f_{t+1} to f_{t+2} remains constant at 50 percent.

We can deal with OLS percentage price changes using a statistical hedging approach explained in Appendix 7D. It turns out that the optimal hedge depends on the current ratio of futures to spot prices, which changes with time. This may call for a dynamic hedging policy that readjusts the hedge as spot and futures prices change through time.

4. HEDGING ESTIMATES BY LINEAR REGRESSION

This section explains how to obtain least squares estimates of hedging coefficients from widely available linear regression software.

Simple Linear Regression

We recall the well-known model of *simple linear regression* of spot price increments S_{t+1} regressed on futures price increments F_{t+1}. (A more detailed review is given in Appendix 6B.) By *linear*, we mean that S_{t+1} is approximated by an expression of the form $a + bF_{t+1}$. The difference $\epsilon_{t+1} = S_{t+1} - a - bF_{t+1}$ is called the *residual*. The objective is to choose the coefficients a and b so that:

1. The approximation is unbiased, meaning $E(a + bF_{t+1}) = E(S_{t+1})$.
2. The residual ϵ_{t+1} has the minimum possible variance.

There is a unique solution to this problem: Choose $b = \beta$, as specified by equation (5), and choose $a = \alpha$, where $\alpha = E(S_{t+1}) - \beta E(F_{t+1})$. The fact that the best choice for b is β follows from the fact that, since a is a constant,

$$\mathrm{var}(\epsilon_{t+1}) = \mathrm{var}(S_{t+1} - bF_{t+1}),$$

and we have already solved this minimum-variance problem under the guise of hedging: we found in Chapter 4 that the variance of $S_{t+1} - bF_{t+1}$ is minimized by choosing $b = \text{cov}(S_{t+1}, F_{t+1})/\text{var}(F_{t+1})$, which is β. Of course, the choice of $a = \alpha$ is dictated by unbiasedness.

Hedging Coefficients from Regression Coefficients

We have discovered a natural coincidence: the optimal hedging coefficient β is the same as the coefficient of the simple linear regression of S_{t+1} on F_{t+1}. This coincidence can be put to use! The regression coefficient reported by standard statistical software packages is the least squares beta estimator $\widehat{\beta}$. Moreover, most such software packages also report several *regression diagnostics*, as shown below in an estimated regression of weekly spot price increments for deutsche marks on weekly nearby futures price increments for deutsche marks, based on 26 consecutive weeks of observations during 1983. We have

$$S_{t+1} = -0.00005 + 0.93468\, F_{t+1} + \hat{\epsilon}_{t+1} \qquad (R^2 = 0.937).$$

$$\phantom{S_{t+1} = } (0.0003) \qquad (0.0501^*) \qquad\quad (0.0013)$$

The key number for hedging purposes is $\widehat{\beta} = 0.93468$. We will not use the estimate of $\widehat{\alpha} = -0.00005$. The diagnostic reported as $R^2 = 0.937$ is the squared estimated correlation between S_{t+1} and $\widehat{\beta}F_{t+1}$, and is a useful measure of the quality of the hedge. An R^2 of 1.0 represents a perfect hedge (no risk); an R^2 of zero represents no hedging power at all. In fact, R^2 is the estimated fraction of variance in the spot deutsche mark position that is eliminated by the optimal hedging position, under the OLS conditions.

The diagnostics reported below the regression equation in parentheses are the least squares estimates of the standard deviations of $\widehat{\alpha}$, $\widehat{\beta}$, and $\hat{\epsilon}_{t+1}$, respectively. These are sometimes called *standard errors*, and indicate the precision of the respective estimates. The asterisk adjacent to the standard error 0.0501 of $\widehat{\beta}$ indicates "statistical significance." In this case, significance means merely that one can reject the hypothesis (with 95 percent probability under special assumptions) that F_{t+1} and S_{t+1} are uncorrelated. It appears, therefore, that the futures contract provides significant hedging power. The asterisk indicating significance appears whenever the ratio of $\widehat{\beta}$ to its standard error is sufficiently large; a rough rule of thumb for large samples under the OLS conditions is a ratio of 2.0 or more. In this example, the ratio, called the *t-statistic*, is actually 18.5, so there is little question that $\widehat{\beta}$ is statistically significant. On some software packages, *t*-statistics are reported in place of standard errors.

An estimated regression and the associated data points are illustrated in Figure 7.5. The *regression line* is fitted to the data points by choosing the *intercept* $\hat{\alpha}$ and the *slope* $\hat{\beta}$ so that the sum of squared vertical distances from the data points to the line is minimized.

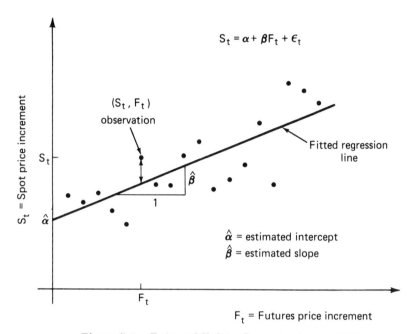

Figure 7.5   Estimated Hedging Regression Line and Data

According to our regression equation, the receivable of 25 million marks described in Section 7.1 has the least squares hedge estimate

$$H = -Q\hat{\beta} = -25,000,000 \times 0.93464 = -23,410,000 \text{ marks.}$$

At 125,000 deutsche marks per contract, this is a short hedge position of 187 contracts, to the nearest whole contract, as reported at the beginning of the chapter.

Hedging by Multiple Linear Regression

In some situations there is an obvious case for hedging a given spot commitment with positions in several different types of futures contracts. As it turns out, hedging positions in each of the futures contracts can be estimated using *multiple linear regression*, the obvious extension of simple linear regression.

Suppose n different futures contracts are under consideration for hedging a spot market commitment. Let S_t denote the spot price increment at time t and let $F_t^{(i)}$ denote the corresponding price increment of the i-th futures contract under consideration. The *multiple linear regression* equation takes the form

$$S_{t+1} = \alpha + \beta_1 F_{t+1}^{(1)} + \beta_2 F_{t+1}^{(2)} + \cdots + \beta_n F_{t+1}^{(n)} + \epsilon_{t+1}.$$

In terms of regression theory, the variables $F_{t+1}^{(1)}, F_{t+1}^{(2)}, \ldots, F_{t+1}^{(n)}$ are called *explanatory* (or sometimes *independent*), and S_{t+1} is called the *explained* (or *dependent*) variable. Again, the regression coefficients $\beta = (\beta_1, \ldots, \beta_n)$ are chosen so as to minimize the variance of the residual ϵ_{t+1}. (The solution for β is reviewed in Appendix 6B.) Equivalently, $(-\beta_1, \ldots, -\beta_n)$ is the collection of futures positions in the respective futures contracts forming the optimal hedge for one unit of the spot asset. If the spot quantity being hedged is Q units, then the optimal futures position in the i-th futures contract is $h_i = -Q\beta_i$, forming the collection $(-Q\beta_1, \ldots, -Q\beta_n)$ of positions in the different contracts. If one were to hedge using the i-th futures contract alone, the optimal futures position would *not* be $-Q\beta_i$ since the simple regression coefficient for the i-th futures contract alone would not be the same as the multiple regression coefficient β_i.

If $\widehat{\beta} = (\widehat{\beta}_1, \ldots, \widehat{\beta}_n)$ are the least squares estimated regression coefficients, then the corresponding least squares estimator for the minimum variance hedging position is

$$(-Q\widehat{\beta}_1, \ldots, -Q\widehat{\beta}_n).$$

Most multiple regression software packages report the regression coefficients $\widehat{\beta}$ as well as the associated regression diagnostics.

Example: Consider the problem of hedging a portfolio of 10,000 shares of Coca-Cola common stock with a position in S&P 500 Index futures and Value Line Average futures. Let:

- S_t denote the change during week t in the share price of Coca-Cola
- $F_t^{(1)}$ denote the change in the nearby S&P 500 Futures Index of the Chicago Mercantile Exchange during week t
- $F_t^{(2)}$ denote the change in the nearby Value Line Futures Index of the Kansas City Board of Trade during week t

The above data were collected for 104 weeks, using Friday closing NYSE stock prices and Friday futures settlement prices for the first week of 1985 through the first week of 1987. A standard statistical software package reported the following estimated regression of S_{t+1} on $F_{t+1}^{(1)}$ and $F_{t+1}^{(2)}$:

$$S_{t+1} = \widehat{\alpha} - 0.038F_{t+1}^{(1)} + 0.132F_{t+1}^{(2)} + \widehat{\epsilon}_{t+1}. \qquad (R^2 = 0.488)$$
$$\phantom{S_{t+1} = \widehat{\alpha} - }(0.04) \qquad\qquad (0.04^*) \qquad\quad (0.72)$$

The estimated hedging coefficients are thus $\widehat{\beta}_1 = -0.038$ and $\widehat{\beta}_2 = 0.132$. The numbers reported in parentheses below these coefficients are estimates of the standard errors of the regression coefficients, as discussed earlier. It appears (from the absence of an asterisk on the appropriate standard error) that the S&P 500 contract may not provide significant hedging ability. We will return to this issue shortly. The reported R^2 corresponds to an estimated 48.8 percent reduction in variance (risk) by hedging. All of these estimates are based, as usual, on the OLS conditions, a major assumption. The least squares hedge estimate is easily calculated as follows. Both the S&P 500 and Value Line contracts pay 500 times their indices at delivery. Since the quantity Q of Coca-Cola shares to hedge is $10,000$, the estimated hedge is $H_1 = -Q\widehat{\beta}_1/500 = 0.76$ S&P 500 contracts and $H_2 = -Q\widehat{\beta}_2/500 = -2.64$ Value Line contracts.

The fact that $\widehat{\beta}_1$ fails the test of statistical significance, however, suggests that one may be better off dropping the S&P 500 contract from the hedge entirely. In that case, the Value Line hedging coefficient $\widehat{\beta}_2 = 0.132$ is *not* an appropriate estimate of the regression coefficient corresponding to a hedge in the Value Line contract alone. Instead, one should estimate a new regression of S_{t+1} on $F_{t+1}^{(2)}$. For our data, the results are

$$S_{t+1} = \widehat{\alpha} + 0.098\ F_{t+1}^{(2)} + \epsilon_{t+1}. \qquad (R^2 = 0.483) \qquad\qquad (9)$$
$$\phantom{S_{t+1} = \widehat{\alpha} + }(0.016^*) \qquad\quad (0.72)$$

The corresponding estimated hedge is

$$H = -Q\widehat{\beta} = \frac{-10,000 \times 0.098}{500} = -1.96 \text{ contracts,}$$

or a short position of about two nearby Value Line contracts. Although the R^2 for this simple regression is reduced (from that of the multiple regression that includes the S&P 500 futures as an additional explanatory variable), the R^2 is not a valid measure for comparing the quality of two regressions with different numbers of explanatory variables.

Incidentally, the Durbin-Watson statistic 2.64 for this regression indicates a relatively high likelihood of autocorrelation in the price increments, as discussed in Appendix 6C. In some cases, advanced econometric techniques are called for in dealing with autocorrelation. We mention some references in the Notes.

5. COMMON HEDGING QUESTIONS

In this section we review some commonly encountered issues of hedging strategy.

Which Futures Contract?

Which type of futures contract provides the maximum risk reduction? When hedging the risk of spot price movements in a given asset, it is often, but not always, true that the optimal futures contract is that delivering the given asset. (An exception is the case of hedging Ginnie Mae mortgage risk, discussed in Appendix 9B.)

Of course, many spot assets are not delivered in any futures market, and one must *cross-hedge*, which means hedge in a futures contract delivering a different but related asset. The general rule for hedging a given quantity of an asset is:

> Choose that futures contract whose price movements have the maximum possible correlation with price movements in the committed spot asset.

Exercise 7.4 asks for a demonstration of the optimality of this rule.

How Many Different Futures Go in a Hedge?

Ignoring transactions costs, estimation risk, and the fact that one can only take positions in whole numbers of contracts, there are no theoretical limits on the number of different futures contracts one would use to hedge a particular commitment. The variance of the total spot plus futures position could always be reduced in principle by including more types of futures contracts in the hedge. Mathematically speaking, this is equivalent to the fact that the standard error of a linear regression can always be reduced by including more explanatory variables. Because one typically uses only statistical estimates of covariances, the estimated variance reduction achieved by including additional types of futures contracts can be illusory, just as can the reported reduction in the standard error of a regression achieved from including unrelated explanatory variables. A hedge based on estimated covariances can in fact be worsened by including unrelated or poorly related futures contracts. Statistical tests of the hypothesis of a significant improvement in the fit of one regression equation over another can be used; some of these tests can be found in sources cited in the Notes. Common sense and an understanding of the economics of the market are always useful in selecting a hedge.

Example: *(Junk Bond Hedge)*   In practice, attention could be focused on those futures contracts that bear some clear economic relationship to the spot commitment. In hedging the purchase or sale price of a bond portfolio, for example, one would tend to look first at interest rate futures of the corresponding maturities. Superior understanding of the risks involved can lead to a better hedge. For example, low-grade corporate bonds have a return that is well correlated with stock returns, since default risk increases with unexpected decreases in share value. One might therefore improve a corporate bond hedge by including both stock index and interest rate futures. Grieves (1986), for example, compares the two regressions:

1. Monthly returns of industrial corporate bonds of Moody's Baa rating regressed on monthly log-price increments of the nearby T-bond futures contract of the Chicago Board of Trade.

2. Monthly returns of industrial corporate bonds of Moody's Baa rating regressed on monthly log-price increments of the nearby T-bond futures contract of the Chicago Board of Trade as well as monthly log-price increments of the nearby S&P 500 Index futures contract of the Chicago Mercantile Exchange.

Regression 2 merely adds S&P 500 futures log-price increments as an additional explanatory variable. Both regressions were based on 31 observations ending January 1985. The R^2 reported for Regression 1 is 0.36; the R^2 reported for Regression 2 is 0.51. Although these figures suggest that an optimal hedge in both T-bond futures and S&P 500 futures provides more variance reduction than a hedge in T-bonds alone, some warnings are in order. *First*, as mentioned earlier, a higher R^2 is not a test of significant reduction in variance. As it turns out, a standard statistical test reported in Grieves's paper shows that one cannot reject the hypothesis that Regression 2 offers a significantly better fit, at a given level of confidence. *Second*, in order to minimize the variance of the value of a position in corporate bonds, the minimum-variance hedging position is obtained from the regression of bond price increments on futures price increments, and not from the regression of returns on log-price increments. Hedging based on regression of log-price increments is discussed in Appendix 7D.

Of course, there is no reason to limit attention to futures contracts. Options and other assets can often improve a hedge. A corporate bond, for example, has many of the characteristics of an option on the value of the firm, and might be better hedged using both options and futures, if an appropriate option can be found.

Which Futures Delivery Date?

An important practical problem is the choice of delivery date. If the spot commitment date is precisely the delivery date of the nearby futures contract in the same commodity, the choice seems clear. Lack of arbitrage implies that the futures price and spot price are the same, or perfectly correlated, at delivery. In principle (ignoring delivery provisions and substitutions), one could therefore obtain a perfect hedge for a fixed quantity of the underlying spot commodity at delivery by taking an equal and opposite position in the futures contract. If these two dates do not coincide, the extent to which the futures price and spot price at the spot commitment date are not perfectly correlated is the delivery basis risk. The delivery basis risk usually rises with increases in the time between the spot commitment date and the futures delivery date. In principle, the futures contract providing the best hedge (maximum risk reduction) would be the one whose delivery date is closest to the spot commitment date, other things being equal.

Of course, "other things" are not equal. *First*, if the closest futures delivery date is before the spot commitment date, the hedge disappears at delivery, and might be replaced with a hedge in the next contract to deliver, or *rolled over*, as is often said. In some cases, it is more convenient to take a position initially in the following contract to deliver, thus eliminating the need to roll over the hedge. *Second*, liquidity often decreases dramatically with the successively later contracts to deliver. The cost of using the less liquid "distant" contracts may be large enough to make hedging in the nearby contract more attractive, and lead to periodic rolling of the hedge into the successive nearby contracts. This liquidity effect receives some discussion in Appendix 7C.

What Are the Effects of Interest on Margin?

So far in our calculations we have not accounted for the daily resettlement feature of futures contracts. The effect of $1 of futures profits or losses today is magnified by the interest paid on that dollar if re-invested until the spot commitment date. This effect, if not accounted for properly, causes one to underestimate the effective standard deviation of futures profits or losses, and therefore can cause over-hedging. The effect turns out to be mild for short hedging periods and low interest rates, and can be corrected by *tailing the hedge*, as shown in Appendix 7B.

Is Integer Rounding OK?

Except in the case of hedging with one futures contract, it is not necessarily true that the best hedge in whole numbers (*integers*) of contracts is obtained by rounding to the nearest integers. It is possible, however, to check the relative quality of several possible integer position combinations. The hedging quality of a given position $y = (y_1, y_2)$ in two different futures contracts, for example, can be estimated as the least squares estimate $\widehat{V}(y)$ of the variance of $S_{t+1} + y_1 F_{t+1}^{(1)} + y_2 F_{t+1}^{(2)}$. One could try various integer combinations $y = (y_1, y_2)$ for a futures position, check $\widehat{V}(y)$ for each, and select the integer combination y^* with the lowest estimated variance $\widehat{V}(y^*)$.

What Is the Total Hedge for Several Different Risks?

Suppose, for example, one is hedging spot positions in both Italian lire *and* Dutch gulden. What is the optimal hedge (the risk-minimizing futures position) for the combined risk? The solution is quite easy, given the following general rule:

Calculate the optimal hedge for each risk separately and add the different hedging positions together.

The optimality of this simple *additivity rule of hedging* is to be demonstrated in Exercise 7.7. The additivity rule works for any number of separate sources of risk, and for hedging each risk with any number of different types of futures contracts.

It is important in applying the additivity rule of hedging to choose an integer number of contracts *after* adding the individual hedges together, not before. Otherwise unnecessary risk can accumulate from rounding errors.

6. HEDGING BY CORPORATIONS

It is commonly believed that firms are better off if they reduce their risk by futures hedging. While this is true in many cases, a careful case for hedging by firms must be based on something more than mere risk aversion.

The Modigliani-Miller Irrelevance Principle

In 1958, Franco Modigliani and Merton Miller published a simple but significant fact: Under standard assumptions, a firm cannot increase its market value, nor better serve its shareholders, merely by changing its debt-equity ratio. Indeed, the reasoning behind this principle implies that any purely financial transaction is irrelevant in this sense. To be sure, the *Modigliani-Miller Irrelevance Principle* depends on the absence of taxes, transactions fees, differences in information, bankruptcy costs, and so on. Nevertheless, the idea forces one into subtle justifications for the financial policy of a firm. In particular, one must overhaul the usual simple explanation of why firms hedge in futures markets. This overly simple justification goes as follows: "By hedging, the firm reduces the riskiness of its total value. Since investors are risk averse, they are willing to pay more for the shares of a firm if its risk is reduced. Thus hedging increases the value of the firm." This statement, left on its own, is easy to contradict, as follows.

Suppose firms A and B are identical in every respect except that firm B hedges its risk using a futures position of y contracts per share. Suppose, in recognition of the risk reduction stemming from this futures position, that the share price p_B of firm B is higher than the share price p_A of firm A. An astute investor can then perform the following arbitrage:

1. Buy one share of firm A.
2. Take a futures position of y contracts.
3. Sell one share of firm B.

Since adopting a futures position requires no initial investment, the net initial cash flow of this strategy is $p_B - p_A > 0$. There is no further cash flow since a share of firm A plus a futures position of y contracts has the same payoff as a share of firm B. This strategy therefore generates profits with no investment or risk. As always, this form of arbitrage is (theoretically) impossible, so our assumption that $p_B > p_A$ must be wrong! Hedging does not necessarily improve the value of firm B. A more careful demonstration of the result is taken up in sources indicated in the Notes.

The Modigliani-Miller Irrelevance Principle is built on the premise that anything a firm can do in futures markets, its shareholders can also do. So if it is advantageous to shareholders to have the value of their shares hedged by a futures position, then the shareholders themselves can hedge. Why should an investor pay a premium for the shares of a hedged firm if that investor can hedge on his or her own at no cost?

The following example illustrates the Modigliani-Miller Irrelevance Principle, and may also serve to limit its scope of application.

Example: The Electric Motor Corporation (EMC), Inc. (a fictional firm), makes significant purchases of copper for the windings and other components of its electric motor products. EMC earns profits, on average, because it has fostered the development of a skilled labor force and has a reputation for incorporating the latest technological advances in motor design. Unfortunately, EMC is also subject to the risk of copper price volatility; a dramatic runup in copper prices can quickly darken the company's profits picture.

The head of EMC's purchasing department, Carol Hausmann, suggests in a memo that EMC reduce its risk of copper costs by taking long positions in Comex copper futures contracts as the company periodically sets its needs for copper during the following quarters. If copper prices increase dramatically, EMC's cost increases will be at least partially offset by profits on its long futures positions. (Likewise, if copper prices decline, EMC's futures losses will be offset by cost savings on its copper purchases.) Hausmann argues that in this way EMC can concentrate on its core manufacturing business, and not be concerned with fluctuations in the copper market that it cannot control.

The chief financial officer of EMC, Kevin Cooper, has authority over the firm's financial policy, and is familiar with the Modigliani-Miller Irrelevance Principle. When he received Hausmann's memo concerning hedging with copper futures, Cooper suggested that they discuss the issue.

Cooper begins their meeting by saying, "In principle, any futures position we take will have no effect on EMC's share price. Assuming we are in business to maximize our shareholders' wealth, should we really get involved in the expense of hiring someone to do our futures trading? Not to mention the brokerage fees and so on."

Hausmann, at first uncertain about Cooper's arguments, asks for an explanation. In only a minute or two, Cooper finishes the standard arguments by saying, "So, you see, anything we can do with futures contracts, our shareholders can do equally well on their own." After acknowledging that her initial motives for futures hedging were overly simple, Hausmann points out a flaw in Cooper's reasoning.

"Kevin, your argument only makes sense if shareholders always know our purchasing plans. Unless we're continually informing every shareholder about the sizes of our copper commitments, how will they know how much to hedge? Anyway, each Comex contract is so large that only our largest shareholders would want to take a position."

Cooper's face reddens slightly with embarrassment as he mentally takes one of his business school professors down a notch.

"I guess you're right," he concedes. "On top of everything you say, there's the fact that the total brokerage fees our shareholders would have to pay, not to mention their time and bother, more than justify the cost of doing the hedging here at EMC."

Motives for Hedging by Firms

The Electric Motor Corporation example illustrates that the Modigliani-Miller Irrelevance Principle must be applied carefully. The scenario included three possible justifications for futures hedging by firms:

1. Firms may have more information than their shareholders concerning the risks involved. Moreover, for strategic reasons, they may not wish to publicize their market commitments for their competitors to learn.

2. Futures contracts tend to be sized for firms and large investors, not for the smaller investor.

3. The transactions costs for hedging within the firm may be smaller than the total transactions costs that would otherwise be incurred by shareholders.

The last justification may not be borne out if investors already hold diversified portfolios of securities. The copper price risk faced by EMC, for example, may already be offset by those EMC shareholders who also own stocks of other firms that produce copper and would therefore profit from an increase in copper prices.

In addition to the three possible justifications for hedging by firms already noted, the following motives are also commonly mentioned:

4. The managers of a firm may not act in shareholders' best interests if their performance in operating the "core business" of the firm is measured by the total profits of the firm. For example, EMC officers (being risk averse) might choose less than the optimal number of motors to produce during periods of high copper price volatility if their performance is being measured by the total profits of EMC. This is known as the *principal-agent* effect. The owner of the firm is the principal; the manager is the agent of the owner.

5. The Modigliani-Miller Irrelevance Principle does not account for bankruptcy costs. For example, if EMC is forced into financial reorganization because of unexpectedly high copper costs (despite the long-run profitability of its core business), then EMC shareholders will bear corresponding reorganizational costs that might not have been necessary had EMC hedged with a futures position.

6. There may be tax-related justifications for hedging. For example, if corporate losses are treated differently for tax purposes than are profits, it may be profitable, on an after-tax basis, for the firm to engage in futures trading.

This list of potential reasons for financial hedging by firms is not exhaustive. Our main purpose here is to replace the naive motive for hedging, "less risk is better," with more careful economic reasoning.

Corporate Futures Trading Programs

Just as the Electric Motor Company example illustrated that futures hedging may improve the welfare of shareholders, the opposite can also occur. A firm engaging in a futures trading program should institute carefully considered policies, procedures, and controls. One possible set of guidelines is:

1. Prepare a policy stating the goals of the firm's futures trading, whether based on risk reduction or profit motives or both, and also providing arguments suggesting how futures trading can accomplish these goals.

2. Institute a study of legal, accounting, financial, and tax implications of futures trading for the firm.

3. Prepare a futures trading strategy, however broadly or narrowly defined, describing how the timing and sizing of contract positions are to be decided and executed. The strategy might be as specific as a set of mathematical formulas and statistical procedures determining

all trades automatically, or as vague as delegation of all trading decisions to one or more employees or consultants. Clearly, the strategy
should be consistent with the policy (1) and the study (2). In particular, the strategy should clearly delineate responsibility for setting,
approving, and transmitting futures orders. It should be ensured
that the FCM handling the firm's account will accept futures orders
only from authorized employees of the firm.

4. Establish a program of oversight and periodic performance evaluation. Oversight should attempt to ensure that the trading strategy
   will be carried out properly, and in particular, that it will not place
   the firm in undue jeopardy. Performance evaluation should check
   the quality of trading decisions and brokerage, and measure the extent to which the trading program is accomplishing its stated policy
   goals. Specific numerical performance measures should be tied to
   each of the specific policy goals whenever possible.

5. Shareholders should be advised of the firm's hedging policy, since
   they may otherwise incorrectly assess the risks they face and inap-
   propriately hedge on their own, unnecessarily adding to their risks.
   Double hedging is not safer, it is riskier.

EXERCISES

7.1 *(Hedging with Heteroskedasticty)* Suppose that the increments of a futures price process $f_1, f_2, \ldots$ and a spot price process $s_1, s_2, \ldots$ satisfy the
OLS conditions, except for the fact that $c_t = \text{cov}(f_{t+1} - f_t, s_{t+1} - s_t)$ and
$v_t = \text{var}(f_{t+1} - f_t)$ can both change with time. (For a frame of reference,
take a time period to be one day.) Suppose that c_t and v_t depend only on
the month of the year. For example, c_t is constant during June, and the
same in June 1984 as in June 1985, in June 1986, and so on; and likewise
for v_t.

(a) Assuming that you know c_t and v_t for all t, calculate the futures
    position on May 27, 1989, that provides a variance-minimizing hedge
    against a commitment to buy 400 units of the spot asset on August
    21, 1989. *Hint: Remember the zero autocorrelation condition and
    what it implies about the variance of a sum of price increments.*

(b) Assuming that you do not know c_t and v_t, but have access to any
    historical spot and futures price data that you would like, outline a

statistical procedure that would give you a hedge based on estimated covariances and variances.

7.2 *(Hedging Project)*   This exercise calls for the preparation of a case study of a hedging problem of your own choice. The various parts of the exercise below will ask you to pose a simple, perhaps imaginary, hedging scenario, to collect appropriate data, to analyze the data statistically, and to recommend a hedge.

(a) *Description of Scenario:*   In 100 words or less, describe the scenario: "Who is hedging how much of what at what date, and why?" Suggest the futures contract or contracts that you will consider, and why.

(b) *Data Collection:*   Collect your own data for the hedging problem. Supply, with your assignment, at least 26 observations on each of the prices or other quantities of interest. You will probably decide to analyze the data with a computer. Sources for data include the statistical annuals of the various futures exchanges. These annuals include related spot market data.

(c) *Data Analysis:*   Using statistical methods, analyze the data for a reasonable estimate of the risk-minimizing futures position(s). You may wish to analyze both price increments and (based on Appendix 7D) log-price increments, suggesting which of these approaches may lead to a better hedging estimate (if either), and why you think so. Be extremely brief! Supply as an appendix any computer output to which you have referred, such as regression equations and diagnostics.

(d) *Hedge Recommendation:*   Based on your analysis, and on any other (brief) reasoning that you may wish to supply, recommend a hedge. State precisely the timing and quantities involved in your hedging strategy, as though they are instructions to a broker.

7.3 Table 7.1 gives the German and Dutch exchange rate data for months 37 through 48, extending from Appendix 7A the data used for the guilder hedging example of Section 7.2.

(a) Estimate the hedging coefficient for this latter 12-month period.

(b) Prepare a plot similar to that shown in Figure 7.2 showing the performance of the hedging position $y = -5$ million deutsche marks (chosen from the data for months 1 through 36) during months 37 through 48.

TABLE 7.1   Guilder-Deutsche Mark Additional Hedging Data

Month No.	Guilder Spot	DM^a Futures
37	0.4895	0.5468
38	0.4843	0.5479
39	0.4907	0.5572
40	0.4924	0.5610
41	0.4873	0.5489
42	0.4857	0.5522
43	0.4787	0.5395
44	0.4891	0.5516
45	0.4838	0.5458
46	0.5112	0.5811
47	0.5438	0.6122
48	0.5626	0.6421

^{a}Nearby contract, end-of-month.

7.4 Consider a hedge at time t in one of two different futures contracts. There are Q units of the asset to be hedged, which has a spot price at time $t + 1$ of s_{t+1}. Suppose that $\mathrm{corr}(f_{t+1}^{(1)}, s_{t+1})$, the correlation of the first futures price with the spot asset price, is higher than $\mathrm{corr}(f_{t+1}^{(2)}, s_{t+1})$, the corresponding correlation for the second type of futures contract.

(a) Show that an optimal hedge in the first futures contract achieves a lower total variance than does an optimal hedge in the second futures contract.

(b) Show that an optimal hedge in both futures contracts simultaneously achieves lower total variance than an optimal hedge in either alone. (This part of the exercise requires some skill in statistics.)

7.5 Based on the data in Appendix 7A, which futures contract, that delivering British pounds, West German marks, or Swiss Francs, would you recommend as a hedge against a commitment to Dutch gulden?

7.6 Based on the data in Appendix 7A, recommend a hedge in one or more of the foreign currency futures for a commitment to buy 20 million Dutch gulden in one month.

7.7 Show the additivity rule of hedging in the following context. Consider a position of Q_1 units of asset number 1 and Q_2 units of asset number 2. Their respective spot prices, $s_{t+1}^{(1)}$ and $s_{t+1}^{(2)}$ are sources of risk to be hedged. Let y_1 be the variance-minimizing futures position in a given futures contract for the first risk $e_1 = Q_1 s_{t+1}^{(1)}$, and likewise let y_2 be the variance-minimizing futures position for the other spot risk $e_2 = Q_2 s_{t+1}^{(2)}$.

(a) Show that $y_1 + y_2$ is the risk-mimimizing futures position for the combined spot commitment $e = e_1 + e_2 = Q_1 s_{t+1}^{(1)} + Q_2 s_{t+1}^{(2)}$.

(b) Extend Part (a) to the case of futures positions in several different futures contracts. (This part of the question requires more advanced statistical skills.)

7.8 (Hedging with a Known Basis) Suppose, changing the example given in Section 7.2, that that Acme Mint's commitment to buy gold is, instead, on October 16, two months before the delivery date of the contract. Calling October 16 "date k," the basis $s_k - f_k$ is not generally zero, and the "equal and opposite" hedging strategy for a zero basis is incorrect. Suppose, however, that the arbitrage formula $f_k = s_k B_{k,T}$ applies, where $B_{k,T}$ is the amount due at date $T =$ December 14 on a riskless loan of \$1 made at date k (October 16). (Corrections and extensions of this formula are discussed in Chapter 5.) Suppose also that, at the current date $t =$ September 15, $B_{k,T}$ can already be accurately estimated at 1.0101 from current Treasury bill prices, assuming that interest rates do not change between t and k.

(a) Show that, if Acme Mint takes a long position of

$$200/B_{k,T} = 200/1.0101 = 198 \text{ contracts,}$$

then its net cost for the gold (spot market cost less futures resettlement profit or loss) is $19{,}800 \times f_t$. Since f_t is known at the date t on which the hedge is established, the total cost of the gold net of the futures profits or losses therefore has no risk at all.

(b) Show that general hedging formula (1) produces the hedge $h = 198$ contracts, by showing that the hedging coefficient is $\beta = 1/B_{k,T}$. In practice, it is impossible to know $B_{k,T}$ exactly in advance, and in any case the cost-of-carry formula does not apply exactly.

7.9 Verify the tailing calculations given in equations (11) and (12) of Appendix 7B.

7.10 (Random Quantity Constraints) Suppose the quantity Q of an asset to be hedged, the spot price s_{t+1} of the asset at the commitment date, and the price f_{t+1} of a futures contract are joint log-normally distributed. That is, their logarithms, denoted X, Y, and Z respectively, are joint normally distributed, as defined in Appendix 4C. Based on Equation (25) from Appendix 7E, calculate the optimal (variance-minimizing) futures position in terms of the means and covariances of X, Y, and Z. Warning: This exercise is a bit advanced mathematically, relative to the others.

7.11 This exercise asks for a verification that the two bond portfolios described in an example in Appendix 7F have the same duration and market value. Portfolio 1 consists of $10 million (face value) worth of 4 year zero-coupon bonds. Portfolio 2 consists of $7.57 million of 2 year zero-coupon bonds and $4 million of 20 year zeros. All bonds are priced to yield a continuously compounding interest rate of 8 percent.

NOTES

On the effect of estimation risk on portfolio choice, the reader should see, for example, the paper by Klein and Bawa (1976). There are many services providing settlement prices for futures contracts. Without endorsing either, two examples are: *Interactive Data Services*, 22 Courtlandt Street, New York, NY 10007-3172; and *Commodity Systems Inc.*, 200 Palmetto Park Road, Suite 200, Boca Raton, FL 33432-9947. Grieves (1986) is the source of the example of corporate bond hedging. Hedging for institutional investment managers is treated by Figlewski (1986).

Johnston (1984) is a typical introductory reference for the regression theory discussed in this chapter. The F-test is a standard test of the relative fit of two different regression equations. The Cochrane-Orcutt method of correcting for serial correlation is also discussed by Johnston (1984). More advanced techniques, including the incorporation of overlapping sampling intervals, are treated in Hansen and Hodrick (1980). For an advanced treatment of regression with autocorrelation and heteroskedasticity, see Amemiya (1985). There are conditions on the log-price increment process (X, Y) leading to the OLS conditions on the price-growth factor process $(\mathcal{F}, \mathcal{S})$ discussed in Appendix 7D; these are the *iid*, or *identically and independently distributed* conditions, which are defined, for example, in Amemiya (1985). A solution for an optimal dynamic hedging strategy under log-normal price assumptions may be found in Duffie and Jackson (1986).

Modigliani and Miller (1958) are of course responsible for the original form of the Modigliani-Miller Irrelevance Principle. The result is extended, under general conditions, to show the irrelevance of corporate hedging policy for the value of the firm in a general multi-period model by Duffie and Shafer (1986), and in an improved form showing irrelevance of shareholder utility by DeMarzo (1987). A recent survey of the topic and literature has been prepared by Miller and McCormick (1988). DeMarzo (1987) gives additional references.

Textbook treatments of international financial markets include Grabbe (1986) and Solnik (1988).

Appendix 7F, on hedging interest rate risk, is based on a wide variety of literature, including Breeden and Giarla (1987), Kidder, Peabody and Company (1987), Klotz (1985), Kopprasch (1985), Jacobs (1982), Toevs and Jacobs (1984), and Yawitz (1986). Additional information on hedging interest rate risk using the immunization approach can be found in the book by Figlewski (1986). The concept in Figure 7.8 of illustrating duration as the center of gravity of the present value of cash flows is drawn from Kopprasch (1985). Smith, Smithson, and Wakeman (1987) contains additional material on swaps.

Appendix 7A: Example Hedging Data

TABLE 7.2   Spot and Futures Price Data
(U.S. $ per unit of foreign currency)

Month	Spot* Dutch Guilder	Nearby Futures* British £ Sterling	German DM	Swiss Franc
1	0.3155	1.4095	0.3670	0.4672
2	0.3397	1.5030	0.3975	0.4836
3	0.3423	1.4615	0.4013	0.4887
4	0.3288	1.4190	0.3805	0.4655
5	0.3248	1.4015	0.3786	0.4621
6	0.3171	1.3750	0.3698	0.4440
7	0.3055	1.3040	0.3512	0.4159
8	0.3068	1.3140	0.3524	0.4237
9	0.2933	1.2380	0.3292	0.4002
10	0.2927	1.2250	0.3334	0.4058
11	0.2864	1.1930	0.3216	0.3927
12	0.2817	1.1550	0.3228	0.3905
13	0.2793	1.1050	0.3247	0.3847
14	0.2654	1.0575	0.3084	0.3606
15	0.2872	1.2265	0.3355	0.3970
16	0.2835	1.2110	0.3266	0.3911
17	0.2872	1.2660	0.3326	0.3965
18	0.2901	1.2840	0.3337	0.3995
19	0.3192	1.3995	0.3633	0.4443
20	0.3193	1.3765	0.3588	0.4368
21	0.3315	1.3850	0.3753	0.4580
22	0.3388	1.4365	0.3839	0.4680
23	0.3539	1.4885	0.3986	0.4819
24	0.3608	1.4370	0.3954	0.4722
25	0.3706	1.3650	0.4315	0.5110
26	0.3986	1.3980	0.4602	0.5480
27	0.3827	1.4385	0.4352	0.5265
28	0.4081	1.5135	0.4689	0.5570
29	0.3848	1.4540	0.4361	0.5240
30	0.4040	1.5215	0.4608	0.5671
31	0.4238	1.4750	0.4813	0.6028
32	0.4319	1.4755	0.4948	0.6144
33	0.4377	1.4295	0.4954	0.6112
34	0.4281	1.3980	0.4854	0.5863
35	0.4475	1.4315	0.5072	0.6099
36	0.4562	1.4325	0.4965	0.5883

*Source: *The Wall Street Journal.*
*Source: *International Monetary Market Yearbook,*
Chicago Mercantile Exchange.

Appendix 7B: Tailing the Hedge

One cannot always ignore the effect on the optimal hedge of daily resettlement and interest on margin accounts. To *tail the hedge* is to correct the size of the hedge for these effects, as described in this appendix. The discussion here will presume for simplicity that:

1. Margin is deposited in the form of interest-bearing assets, with interest credited daily.

2. Interest rates do not change during the hedging period.

3. Initial and maintenance margin are set at the same level.

4. Excess margin is not withdrawn (or is transferred to a reserve fund bearing interest at the same rate), while margin calls are met by borrowing at the same interest rate.

We still presume that the objective is to calculate the futures position that minimizes the variance of the total final position, and adopt the same scenario leading to the hedge shown in equation (8).

Let B denote the value after one day of \$1 invested risklessly at the interest rate paid on margin deposits. Then the value of the initially deposited \$1 after two days is B^2, after three days is B^3, and so on. For example, if the annual interest rate on a continually compounding basis is r, then

$$B = \exp\left(\frac{r}{365.25}\right),\qquad (10)$$

which is a number that is typically close to 1.0, but not so close that large money fund managers are willing to wait overnight to invest cash. If $r = 10$ percent, for instance, then $B = 1.000274$, which represents almost 3 basis points. (A *basis point*, in this context, is 0.01 percent.)

Suppose the futures position y is adopted for K days at day t. Under our assumptions, the futures gains (or losses) yF_{t+1} over the first day of the hedge are invested in the margin account for $K - 1$ days, yielding $B^{K-1}yF_{t+1}$ when the final position is calculated at day $t + K$. Similarly, the second day's gains yield $B^{K-2}yF_{t+2}$ at day $t + K$, and so on. The variance of the final position determined by Q units of the spot asset whose price changes from s_t to s_{t+K} is thus

$$V(y) = \mathrm{var}[Q(s_{K+t} - s_t) + B^{K-1}yF_{t+1} + B^{K-2}yF_{t+2} + \cdots + yF_{t+K}].$$

Under the OLS conditions on spot and futures price increments, this reduces to

$$V(y) = \text{var}[KQS_{t+1} + (B^{K-1} + B^{K-2} + \cdots + B + 1)yF_{t+1}], \quad (11)$$

which is instructive to verify as an exercise. Once again doing the calculations leading to $V'(y) = 0$, we have the minimum variance futures position

$$y = -a(B,K)Q\beta,$$

where

$$a(B,K) = \frac{K}{1 + B + B^2 + \cdots + B^{K-1}}. \quad (12)$$

The coefficient $a(B,K)$ is called the *tailing factor*. The *tailed optimal hedge* is therefore $a(B,K)h$, where $h = -Q\beta$ is the "un-tailed" hedge shown earlier. The least squares estimator for the tailed hedge is $a(B,K)H$, where $H = -Q\widehat{\beta}$.

Sample values of the tailing factor $a(B,K)$ are given in Table 7.4, based on different scenarios for interest rates and hedging periods. Although the effect of tailing only becomes significant with long hedging periods or high interest rates, the effect is always to reduce the magnitude of the optimal hedging position. Of course, one could achieve even lower variance, under our assumptions, by periodically "re-tailing" the hedge, rather than maintaining a fixed position for the entire hedging period. If re-tailing daily (which may be excessive given transactions costs), the tailed optimal hedge with K days remaining is $B^{-K}h$, as can easily be shown in an exercise. Monthly re-tailing, for example, is also easily calculated.

TABLE 7.3   Tailing Factors

Interest	Hedging Period (Days)			
Rate (%)	10	100	500	1000
10	0.999	0.987	0.933	0.869
20	0.998	0.973	0.870	0.751

With continuous payments and continuous-compounding at the interest rate r, the denominator of (12) can be recognized as the future value of an annuity factor

$$A_{t,T} = \frac{\exp[r(T-t)] - 1}{r},$$

as defined in Section 5.2, where the length $T - t$ of the hedging period is measured in years. With that convention, the tailing factor is

$$a(r, T - t) = \frac{r(T - t)}{\exp[r(T - t)] - 1}.$$

Appendix 7C: Liquidity and Time to Delivery

Liquidity, measured perhaps by daily volume of trade, affects the cost of making a trade. With a low volume of trade, a market order to sell, for example, might have little chance of arriving at the market at about the same time as a corresponding market order to buy, and might have to be executed at a price low enough to induce a trader to hold the position on the trader's own account until an offsetting order arrives. The lower the volume of trade, the greater are the risk and opportunity cost for the accommodating trader, and the lower will be the price required to induce the trader to take the long position. Similarly, a market order to buy would typically be executed at a premium during inactive trading periods. The *bid-ask spread*, a term usually reserved for specialist markets such as the New York Stock Exchange, is the difference between the price at which a market order to buy would be executed and the price at which a market order to sell would be executed. Unlike the bid-ask spread in specialist markets, the bid-ask spread on a futures market is not quoted, and is impossible to measure directly. It nevertheless represents part of the total costs of transactions services. In Section 5.3, we called this the "market impact" portion of transactions costs.

Now, let us suppose that there is some natural tendency for trade to be more active in the contracts sooner to deliver. (This is true in many markets.) With somewhat more liquidity in the nearby contracts, the higher market impact costs facing hedge-motivated trades in the later-to-deliver contracts will cause some of these trades to be replaced with trades in contracts sooner to deliver. Of course, this would further skew liquidity in favor of nearby contracts, and the effect could feed back on itself to the point of having a high fraction of futures trades in a particular commodity concentrated in the nearby contract. The actual distribution of liquidity (measured by annual volume of trade) segregated by the nearness of the delivery date is shown in Figure 7.6 for S&P 500 Stock Index Futures Contracts (Chicago Mercantile Exchange), U.S. Treasury Bond Futures Contracts (Chicago Board of Trade), and wheat futures contracts (Chicago Board of Trade). The two financial futures contracts show a dramatic increase in liquidity with the nearness of the contract delivery date, while the effect is less pronounced with the wheat contract. Presumably, those hedging distant commitments with the financial futures contracts find that the nearby contract offers a reasonable hedging alternative to the contract whose delivery date is closest to the commitment date; the liquidity of the nearby contract is far superior. In the wheat market, however, perhaps hedgers facing spot commitments far into the future find that the nearby contract is not a good hedge. Perhaps this is because the difficulty of short selling wheat (in the way that financial securities are short sold) prevents a close arbitrage price relationship from holding between the nearby and distant futures prices. As shown in an exercise, an arbitrage price relationship (coupled with low interest rate uncertainty) allows most of the basis risk to be eliminated with an appropriately sized hedge.

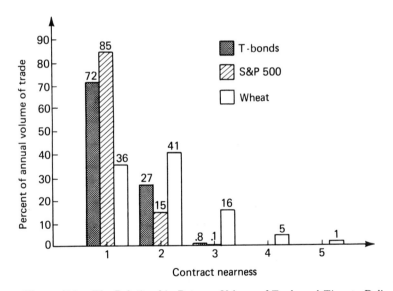

Figure 7.6   The Relationship Between Volume of Trade and Time to Delivery

There may also be speculative reasons (related to differences in information among traders) to believe that liquidity may be concentrated in a similar fashion. [See Admati and Pfleiderer (1988) for a model with a related property.]

These comments on liquidity are casually presented, but are supported at least by the observed distribution of trading volume across the various delivery dates of most types of futures. A conclusion is that there may be grounds for hedging with a futures contract delivering much sooner than the spot commitment date, even if contracts delivering closer to the commitment date are available. For example, one might hedge always in the nearby contract and *roll over* the hedge as the delivery date on the nearby contract approaches. For reasons also related to liquidity, a large hedge would be rolled over gradually, not as a single order.

Appendix 7D: Hedging Percentage Price Growth

If percentage price changes, rather than price increments, satisfy the OLS conditions, then linear regression based on price increment data will not generate the best estimators for the hedging coefficient β. As the current price becomes larger, so will the variance of the subsequent price increment increase, as illustrated in Chapter 6. We now review methods for estimating β based on OLS price growth. In reality, of course, neither price increments nor price growth satisfy the OLS conditions exactly, and judgment or more sophisticated approaches are often called for.

Price Growth Betas

Given stochastic futures and spot price processes, $f = (f_1, f_2, \ldots)$ and $s = (s_1, s_2, \ldots)$ respectively, let $\mathcal{S}_t = s_t/s_{t-1}$ and $\mathcal{F}_t = f_t/f_{t-1}$ denote the *price growth factors* for spot and futures, respectively. Since $s_{t+1} = s_t \mathcal{S}_{t+1}$ and $f_{t+1} = f_t \mathcal{F}_{t+1}$, we know at time t that

$$\text{cov}(f_{t+1} - f_t, s_{t+1} - s_t) = s_t f_t \, \text{cov}(\mathcal{F}_{t+1}, \mathcal{S}_{t+1})$$

and that $\text{var}(f_{t+1} - f_t) = f_t^2 \, \text{var}(\mathcal{F}_t)$. It follows that the hedging coefficient is

$$\beta = \frac{\text{cov}(f_{t+1} - f_t, s_{t+1} - s_t)}{\text{var}(f_{t+1} - f_t)} = \frac{s_t}{f_t} \beta^G, \tag{13}$$

where

$$\beta^G = \frac{\text{cov}(\mathcal{F}_{t+1}, \mathcal{S}_{t+1})}{\text{var}(\mathcal{F}_{t+1})}$$

is the regression coefficient for spot price growth $\mathcal{S}_{t+1}$ regressed on futures price growth $\mathcal{F}_{t+1}$. Given data, one can obtain the least squares estimator

$\widehat{\beta}^G$ for β^G. For a commitment of Q units of the spot asset at time $t+1$, the corresponding least squares estimator of the optimal hedge at time t is

$$H_t = -Q\frac{s_t}{f_t}\,\widehat{\beta}^G. \tag{14}$$

This calculation only applies to spot commitments one period into the future, so one must either obtain an estimate of β^G with data intervals equal to the time period of the hedge or adopt a dynamic hedging strategy. Both of these alternatives will be discussed shortly.

Hedging with Normally Distributed Price Growth Rates

A common, although sometimes unjustified, assumption is that the price growths $\mathcal{F}_{t+1}$ and $\mathcal{S}_{t+1}$ are log-normally distributed, which is to say that the log-price increments $X_{t+1} = \log(\mathcal{F}_{t+1})$ and $Y_{t+1} = \log(\mathcal{S}_{t+1})$ are normally distributed, a property explained in Appendix 4C. (Empirical tests of the log-normality assumption are discussed in Section 6.6.) The log-price increment X_{t+1} is the continuously compounding rate of growth in prices represented by the change from f_t to f_{t+1} during one time period (and likewise for Y_{t+1}). A calculation made in Appendix 7E shows that, with log-normality,

$$\beta^G = Jb^G, \tag{15}$$

where

$$J = \exp\left(E(Y_{t+1}) - E(X_{t+1}) + \frac{[\mathrm{var}(Y_{t+1}) - \mathrm{var}(X_{t+1})]}{2}\right) \tag{16}$$

and

$$b^G = \frac{\exp[\mathrm{cov}(X_{t+1}, Y_{t+1})] - 1}{\exp[\mathrm{var}(X_{t+1})] - 1}. \tag{17}$$

The variance-minimizing hedge for a commitment to Q units of the spot asset one period hence is therefore

$$h_t = -Q\frac{s_t}{f_t}Jb^G. \tag{18}$$

Once again, we point out that the hedging coefficient β^G in the case of OLS price growth depends on the length of the time interval, as opposed to the case of OLS price increments.

Example: Suppose that $E(X_{t+1}) = E(Y_{t+1}) = 0.3$, that $\text{sdev}(X_{t+1}) = \text{sdev}(Y_{t+1}) = 0.20$, and that $\text{corr}(X_{t+1}, Y_{t+1}) = 0.5$. These could be typical figures for annual periods. In this case, $J = 1$, and

$$\beta^G = b^G = \frac{\exp(0.02) - 1}{\exp(0.04) - 1} = 0.495.$$

If one incorrectly substituted for β^G the log-price increment regression coefficient

$$\beta^L = \frac{\text{cov}(X_{t+1}, Y_{t+1})}{\text{var}(X_{t+1})} = 0.500, \tag{19}$$

the damage would not be too severe in this example. Taking another case, if $\text{corr}(X_{t+1}, Y_{t+1}) = 0.9$ and all other parameters are the same, then $\beta^G = b^G = 0.899$, while $\beta^L = 0.9$.

As suggested by the example, for typical estimates of variances of log-price increments, b^G and β^L indeed do not differ by a great deal. Furthermore, when hedging with a futures contract delivering the same asset being hedged, it is often the case that J need not depart from 1 by much. In such a situation, the hedging position

$$h_t^L = -Q\frac{s_t}{f_t}\beta^L, \tag{20}$$

substituting the log-price increment regression coefficient β^L for the price growth regression coefficient β^G, will not result in a hedge differing drastically from the optimal hedge h_t given by equation (18), at least for small time intervals. The hedging position h_t^L has in fact often been suggested in practice, although we can see that it is not strictly speaking optimal.

Dynamic Hedging in the Log-Normal Case

It can be shown that as the length of the time interval under consideration becomes smaller and smaller, the optimal hedge h_t given by (18) converges to the hedging position h_t^L given by equation (20). Furthermore, if log-price increments satisfy the OLS conditions, then the regression coefficient β^L does not depend on the length of the time interval, analogously with the case of OLS price increments discussed in Section 7.3. These facts suggest that, if the hedger has the ability to adjust the hedging position continually through time, then the optimal position at any time t is merely the position h_t^L given by equation (20). Although the calculations are too extensive to review here,

Duffie and Jackson (1987) show that this is indeed the case if the futures price process is a martingale (meaning no expected futures profits or losses). It is not true, in general, if the futures price is not a martingale. Generally speaking, the opportunity to adjust the hedge dynamically through time in response to changing prices and new information results in superior risk reduction.

Alternative Estimators for Price Growth Betas

We have discussed the risk-minimizing hedge in the case of OLS price growth. It is not immediately clear, however, how one should estimate the coefficient β^G determining the optimal hedge. There are three obvious possibilities:

1. Obtain the OLS estimator $\widehat{\beta}^G$, based on the observed growth factors: $(\mathcal{F}_1, \mathcal{S}_1), (\mathcal{F}_2, \mathcal{S}_2), \ldots$. This leads to the hedge

$$H_t = -Q \frac{s_t}{f_t} \widehat{\beta}^G. \tag{21}$$

2. Obtain the OLS estimator $\widehat{\beta}^L$ for β^L, the log-price increment regression coefficient. Under our presumption that β^G and β^L do not differ drastically for practical purposes, one could consider the hedge

$$H_t^L = -Q \frac{s_t}{f_t} \widehat{\beta}^L. \tag{22}$$

3. Let $C(X, Y)$ denote the least squares estimator for $\mathrm{cov}(X_{t+1}, Y_{t+1})$, let $V(X)$ denote the least squares estimator for $\mathrm{var}(X_{t+1})$, let $V(Y)$ denote the least squares estimator for $\mathrm{var}(Y_{t+1})$, and finally let $\overline{X}$ and $\overline{Y}$ denote the respective least squares estimators for $E(X_{t+1})$ and $E(Y_{t+1})$. If we substitute everywhere in equations (16) and (17) these estimators for the true (unknown) parameters, we obtain

$$\overline{J} = \exp\left(\overline{X} - \overline{Y} + \frac{[V(X) - V(Y)]}{2}\right)$$

and

$$\overline{b}^G = \frac{\exp[C(X, Y)] - 1}{\exp[V(X)] - 1}.$$

The estimator

$$\overline{\beta}^G = \overline{J}\, \overline{b}^G \tag{23}$$

can be shown to be a biased estimator for β^G. On the other hand, under the OLS conditions, the bias is not generally large, and shrinks to zero as the number of observations gets large. Moreover, this estimator $\overline{\beta}^G$ has certain attractive efficiency properties when the price growth factors are OLS and log-normal, although we will not make the effort to describe these efficiency properties here. In short, one can also make a case for the estimated hedge

$$\overline{H}_t = -Q\frac{s_t}{f_t}\overline{\beta}^G. \tag{24}$$

Now, which hedging estimate should one take, that given by (21), (22), or (24)? This is not easily resolved, although we now review evidence that it doesn't matter a great deal in some cases.

Monte Carlo Simulation Check of Hedging Estimates

We can check the performance of the three hedges suggested above by Monte Carlo simulation, referring to Tables 7.5, 7.6, and 7.7. Each table shows four trials for each of several choices for T, the number of simulated time periods of data. The simulations are based on pseudo-normal pseudo-randomly generated observations of X_t and Y_t, all with the means, standard deviations, and correlations indicated in the tables. The particular random number generator used for these tables is that available with the GAUSS programming language; however, many software packages support their own random number generators.

The key comparisons to make in these three tables are the differences between the trial outcomes of the estimators and the true underlying beta shown at the top of the table. [We recall that $\widehat{\beta}^L$ is the OLS estimator for β^L, that $\widehat{\beta}^G$ is the OLS estimator for β^G, and that $\overline{\beta}^G$ is a special biased estimator for β^G given by equation (23).] The estimators improve, on average, as the number of observations increases. In principle, each of these estimators will converge under fairly general assumptions to the true underlying betas, but their rates of convergence may vary. This Monte Carlo simulation approach can be applied under other statistical models for price increments.

Example: We return to the simple scenario presented in Section 7.1 of a commitment to sell 25 million deutsche marks, hedging with the nearby deutsche mark futures contract. Assuming OLS price growth, we might be inclined, on the basis of our previous discussion, to regress the spot log-price increment $Y_{t+1} = \log(s_{t+1}) - \log(s_t)$ on the futures log-price increment

TABLE 7.4   Monte Carlo Hedging Estimates (Case I)

Case I: $\mathrm{sdev}(X_t) = \mathrm{sdev}(Y_t) = 0.20$; $\mathrm{corr}(X_t, Y_t) = 0.5$; $\overline{X}_t = \overline{Y}_t = 0.3$; $\beta^G = 0.505$ $\beta^L = 0.500$				
Observations	Trial	$\overline{\beta}^G$	$\widehat{\beta}^L$	$\widehat{\beta}^G$
$T = 10$	1	1.025	1.095	1.058
	2	0.292	0.308	0.403
	3	0.438	0.463	0.434
	4	1.115	1.101	1.314
$T = 100$	1	0.473	0.475	0.467
	2	0.590	0.594	0.594
	3	0.451	0.456	0.485
	4	0.544	0.540	0.536
$T = 1000$	1	0.486	0.480	0.484
	2	0.490	0.484	0.479
	3	0.515	0.509	0.503
	4	0.525	0.518	0.523

TABLE 7.5   Monte Carlo Hedging Estimates (Case II)

Case II: $\mathrm{sdev}(X_t) = \mathrm{sdev}(Y_t) = 0.20$; $\mathrm{corr}(X_t, Y_t) = 0.9$; $\overline{X}_t = \overline{Y}_t = 0.3$; $\beta^G = 0.902$ $\beta^L = 0.900$				
Observations	Trial	$\overline{\beta}^G$	$\widehat{\beta}^L$	$\widehat{\beta}^G$
$T = 10$	1	0.970	0.956	0.964
	2	1.142	1.094	1.077
	3	0.812	0.819	0.836
	4	1.052	1.013	0.958
$T = 100$	1	0.873	0.870	0.872
	2	0.926	0.927	0.934
	3	0.963	0.954	0.938
	4	0.869	0.857	0.852
$T = 1000$	1	0.897	0.870	0.872
	2	0.876	0.876	0.884
	3	0.924	0.923	0.918
	4	0.902	0.900	0.891

$X_{t+1} = \log(f_{t+1}) - \log(f_t)$. For the same data used earlier to obtain the estimated price increment regression equation shown in Section 7.4, we obtain

TABLE 7.6   Monte Carlo Hedging Estimates (Case III)

Case III: sdev$(X_t) = 0.20$; sdev$(Y_t) = 0.40$; corr$(X_t, Y_t) = 0.5$, $\overline{X}_t = \overline{Y}_t = 0.3$; $\beta^G = 1.062$; $\beta^L = 1.000$				
Observations	**Trial**	$\overline{\beta}^G$	$\widehat{\beta}^L$	$\widehat{\beta}^G$
$T = 10$	1	0.564	0.642	0.876
	2	0.819	0.814	0.581
	3	0.929	0.934	0.870
	4	1.300	1.526	2.063
$T = 100$	1	0.967	0.933	0.954
	2	1.005	0.987	0.994
	3	1.071	1.000	1.162
	4	1.530	1.414	1.420
$T = 1000$	1	1.070	1.021	1.082
	2	1.014	0.969	1.033
	3	1.026	0.960	1.027
	4	0.992	0.944	1.050

the following estimated log-price increment regression:

$$Y_{t+1} = \widehat{\alpha} + 0.940 \ X_{t+1} + \epsilon_{t+1}. \qquad (R^2 = 0.935)$$

$$(0.052^*) \qquad (0.0034)$$

The "fit," measured say by R^2, seems to be about the same as that of the price-increment regression estimated in Section 7.4. The estimate $\widehat{\beta}^L = 0.940$ for β^L is statistically significant (in the usual sense), judging from its relatively low standard error estimate of 0.052.

Suppose the current exchange rate is $s_t = \$0.60$ per deutsche mark and the current futures price for nearby delivery is $f_t = \$0.62$ per guilder. Then, referring to equation (22), we have the hedging estimate

$$H_t^L = -25{,}000{,}000 \times \frac{0.60}{0.62} \times \frac{0.940}{125{,}000} = -182 \ \text{(contracts)}.$$

Since β^L is not equal to β^G, this hedging estimate is biased. On the other hand, the net effect in this particular situation is not likely to be severe, especially considering the effect of estimation error. It is indeed common practice to base hedging calculations on the approach taken in this example.

Once again, we point out that, even ignoring estimation error, this hedging calculation is only accurate for short hedging periods. If the ratio of spot to futures price changes significantly during the period of hedging, it is generally advisable to readjust the hedge with changes in the spot-futures price ratio. This dynamic hedging strategy is optimal if the futures price is a martingale, as shown in Duffie and Jackson (1986).

The Multi-Contract Case

Suppose one is choosing the variance-minimizing hedging position in n different futures contracts for a commitment to Q units of a spot asset with price growth factor $\mathcal{S}_{t+1}$ from date t to date $t+1$. Given the respective price growths factors $\mathcal{F}_{t+1}^{(1)}, \mathcal{F}_{t+1}^{(2)}, \ldots, \mathcal{F}_{t+1}^{(n)}$ of the n futures contracts, we can estimate the multiple regression equation

$$\mathcal{S}_{t+1} = \alpha + \beta_1^G \mathcal{F}_{t+1}^{(1)} + \beta_2^G \mathcal{F}_{t+1}^{(2)} + \cdots + \beta_n^G \mathcal{F}_{t+1}^{(n)} + \epsilon_{t+1}.$$

The corresponding estimates $\widehat{\beta}_1^G, \ldots, \widehat{\beta}_n^G$ of the multiple regression coefficients then imply the futures position

$$H_t^i = -Q \frac{s_t}{f_t^{(i)}} \widehat{\beta}_i^G$$

in the i-th contract (whose current futures price is $f_t^{(i)}$) for each i. It is common, however, to substitute for $\widehat{\beta}_i^G$ the estimated regression coefficient $\widehat{\beta}_i^L$ from the corresponding log-price increment regression

$$Y_{t+1} = \alpha + \beta_1^L X_{t+1}^{(1)} + \cdots + \beta_n^L X_{t+1}^{(n)} + \epsilon_{t+1},$$

where $Y_{t+1} = \log{(\mathcal{S}_{t+1})}$ and $X_{t+1}^{(i)} = \log\left(\mathcal{F}_{t+1}^{(i)}\right)$.

An application of this approach to Ginnie Mae mortgage hedging is shown in Appendix 7F.

Appendix 7E: Log-Normal Hedging Calculations

This appendix provides the calculation of the hedging coefficient β under the assumption that the futures and spot log-price increments, $\log(f_{t+1}) - \log(f_t)$ and $\log(s_{t+1}) - \log(s_t)$, are normally distributed. The calculation is needed for equations (15)–(18).

First, suppose that W and Z are jointly normally distributed random variables. It can be shown as an exercise [using the formula for $E(e^W)$ given in Appendix 4C] that

$$\begin{aligned}
&\text{cov}[\exp(W), \exp(Z)] \\
&= \exp\left(\overline{W} + \overline{Z} + \frac{[\text{var}(W) + \text{var}(Z)]}{2}\right)(\exp[\text{cov}(W, Z)] - 1).
\end{aligned} \quad (25)$$

Applying this to the case $W = Z$, we also have the formula

$$\text{var}[\exp(W)] = \text{cov}[\exp(W), \exp(W)] = \exp[2\overline{W} + \text{var}(W)](\exp[\text{var}(W)] - 1).$$

If $X_{t+1} = \log(f_{t+1}/f_t)$ and $Y_{t+1} = \log(s_{t+1}/s_t)$ are jointly normally distributed, we then have

$$\text{cov}(f_{t+1} - f_t, s_{t+1} - s_t) = f_t s_t UV,$$

where

$$U = \exp\left(\overline{X}_{t+1} + \overline{Y}_{t+1} + \frac{[\text{var}(X_{t+1}) + \text{var}(Y_{t+1})]}{2}\right)$$

and

$$V = \exp[\text{cov}(X_{t+1}, Y_{t+1})] - 1.$$

Likewise,

$$\text{var}(f_{t+1} - f_t) = f_t^2 \exp\left[2\overline{X}_{t+1} + \text{var}(X_{t+1})\right](\exp[\text{var}(X_{t+1})] - 1).$$

This leaves

$$\beta = \frac{\text{cov}(f_{t+1} - f_t, s_{t+1} - s_t)}{\text{var}(f_{t+1} - f_t)} = \frac{s_t}{f_t}\beta^G = \frac{s_t}{f_t}Jb^G, \quad (26)$$

where J and b^G are given by equations (16) and (17) respectively.

Appendix 7F: Hedging Interest Rate Risk

A potential change in interest rates is a risk faced by almost any investor or firm in the economy. A homeowner with a variable rate mortgage worries about a rise in interest rates; a pension fund manager about to reinvest the fund in T-bills worries about a decline in interest rates; and the manager of a savings and loan association, which typically pays short term rates to its depositors and earns long term rates on mortgages, is concerned about a decline in long term rates relative to short term rates.

Although the general principles of hedging discussed in Chapter 7 apply in particular to interest rate commitments, the problem of interest rate risk is sufficiently widespread to warrant special treatment here.

We will begin with a discussion of several important measures of interest rate risk: price elasticity, duration, and convexity. These concepts are useful guideposts in setting and adjusting a hedge against interest rate changes.

Bond Elasticity

Although there are exceptions to the rule, the sensitivity of bond prices to interest rate changes is greater for bonds of longer maturity. Consider, for example, the effect of interest rate changes on 1-year and 10-year zero-coupon bonds. Let $P_t(r)$ denote the price per dollar of face value of a zero-coupon bond with t years to maturity yielding a continuously compounding interest rate of r. We know that $P_t(r) = e^{-rt}$. (See Section 5.1 for details.) Assuming the 1-year and 10-year bonds both yield a continuously compounding rate of 11 percent, their prices are

$$P_{10}(0.11) = e^{-0.11 \times 10} = 0.3329$$
$$P_1(0.11) = e^{-0.11 \times 1} = 0.8958.$$

An increase in the continuously compounding yield to 12 percent reduces the respective bond prices to

$$P_{10}(0.12) = e^{-0.12 \times 10} = 0.3012$$
$$P_1(0.11) = e^{-0.12 \times 1} = 0.8869.$$

The price of the 10-year bond price has suffered more dramatically than that of the 1-year bond. Figure 7.7 shows this general effect in a plot of $P_1(r)$ and $P_{10}(r)$ at various levels of r. The first derivative $P'_{10}(r)$ gives the rate of change in the price of the 10-year bond per percentage point increase in r. In other words, $P'_{10}(r)$ is the slope of the function $P_{10}(r)$. Dividing $P'_{10}(r)$ by $P_{10}(r)$, we get the percentage rate of price decline per unit of interest rate change, which is called the *bond elasticity*

$$\mathcal{E}_{10}(r) = \frac{P'_{10}(r)}{P_{10}(r)}.$$

Since the derivative of $P_t(r) = e^{-rt}$ with respect to r is merely $P'_t(r) = -te^{-rt}$, we can easily calculate the elasticity

$$\mathcal{E}_t(r) = \frac{-te^{-rt}}{e^{-rt}} = -t.$$

In other words, for zero-coupon bonds, (minus) elasticity and maturity are the same thing! The price of the 10-year bond changes at a rate of $\mathcal{E}_{10}(r) = -10$ percent per unit increase in its continuously compounding interest rate r, at any level of r. The 1-year bond price elasticity is always $\mathcal{E}_1(r) = -1$ percent.

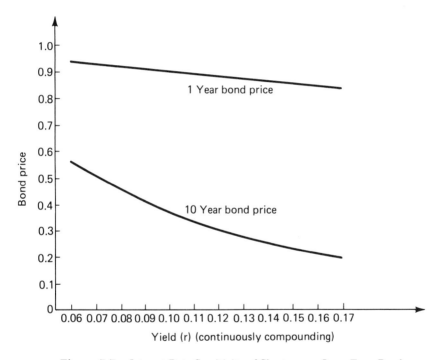

Figure 7.7   Interest Rate Sensitivity of Short versus Long Term Bonds

Bond elasticity, being a marginal rate of change, is not exactly equal to the total percentage price change for a sudden jump in interest rates of 1 percent. For example, the change from 11 percent to 12 percent in continuously compounding yield generates a total percentage change in the 10-year bond price of

$$\frac{P_{10}(0.12) - P_{10}(0.11)}{P_{10}(0.11)} = \frac{0.3012 - 0.3329}{0.3329} = -0.0952 = -9.52 \text{ percent.}$$

This is not exactly equal to the price elasticity $\mathcal{E}_{10}(r) = -10$ percent since the slope $P'_{10}(r)$ changes slightly between $r = 11$ percent and $r = 12$ percent. Nevertheless, for small changes in interest rates, the bond price elasticity and total percentage price decline divided by the interest rate change are approximately the same.

Elasticity and Duration of Coupon-Bearing Bonds

We have just seen that a zero-coupon bond's maturity and its price sensitivity to interest rate changes (elasticity) are the same thing. This useful fact is extended to coupon-bearing bonds as follows.

First of all, the maturity (time to repayment of principal) of a coupon-bearing bond is only a vague measure of its interest rate sensitivity since it ignores the effect of interim coupon payments, which tend to reduce the bond's interest rate sensitivity. Consider a 2-year "zero" and a 2-year 15-percent coupon bond, both priced to yield 10 percent interest, continuously compounding. The price $P_{0,2}(0.10)$ of the 2-year zero is $e^{-0.10\times2} = 0.8187$ (dollars per dollar of face value). In general, we let $P_{c,t}(r)$ denote the price of a c-percent annual coupon bond of maturity t years yielding a continuously compounding interest rate r. The price $P_{15,2}(0.10)$ of the 15-percent coupon 2-year bond at $r = 10$ percent, for example, is given by

$$P_{15,2}(0.10) = e^{-0.10\times1} \times 0.15 + e^{-0.10\times2} \times 1.15$$
$$= 0.9048 \times 0.15 + 0.8187 \times 1.15$$
$$= 0.1357 + 0.9415 = 1.0772.$$

The first term, $e^{-0.10\times1} \times 0.15$, is the discounted presented value of the first-year coupon of 15 cents per dollar of face value; the second term is the discounted present value of the coupon plus principal in 2 years.

An increase in r to 11 percent gives the new prices $P_{0,2}(0.11) = 0.8025$ and $P_{15,2}(0.11) = 1.0573$. The zero coupon price is reduced 1.98 percent by the rate increase; the 15-percent coupon bond price is reduced 1.85 percent. The coupon bond is less seriously affected because the present value of the first-year coupon is proportionately less affected by rate changes than the present value of the principal repayment in 2 years. We can account for this effect by an adjusted measure of a bond's maturity known as its *duration*.

The duration of a bond is the weighted average maturity of all cash flows stemming from the bond. The weight applied to the maturity of each bond payment is the present discounted value of that payment as a fraction of the total price of the bond. The duration of the 2-year 15-percent coupon bond at a continuously compounding interest rate of r is therefore given by the formula

$$D_{15,2}(r) = \frac{e^{-r \times 1} \times 0.15}{P_{15,2}(r)} \times 1 \text{ year} + \frac{e^{-r \times 2} \times 1.15}{P_{15,2}(r)} \times 2 \text{ years}.$$

At $r = 10$ percent,

$$D_{15,2}(0.10) = \frac{0.1357}{1.0772} \times 1 \text{ year} + \frac{0.9415}{1.0772} \times 2 \text{ years}$$

$$= 0.1260 \text{ years} + 1.7481 \text{ years} = 1.8741 \text{ years}.$$

This is less than the duration $D_{0,2}(r)$ of the zero-coupon 2-year bond, which is obviously equal to 2 years. Using an idea presented in Kopprasch (1985), Figure 7.8 illustrates the duration of a coupon-bearing bond as the center of gravity of the maturities of its discounted cash flows.

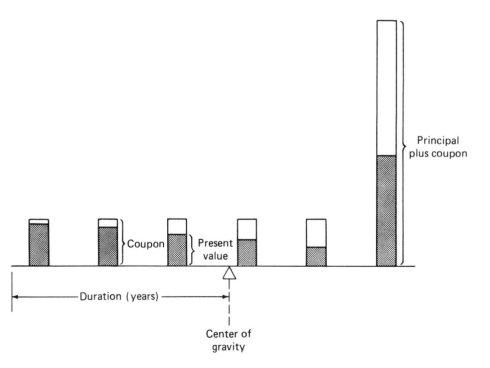

Figure 7.8   Duration as Center of Gravity of Payment Dates

The duration $D_{c,t}(r)$ of a t-year c-percent coupon bond yielding r (continuously compounding) is given by the weighted sum

$$D_{c,t}(r) = \frac{e^{-r \times 1} \times c \times 1 + e^{-r \times 2} \times c \times 2 + \cdots + e^{-r \times t}(100 + c) \times t}{100 \times P_{c,t}(r)},$$

where $P_{c,t}(r)$ is the bond's price. As with zero coupon bonds, the price elasticity $\mathcal{E}_{c,t}(r)$ of a t-year c-percent coupon bond yielding a continuously compounding interest rate of r is given by the formula

$$\mathcal{E}_{c,t}(r) = \frac{P'_{c,t}(r)}{P_{c,t}(r)},$$

the percentage rate of change in the bond price per unit change in the interest rate r. Using the rule for derivatives,

$$\frac{d}{dr}\left(e^{-rt}c\right) = -te^{-rt}c,$$

it is easy to calculate the derivative $P'_{c,t}(r)$ and check (from the preceding three equations) that

$$\mathcal{E}_{c,t}(r) = -D_{c,t}(r),$$

or, in words,

$$\text{elasticity} = -\text{duration}.$$

As with the zero coupon bond, the sensitivity of bond prices to interest rate changes is given directly by the duration of the bond.

The definition of duration we have taken here is often called *Macaulay duration*. When working with simple interest rates rather than continuously compounding rates, a slightly different notion called *modified duration* generates a formula that equates simple elasticity (the percentage rate of change in price for a unit change of simple interest rates) with (minus) modified duration. One may consult sources indicated in the Notes for the details.

Yield Curve Effects

So far, we have implicitly assumed a flat yield curve since we have discounted all cash flows at a fixed continuously compounding rate of r. Suppose, on the other hand, that there are cash flows $F_1, F_2, \ldots, F_n$ at respective times $t_1, t_2, \ldots, t_n$ (which need not be equally spaced), and that the yield curve

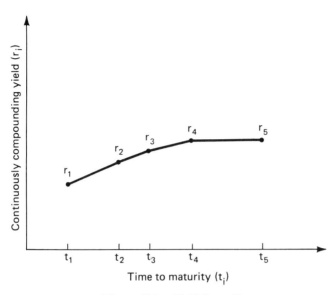

Figure 7.9   Yield Curve Data

applies a continuously compounding interest rate of r_i to payments of maturity t_i as shown in Figure 7.9.

Consider a bond (or portfolio of bonds) whose price is P with a dollar cash flow of F_i at time t_i for each i. The *duration* of this bond (or bond portfolio) is once again its present value weighted sum of maturities

$$D = w_1 t_1 + w_2 t_2 + \cdots + w_n t_n, \tag{27}$$

where the weight w_i applied to maturity t_i is given by

$$w_i = \frac{e^{-r_i t_i} F_i}{P},$$

the fraction of the total price P of the portfolio represented by the present value $e^{-r_i t_i} F_i$ of the i–th cash flow.

A natural measure of price sensitivity for the bond portfolio is the percentage rate of change of the portfolio price per unit upward shift of the entire yield curve. We call this the *portfolio elasticity*. Although we shall not produce the calculations, they are easy and show that the portfolio elasticity $\mathcal{E}$ is once again (minus) the duration D.

Example: Consider a portfolio made up of

- $10 million (face value) worth of zero-coupon 2-year bonds yielding 6 percent continuously compounding.

- $20 million (face value) worth of zero-coupon bonds yielding 7 percent continuously compounding and maturing in 4.25 years.

- $25 million (face value) worth of zero-coupon bonds yielding 9 percent continuously compounding and maturing in 21.3 years.

The "spread sheet" style duration calculations are shown in Table 7.7. As shown, the portfolio's duration is 5.8 years. This implies that the price of the bond portfolio goes down at a rate of 5.8 percent per unit upward shift in all interest rates on the yield curve. Unfortunately, the yield curve does not generally shift directly upward or downward to a new parallel curve; it can also "tilt" and "bend" unpredictably as long term rates rise relatively more or less than short term rates. With arbitrary (non-parallel) movements in the yield curve there is no single accurate measure of price sensitivity to interest rates. For the greatest possible accuracy, one must measure sensitivity relative to interest rates at each of the various maturities.

TABLE 7.7   Example Duration Calulations

Maturity t_i (years)	Yield[a] r_i	Discount $e^{-r_i t_i}$	Pay F_i ($m.)	Value $e^{-r_i t_i} F_i$ ($m.)	Weight[b] w_i	Weighted t_i (years)
2.00	6%	0.887	10	8.87	0.324	0.648
4.25	7%	0.743	20	14.86	0.542	2.304
21.30	9%	0.147	25	3.67	0.134	2.854
TOTAL	—	—	—	27.40	1.000	5.806

[a]The yield is shown on a continuously compounding basis.
[b]The weight w_i is $e^{-r_i t_i} F_i / 27.40$.

Convexity

An examination of the duration (or equivalently, as we have seen, elasticity) of a bond does not tell the full story of its percentage price response to yield changes. Figure 7.10 shows how the prices of two different bond portfolios with the same price and the same duration (or equivalently, the same elasticity) depend on yield changes. The market value of Portfolio 2 declines more slowly with increases in yield, and rises more quickly with decreases in yield, than that of Portfolio 1. Of the two curves defining price response, that of Portfolio 2 has more *convexity*, even though both have the same *slope* (duration). *Convexity* is a measure of the degree of inward curvature of the price curve. We will soon give a formula for convexity.

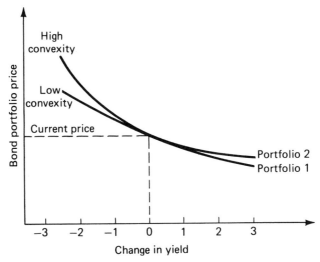

Figure 7.10   Low and High Convexity Bond Portfolios

Example: Suppose Portfolio 1 consists of $10m. ($10 million, face value) of 4-year zero-coupon bonds, while Portfolio 2 consists of $7.57m. (face value) of 2-year zeros and $4m. of 20-year zeros. Suppose, for simplicity, that the yield curve is flat at a continuously compounding rate of 8 percent.

The elasticity of Portfolio 1 is -4 (since it's duration is clearly 4 years). The price of Portfolio 1 is $e^{-0.08 \times 4} \times \$10m. = \$7.26m.$ Portfolio 2 was constructed to have the same duration and price, respectively, as those of Portfolio 1. (This should be checked by the reader as an exercise.)

An increase in continuously compounding yields to 10 percent causes the price of Portfolio 1 (the four-year bond) to drop from $7.26m. (that is,

$e^{-0.08 \times 4} \times \$10m.$) to $\$6.70m.$, a decline of 7.7 percent in market value. The value of Portfolio 2, however, declines to

$$e^{-0.10 \times 2} \times \$7.57m. + e^{-0.10 \times 20} \times \$4m. = \$6.74m.,$$

which represents a smaller decline of 7.16 percent in value.

Likewise, a drop in yields from 8 percent to 6 percent causes the value of Portfolio 1 to increase to $\$7.87m.$, a rise in value of 8.4 percent. The move down to a 6-percent yield improves the value of Portfolio 2 relatively more; its new market value is $\$7.91m.$, which is 9.0 percent higher than its value at an 8-percent yield.

In summary, Portfolio 2 has more convexity than Portfolio 1: its value rises more sharply and drops more gradually in response to interest rate changes.

Clearly, the general rule is: "Convexity is good." Of course, since more convexity is better, there is a price to pay in the market for bonds of relatively greater convexity. The mathematical definition of convexity is

$$C(r) = \frac{P''(r)}{P(r)},$$

where $P(r)$ is the price of the bond (or bond portfolio) as a function of the yield r and $P''(r)$ denotes the second derivative of $P(r)$.

For a zero-coupon bond of maturity t, the price per dollar of face value is $P(r) = e^{-rt}$, which has the second derivative $P''(r) = t^2 e^{-rt}$. The convexity is therefore

$$C(r) = \frac{P''(r)}{P(r)} = t^2.$$

The convexity of a bond portfolio with cash flow of F_i at time t_i (with an associated continuously compounding interest rate of r_i), for times $t_1, \ldots, t_n$ (as shown in Figure 7.9), is the weighted sum of squared maturities:

$$C = w_1 t_1^2 + w_2 t_2^2 + \cdots + w_n t_n^2,$$

where the weight $w_i = e^{-r_i t_i} F_i / P$ is the same as that used in the formula (27) for the duration of the portfolio.

Example: Consider once again the bond portfolio described in Table 7.7. The weights w_1, w_2, and w_3 used to calculate duration can be re-used for an easy calculation of convexity. We have

$$C = w_1 \times 2^2 + w_2 \times 4.25^2 + w_3 \times 21.3^2$$
$$= 0.324 \times 4 + 0.542 \times 18.06 + 0.134 \times 453.69$$
$$= 71.88 \text{ years}^2.$$

The units of convexity, years squared, are not immediately of interest; it is best to think of convexity merely as the curvature of the portfolio's price-yield curve, with higher curvature preferred for a given duration.

Unless two bond portfolios have the same duration, a comparison of their convexities need not lead one portfolio to be favored over the other. For instance, the calculated portfolio convexity of 71.88 years^2 is inferior to that of a 9-year zero-coupon bond (since $9^2 > 71.88$), but the zero-coupon bond has a higher duration (9 years > 5.81 years), implying greater interest rate sensitivity.

Due to a mathematical rule known as *Jensen's Inequality*, it is always true that a bond portfolio (involving more than a single payment) with the same duration as that of a zero-coupon bond always has higher convexity than that of the zero-coupon bond.

FORTRAN code for the duration and convexity of coupon bonds as well as general bond portfolios is provided at the end of this appendix.

Duration and Convexity of Callable Bonds

The calculations of duration and convexity can be extended to cover bonds with a *call provision*, a clause in the bond contract allowing the seller of the bond to cancel the obligation at certain times by immediately repaying the principal. Call provisions can be complicated by terms restricting the timing or nature of the repayment provision.

Example: To take an unrealistically simple case, suppose that a 2-year 15-percent-coupon bond has a call provision allowing repayment (at the option of the borrower) 1 year before maturity. Clearly, the bond will be called (by an astute borrower) if and only if the 1-year simple rate of interest prevailing at the call date is less than 15 percent, since the borrower has the option of paying the prevailing 1-year rate for the last year of the loan rather than the 15-percent coupon rate. The price (per dollar of face value) of the callable bond at the call date is therefore 1.00 if the 1-year interest rate is below 15 percent [which is a continuously compounding rate of $r = \log(1.15) = 0.14 = 14$ percent], and otherwise the bond will sell at its discounted value $P(r) = e^{-r \times 1} \times 1.15$ at any continuously compounding rate r above 14 percent. The curve defining bond price at the call date, shown in Figure 7.11, therefore indicates *negative convexity*, at least in the vicinity of the coupon rate.

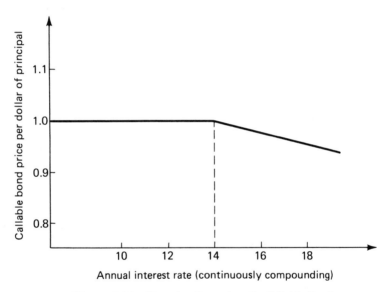

Figure 7.11   Negative Convexity of a Callable Bond

Pass-through mortgages such as Government National Mortgage Association (GNMA or "Ginnie Mae") certificates form a major class of callable bonds which generally exhibit negative convexity. (Appendix 9B discusses the role that the call provision played in the demise in popularity of the GNMA futures contract traded on the Chicago Board of Trade.) Transactions costs and individual factors often prevent GNMA mortgages from being called when it might otherwise seem optimal for homeowners to replace high interest mortgages with lower interest loans. Based on the estimated fraction of mortgages of a given coupon rate that are called at a given interest rate (such figures have been made available, for example, by Salomon Brothers), one can ultimately construct for a given portfolio of pass-through mortgages an estimate of the duration and convexity of the mortgage portfolio. Later in this appendix we estimate a futures hedge for Ginnie Mae mortgage commitments. Because of the call provision, the hedge is improved by including short-term interest rate futures.

Immunization and Duration Matching

Immunization means the adjustment of a portfolio of fixed income liabilities and assets so that the net interest rate risk is reduced or, in the ideal case, eliminated. *Duration matching* is an immunization strategy that calls for adjusting one's fixed income asset portfolio so that it has the same duration and the same market value as one's fixed income liabilities. In this way, a rise in interest rates causes the same marginal gain from reduced liabilities as the marginal loss from reduced asset value, and the portfolio is thereby effectively hedged against small interest rate changes.

Example: Suppose the yield curve is flat at 8 percent continuously compounding, and consider assets made up of $10m$. face value of 4-year zero-coupon bonds, and liabilities comprised of $7.57m$. face value of 2-year zero coupon notes and $4m$. of 20-year zero coupon notes. This situation was reviewed in an earlier example. The asset and liability portfolios have the same market value ($7.26m$.) and the same duration (4 years). The rate of change of the total market value of assets less liabilities with shifts in the yield curve up or down from 8 percent is therefore zero.

Immunization is only effective in this scenario for small shifts in the yield curve. As the yield curve moves down from 8 percent to 6 percent, the duration of the liability portfolio increases from 4 years to 4.75 years, while the duration of the asset portfolio remains fixed at 4 years. In other words, the value of the liability portfolio becomes more sensitive to rate changes as rates go down. The total effect of a decline in rates from 8 percent to 6 percent is an increase in the value of the asset portfolio from $7.26m$. to $7.87m$., while the liability portfolio moves up in value from $7.26m$. to $7.91m$. The $0.61m$. improvement on the asset side is more than offset, unfortunately, by the $0.65m$. loss on the liability side, for a net loss of approximately $40,000. The loss is due to a mismatch in convexity. If the asset and liability portfolios had been constructed with the same convexity, the net effect on the total portfolio value due to changes in rates of this kind would be approximately zero. Of course, duration matching alone was enough to eliminate a large fraction of the interest risk. (Had the assets been held in cash rather than 4-year bonds, the total loss would have been the increase in liability value, $650,000.)

This example shows that duration matching is not necessarily effective unless care is taken to match convexity as well. Alternatively, one can match duration dynamically as rates change. That is, as the yield curve moves down from 8 percent to 6 percent, the portfolio of liabilities might be continuously rebalanced by increasing short term liabilities relative to long term liabilities so as to always maintain a liability duration of 4 years. Alternatively, one could adjust the asset duration, gradually increasing it so as to always match the liability duration.

Immunization with Futures Positions

In the previous example, the liability portfolio of 2-year and 20-year bonds could have been hedged with futures positions. Since there is both short and long term interest rate risk, it is best to consider both short and long term interest rate futures. If it could be guaranteed, however, that the yield curve would move up and down in a parallel fashion, then one could use a single position in, say, 90-day Treasury bill futures to offset the risks. (This is unrealistic, and we will shortly offer a better recommendation.) The recommended position in T-bill futures could be calculated from the general formula:

futures resettlement profit $=$ $-$ change in portfolio value.

Let

- Δf denote the change in T-bill futures price per unit upward shift in the yield curve.
- y denote the futures position.
- ΔV denote the change in the value of the portfolio per unit upward shift in the yield curve.

We can then re-write the above formula more specifically as

$$y \, \Delta f = -\Delta V.$$

Solving, the recommended futures position is $y = -\Delta V/\Delta f$. This is the futures position that, in principle, generates resettlement profits (or losses) that exactly offset changes in the value of a portfolio being hedged.

Example: Consider once again our simple example of a liability portfolio consisting of $\$7.57m$. in 2-year zeros and $\$4m$. in 20-year zeros. Again assuming the yield curve only makes parallel movements, a downward shift in the yield curve from 8 percent to 7 percent increases the value of the liabilities from $\$7.26m$. to $\$7.57m$., or $\Delta V = -\$310,000$. The spot price of $\$1m$. (face value) worth of 90-day (0.25-year) Treasury bills (the deliverable on one futures contract) would change from $e^{-0.25 \times 0.08} \times \$1m. = \$980,200$ to $e^{-0.25 \times 0.09} \times \$1m. = \$977,750$. Assuming for simplicity that the futures contract is about to deliver, the futures and spot T-bill prices coincide, so $\Delta f = \$977,750 - \$980,200 = -\$24,500$. The recommended futures position is therefore

$$y = -\frac{\Delta V}{\Delta f} = -\frac{-\$310,000}{-\$24,500} = -12.66 \text{ contracts},$$

or about 13 T-bill contracts short.

One would need a great deal of confidence in the assumption of parallel movements of the yield curve in order to trust this hedge. Given the fact that the portfolio being hedged is made up of 2-year and 20-year notes, unpredictable relative movements of short and long term rates would normally make the calculated T-bill futures hedge a relatively poor means of reducing interest rate risk.

A more prudent futures hedging strategy calls for positions in both short and long term interest rate futures contracts in order to independently hedge the effects of interest rate movements on the short and long ends of the yield curve. For example, the U.S. Treasury bond futures contract could be effective against changes in the market value of the 20-year notes, while the U.S. T-bill contract, the Eurodollar contract, or the 5-year Treasury note contract could be used to hedge against changes in the value of the 2-year notes making up the short term portion of the liability portfolio in this example.

As to how to select the composition of the hedge, in order to account for basis risk and for correlation between short and long term interest rate changes, it seems conservative and appropriate to adopt the straightforward minimum variance procedures outlined in the body of Chapter 7. For instance, one can create a data file containing the market value of the liability portfolio (or a suitable proxy) for each of a number of historical time periods. With corresponding futures price data for short and long term interest rate futures prices, one can estimate the minimum variance hedging coefficients by estimating the appropriate multiple regression coefficients, as explained in Section 7.4 and Appendix 7D.

The following example illustrates the importance of both long and short term interest rate futures in hedging the value of pass-through mortgage loans. The example uses (with permission) data and calculations provided by John Wyche, a former student, as part of his response to Exercise 7.2.

Example: The Palo Alto Savings and Loan, a (fictional) lender, has contracted to sell 30 days from now $30 million (face value) of 15-year callable 9.5-percent mortgages to the Government National Mortgage Association (GNMA, or Ginnie Mae). Since the value of these mortgages represents a significant fraction of Palo Alto Savings and Loan's market value, management has decided to hedge the price to be received for the mortgages with an interest rate futures position. Palo Alto S&L has decided to hedge the effects of long term interest rate risk with U.S. Treasury bond futures (traded on the Chicago Board of Trade). Since the mortages are callable, their value may also bear some relationship to short term rates. For this reason, a position in 3-month Eurodollar futures (traded on the Chicago Mercantile Exchange) will also be considered.

Following the prescription outlined in Appendix 7D, data for 97 weeks (May 15, 1986 to March 24, 1988) on the log-price increments (Y_t) of Ginnie Mae mortgage-backed 9.5-percent coupon securities were regressed on the corresponding time series for U.S. Treasury bond futures $(X_t^{(1)})$ and Eurodollar futures $(X_t^{(2)})$, using log-price increments for the nearby contract in each case. The estimated regression equation is

$$Y_t = 0.0001 + 0.204\,X_t^{(1)} + 1.51\,X_t^{(2)} + \epsilon_t. \qquad (R^2 = 0.711)$$

$$(0.034^*) \qquad (0.245^*) \qquad (0.005)$$

The regression coefficients easily pass (at standard confidence levels, under standard asssumptions) tests of statistical significance. The spot price of 9.5-percent coupon GNMA mortgage coefficients is currently 99.5625 percent of face value. The current T-bond futures price for nearby delivery is 90.50. The

current 3-month Eurodollar nearby futures index is 92.67. As with the calculations of T-bill futures prices shown in Section 6.2, the resttlement payments
on a Eurodollar position are actually one quarter of the change in the Eurodollar futures index. Following the analysis in Appendix 7D, the estimated
risk-minimizing hedge is therefore made of the following futures positions:

$$\text{T-bond position} = 0.2042 \times \frac{99.5625}{90.50} \times \$10 \text{ million} = -\$2.246 \text{ million,}$$

or a short position of about 22 contracts of $100,000 (face value) each, and

$$\text{Eurodollar position} = -1.51 \times \frac{99.5625}{92.67} \times \frac{1}{4} \times \$10 \text{ million} = -\$4.06 \text{ million,}$$

or a short position of about 4 contracts.

The R^2 of 0.711 indicates an estimated reduction in risk (variance of
the hedged value of the mortgages) of about 71 percent can be achieved by
using this combined futures position. This is superior to the estimated risk
reduction that can be achieved solely with T-bond futures, or solely with
Eurodollar futures (as can be shown by estimating the corresponding simple
linear regressions).

Based on additional regressions not reported here, Palo Alto S&L determined that Eurodollar and T-bond futures together provided a better hedge
than a combined position in T-bill and T-bond futures. The Eurodollar contract, moreover, has recently been far more liquid than the T-bill contract,
and therefore seems superior to the T-bill futures contract for the short term
portion of the hedge. Further tests also showed that the U.S. Treasury note
futures contract (delivering 6–10 year U.S. T-notes and traded on the CBOT)
does not appear to give a significantly better fit when added to the above regression equation as an additional explanatory variable (again using log-price
increment data).

Swaps

A recent innovation in capital markets, *swaps* comprise a class of asset exchanges between two parties that typically involve swapping one set of cash
flows for another. The cash flows are usually coupon payments on a bond,
or more generally, interest payments due on loans for which there may not
be a secondary market. With a *currency swap*, the cash flows received by
one party are in a different currency than the cash flows paid by that party.

With an *interest rate swap*, the cash flows paid by one party are fixed in advance, for example as the coupon payments on a fixed rate loan, while the cash flows received by that party are variable, for example based on a *floating interest rate* such as the London Interbank Offered Rate (LIBOR). There are combinations of currency and interest rate swaps, and many variations such as optional payment periods or staged drawdowns in the principal underlying the loan payments.

In some cases, a swap is negotiated on the basis of additional initial payments to one party or the intermediary. For example, an *off-market-rate swap* involves some initial payment from the fixed-rate payer to the floating-rate payer if the fixed rate is below currently set fixed rates for comparable loans, or a payment from the floating rate payer to the fixed rate payer under the opposite condition. Interest rate swaps, denominated in U.S. dollars (and therefore occasionally referred to as *dollar swaps*), appeared later than currency swaps, but have since come to be the more prevalent of these two basic forms of swaps. A variation is the *basis rate swap*, an exchange of cash flows based on different floating rates, such as a swap of the commercial paper rate for LIBOR. The bulk of swaps are intermediated by the large U.S. commercial and (to a lesser extent) investment banks. Prominent intermediaries include Citicorp, Chemical Bank, Bankers Trust, Chase, and Morgan Stanley. It has been increasingly common for a bank to take one side of a swap as its own position.

One normally thinks of a forward contract as an agreement to exchange assets at a particular date. From an abstract point of view, a swap is merely a forward agreement to exchange assets at a number of dates in the future. One could easily imagine a new type of futures contract, one calling for a series of cash settled payments from the short to the long in return for a series of fixed payments from the long to the short. The usual notion of a futures price would in this case be the amount paid by the long to the short at delivery, that is, at the date the series of payments begins, as in the manner of an off-the-market interest rate swap. Such a futures market does not yet exist.

The recent growth of swap transactions seems to be due, in large part, to the fact that swaps allow firms to design various cash flow hedges that cannot be easily constructed by using previously available security markets. In particular, the futures and forward markets do not typically deliver more than 1 or at most 2 years ahead, whereas interest rate or foreign currency payments and receivables may be staged over much longer periods. Interest rate swaps, for example, can be arranged for up to 15-year terms. The growth of the swap market, moreover, has promoted yet further growth by allowing reduced transactions fees accompanied by ever greater liquidity and convenience.

Example: (An Interest Rate Swap)   This sort of example can be found in advertising paid for by swap intermediaries, who have an obvious incentive to portray swaps as hedges as well as profit sources. Two companies, say A and B, must each raise $100 million in debt financing for five years. For reasons such as relative credit ratings, tax considerations, access to different markets, or other institutional considerations, company A has a cost advantage in fixed rate borrowing over floating rate borrowing, relative to company B. Specifically, Company A can float 5-year commercial paper at fixed 8.80-percent coupon payments, and borrow at one quarter of a percent over the 6-month LIBOR. (The interest is stated on a semi-annual basis; interest payments on the commercial paper of 4.4 percent of the principal would be due each 6 months.) Company B, on the other hand, pays a fixed rate of 10.00 percent or a floating rate of 0.75 percent over LIBOR. Now suppose Company A indeed issues the commercial paper, and pays the 6-month LIBOR rate payments on the principal to Company B, via a bank. Company B actually borrows at LIBOR plus 0.75 percent, and makes payments at a fixed rate of 8.90 percent to Company A (via the same intermediary bank). The series of cash flows is illustrated in Figure 7.12 The net effect is that Company A pays at LIBOR less 0.10 percent, while Company B pays a fixed rate of 9.65 percent.

One way of looking at this example is that the two parties have engaged in an arbitrage: both are strictly better off, have a "saving" of 35 basis points from the swap. Some of these basis points go to the bank for its services. Of course, the fact that Company B must pay more than company B for fixed rate funding indicates that it may have a higher default risk, which must be borne by the bank or perhaps by Company A, depending on the contractual arrangements. Such a swap may or may not be motivated by the suggested cost advantage to both parties. A simpler justification for swap transactions is hedging. Company B, for example, may wish to hedge the uncertainty inherent in changes in LIBOR over the loan period; Company A may be relatively more willing to bear that risk. From this point of view, it may have been better for Company B to swap away only a fraction of its original floating rate commitment.

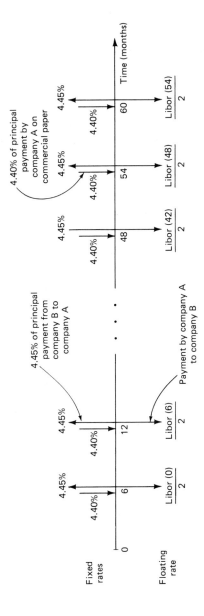

Figure 7.12 Interest Rate Swap Cash Flow

Example: (Currency Swap)   A currency swap may be designed to reduce foreign exchange risk. For example, one could hedge the market value of foreign income streams by swapping domestic interest expenses for foreign interest expenses. Another reason for currency swaps may be a relative cost (interest rate) advantage of firms borrowing in their home countries. A cost advantage could be due to legal barriers separating lenders from potential borrowers in foreign countries, differential tax considerations, or perhaps governmental restrictions on international capital flows. Figure 7.13 portrays a currency swap between a U.S. firm that wishes to create Swiss Franc borrowing and a Swiss firm that wishes to create U.S. dollar borrowing. The U.S. firm can borrow at 10.50 percent in the U.S. dollar market and 4.2 percent in the Swiss Franc market, while the Swiss firm can borrow at 10.80 percent in the U.S. dollar market and 4.0 percent in the Swiss Franc market. An intermediary bank has arranged for them to swap their home currency borrowing costs, at a saving of 15 basis points to each, the remainder going to the bank.

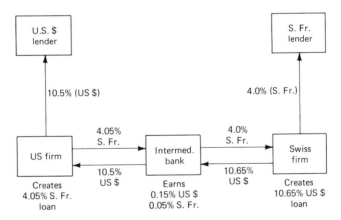

Figure 7.13   A Currency Swap

FORTRAN Code for the Duration and Convexity of Bond Portfolios

The calculations explained earlier in this appendix for the duration and convexity of bond portfolios are easily left to the computer. The following FORTRAN code, prepared by Stephen Fan under the direction of the author, has been debugged and used.

```
      Program MAIN
c
c  ********************************************************************
c  * This program calculates DURATIION and CONVEXITY for:            *
c  *    1 - a portfolio of zero coupon bonds (ZDRATN, ZCNVEX)        *
c  *    2 - a coupon bearing bond (CDRATN, CCNVEX)                   *
c  * Coding by Stephen Fan at the direction of the author            *
c  ********************************************************************
c
c Variable Definitions
c ** For zero coupon bond portfolio
c
c   t(i): maturity of i-th bond from now
c   r(i): continuous compounding interest rate of i-th bond
c   f(i): amount of payment of i-th bond
c      n: total number of bonds
c
c ** For coupon bearing bond
c
c      c: coupon rate
c     ff: first coupon payment from now
c     tt: regular interval of coupon payment
c     xm: time to maturity from now
c      y: yield to maturity
c      p: present value of bonds (per dollar face value)
c      k: flag of whether to use y or p to do calculations
c      k = 1, use y (yield to maturity)
c      o/w, use p (present value of bond)
c
      dimension t(100),r(100),f(100)
c
c Choose calculation desired
c
  100 write (*,500)
  500 format(1x,'Please enter calculation desired:',/,
     *3x,'1 for calculation of a portfolio of Z-Coupon Bonds',/,
     *3x,'2 for calculation of a coupon bearing bonds',/,
     *3x,'3 for end of calculation',/)
c
      read (*,*) ik
      if (ik.eq.2) goto 200
      if (ik.eq.3) goto 900
c
c Zero Coupon Bond Calculation
c Input for zero coupon bond portfolio
c
      write(*,1000)
      read (*,*) n
      do 1 i=1,n
      write(*,1050) i
      read (*,*) t(i),r(i),f(i)
c
c convert interest rate to fraction
c
```

```
        r(i) = r(i)/100.
      1 continue
c
c call function routine
c
        ZDURA = ZDRATN(t,r,f,n)
        ZCONV = ZCNVEX(t,r,f,n)
c
c Write result for the portfolio of zero coupon bonds
c
        write (*,2000) ZDURA,ZCONV
        goto 100
c
c Coupon Bearing Bond Calculation
c
      200 continue
c
c Input for coupon bearing bond
c
        write (*,1100)
        read(*,*) c,ff,tt,xm,k,x
c
c convert coupon rate to fraction
c
        c = c/100.
c
        if(k.eq.2) goto 205
c
c convert yield to maturity to fraction
c
        y = x/100.
        p = 0.0
        goto 220
c
      205 y=0.0
        p = x
c
c call calculation subroutines
c
      220 CDURA = CDRATN(c,ff,tt,xm,y,p,k)
        CCONV = CCNVEX(c,ff,tt,xm,y,p,k)
c
c Write result for the coupon bearing bond
c
        write (*,2050) CDURA,CCONV
        goto 100
c
      900 stop
c
     1000 format(1x,'Please enter total no. of zero coupon bonds ',
      *            'in the portfolio:',/)
     1050 format(1x,'Please enter following parameters for Z-Bond # ',
      *        i3,':',/,
      *        3x,'t: time to maturity from now',/,
```

```
      *          3x,'r: continuous compound rate (%)',/,
      *          3x,'f: final payment of bond',/)
 2000 format(1x,'The Duration of Z-Bond Portfolio is: ',f10.3,/,
      *          1x,'The Convexity of Z-Bond Portfolio is: ',f10.3,/)
 1100 format(1x,'Please enter following parameters for the coupon ',
      *          'bearing bond:',/,
      *          3x,'c: coupon rate (%)',/,
      *          3x,'f: time to first coupon payment from now',/,
      *          3x,'t: regular coupon paying interval',/,
      *          3x,'m: time to maturity from now',/,
      *          3x,'k: whether inputting p or y next 1 for y;',
      *                                ' 2 for p',/,
      *          3x,'y or p:',/,
      *          3x,'   where   y: yield to maturity (%)',/,
      *          3x,'           p: present value of bond ',
      *                         '(per dollar face value)',/)
 2050 format(1x,'The Duration of Coupon Bond is: ',f10.3,/,
      *          1x,'The Convexity of Coupon Bond is: ',f10.3,/)
c
      end
c
c
c
      FUNCTION ZDRATN(t,r,f,n)
c
c **********************************************************************
c *   This function calculates the DURATION for a portfolio of     *
c * zero coupon bonds with different interest rates and maturity   *
c **********************************************************************
c Variable Definitions
c   t(i): maturity of i-th bond from now
c   r(i): continuous compound interest rate of i-th bond (fraction)
c   f(i): amount of payment of i-th bond
c     n: total number of bonds
c
      dimension t(n),r(n),f(n)
c
c calculate overall present value of bond portfolio
c
      p = 0.0
      do 1 i = 1,n
      p = p + exp(-r(i)*t(i)) * f(i)
    1 continue
c
c calculate duration of portfolio
c
      d = 0.0
      do 2 i = 1,n
      d = d + exp(-r(i)*t(i))*f(i)/p * t(i)
    2 continue
c
      ZDRATN = d
c
      return
```

```
      end
c
c
c
      FUNCTION ZCNVEX(t,r,f,n)
c
c  ********************************************************************
c  *    This function calculates the CONVEXITY for a portfolio of   *
c  *  zero coupon bonds with different interest rates and maturities*
c  ********************************************************************
c Variable Definitions
c   t(i): maturity of i-th bond from now
c   r(i): continuous compound interest rate of i-th bond (fraction)
c   f(i): amount of payment of i-th bond
c      n: total number of bonds
c
      dimension t(n),r(n),f(n)
c
c calculate overall present value of bond portfolio
c
      p = 0.0
      do 1 i = 1,n
      p = p + exp(-r(i)*t(i)) * f(i)
    1 continue
c
c calculate CONVEXITY of portfolio
c
      c = 0.0
      do 2 i = 1,n
      c = c + exp(-r(i)*t(i))*f(i)/p * t(i)**2
    2 continue
c
      ZCNVEX = c
c
      return
      end
c
c
c
      FUNCTION CDRATN(c,f,t,xm,y,p,k)
c
c  ********************************************************************
c  *    This function calculates the DURATION of  coupon bearing    *
c  *    bonds with known yield to maturity or present bond value    *
c  ********************************************************************
c Variable Definitions
c      c: coupon rate (fraction)
c      f: first coupon payment from now
c      t: regular interval of coupon payment
c     xm: time to maturity from now
c      y: yield to maturity (fraction)
c      p: present value of bonds (per dollar face value)
c      k: flag of whether to use y or p to do calculations
c         k = 1, use y (yield to maturity)
```

```
c              o/w, use p (present value of bond)
c
c
c calculate number of payments excluding first one
c
      n = int((xm-f)/t)
c
c check consistency of user specified t, f, xm
c
      e = t*n+f
      if(abs(e-xm).gt.0.001) goto 999
c
      nn = n - 1
      if (k.eq.1) goto 100
c
c calculate equivalent continuously compounding rate from p
c by Newton-Raphson Method
c
      r0=.01
c
  111 x = exp(-f*r0) * c*t
      xp = -f * exp(-f*r0) * c*t
      do 1 i = 1,nn
      x = x + exp(r0*(-f-i*t)) * c*t
      xp = xp - (f+i*t) * exp(r0*(-f-i*t)) * c*t
    1 continue
      x = x + exp(-r0*xm) * (1.+c*t) - p
      xp = xp - xm * exp(-r0*xm) * (1.+c*t)
      r1 = r0 - x/xp
      if(abs(r0-r1).le..00001) goto 222
      r0 = r1
      goto 111
c
  222 r = r0
c
c convert continuously compounding
c interest rate to yield to maturiry
c
      y = (exp(r*t)-1.)/t
      write (*,*) 'equivalent yield to maturity = ',y
      goto 200
c
  100 continue
c
c calculate present value of bond from input of y
c
      p = (1.+y*t)**(-f/t) * c*t
      do 333 i=1,nn
      p = p + (1+y*t)**(-f/t-i) *c*t
  333 continue
      p = p + (1+y*t)**(-xm/t) * (1.+c*t)
      write (*,*) 'equivalent present value = ',p
c
  200 continue
```

```
c
c calculate DURATION
c
      d = (1+y*t)**(-f/t) *c*t/p * f
      do 2 i = 1,nn
      d = d + (1+y*t)**(-f/t-i) *c*t/p * (f+i*t)
    2 continue
      d = d + (1+y*t)**(-xm/t) *(1.+c*t)/p * xm
c
      CDRATN = d
c
      return
c
  999 write(*,*) '*** inconsistent input of "f", "t", "m" ***'
      stop
      end
c
c
c
      FUNCTION CCNVEX(c,f,t,xm,y,p,k)
c
c **********************************************************************
c *    This function calculates the CONVEXITY for coupon bearing    *
c *    bonds with known yield to maturity or present bond value     *
c **********************************************************************
c Variable Definitions
c     c: coupon rate (fraction)
c     f: first coupon payment from now
c     t: regular interval of coupon payment
c     xm: time to maturity from now
c     y: yield to maturity (fraction)
c     p: present value of bonds (per dollar face value)
c     k: flag of whether to use y or p to do calculations
c        k = 1, use y (yield to maturity)
c           o/w, use p (present value of bond)
c
c
c calculate number of payments excluding first one
c
      n = int((xm-f)/t)
c
c check consistency of user specified t, f, xm
c
      e = t*n+f
      if(abs(e-xm).gt.0.001) goto 999
c
      nn = n - 1
      if (k.eq.1) goto 100
c
c calculate equivalent continuous compound rate from p
c by Newton-Raphson Method
c
      r0=.01
c
```

```fortran
  111 x = exp(-f*r0) * c*t
      xp = -f * exp(-f*r0) * c*t
      do 1 i = 1,nn
      x = x + exp(r0*(-f-i*t)) * c*t
      xp = xp - (f+i*t) * exp(r0*(-f-i*t)) * c*t
    1 continue
      x = x + exp(-r0*xm) * (1.+c*t) - p
      xp = xp - xm * exp(-r0*xm) * (1.+c*t)
      r1 = r0 - x/xp
      if(abs(r0-r1).le..00001) goto 222
      r0 = r1
      goto 111
c
  222 r = r0
c
c convert continuously compounding
c interest rate to yield to maturity y
c
      y = (exp(r*t)-1.)/t
      goto 200
c
  100 continue
c
c calculate present value of bond from input of y
c
      p = (1.+y*t)**(-f/t) * c*t
      do 333 i=1,nn
      p = p + (1+y*t)**(-f/t-i) *c*t
  333 continue
      p = p + (1+y*t)**(-xm/t) * (1.+c*t)
c
  200 continue
c
c calculate CONVEXITY
c
      c = (1+y*t)**(-f/t) *c*t/p * f**2
      do 2 i = 1,nn
      c = c + (1+y*t)**(-f/t-i) *c*t/p * (f+i*t)**2
    2 continue
      c = c + (1+y*t)**(-xm/t) *(1.+c*t)/p * xm**2
c
      CCNVEX = c
c
      return
c
  999 write(*,*) '*** inconsistent input of "f", "t", "m" ***'
c
      return
      end
```

8

OPTIONS AND FUTURES OPTIONS

This chapter is an overview of options and futures options, securities that have an important relationship with futures markets. We will also describe the synthetic creation of an option via a dynamic futures trading strategy. With the S&P 500 Index futures contract, a version of this strategy this has become known as *portfolio insurance*. Appendix 8A reviews the Black-Scholes option pricing formula and its extension to futures options. Appendix 8B supplies FORTRAN coding for the various Black-Scholes calculations that would normally be done on a computer.

1. OPTIONS

Basic Option Concepts

A *call option* on an asset at an *exercise price* of K is a contract giving its owner the right, but not the obligation, to purchase the asset for the price K. An option generally cannot be exercised after a given *expiration date*. The exercise price is also known as the *strike price*. The expiration date is also known as the *expiry date*. A *European option* can only be exercised at its expiration date; an *American option* may be exercised early. The price of an option is also referred to as the *option premium*.

Example: Suppose that on May 17 an American call option on IBM common stock for June expiration at an exercise price of $105 is selling for $6.75, while IBM is trading at $110\frac{1}{8}$ per share. The option can be exercised immediately; the exercised option is worth $5\frac{1}{8}$ since the share bought for $105 can immediately be resold for $110\frac{1}{8}$. Since the option currently trades at a price

Chapter Outline

greater than $5\frac{1}{8}$, it would be silly to exercise the option rather than sell it or hold it until a later date. If the option is held to expiration in June, it will be worthless if IBM trades at less than $105 per share at expiration, and otherwise will be worth the excess of the share price at expiration over the exercise price of $105. For example, if IBM trades at $109 at expiration, the option to buy at $105 is worth $4 at that time.

A *put option* gives the buyer the right, but not the obligation, to sell the underlying asset at a given exercise price by a given expiration date. Extending the last example, the corresponding June put on IBM at an exercise price of $105 is selling on May 17 for $\frac{11}{16}$. Traders apparently place this low a value on the put because they feel that the price of IBM has a low probability of falling so far as to make the put worth exercising. Certainly, the put should not be exercised until at least the first time IBM drops below $105, which may not happen before expiration.

Options are commonly issued with a selection of strike prices and a series of expiration dates. Typical expiration sequences are monthly, for at least three months from the current date, with new options added each time an expiration date passes. Strike prices are chosen to bracket the current asset price. As the price of the underlying asset changes, additional options are made available for trade so that, at the beginning of each day's trade, there is always at least one strike price traded on each side of the current asset price.

The 1970s witnessed a major expansion in the markets for options on common stocks. The surge in popularity of financial futures in the 1980s has spawned corresponding markets in options and futures options on various indices, commodities, and other financial instruments. Futures options, described in the next section, often differ from options in their margining provisions.

Example: (S&P 500 Index Options)   Figure 8.1 shows prices of selected index options as reported on a typical day by *The Wall Street Journal.* Options on the S&P 500 Index are currently traded at the *Chicago Board Options Exchange* (CBOE). There is also an S&P 500 futures option, traded at the Chicago Mercantile Exchange, although its settlement provisions are somewhat different from those of the CBOE index options, as described later in the chapter. The payoff at expiration of an S&P 500 call option with an exercise price of 250, for example, is shown in Figure 8.2. If the S&P 500 Index at expiration, S_T, is higher than the exercise price $K = 250$, the option holder will exercise the option by "buying the index" for 250. The contract actually provides for a cash settlement of $S_T - 250$ to the option buyer in this case, and a payment of $S_T - 250$ from the option seller, who is more commonly referred to as the *option writer.* If $S_T \leq 250$, the option is not exercised, and no payments are made to or from buyer or writer.

Put-Call Parity

The expiration payoff to the buyer of an S&P 500 Index European put at an exercise price of $K = 250$ is shown in Figure 8.3. Ignoring dividends, one can produce the payoff shown in Figure 8.2 of the corresponding call option by the following strategy:

1. Invest the current index S_t in the S&P 500 tracking portfolio, the portfolio of stocks whose value tracks the S&P 500 Index, as explained in Chapter 5.

INDEX TRADING

Tuesday, November 29, 1988

OPTIONS
CHICAGO BOARD

S&P 100 INDEX

Strike Price	Calls—Last Dec	Calls—Last Jan	Calls—Last Feb	Puts—Last Dec	Puts—Last Jan	Puts—Last Feb
230	26⅝	....	....	3/16	11/16	1 7/16
235	21⅜	....	....	¼	1	1⅞
240	19	19¼	....	7/16	1½	2⅝
245	14¼	16⅞	17¾	13/16	2 3/16	3¾
250	9½	12½	14	1½	3⅛	4⅞
255	5½	8⅞	11	2⅝	4⅞	6¼
260	2 9/16	5¾	8	4¾	6⅞	8½
265	⅞	3½	5½	8¼	9⅝	....
270	¼	1⅞	3⅝	12⅞	13⅝	....
275	1/16	15/16	2⅛	18	....	20
280	1/16	7/16	1 3/16	22¾	....	....
285	....	3/16	....	....	....	....

Total call volume 104,407 Total call open int. 324,782
Total put volume 99,270 Total put open int. 322,245
The index: High 258.44; Low 255.16; Close 258.00, 2.36.

S&P 500 INDEX

Strike Price	Calls—Last Dec	Calls—Last Jan	Calls—Last Mar	Puts—Last De	Puts—Last Jan	Puts—Last Mar
230	39	....	....	....	....	1
240	....	....	....	3/16	¾	2 7/16
245	....	....	....	¼	1 1/16	2½
250	....	....	....	¼	1⅜	4
255	....	....	22½	½	2	4¼
260	12	....	18⅞	¾	3	5⅛
265	7¾	9⅞	14⅛	1 9/16	4⅞	6¾
270	4¼	7¾	12⅛	3	5¼	8
275	1 13/16	....	9⅝	5¼	8⅞	....
280	9/16	3¼	6½	11⅜	10¾	....
285	⅛	1½	5	16¼	....	16⅛
290	1/16	....	2 15/16	21½	....	21
295	....	....	....	24	....	....
300	....	....	....	....	....	1 5/16
325	....	....	....	54	....	....

Total call volume 13,669 Total call open int. 229,678
Total put volume 18,666 Total put open int. 247,087
The index: High 271.31; Low 268.13; Close 270.91, +2.27.

NEW YORK

NYSE INDEX OPTIONS

Strike Price	Calls—Last Dec	Calls—Last Jan	Calls—Last Feb	Puts—Last Dec	Puts—Last Jan	Puts—Last Feb
135	....	....	....	1/16	5/166	⅞
140	....	....	....	1/16	⅝	....
142½	....	....	....	3/16	....	....
145	8⅜	9¾	....	¼	1⅛	2¼
147½	....	....	....	½	1¾	....
150	3 15/16	....	....	1	2¼	....
152½	2⅛	4	....	1⅞	....	....
155	⅞	2¾	....	4	....	5¾
157½	⅜	....	....	....	....	....
160	⅛	15/16	....	....	7½	....

Total call volume 1,246. Total call open int. 5,590.
Total put volume 1,859. Total put open int. 8,120.
The index: High 152.58; Low 151.03; Close 152.43, +1.18.

PACIFIC

FINANCIAL NEWS COMPOSITE INDEX

Strike Price	Calls—Last Dec	Calls—Last Jan	Calls—Last Mar	Puts—Last Dec	Puts—Last Jan	Puts—Last Mar
180	11⅝	....	....	⅜	....	....
185	7⅛	....	....	⅞	....	....
190	3⅛	....	....	1⅞	3¾	....
195	15/16	5⅞	....	4⅜	5⅞	....
200	....	1¼	....	8⅞	8⅞	....

Total call volume 212 Total call open int. 2,197
Total put volume 524 Total put open int. 4,272
The index: High 191.62; Low 189.32; Close 191.21, +1.60.

Figure 8.1 A Sample of Published Index Option Prices from *The Wall Street Journal*

2. Pay the put price P_t for one S&P 500 put option with the same exercise price K and expiration date T as those of the call option.

3. Borrow $KZ_{t,T}$ risklessly until expiration, where $Z_{t,T}$ is the price at time t per dollar of face value of a zero coupon bond riskless bond maturing at date T.

As shown in Table 8.1, the net payoff of this strategy for the two possible cases, $S_T \le K$ and $S_T > K$, is indeed the same as the payoff of the call option. The total cost of this strategy is $S_t + P_t - KZ_{t,T}$. Using our usual arbitrage arguments, we therefore deduce the following *put-call parity formula* for the current price C_t of the call option in the absence of arbitrage, transactions

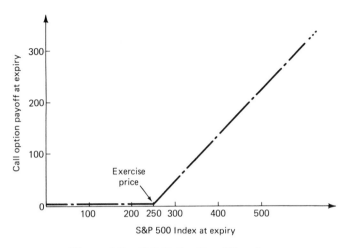

Figure 8.2   Call Option Payoff Function

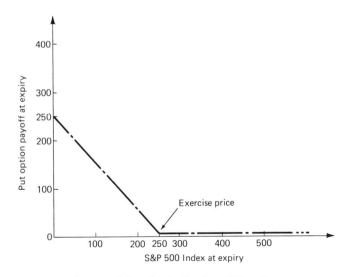

Figure 8.3   Put Option Payoff Function

TABLE 8.1   Put-Call Parity Strategy

	Cost at t (at Parity)	Payoff at T	
		Case: $S_T \leq K$	Case: $S_T > K$
Stock Portfolio	S_t	S_T	S_T
Put	P_t	$K - S_T$	0
Loan	$-KZ_{t,T}$	$-K$	$-K$
Total	$S_t + P_t - KZ_{t,T}$	0	$S_T - K$

costs, or dividends:

$$C_t = S_t + P_t - KZ_{t,T}. \tag{1}$$

A put-call parity formula has also been developed for European options on assets with dividends, under special conditions explained in a source indicated in the Notes to this chapter. Exercise 8.1 explores put-call parity for futures options that are marked to market.

2. FUTURES OPTIONS

Background

Today's markets for futures options can be traced back almost to the beginning of American futures markets, when traders at the Chicago Board of Trade protected themselves by buying and selling *privileges*, an early synonym for commodity options. Initially, most privileges were traded with expiration on the next trading day. Gradually, the general trading of privileges expanded. After the Chicago Board of Trade attempted to halt trading in privileges (which were widely believed to be a vehicle for gambling), the contracts were modified cosmetically, called *indemnities*, and trading resumed. The Futures Trading Act of 1921 attempted to inhibit the trading of privileges with a stiff tax, but this measure was found to be unconstitutional, and privilege trading continued unabated until the Commodity Exchange Act of 1936 prohibited trading in options on those commodities in which futures trading was regulated. Meanwhile, unregulated commodity options trading continued. Although *Mocatta options* (also known as *dealer options*), those written by firms owning the underlying assets, or *commercial options*, those sold to a purchaser with a business requirement for the assets, caused few serious problems, various scandals and frauds in commodity options led the CFTC to suspend commodity options trading in the U.S. in 1978. Since then, exchange-traded commodity and financial futures options have been gradually authorized; trading in these markets by registered dealers has grown to significant proportions.

Futures options, the name commonly applied to options on futures contracts, are now an important fixture on the financial scene. A summary of traded futures options is provided in Appendix 9D. A sample of futures options prices as reported daily in *The Wall Street Journal* is shown in Figure 8.4.

Futures options are typically traded on the same exchanges at which the underlying futures contracts are traded, and are usually executed and cleared following the same or similar procedures used for futures. The principal differences concern margining and resettlement practices, which vary widely. We shall try to make a distinction here between a futures option in its purest form, with daily margin and resettlement features like those of a futures contract, and a *conventional option*. A conventional call option, for example, requires payment of the option premium when purchased, and at exercise pays the buyer any excess of the underlying asset price over the exercise price. A *pure futures option*, on the other hand, calls for the buyer to receive (or pay) daily any change in the futures option price in order to mark the buyer's margin account to market. This distinction between "conventional" and "pure" futures options is not widely appreciated.

Strictly speaking, a pure futures option is not an option at all. It is, rather, a futures contract that delivers the corresponding conventional option at expiration. The futures options traded at the London International Financial Futures Exchange (LIFFE) have resettlement provisions that, in principle, make these more like pure than conventional futures options. The futures options traded on American exchanges are hybrids of the two extremes.

Example: (Pure Futures Options) We shall treat the S&P 500 futures option in this example as though it is a pure futures option. The actual resettlement features of this contract are much more complicated and are summarized later in this section.

COMMODITY FUTURES OPTIONS

Monday, December 19, 1988.

–AGRICULTURAL–

CORN (CBT) 5,000 bu.; cents per bu.

Strike	Calls–Settle			Puts–Settle		
Price	Mar-c	May-c	Jly-c	Mar-p	May-p	Jly-p
260	23¾	30	35	1⅜	2¾	6½
270	15¾	22¼	29	2¾	6	10½
280	10	16¼	24	7	10½	15
290	5¾	12¼	19½	12¾	15½	20½
300	3½	9	16	20	21½	26½
310	2	7	12½	29	29	33

Est. vol. 5,500, Fri vol. 3,039 calls, 3,117 puts
Open interest Fri 56,387 calls, 38,448 puts

SOYBEANS (CBT) 5,000 bu.; cents per bu.

Strike	Calls–Settle			Puts–Settle		
Price	Mar-c	May-c	Jly-c	Mar-p	May-p	Jly-p
750	64	100	92	8¼	19½	28
775	47	83	78	15½	28	38½
800	34	67	66½	27	40	51
825	24	55	57	42	54	67½
850	16½	46	50	59	70½	....
875	12	37	43	78	88	....

Est. vol. 7,000, Fri vol. 6,122 calls, 3,722 puts
Open interest Fri 41,199 calls, 17,177 puts

SOYBEAN MEAL (CBT) 100 tons; $ per ton

Strike	Calls–Settle			Puts–Settle		
Price	Mar-c	May-c	Jly-c	Mar-p	May-p	Jly-p
250	14.30	17.10	17.50	5.70	11.25	....
255	11.60	14.75	....	7.85	....	....
260	9.25	12.65	14.00	10.50	....	....
265	7.50	11.10	....	....	....	....
270	6.00	10.00	....	....	....	....
275	5.00	....	....	....	....	....

Est. vol. 250, Fri vol. 1,080 calls, 697 puts
Open interest Fri 5,240 calls, 2,907 puts

SOYBEAN OIL (CBT) 60,000 lbs.; cents per lb.

Strike	Calls–Settle			Puts–Settle		
Price	Mar-c	May-c	Jly-c	Mar-p	May-p	Jly-p
22	2.150	....	....	.400	.600	.650
23	1.400	2.200	....	.650	....	....
24	.850	1.700	2.100	1.150	....	1.450
25	.500	1.300	1.800	1.800	....	....
26	.380	1.000	1.450	2.600	....	2.550
27	.250	.600	1.150	....	....	....

Est. vol. 200, Fri vol. 327 calls, 59 puts
Open interest Fri 3,448 calls, 1,387 puts

WHEAT (CBT) 5,000 bu.; cents per bu.

Strike	Calls–Settle			Puts–Settle		
Price	Mar-c	May-c	Jly-c	Mar-p	May-p	Jly-p
420	24¾	23½	....	5	....	....
430	17½	18½	9½	9	....	....
440	12⅝	14	....	13¼	....	....
450	8½	10	....	19	36	....
460	6½	5½	....	....	....	....
470	4½	....	....	....	53	....

Est. vol. 2,000, Fri vol. 743 calls, 977 puts
Open interest Fri 16,888 calls, 16,115 puts

–OIL–

CRUDE OIL (NYM) 1,000 bbls.; $ per bbl.

Strike	Calls–Settle			Puts–Settle		
Price	Feb-c	Mar-c	Ap-c	Feb-p	Mar-p	Apr-p
14	1.86	1.64	1.62	0.05	0.23	0.37
15	0.98	0.93	0.96	0.15	0.50	0.69
16	0.30	0.43	0.52	0.47	0.98	1.94
17	0.06	0.16	0.26	1.22	1.70	....
18	0.02	0.06	0.11	2.18	....	....
19	0.01	....	....	....	....	....

Est. vol. 8,675; Fri vol. 6,805 calls; 10,335 puts
Open interest Fri; 58,618 calls; 90,736 puts

HEATING OIL No.2 (NYM) 42,000 gal.; $ per gal.

Strike	Calls–Settle			Puts–Settle		
Price	Feb-c	Mar-c	Ap-c	Feb-p	Mar-p	Apr-p
4600	.0405	.0270	....	.0030	.0160	....
4800	.0220	.0175	....	....	....	....
5000	.0110	.0105	....	.0135	....	....
5200	.0040	.0060	....	....	....	....
5400	.0020	....	....	....	....	....
5600	....	....	....	....	....	....

Est. vol. 201; Fri vol. 834 calls; 67 puts
Open interest Fri; 2,934 calls; 545 puts

–LIVESTOCK–

CATTLE-FEEDER (CME) 44,000 lbs.; cents per lb.

Strike	Calls–Settle			Puts–Settle		
Price	Jan-c	Mar-c	Apr-c	Jan-p	Mar-p	Apr-p
80	4.00	4.07	3.85	0.15	1.05	1.45
82	2.30	2.77	2.70	0.45	1.75	2.27
84	1.00	1.67	1.80	1.15	2.70	....
86	0.35	0.97	1.00	2.50	4.00	....
88	0.12	0.50	0.60	....	....	....
90	0.05	0.22	....	....	....	....

Est. vol. 630, Fri vol. 242 calls, 471 puts
Open interest Fri; 3,624 calls, 7,213 puts

CATTLE-LIVE (CME) 40,000 lbs.; cents per lb.

Strike	Calls–Settle			Puts–Settle		
Price	Feb-c	Apr-c	Jun-c	Feb-p	Apr-c	Jun-p
70	3.50	5.45	4.60	0.27	0.52	1.05
72	1.92	3.85	3.35	0.70	0.90	1.75
74	0.87	2.52	2.27	1.65	1.55	2.65
76	0.32	1.52	1.50	3.10	2.50	3.82
78	0.12	0.85	0.95	4.90	....	....
80	0.05	0.45	0.55	....	....	....

Est. vol. 3,459, Fri vol. 1,208 calls, 2,993 puts
Open interest Fri; 30,648 calls, 31,519 puts

HOGS–LIVE (CME) 30,000 lbs.; cents per lb.

Strike	Calls–Settle			Puts–Settle		
Price	Feb-c	Apr-c	Jun-c	Feb-p	Apr-p	Jun-p
42	4.42	4.00	....	0.15	0.82	0.40
44	2.70	2.65	....	0.42	1.40	0.80
46	1.35	1.70	4.85	1.02	2.40	1.27
48	0.62	1.10	3.70	2.35	....	2.10
50	0.30	0.65	2.70	....	....	....
52	0.12	0.35	1.85	5.85	....	....

Est. vol. 489, Fri vol. 380 calls, 171 puts
Open interest Fri; 5,139 calls, 2,991 puts

Source: *The Wall Street Journal*

Figure 8.4 A Sample of Published Commodity Futures Options Prices

On Tuesday, July 19, 1988, the Chicago Mercantile Exchange S&P 500 Futures Option contract with a strike price of 270 and September 1988 expiration had a settlement price of 8.95. (Each futures option contract is re-settled at $500 times the published futures option price.) Suppose the Wealthy Equity (WE) Fund, a fictional mutual fund, bought 20 of these futures options contracts on July 19 at the settlement price, and the July 20 settlement price turned out to be 9.10. The WE fund deposited the required initial margin. Assuming 100 percent variation, the WE Fund margin account would be credited on the morning of July 21 with the collect

$$\$500 \times (9.10 - 8.95) \times 20 = \$1,500.$$

Variation collects or pays would continue in this manner, crediting the WE Fund account whenever the futures option settlement price rises, and debiting the account whenever the futures option settlement price falls, until the futures option position is offset (by executing a sell order for 20 futures options contracts) or until the futures option contract expires.

Suppose the futures option premium settles at 14.00 on the day before expiration of the contract and that the underlying S&P 500 futures contract settles at 286.00 on the option expiration date (which need not be the futures delivery date). The futures option contract must therefore settle at 16.00 on the expiration date (the excess of the futures price 286.00 over the strike price of 270.00). If the WE Fund futures option position were held to expiration, it would be credited with the final day's change in the futures option premium, $16.00 - 14.00 = 2.00$, for a final collect of $\$500 \times 2.00 \times 20 = \$20,000$. The WE Fund would then automatically be assigned a futures position of 20 contracts (long).

As it happens, the S&P 500 Index Option traded on the Chicago Board Options Exchange, for September, 1988 expiration and the same 270.00 strike price, closed on July 19 at $8\frac{3}{4}$, a bit lower than the CME futures option premium of 8.95 for the same day. The discrepancy between the index option and futures option prices could be due to the resettlement features of the futures option. Of course, other institutional reasons could lie behind this price difference. To repeat, the actual futures option margin procedures of the CME, which are reviewed later in this section, are actually more complicated than suggested by this simple example.

Conventional versus Pure Futures Options

For the astute reader who has mastered the cost-of-carry formula in Chapter 5, the distinction between conventional and pure futures options may explain some of the excess of certain futures options prices over corresponding conventional option prices. The pure futures options price is (under the assumptions of the cost-of-carry formula) the forward price of the underlying option, which is the price of the underlying option multiplied by the payback on $1 borrowed risklessly until expiration. That is, if $O_{t,T}$ denotes the price at time t of a given conventional European option with expiration at T, and if the assumptions of the theoretical futures price apply (as stated in Chapter 5), then the corresponding pure futures option price is $O_{t,T}^F = B_{t,T} O_{t,T}$, where $B_{t,T} = 1/Z_{t,T}$ is the payback at time T per dollar invested at time t in riskless bonds maturing at T.

Examples of conventional options and futures options both traded on the same underlying asset can be gleaned from Appendix 9D. Some futures options have settlement procedures that are more like those of conventional options. The reader should consult a futures commodity merchant or other broker for the latest contract provisions before trading.

Example: (Futures Options Margins at the CME) The margin requirements of the CME for futures options are quite complicated, but we can summarize the provisions of the *Clearing House Manual of Operations* of the Chicago Mercantile Exchange as follows.

Margin requirements are based on three categories:

1. Clearinghouse margins, the amounts clearing members must deposit with the clearinghouse.

2. Floor trader margins, the amounts clearing firms must collect from members' accounts.

3. Public customer margins, the amounts to be collected from non-members.

As usual, the amounts required by the clearinghouse are minimums; firms may require more from their customers. Provided 50 percent of the account equity is owned by members, customer accounts are allowed to be treated much as those of members.

Clearinghouse margins (per option) are broken into two components: *equity margin* and a *risk factor component*. The equity component is merely the settlement futures option price, which is marked to market each day. The risk factor component is the *delta* of the option (a number between 0 and 1 which is defined in the following section) multiplied by a *Designated Dollar Amount (DDA)* which is usually the underlying futures margin. Long futures options positions are credited with the equity, while short positions are debited the equity. The delta of an option is roughly the amount the option price changes for each dollar change in the underlying futures price, which explains its role in the risk factor component of margins.

For example, suppose a clearing member sells one call option on Canadian dollars at the futures option settlement price, say 1.50 cents (U.S.) per \$100,000 (Canadian). (The underlying futures contract delivers 100,000 Canadian dollars.) The clearing firm receives the option premium, $\$0.015 \times 100,000 = \$1,500$. Suppose the delta of this option is 0.3 and the Designated Dollar Amount is the futures margin, say \$3,000. Then the clearing firm's margin account is debited the total amount $\$1,500 + 0.3 \times \$3,000 = \$2,400$. The total margin of any clearing firm in excess of \$25,000 can be replaced with Treasury bills, as explained in Chapter 3.

Suppose the futures option premium settles the following day at 0.012, and that the call's delta is re-calculated by the clearinghouse at 0.25 based on the new premium. The new total margin requirement is

$$\$0.012 \times 100,000 + 0.25 \times \$3,000 = \$1,950.$$

The reduction from the previous day in the total margin required, $\$2,400 - \$1,950 = \$450$, is credited to the clearing firm's margin account. The margin account is marked to market in this fashion until the position is offset or expiration.

If the clearing firm's futures option position had been long rather than short, the required margin at the original settlement price of 0.015 is the risk factor component of $0.3 \times \$3,000 = \$900$ less the equity value of the option, \$1,500. In this case, the net credit to the margin account is \$600, which can be applied to required margins on other positions. (As usual, however, the \$600 could not be applied to meet variation margins because, as explained in Chapter 3, variation margin must always be deposited in cash.) If, on the other hand, the delta of the option had been 0.6, then the risk factor component of $0.6 \times \$3,000 = \$1,800$ exceeds the equity margin, but no margin is required of a long option position in this situation.

Margin requirements for floor traders are much like those for clearing firms; we will not give any details here. Public customer margins, however, are quite different. The long merely pays the futures option premium in full. The short's position is marked to market according to changes in the futures option premium. The short must also deposit the futures margin for the underlying futures contract (whether speculative or hedge margin, as appropriate), less one-half of the amount by which the option is out of the money (for a call, any excess of the exercise price over the current futures price; for a put, any excess of futures price over the exercise price). Obviously, a short position, if *naked* (not covered by an offsetting futures or option position), is subject to much larger potential losses than a long position, explaining this difference in the treatments of longs and shorts. For spread positions (combinations of long and short option-futures or option-option positions), the requirements are more complicated, and we will not review them here.

3. PORTFOLIO INSURANCE

Figure 8.5 is a graph of the payoff of three hypothetical portfolios against the value S_T of the S&P 500 Index one year hence. The first portfolio, whose payoff is labeled "pure stock" and shown by the 45° solid line, is the payoff of the S&P 500 tracking portfolio, which is S_T itself. The current price of this tracking portfolio is the current S&P 500 Index, S_t. The horizontal dashed line in Figure 8.5 indicates the payoff of an investment of S_t dollars in one-year riskless bonds. The dotted line indicates the payoff of a portfolio made up of $S_t/2$ dollars' worth of the tracking portfolio of stocks and $S_t/2$ dollars' worth of the bonds. One can adjust the fraction of the portfolio held in stocks, with the remainder held in bonds, so as to generate an entire family of straight-line payoff functions. With fixed proportions, only straight-line payoffs of this sort are possible.

The remainder of this section describes a dynamic trading strategy called *portfolio insurance* that (under the right assumptions) produces a nonlinear payoff such as that shown in Figure 8.6. It has been claimed that such a payoff scheme is attractive to some investors in that it provides for limited losses and unlimited gains. The restrictions on investor risk attitudes consistent with the optimality of portfolio insurance, however, are quite severe, as shown in sources cited in the Notes.

Portfolio Insurance with Options

Based on the previous put-call parity calculations, we can construct the portfolio insurance payoff shown in Figure 8.6 using options in two obvious ways:

1. *Call Strategy*: Buy one European S&P 500 call option with exercise price K and expiration date T at the call price C_t. Invest $KZ_{t,T} - P_t$ in riskless bonds maturing at T. The total cost, according to the put-call parity formula (1), is the current index S_t.

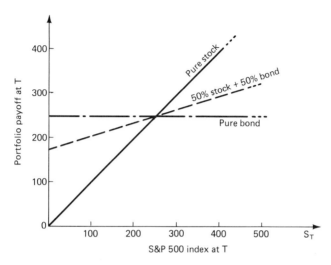

Figure 8.5   Fixed Stock-Bond Portfolio Payoffs

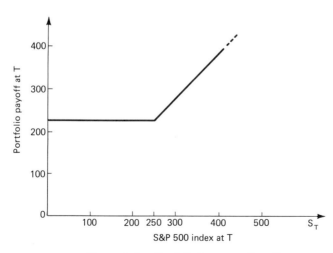

Figure 8.6   Portfolio Insurance Payoff

2. *Put Strategy*:   Invest S_t in the S&P 500 tracking portfolio, buy one
European S&P 500 put with exercise price K and expiration date T
at a cost of P_t, and borrow P_t risklessly until T.

As shown in Table 8.2, both these strategies generate the payoff plotted in
Figure 8.5; with put-call parity, both require an initial investment of the
current index, S_t.

TABLE 8.2   Portfolio Insurance: Option Strategy Payoffs

	Cost at t (at Parity)	Payoff at T $(B_{t,T} = 1/Z_{t,T})$	
		Case: $S_T \leq K$	Case: $S_T > K$
Strategy (1):			
Call Option	C_t	0	$S_T - K$
Bonds	$KZ_{t,T} - P_t$	$K - P_t B_{t,T}$	$K - P_t B_{t,T}$
Total	S_t	$K - P_t B_{t,T}$	$S_T - P_t B_{t,T}$
Strategy (2):			
Stock	S_t	S_T	S_T
Put Option	P_t	$K - S_T$	0
Bonds	$-P_t$	$-P_t B_{t,T}$	$-P_t B_{t,T}$
Total	S_t	$K - P_t B_{t,T}$	$S_T - P_t B_{t,T}$

Synthetic Portfolio Insurance

A method of obtaining portfolio insurance, or at least approximate portfolio insurance, that has been popular in the past among large equity fund
managers is *synthetic portfolio insurance*—a dynamic futures trading strategy that produces the payoff of a put option. The theoretical possibility of
such a strategy became apparent with the advent in 1973 of the Black-Scholes
option pricing formula, described in Appendix 8A. Although extensions of
the Black-Scholes model show that synthetic portfolio insurance is possible
under fairly general theoretical assumptions concerning price movements, it

is possible to solve for the appropriate futures strategy only under extremely restrictive assumptions, such as those described in Appendix 8A. Under these assumptions, let

- $N(x)$ denote the probability that a normally distributed random variable (with zero mean and variance equal to one) is less than x. (See Appendix 4D for a definition of normal random variables.)

- σ (sigma) denote the *volatility* of the annual return on the S&P 500 Index, or more precisely, the standard deviation of the continuously compounding annual S&P 500 return (this is the standard deviation of the log-price increment, $\log(S_T) - \log(S_t)$, where $T - t = 1$ year).

- r denote the (assumed constant) continuously compounding annual interest rate on riskless borrowing or lending.

How are these quantities $N(x)$, σ, and r estimated? Appendix 8B includes FORTRAN code for a simple and approximate method of computing $N(x)$, the cumulative normal distribution function; this is shown as a function subroutine named CUNORM. In order to estimate σ, the volatility parameter, one can use least squares estimates based on historical data, as discussed in Chapter 6, but a more common and perhaps more reliable method is to use the volatility implicit in options prices, as described in Appendix 8A. FORTRAN code for implied volatility, based on two different methods, is provided in Appendix 8B. One method calculates the implicit volatility of the *nearest-to-the-money option*, that option whose strike price is closest to the current price of the underlying asset. This method is popular because the Black-Scholes formula tends to be more accurate in practice for nearer-to-the-money options. The FORTRAN code for estimating the implicit volatility of any option is shown in Appendix 8B as the function subroutine XIMPVOL. The second method, coded as a function subroutine PIMPVOL, calculates a weighted average of the implicit volatilities of the various available options. The continuously compounding interest rate r can be estimated as

$$\widehat{r} = \frac{\log(10,000) - \log(\text{BILL}_t)}{T_m - t}, \tag{2}$$

where BILL_t denotes the current price of a $10,000 face-value T-bill whose maturity date T_m is close to the terminal date T of interest. [Equation (2) follows from Equation (2) of Chapter 5.]

Suppose there is also a futures contract whose delivery date is the same as the expiration date T of the option. Also, suppose the futures price is given by the theoretical forward price $f_t = e^{r(T-t)}S_t$. As it turns out, under the assumptions of the Black-Scholes model, the equivalent portfolio insurance options strategies (1 and 2) described above are also equivalent to a third dynamic strategy:

3. *Synthetic Portfolio Insurance Strategy*

    a. Invest S_t dollars in the S&P 500 portfolio

    b. At each time s between t and T adopt a futures position of

$$y_s = Z_{s,T}\Delta_s, \qquad (3)$$

    where

$$\Delta_s = N\left(\frac{\log(f_s/K)}{\sigma\sqrt{T-s}} + \frac{\sigma\sqrt{T-s}}{2}\right) - 1. \qquad (4)$$

    c. Borrow (lend) risklessly all resettlement losses (profits).

The term Δ, called the *delta* or, alternatively, the *hedge* of the put option with strike price K, is approximately the change in the put price for each dollar change in the underlying index S_t. (Formally, it is the derivative of the put price with respect to the current index S_t. Further details are given in Appendix 8A. A FORTRAN-coded subroutine function DELTA, shown in Appendix 8B, can be used to calculate Δ on a computer.) Thus, for any two times a and b that are close together, $P_a - P_b$ is approximately equal to $\Delta_b(S_a - S_b)$. It follows that, at time s, one could substitute a fraction Δ_s of the portfolio of stocks whose value tracks the index S_s in place of a portfolio consisting of a single put option, since these two portfolios have approximately the same changes in market value over short time intervals. Each time the index S_s changes appreciably, the corresponding Δ_s changes, so one would continually adjust the fraction Δ_s of the tracking portfolio held in order to maintain a trading strategy whose profits track those of the put option. This fact is actually the key to synthetic portfolio insurance.

Of course, it is not always practical to adjust a portfolio consisting of 500 different stocks every time the index S_s moves, but we know, under the assumptions of the theoretical futures price discussed in Chapter 5, that the current futures price at any time s is $f_s = S_s B_{s,T}$, where $B_{s,T} = 1/Z_{s,T}$ is the payback at time T per dollar invested at time s in riskless bonds maturing at T. Thus, rather than holding a fraction Δ_s of the index tracking portfolio, one could substitute with a futures position of $\Delta_s/B_{s,T} = \Delta_s Z_{s,T} = y_s$. (This would not work if the bond price process $Z_{s,T}$ is too risky. Here, we are assuming that there is no uncertainty in movements of $Z_{s,T}$.) This explains the portfolio insurance futures strategy y_s given by equation (3).

It can be seen that Δ_s is negative, implying a short futures position at all times, and also that Δ_s becomes more negative as the index S_s falls. (This is illustrated in in Figure 8.8 of Appendix 8A.) These properties of Δ imply that the synthetic portfolio insurance strategy sells futures in a falling stock market (and buys in a rising market). For this reason, portfolio insurance is accused of adding momemtum to the Stock Crash of October, 1987, as explained in Appendix 5B.

Appendix 8A provides an adjustment to the synthetic strategy (3) for cases in which the terminal date T of the strategy is not the delivery date of the futures contract.

Since the synthetic insurance strategy for producing portfolio insurance requires continuous adjustment of the futures position, a physical impossibility, it is common practice to adjust the futures position only when the theoretical futures position y_s prescribed by equation (3) moves sufficiently far away from the last established position. Interpretations of "sufficiently far" are based on such realistic factors as transactions costs. Because of this limitation on practical strategies, and because the theoretical model for price movements underlying equation (3) is far from exact, practical synthetic portfolio insurance strategies produce only an approximation to the payoff shown in Figure 8.6.

Of course, none of the calculations are specific to the S&P 500 Index contracts. The same principles apply to any market in which the Black-Scholes option pricing approach applies. One of the key assumptions of the Black-Scholes model is that the futures price f_t changes continuously, that is, if one plotted the index against time, there can be no gaps in the plot. If the futures price jumps discontinuously, or "gaps," as it is often expressed, then one cannot approximate the effect of the sudden change in the put price by gradually changing the futures position. For example, for the oil futures market, an announcement by OPEC of major changes in oil production quotas would cause the price of the New York Mercantile Exchange crude oil futures price to gap, creating a hazard for synthetic portfolio insurance. Although the stock price changes that occured during the Stock Crash of October 1987 were of unprecedented magnitude, the effect of gaps in the S&P 500 futures index was not so severe as to prevent certain funds from obtaining most of the theoretical protection offered by portfolio insurance. Many other users of synthetic portfolio insurance, however, did not adjust their futures positions quickly enough with falling stock prices to obtain even an approximation to the theoretical protection.

Given the transactions costs of frequently buying and selling futures, and the fact that one can only obtain an approximation to the payoff shown in Figure 8.6, why is the synthetic insurance strategy still an attractive alternative to the more direct call or put option strategies for portfolio insurance? Several reasons have been offered by those practicing portfolio insurance:

1. Futures contracts tend to be more liquid than options contracts, and therefore involve smaller market-impact transactions costs.

2. In principle, dynamic futures strategies can produce a much larger variety of effective exercise prices and expiration dates than the selection available directly on options markets.

3. Going even further, dynamic futures strategies can produce an unlimited variety of nonlinear payoff schemes that cannot be generated by fixed positions in options or futures alone.

The third reason pertains not to portfolio insurance itself, but to the general potential for producing payoff patterns tailor made to the risk attitudes and other specifications of individual investors. Some of these variants are treated in sources cited in the Notes. Appendix 5B discusses the role of portfolio insurance in the Stock Crash of 1987. As explained there, portfolio insurance has become much less popular since the Stock Crash of 1987. The basic principle, however, of using a dynamic futures strategy to adjust a portfolio's payoff pattern is still popular in many forms.

EXERCISES

8.1 (Put-Call Parity) For this exercise, use prices shown in the financial press for the first business day after the exercise is assigned. Use the CBOE S&P 500 index option prices and CME S&P 500 futures options prices for the third nearest expiration month. Take the call and put with the nearest exercise price above the current S&P 500 index. For interest rates, use the 90-day LIBOR rate. Ignore dividends and transactions costs.

(a) State the current index call and put option prices, C_t and P_t, the corresponding futures option prices, C_t^F and P_t^F, as well as the price

$Z_{t,T} = 1/B_{t,T}$ at time t per dollar return at the option expiration
date T, based on the LIBOR rate.

(b) State the amount by which the call price C_t exceeds the call option
price theoretically based on put-call parity.

(c) Assuming no transactions costs or arbitrage possibilities, show that,
if the futures option is a "pure " futures option in the sense of Section
8.2, then its price C_t^F satisfies the following put-call parity formula
for pure futures options: $C_t^F = S_t B_{t,T} + P^F - K$. Then check the formula against the actual prices. That is, state the amount by which
C_t^F exceeds its theoretical value according to this formula. (Hint:
Under the assumptions of the theoretical futures price, because pure
futures options are effectively forwards on the options, use the theoretical forward prices $C_t^F = C_t B_{t,T}$ and $P_t^F = P_t B_{t,T}$.)

8.2 (Black-Scholes Implicit Volatility)   Using the Black-Scholes formula (7)
for pure futures options provided in Appendix 8A, calculate the pure
futures call option price for delivery of crude oil (New York Mercantile
Exchange) at the third-out delivery month, taking the nearest available
exercise price above the current futures settlement price for that delivery
month. Use the 90-day LIBOR rate in order to calculate the continuously compounding interest rate r. Assume that the volatility parameter
σ is 0.40. Use a table (available in most statistics books) for the standard normal distribution function $N(\cdot)$, or use software such as that in
Appendix 8B. Use prices as reported in the financial press on the first
business day after this exercise is assigned. If the futures option price
you calculate is higher than that reported in the financial press for the
same futures option, decrease the assumed σ from 0.40 to 0.35, and re-
calculate the Black-Scholes price. Likewise, if the futures option price
you calculated is lower than the reported price, increase σ by 0.05 and
try again. Repeat this strategy until you find the value of σ that brings
the Black-Scholes formula closest to the reported futures option price,
obtaining the *Black-Scholes implicit volatility* $\bar{\sigma}$ to the nearest 0.05. This
is roughly the algorithm used in the implicit volatility program of Appendix 8B. (Of course, the computer can quickly achieve $\bar{\sigma}$ to the nearest
0.01.)

8.3 Draw the payoff curve, to be compared with that in Figure 8.6, for an
investment at time t in two parts: (i) $S_t/2$ (half the current S&P 500
Index) in the S&P 500 tracking portfolio, and (ii) $S_t/2$ invested in the
portfolio insurance strategy. By varying the fraction of a portfolio which

is "insured" in this manner, one can create a range of non-linear payoffs.

NOTES

The definitive reference on options is *Option Markets*, by Cox and Rubinstein (1985). A somewhat shorter book by Jarrow and Rudd (1983) is also recommended, and treats put-call parity with dividends. Further institutional information can be obtained from the books by from McMillan's (1986) and Gastineau (1988). The regulatory history of commodity options can be gleaned from Markham (1987). Details on the margin and resettlement provisions for futures options at the Chicago Mercantile Exchange can be found in Section 4 of the *Clearing House Manual of the Chicago Mercantile Exchange*. Fitzgerald (1987) points out that the resettlement procedures of the LIFFE futures options make them much like what we have called a pure futures option, in contrast with many U.S. futures options.

Black and Scholes (1973) are of course responsible for the Black-Scholes option pricing formula. Merton (1973) made central contributions to the development of the theory of option pricing. Rubinstein (1987) and Varian (1987) give simple expositional treatments of the ideas behind the Black-Scholes model. Some of the many theoretical developments of the Black-Scholes model are reviewed by Duffie (1988), which also provides a full definition of Brownian Motion supplanting the informal definition in Appendix 8A. Geske and Torous (1987) suggest a practical method for improving the estimation of the volatility parameter σ for option pricing. Black (1976) extended the Black-Scholes formula to options on futures. This formula was further studied by Ramaswamy and Sundaresan (1985), and further extended for futures options and other continually resettled claims by Duffie and Stanton (1988).

The issue of what risk attitudes imply the optimality of portfolio insurance is examined by Leland (1980) and Beninga and Blume (1985). Some practical questions concerning the feasibility of program trading are treated by Asay and Edelsberg (1986). Simplified or alternative forms of portfolio insurance are discussed by Perold and Sharpe (1987), Rubinstein (1985), Black and Jones (1987), Brennan and Schwartz (1987), and Grossman and Vila (1988a, 1988b). Some of the related issues in practical applications are treated by Hill and Jones (1988). Merton (1971) originated the approach to optimal continuous-time portfolio selection. Grossman (1988a, 1988b) provides a theoretical analysis of the implications of portfolio insurance for the

Appendix 8A: The Black-Scholes Option Pricing Formula

underlying asset volatility. A closely related alternative to portfolio insurance, *superhares* is collection of funds developed by Leland O'Brien Rubinstein to avoid some of the impact of portfolio insurance on stock markets that could occur in periods such as the Stock Crash of 1987. Based on concepts developed by Nils Hakansson, supershares are briefly described in *The Wall Street Journal*, November 30, 1988, and in "The Market Place" column of *The New York Times*, December 8, 1988.

Appendix 8A: The Black-Scholes Option Pricing Formula

This appendix briefly reviews the Black-Scholes option pricing formula and related concepts. FORTRAN codes for the required calculations are provided in Appendix 8B.

The Advent of Black-Scholes

In 1973, Fisher Black and Myron Scholes published their now-famous formula for the price of a call option, under assumptions to be described shortly. The assumptions were surprising at the time because they had nothing to do with investor risk attitudes, given the assumed behavior of the underlying asset prices. The formula is correct under its assumptions because if it were not, it would be possible to perform unlimited riskless arbitrage. The basic idea of the Black-Scholes assumptions are that:

1. Returns are normally distributed.

2. Returns during separate time periods are not correlated.

3. Returns have the same mean and standard deviation (risk) over any two time periods of equal length.

4. Traders are able to continually adjust their portfolios without transactions costs.

None of these assumptions (which are explained in more detail later in this appendix) is, strictly speaking, correct, but the formula works reasonably well and has revolutionized options markets and spawned offshoots such as portfolio insurance. The formula also allows one to estimate the volatility of the asset underlying the option, which is useful for other purposes. The concept and calculation of implied volatility are reviewed later in this appendix.

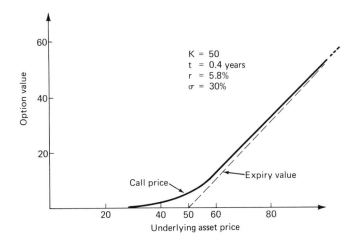

Figure 8.7   Black-Scholes Call Option Values

The Black-Scholes Formula

Under the assumptions of Black-Scholes, the price C of a European call option with exercise price K and T years remaining until expiration is

$$C = SN(h) - Ke^{-rT}N(h - \sigma\sqrt{T}),\qquad(5)$$

where

- for any number x, $N(x)$ is the probability that a standard normal (zero mean, unit variance) random variable is less than x.
- S is the current price of the underlying asset.
- r is the continuously compounding interest rate assumed to apply until expiration.
- σ (sigma) is the standard deviation of the continuously compounding annual return of the underlying asset.
- h is given by the formula

$$h = \frac{\log\left(e^{rT}S/K\right)}{\sigma\sqrt{T}} + \frac{\sigma\sqrt{T}}{2}.$$

Figure 8.7 shows the Black-Scholes price of a call option as a function of the underlying asset price, and also shows the expiration value of the call. The current option prices always lie above the expiration value.

Example: A European call option with four months to expiration ($T = 0.33$ years) on a stock selling at $S = \$40$ per share, with an exercise price of $K = \$40$, an interest rate of $r = 0.12$ (12 percent continuous compounding), and a volatility of $\sigma = 0.30$ (30 percent standard deviation per year), has the theoretical Black-Scholes value of $C = \$3.55$ from Equation (5).

Futures Option Prices

A pure futures option (that is, a contract that is marked to market in the manner of a futures contract) is effectively a futures contract delivering the underlying option on the expiration date T. Even if the underlying option is not traded, the theoretical value of the underlying option, $O_{t,T}$ at time t, is still that given by that Black-Scholes formula. Moreover, the same asumptions that produce the Black-Scholes formula allow one to assume that the underlying option is in fact traded, since its payoff can be synthesized with a dynamic futures strategy. Now, also assuming that the assumptions of the theoretical futures price formula developed in Chapter 5 apply to the futures option, we know that the arbitrage-free price of the pure futures option is $O_{t,T}^F = O_{t,T} B_{t,T}$. The Black-Scholes assumptions imply that $B_{t,T} = e^{r(T-t)}$, where r is the (assumed constant) continuously compounding interest rate. Taking the Black-Scholes call price C given by (5), for example (and substituting $T - t$ for the time remaining in the option), we have the Black-Scholes futures option price

$$C_{t,T}^F = e^{r(T-t)} C = e^{r(T-t)} S_t N(h) - K N(h - \sigma\sqrt{T-t}), \qquad (6)$$

where

$$h = \frac{\log(e^{r(T-t)} S_t / K)}{\sigma\sqrt{T-t}} + \frac{\sigma\sqrt{T-t}}{2}.$$

If there is in fact a futures contract delivering the underlying asset on the same expiration date T, we know that the current futures price is theoretically $f_{t,T} = e^{r(T-t)} S_t$, so based on (6) we can also write the somewhat simpler formula:

$$C_{t,T}^F = f_{t,T} N(h) - K N(h - \sigma\sqrt{T-t}), \qquad (7)$$

where

$$h = \frac{\log(f_{t,T}/K)}{\sigma\sqrt{T-t}} + \frac{\sigma\sqrt{T-t}}{2}.$$

The volatility parameter σ is always taken to be that of the underlying asset price. If the underling asset price is not readily observable (which is often the case in practice), one could subsitute the estimated volatility as measured from observations of the theoretical underlying asset price $S_t = f_{t,T}/B_{t,T}$.

If one is literally dealing with a conventional option on a futures contract (an option that is not marked to market), as opposed to a pure futures option, then formula (7) is not appropriate. If the expiration date of the option is the same as the delivery date of the futures, then the price of the conventional option is the same as the price of the option on the underlying asset. Otherwise, simple adjustments apply based on the theoretical futures price formula.

In practice, the margin procedures of (resettled) futures options would seem to make the actual futures option price some hybrid of:

1. the pure futures option price, that is, the futures price of a futures contract with cash settlement at $\max(f_T - K, 0)$ on the expiration date T (where f_T is the futures price on that date), and

2. the current price of a conventional option paying $\max(f_T - K, 0)$ on the expiration date T of the option.

Option Deltas

The *delta* of a particular option, denoted Δ, is useful knowledge for hedging purposes. Over short periods of time, holding one option is equivalent for purposes of risk and return to holding Δ shares of the underlying asset. Thus, for example, if the delta of a particular option is $\Delta = 0.25$, one can hedge 10 shares of the asset for a "short" period of time by holding $-10/\Delta = -40$ options during that period. For this reason, the delata of an option is often called the *hedge of the option*. Under the Black-Scholes assumptions, the delta of a call option is equal to $N(h)$, where N and h are defined with Equation (5). The delta of a put option is 1 minus the delta of the corresponding call option, as shown in Figure 8.8.

Option Gammas

The *gamma* of an option is the rate of change in the option's delta per unit change in the underlying asset price (formally, the derivative of the delta with respect to the asset price). The gamma (written as the Greek letter γ) is a measure of the sensitivity of the hedge to changes in the underlying asset price. For example, if $\gamma = 0.025$ and $\Delta = 0.20$, then an increase of $2 in the underlying asset price increases Δ by $2 \times 0.025 = 0.05$ to a new delta of 0.25, so

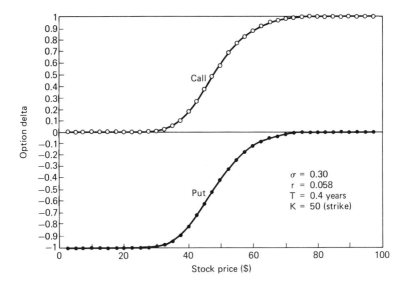

Figure 8.8   Black-Scholes Put and Call Option Deltas

a hedge for 10 shares of the underlying asset should be scaled down from -50 to -40 options. A gamma that is large in magnitude is therefore a warning that option hedging positions are relatively sensitive to the underlying asset price and should therefore be adjusted relatively frequently.

Gamma (as measured by the Black-Scholes method) is also useful as an indicator of whether the value of the option will go up or down in response to an unexpected increase in the volatility of the underlying asset. A positive gamma indicates that investing in the option is a "bet" in favor of greater volatility; a negative gamma is a bet in favor of lower volatility. Under the Black-Scholes assumptions, the gamma of a call is the same as the gamma of the corresponding put.

Theta

The *theta* (θ) of an option is the rate at which the option value decreases, other things being equal, as the time remaining to expiration decreases. In other words, θ is the derivative of the Black-Scholes option pricing formula with respect to the time until expiration. As the expiration date of the option approaches, the curve for the option price shown in Figure 8.7 drops down to the expiration value of the option shown in that figure. This is because the excess of the current option price over the expiration value (at the same underlying asset price) reflects the possibility that a random change in the underlying asset price will occur to the favor of an option holder. As the expiration date approaches, there is less and less time for such a favorable event to occur, and the option price declines, holding the price of the underlying asset fixed.

Implicit Volatility

Not surprisingly, other things being equal, an option is worth more if the volatility of the underlying asset is greater. Higher volatility increases the likelihood that the price of the underlying asset at expiration will be far away from the exercise price; a price far below makes no difference to the holder of a call option since the option need not be exercised; a price far above, however, is valuable to the call holder. This relationship, "higher volatility implies higher call price," works the other way as well: "higher call price implies higher volatility." The volatility of the underlying asset can in fact be measured in terms of the call price, under certain assumptions. Under the Black-Scholes assumptions, for example, the volatility σ (measured as the standard deviation of the continuously compounding annual return), is given as a continuous function

$$\sigma = V(C, S, K, r, T),$$

where, just as in the Black-Scholes option pricing formula, C is the call price, S is the underlying asset price, K is the exercise price, r is the continuously compounding interest rate, and T is the number of years to expiration. Since C, S, K, r, and T are all available from market data, we should be able to plug them into the function V to get the volatility σ. It is not quite that simple, however, since V can only be calculated by an iterative procedure that converges to the volatility σ after several rounds of calculations, which are typically done on a computer. The computer is usually programmed to stop once the procedure has come within, say, 1 percent of the correct value. A commonly used iterative procedure is used in the FORTRAN code for implicit volatility supplied in Appendix 8B. Of course, one can also obtain the volatility implied by the put option price in a like fashion.

If there are several options on the same underlying asset, with different strike prices and expiration dates, they would all have the same implied volatility σ if the Black-Scholes assumptions were all correct. Since these assumptions are not strictly correct, five different options, for example, will have five different implied volatilities, $\sigma_1, \sigma_2, \sigma_3, \sigma_4$, and σ_5. Which one should be believed? The usual practice is to calculate a weighted average

$$\overline{\sigma} = w_1 \sigma_1 + w_2 \sigma_2 + \cdots + w_5 \sigma_5.$$

The weights (w_1 through w_5) are usually larger for *closer-to-the-money options*, that is, for those options whose exercise prices are closer to the current underlying asset price. This practice is due to the fact that the Black-Scholes formula is typically more accurate for closer-to-the-money options. Some practitioners merely apply all of the weight to the closest-to-the-money option. This works roughly as well as more sophisticated weighting schemes, according to some of the finance literature. Some users take the average of the implicit volatilities of the nearest-to-the-money call and the nearest-to-the-money put. The weighting scheme used in the FORTRAN code for implicit volatility given in Appendix 8B uses weights proportional to the square of the derivative of the call option price with respect to the volatility parameter.

Example: (Volatilities of the S&P 500 Index) According to *Market Perspectives* (Volume 6, Number 8, October, 1988), a newsletter published by the Chicago Mercantile Exchange, the estimated volatility parameter σ for S&P 500 stock index based on historical observations over the previous 30 days was 34.4 percent as of September 1, 1988. This is the ordinary least squares estimate of the standard deviation of the ratio of consecutive stock indices, based on 30 observations. The estimate is multiplied by $\sqrt{252}$, on the basis of an assumption that the price moves on the (approximately) 252 business days of the year. Theoretically speaking, σ should be based on the logarithm of the ratio of consecutive days' prices, rather than on the ratio itself. As explained in Appendix 6D, however, for small periods (such as one day), the two standard deviations would be approximately the same over such a short time period.

The S&P 500 implied volatility as of the same date was 27.8 percent. This is the average of the implied volatilities (according to the Black-Scholes formula) of the nearest-to-the-money put and call. (See the *Market Perspectives* newsletter for more details.)

The maximum historical volatility estimate during the previous year was 123.3 percent, reached on November 23, 1987 (for a 30-day period shortly following the Stock Crash of 1987). The all-time high for the implicit volatility estimate is 95.1 percent, reached on October 26, 1987. Obviously, with sudden unexpected changes in volatility, the implicit volatility should react more quickly than the historical volatility estimate. On the other hand, the implict volatility is based on strong assumptions in addition to those required for the validity of the of the historical estimate (OLS conditions on asset returns).

Underlying Assumptions

The basis for the Black-Scholes formula for an option's price is the existence of a strategy for continually trading the asset underlying the option, in combination with riskless borrowing and lending, that replicates the payoff of the option. Unless the price of the option is the same as the initial investment required for the replicating strategy, arbitrage is possible. The assumption required of the underlying asset price process is that it has OLS log-price increments, but even more! We need a version of the OLS conditions that applies not only at given time intervals of a fixed length, but somehow continuously through time. This continuous-time version of the OLS conditions is called the *Brownian Motion* property. In a continuous-time setting, a stochastic process is a collection X of random variables, made up of one random variable $X(t)$ for each time t, whether t is an integer (whole number) or not. In rough terms, a stochastic process X is a Brownian Motion if, for any times $t_1, t_2, \ldots, t_n$ chosen in strictly increasing order, the *normalized increments* $Y_1, Y_2, Y_3, \ldots, Y_{n-1}$ are jointly normally distributed with zero means and satisfy the OLS conditions when defined by

$$Y_1 = \frac{X(t_2) - X(t_1)}{\sqrt{t_2 - t_1}}, \ Y_2 = \frac{X(t_3) - X(t_2)}{\sqrt{t_3 - t_2}}, \ \ldots, \ Y_{n-1} = \frac{X(t_n) - X(t_{n-1})}{\sqrt{t_n - t_{n-1}}}.$$

A more careful mathematical definition of Brownian Motion is given in a source cited in the Notes. In order for the Black-Scholes option pricing formula to apply to options on an asset with a price process S, we must assume that the stochastic process X defined by $X(t) = \log[S(t)] - at$ is a Brownian Motion for some constant a. (Indeed, this implies that S has OLS log-price increments at fixed time intervals, and even more.) We must also assume riskless borrowing or lending at some continuously compounding annual interest rate r, and no transactions costs. The volatility parameter σ (sigma) of the underlying asset is the standard deviation of a one-year log-price increment, $X_t - X_{t-1}$.

Replicating an Option by Trading Stock

Under the Black-Scholes assumptions, the security trading strategy required to produce the payoff of a call option is to hold at each time t until expiration a portfolio consisting of Δ_t units of the underlying asset and $C_t - \Delta_t S_t$ dollars' worth of short-term riskless lending, where Δ_t is the delta of the call option at time t, S_t is the price of the underlying asset at time t, and C_t is the option price at time t. Since Δ_t changes continuously with movements in the asset price S_t, this strategy is not practically implementable, but can be approximated by adjusting the asset position with some degree of frequency. By applying put-call parity, the corresponding put option payoff can be replicated by a strategy of holding $\Delta_t - 1$ units of the asset and $P_t - (\Delta_t - 1)S_t$ worth of short-term riskless lending, where P_t is the current price of a European put option with the same exercise price K and expiration date T. In principle, this again requires continual adjustment of the positions in asset and bond.

Replicating an Option by Trading Futures

If there is a futures contract on the underlying asset with delivery at some date $T' \geq T$, and the futures price follows the theoretical futures price formula $e^{r(T'-t)}S_t$, it is not hard to see that one can also replicate the call payoff by the continually adjusted futures position $e^{-r(T'-t)}\Delta_t$, with C_t invested in short-term riskless lending. Likewise, to replicate the put option payoff, one could adopt a continually adjusted futures position of $y_t = e^{-r(T'-t)}(\Delta_t - 1)$, always maintaining P_t worth of riskless bonds. This is the strategy shown in Section 8.3 as equation (3).

Appendix 8B: Black-Scholes FORTRAN Codes

This appendix includes all of the FORTRAN code required to estimate the various Black-Scholes quantities described in this chapter. The code was prepared by Stephen Fan under the direction of the author, and has been debugged and used. The package includes:

- CUNORM, which estimates the cumulative normal distribution function by a standard polynomial approximation found in Cox and Rubinstein (1985).

- XBS, the Black-Scholes option pricing formula.

- **DELTA**, the delta (Δ), or *hedge*, as it is sometimes called, of a call or put option.

- **GAMMA**, the gamma (γ) of an option.

- **THETA**, the theta (θ) of an option.

- **XIMPVO**, the implicit volatility (σ), using a Newton-Raphson numerical search.

- **PIMPVO**, the implicit volatility (σ) of a collection of options on the same underlying asset, weighted by the square of the derivative of the Black-Scholes formula with respect to the volatility (σ) parameter.

Code for Cumulative Normal Distribution Approximation

```
      Function CUNOM(d)
c
c     ***********************************************************
c     *   This function calculates the cumulative normal       *
c     *   distribution using a polynomial approximation         *
c     *   See Cox and Rubinstein (1985) for details.           *
c     ***********************************************************
c
c Assign values of constants of polynomial
c
      pi = 3.141516
      b1 = .319381530
      b2 = -.356563782
      b3 = 1.781477937
      b4 = -1.821255978
      b5 = 1.330274429
      a  = .2316419
c
      x  = 1./(1.+a*abs(d))
c
      cunom = 1. - 1./sqrt(2.*pi)*exp(-0.5*d**2)*
     *         (b1*x+b2*x**2+b3*x**3+b4*x**4+b5*x**5)
      if (d.lt.0.0) goto 200
      goto 300
  200 cunom = 1. - cunom
  300 return
      end
```

Code for Black-Scholes Option Pricing Formula

```fortran
      Function XBS(id,r,t,xk,s,sigma)
c
c     **************************************************
c     * This function calculates option price by      *
c     * Black-Scholes formula                          *
c     **************************************************
c     Variables:
c        id: 1 for call; 2 for put
c         r: riskless continuous compound interest rate
c         t: time remaining till expiration of the option in years
c        xk: striking price of the option
c         s: underlying asset (stock) price
c     sigma: volatility
c
c Check if CALL or PUT
c
      if (id.ne.1) goto 100
c
c Calculation for CALL option
c
c Calculate parameters d1,d2
c
      d1 = (alog(s/xk)+r*t)/(sigma*sqrt(t)) +
     *     0.5*sigma*sqrt(t)
      d2 = d1 - sigma*sqrt(t)
c
c Calculate the value of cumulative S.N.D. of d1 & d2
c
      xnd1 = cunom(d1)
      xnd2 = cunom(d2)
c
c Calculate CALL option price
c
      xbs = s*xnd1 - xk*exp(-r*t)*xnd2
      goto 1000
c
c Calculation for PUT option
c
c Calculate parameter d1,d2
c
  100 d1 = (alog(xk/s)-r*t)/(sigma*sqrt(t)) -
     *     0.5*sigma*sqrt(t)
      d2 = d1 + sigma*sqrt(t)
c
c Calculate the value of cumulative S.N.D. of d1 & d2
c
      xnd1 = cunom(d1)
      xnd2 = cunom(d2)
c
c Calculate PUT option price
c
      xbs = xk*exp(-r*t)*xnd2 - s*xnd1
 1000 return
      end
```

Code for Option Delta (Hedge)

```
      Function DELTA(id,r,t,xk,s,sigma)
c
c     ************************************************************
c     *  This function calculates value of 1st derivative of  *
c     *  Black-Scholes formula wrt stock price                *
c     ************************************************************
c     Variables:
c         id: option id: 1 for call, 2 for put
c          r: riskless continuous compound interest rate
c          t: time remaining till expiration of the option in years
c         xk: striking price of the option
c          s: underlying asset (stock) price
c      sigma: volatility
c
c
c Calculate parameter d1
c
      d1 = (alog(s/xk)+r*t)/(sigma*sqrt(t)) +
     *     0.5*sigma*sqrt(t)
c
c Calculate the derivative for CALL or PUT option
c
      if(id.eq.1) delta = cunom(d1)
      if(id.eq.2) delta = cunom(d1) - 1
c
      return
      end
```

Code for Option Gamma

```
      Function GAMMA(r,t,xk,s,sigma)
c
c     ************************************************************
c     *  This function calculates value of 2nd derivative of  *
c     *  Black-Scholes formula wrt stock price                *
c     ************************************************************
c     Variables:
c          r: riskless continuous compound interest rate
c          t: time remaining till expiration of the option in years
c         xk: striking price of the option
c          s: underlying asset (stock) price
c      sigma: volatility
c
c
      pi = 3.141516
c
c Calculate parameter d1
c
```

```
      d1 = (alog(s/xk)+r*t)/(sigma*sqrt(t)) +
     *      0.5*sigma*sqrt(t)
c
c Calculate the derivative
c
      gamma = 1./sqrt(2.*pi)*exp(-0.5*d1**2) *
     *        1./(sigma*s*sqrt(t))
c
      return
      end
```

Code for Option Theta

```
      Function THETA(id,r,t,xk,s,sigma)
c
c     ************************************************************
c     *  This function calculates the 1st derivative of         *
c     *  Black-Scholes formula wrt time                         *
c     ************************************************************
c     Variables:
c         id: option id: 1 for call, 2 for put
c          r: riskless continuous compound interest rate
c          t: time remaining till expiration of the option in years
c         xk: striking price of the option
c          s: underlying asset (stock) price
c      sigma: volatility
c
c
      pi = 3.141516
c
c Calculate parameter d1,d2
c
      d1 = (alog(s/xk)+r*t)/(sigma*sqrt(t)) +
     *      0.5*sigma*sqrt(t)
      d2 = d1 - sigma*sqrt(t)
c
c Check if CALL or PUT option
c
      if(id.ne.1) goto 100
c
c Calculate the derivative for CALL option
c
      theta = - 0.5*s*sigma/sqrt(t) *
     *          1./sqrt(2.*pi)*exp(-0.5*d1**2) -
     *          r*xk*exp(-r*t)*cunom(d2)
      goto 1000
c
c Calculate the derivative for PUT option
c
  100 theta = - 0.5*s*sigma/sqrt(t) *
     *          1./sqrt(2.*pi)*exp(-0.5*d1**2) -
     *          r*xk*exp(-r*t)*cunom(d2) +
```

```
        *        r*xk*exp(-r*t)
c
 1000 return
      end
```

Code for Option's Implicit Volatility

```
      Function ximpvo(id,op,r,t,xk,s,sig,tol)
c     *********************************************************
c     *  This function solves the implicit volatility of an  *
c     *  option for Black-Scholes formula using Newton-       *
c     *  Raphson method                                       *
c     *********************************************************
c     Variables:
c        id: 1 for call; 2 for put
c        op: option prices
c         r: riskless continuous compound interest rate
c         t: time remaining till expiration of the option in years
c        xk: striking price of the option
c         s: underlying asset (stock) price
c        sig: first guess of volatility
c        tol: tolerance of convergence for implicit volatility
c
      pi = 3.141516
      kk = 0
      sigma1 = 0.0
c
c First guess of volatility
c
      sigma = sig
c
c Calculate the derivative of B-S formula wrt sigma
c
  100 d1 = (alog(s/xk)+r*t)/(sigma*sqrt(t)) +
     *     0.5*sigma*sqrt(t)
      fx = s*sqrt(t)/sqrt(2.*pi)*exp(-0.5*d1**2)
c
c Calculate the error of first guess of sigma
c
      bs = xbs(id,r,t,xk,s,sigma)
      err = bs - op
c
c Check if the guessed volatility acceptable
c
      dsigma = sigma - sigma1
      if (abs(err).le.tol.and.abs(dsigma).le.tol)
     *   goto 1000
c
      sigma1 = sigma
      sigma = sigma - (err/fx)
      kk = kk+1
      go to 100
```

```
c
c Return final acceptable implicit volatility value
c
 1000 ximpvo = sigma
c
      return
      end
```

Code for Implicit Volatility of a Collection of Options

```
      Function pimpvo(n,id,op,r,t,xk,s,sig,tol)
c     ************************************************************
c     * This subroutine calculates implicit volatility of        *
c     * a portfolio of options of the same underlying stock      *
c     * ---weighted according to (dBS/dSIGMA)**2                  *
c     ************************************************************
c     Variables:
c        id: 1 for call; 2 for put
c        op: option prices
c         r: riskless continuous compound interest rate
c         t: time remaining till expiration of the option in years
c        xk: striking price of the option
c         s: underlying asset (stock) price
c       sig: first guess of volatility
c       tol: tolerance of convergence for implicit volatility
c
c
      dimension op(n),xk(n),id(n),t(n)
c
c Initialization
c
      pi = 3.141516
      wsig = 0.0
      wsum = 0.0
c
      do 1 i=1,n
c
c Calculate impicit volatility for individual option
c
      sigma = ximpvo(id(i),op(i),r,t(i),xk(i),s,sig,tol)
      write(5,100) i,sigma
      write(24,100) i,sigma
  100 format(1x,' sigma(',i1,') = ',f10.3)
c
c Calculate weight for each option
c    Weighted according to (dBS/dSIGMA)**2
c
      d1 = (alog(s/xk(i))+r*t(i))/(sigma*sqrt(t(i))) +
     *     0.5*sigma*sqrt(t(i))
      w = s*sqrt(t(i))/sqrt(2.*pi)*exp(-0.5*d1**2)
      w = w**2
c
```

```
c Sum up weighted sigma and weights so far
c
      wsig = wsig + w * sigma
      wsum = wsum + w
c
    1 continue
c
c Calculate weighted implicit volatility
c
      pimpvo = wsig/wsum
c
      return
      end
```

9

REGULATION
AND DESIGN OF FUTURES

This chapter reviews the basic regulatory structure of futures markets, as well as the design of futures contracts. As an example of contract design, the chapter includes a description of the the U.S. Treasury bond futures contract of the Chicago Board of Trade. Appendices A–C review, respectively, the Silver Crisis of 1980, design problems responsible for the demise of the GNMA (Ginnie Mae) CDR futures contract, and a simple model of optimal contract innovation by exchanges. Appendix D is a summary of currently traded futures and related options contracts, while Appendix E lists the world's futures exchanges and clearinghouses.

1. OVERVIEW

The story of futures markets is one of entrepreneurs pursuing an economic advantage by organizing the forward exchange of commodities and financial instruments, subject to the oversight of government agencies acting on behalf of the public. Why are certain futures markets organized and not others? What determines the provisions of a futures contract and how are these provisions enforced? When do the interests of a futures exchange run counter to those of the public? What is the regulatory structure to be imposed? These are some of the issues to be faced here.

Exchange and Social Incentives

The members of a futures exchange have three basic incentives for making a particular contract available for trade. *First*, some exchange members are at risk on related spot markets and benefit from the availability of insurance at competitive prices. *Second*, some members can expect to profit from

Chapter Outline

speculative positions taken on their own accounts, perhaps via superior technical or fundamental market analysis. *Third*, and of mounting relative importance, many members of an exchange profit from the provision of transactions services to the public at large. Brokerage profits can be direct commission charges, or can also accrue to traders that make a market by taking positions on their own accounts, absorbing imbalances in outside order flow. For this reason there is a natural incentive to open markets that will be "popular," that is, have a high volume of trade.

It is generally believed that the public can benefit in at least the following essential ways from the introduction of a futures contract. *First*, just as do exchange members, many members of the public can benefit from the availability of insurance markets: hedgers can reduce their risk; speculators (by which we mean those not trading principally for risk reduction) expect to profit, on average in return for bearing the risk. *Second*, futures markets can amalgamate and promulgate diversely held information on spot market conditions. For example, production, consumption, product pricing, and investment decisions can often be improved by learning the information impounded in related futures prices. There is a strong incentive—trading profits—for this information to be gathered, analyzed, and impounded. This second, *price discovery* role of futures markets is not easily modeled, but is widely agreed to be important. *Third*, because of the efficient institutional structure of futures markets, a futures position can act as a proxy for a spot market position, often with better liquidity and lower transactions costs. An example is the use of stock index futures for portfolio insurance, asset allocation, and related purposes.

It is also known that, under special circumstances, the public might be made worse off by the introduction of a futures market. Hart (1975), for example, shows a pathological example in which every agent is made worse off by *innovation*, the introduction of a new futures contract. Generally, however, one should expect that many agents will be made better off by innovation, while some, perhaps, will be made worse off. This makes regulatory policy difficult, especially since the effects of innovation are not well modeled or understood. Basically, government policy has been to "let the market decide," and to step in mainly in order to prevent manipulation (*corners* and *squeezes*), to inhibit fraud, and to limit "disruptive" effects on spot markets. Justification of regulatory policy and the form it should take are heavily contested issues.

Contract Design Features

Aside from the choice of commodity type and delivery dates, a futures exchange has many design features at its disposal, including:

1. *Delivery provisions*, which include an array of timing, location, and substitution options, or cash settlement provisions.

2. *Trading rules*, such as trading hours, choice of auction format, and privileges for various trader designations.

3. *Price limits*, daily maximum and minimum futures prices.

4. *Quantity limits*, especially on speculators' positions.

5. *Margin requirements*, for clearing and customer accounts, by account category.

Each of these design features plays a significant role in determining the popularity (or trading volume) and integrity of futures contracts. Aside from margin requirements, each of these contract design features are subject to the approval of the CFTC. An exchange (subject to approval of the CFTC) also has an important measure of flexibility in the overall design of the market: its auction format, physical layout, location, committee structure, clearing procedures, arbitration process, information dissemination, and so on.

2. REGULATORY FRAMEWORK

Futures market regulations in the United States have taken several basic forms:

1. *Registration of market participants*, including the exchanges themselves, traders, futures commodity merchants (FCMs), and associated persons.

2. *Approval of new contracts*, including some of the design features mentioned above.

3. *Mandatory risk disclosure*, intended to ensure that public customers understand the nature of their contracts.

4. *Enforcement, arbitration, and reparation provisions*, including legal authority to impose penalties and to initiate, prosecute, and adjudicate legal cases.

Legislative Background

The Chicago Board of Trade was established in 1859 under an Illinois state charter. Until the (federal) Cotton Futures Trading Act of 1914, government regulation of futures trading occurred at the state level; some states banned futures trading during some periods. The centerpiece of futures market regulatory legislation is the *Commodity Exchange Act (CEA)*, the new name given in 1936 to the *Grain Futures Act* of 1922. Historically the responsibility of the U.S. Department of Agriculture, futures legislation was principally directed toward agricultural commodities until the 1970s. A key development was the establishment in 1974 of the Commodity Futures Trading Commission (CFTC), under an amendment to the CEA. The CFTC was given exclusive jurisdiction over trade on all organized U.S. futures markets, with authority to approve, disapprove, or amend rules and regulations of commodity exchanges relating to futures contracts, except for the regulation of margins, which was left to the exchanges themselves. The CFTC was also given emergency powers, and among other powers, authority:

1. To seek redress in the courts.

2. To impose fines.

3. To review disciplinary and membership decisions of exchanges.

4. To oversee arbitration and reparations procedures for customer complaints.

5. To establish and register self-regulatory organizations of futures market participants, or *registered futures associations*, the primary example being the *National Futures Association*.

6. To establish several classes of *registrants*, including *associated persons of FCMs, commodity trading advisors, commodity pool operators*, and (with the *Futures Trading Act of 1978*), *introducing brokers, associated persons of commodity trading advisors*, and *associated persons of commodity pool operators*.

7. With the Futures Trading Act of 1978, to develop an industry fee system to offset regulatory costs.

As an independent commission of the federal government, the CFTC has a staff organized into the following divisions:

- *Trading and Markets Division*, in charge of regulating the "boards of trade" (the statutory term for exchanges), auditing, and registration.

- *Enforcement Division*, responsible for legal action either in the courts or directly before the CFTC.

- *Division of Economic Analysis*, which supports the CFTC with economic research.

The responsibilities and histories of these divisions of the CFTC are outlined by Markham (1987).

With the introduction of financial futures (beginning in 1972 with the approval of foreign currency futures, followed quickly by new futures contracts for Treasury bills and Government National Mortgage Association certificates), a number of U.S. government bodies expressed jurisdictional rights over some aspects of futures trading. Chief among these were the Securities and Exchange Commission (SEC), the Federal Reserve Board (Fed), and the U.S. Treasury Department (Treasury). Just after the approval of the GNMA futures contract, the SEC chairman, Roderick Hills, wrote to the

CFTC chairman, William Bagley, stating his concern that the CFTC and SEC had overlapping jurisdictions, principally over contracts for the delivery of securities, the domain of the SEC. Hills expressed reservations about the effects of financial futures contracts on markets for the underlying securities. In a well known memorandum, Bagley responded by emphasizing that the legislated jurisdiction of the CFTC over futures trading supersedes that of other state and federal authorities. Federal Reserve and Treasury officials expressed concern over the effect on spot markets of trading in futures for the delivery of U.S. government debt instruments; they were, respectively, worried about the potential impact on monetary policy and on the ability of the U.S. government to finance its debt. The Federal Reserve is also empowered to establish limits on the purchase of stocks on margin. Both the SEC and the Federal Reserve were concerned about potential destabilization of stock markets with the introduction of stock index futures, particularly without margin regulations. (The CFTC does not regulate futures margins, which are conceptually quite different from stock margins. Stock margins are a form of down payment; futures margins are a form of collateral.)

Studies were undertaken, compromises were made, and some concerns were allayed. Further amendments to the CEA in the Futures Trading Act of 1982 re-emphasized the jurisdiction of the CFTC over all organized futures trading, and required that the CFTC inform and seek the views of the SEC, the Treasury, and the Fed of any CFTC activities relating to their respective jurisdictions. In some cases (for example, on the question of margins and the authority of the Federal Reserve), the SEC, Fed, and Treasury have reserved their respective jurisdictional rights to act, though they have rarely done so. The SEC was also given effective veto power at this time over approval of new security (stock or bond) index futures contracts, based on three criteria:

1. The contract must settle in cash.

2. The contract must not be susceptible to manipulation.

3. The underlying index must reflect the market for all or a substantial segment of publicly traded equity or debt securities.

In splitting the potential markets for financial futures and options into the jurisdictions of the SEC and CFTC, it was legislated that the SEC would regulate options on securities other than futures, foreign currencies (traded on a domestic exchange), and stock groups or indices. The CFTC was to regulate futures, as well as options on futures, on "exempted securities" (such as GNMA certificates but not including municipal securities), certificates of deposit, "broad-based" groups of stocks (or stock indices), and options on foreign currencies that are not traded on a domestic exchange.

A number of incidents, such as the Silver Crisis of 1980 (see Appendix 9A) and the Stock Crash of 1987 (see Appendix 5B), have focused further scrutiny on the regulatory ability of the CFTC. There has even been speculation in the press that the CFTC will eventually be eliminated and its powers assumed by the SEC (which is seen as having a significantly less laissez-faire attitude than the CFTC), or that the Fed will become a supervisor of the functions of both the SEC and the CFTC, as recommended in the Brady report on the Stock Crash of 1987 (Appendix 5B). Although the Fed has expressed a lack of interest in assuming such a role, in a controversial move the SEC voted in May, 1988 to apply to Congress for regulatory authority over all stock index futures. At this writing, however, there is no sign of action in these directions, and the CFTC remains the principal regulator of U.S. futures markets.

Many more details on the history and jurisdictional structure of futures market regulation, including coverage of British futures markets, can be found in sources cited in the Notes.

Self-Regulation

Futures exchanges and futures commodity merchants, acting individually and collectively, themselves adopt many procedures that limit manipulation, inhibit fraud, and promote the stability and integrity of futures and related markets. As these are also regulatory goals, the term *self-regulation* has been applied. This term may seem inappropriate since exchanges and FCMs clearly make choices in their own interests, whether to promote the volume of trade in a particular contract by guaranteeing its integrity, or to garner the commercial value of a long-term reputation for financial soundness and fair treatment of the public. In these terms, any firm selling a level of quality in its products is "self-regulating." Presumably, "regulation" in fact refers to legal limits on economic agents that might otherwise act against the public interest.

In addition to controls exercised by exchanges and FCMs over their own activities, the *National Futures Association (NFA)*, a private-membership association established and registered by the CFTC, sets standards and conducts tests for the registration of various types of professionals working in the futures industry. The NFA has four registration categories:

1. Futures commodities merchants
2. Introducing brokers

3. Commodity pool operators

4. Commodity trading advisors

The NFA also registers associated persons with respect to these categories. As with other professional associations, membership in the NFA conveys the benefits accruing to those who can claim to be subject to the rules and disciplinary powers of the association. NFA rules cover advertising, account handling, order execution, and accounting. Penalties currently include fines of up to $100,000 and loss of membership. Customers of the futures industry can obtain compensation for violation of NFA rules through arbitration procedures governed by the NFA.

Justifying Regulation

Well-known economic principles show that, under specified general conditions, free market competition leads to an efficient allocation of resources. By *efficient*, we mean that no other feasible resource allocation mechanism can make every agent at least as well off, and some better off. This focuses attention on two situations in which regulation may (or may not) be justified in order to correct or reduce inefficiencies:

1. The conditions implying the efficiency of competitive markets need not actually apply.

2. Some agents do not behave competitively (take the formation of prices as given), but rather attempt to manipulate prices.

One may also consider the broad philosophical question: "Is the mere efficiency of a free market allocation a sufficiently strong reason not to interfere?" It suffices here to say that justice, equity, and individual freedom and rights are additional goals that are sometimes difficult to reconcile with one another or with efficiency. In any case, even if a free market allocation of resources is not efficient, it is far from granted that regulations are philosophically justified or can improve the allocation. Regulations are themselves costly, and sometimes correct one source of inefficiency or injustice while causing several others. As we continue in this chapter, we will come across cases in which one or both of the potential justifications for regulation listed above may apply. Readers interested in the "conditions" sufficient for the efficiency of competitive markets may consult sources mentioned in the Notes.

3. DELIVERY OPTIONS

Perhaps the most important design feature of a futures contract is the available set of delivery options. Assuming the short is allowed to choose among the available grades, locations, and delivery times, and does so rationally, the short will meet the delivery requirements of the futures contract in the cheapest possible manner. The futures price before delivery must therefore reflect this option to make the cheapest possible delivery, rather than reflecting the standard default delivery.

Example: Suppose a particular wheat futures contract allows substitution of Number 2 hard wheat in Kansas City for the standard Number 2 soft wheat in Chicago. If hard wheat in Kansas City can be delivered at \$3.31 per bushel, while delivering soft wheat in Chicago costs \$3.34 per bushel, then the short will clearly opt for the hard wheat delivery in Kansas City. The futures price at delivery would then be \$3.31, or else arbitrage may be possible. If the contract specifies, however, that substitution of the hard wheat in Kansas City occurs at a discount of 4 cents per bushel off the futures price at delivery, then the short will prefer to deliver soft wheat in Chicago, since the hard is only 3 cents per bushel cheaper than the soft. In this case, the futures price at delivery would be \$3.34, the price of the cheapest-to-deliver. (The effective price of the hard is \$3.31 plus the loss of 4 cents per bushel as a substitution cost.) Finally, if the soft were selling instead at \$3.36 per bushel at delivery, then the short would deliver the hard, incur the substitution discount of 4 cents per bushel, and the futures price at delivery would be \$3.31 + \$0.04 = \$3.35 per bushel. Weeks or months before delivery, the current futures price reflects market expectations of what the cheapest-to-deliver grade and location will be at the delivery date.

Among other effects, delivery options can reduce the ability of the contract to hedge the risk faced by those with spot market commitments in the standard delivery grade. Appendix 9B, for example, relates how the delivery option on the GNMA (Ginnie Mae) CDR futures contract was ultimately responsible for the demise of that contract. The cheapest-to-deliver grade under the terms of the GNMA futures contract was qualitatively so much different from the standard deliverable grade that, for the bulk of GNMA hedgers, the GNMA futures contract was inferior to the U.S. Treasury bond futures contract.

If delivery options complicate the valuation of a futures contract and tend to degrade the hedging quality of the contract for the "standard" hedger, why are these options written into the contract? A futures contract without delivery options forces the short to draw from a single narrowly defined stock of assets in order to make delivery. If the spot market for this particular type of asset is small, there is the potential for manipulation, such as a *corner*, in which effectively all of the asset is controlled by a single agent or group of agents acting collusively, or a *short squeeze*, in which enough of the deliverable is held off the spot market to prevent the short from obtaining the required deliverable except at an exorbitant price. Appendix 9A reviews what is usually described as an attempt by the Hunt brothers to corner the silver market, an attempt that culminated in the Silver Crisis of 1980. Presumably, a futures exchange, perhaps influenced by the contract approval authority of the CFTC, feels that offering the short the option to substitute with grade, location, or time enlarges the pool of deliverable assets enough to inhibit manipulation. In some cases, delivery substitutions may also increase hedging interest in the contract by providing a better hedge for spot commitments in the substitution grades. Finally, delivery options make it more convenient to deliver against the contract for shorts who have access to a substitution grade, or who have stockpiles in an alternate delivery location.

4. THE CBOT T-BOND FUTURES CONTRACT DESIGN

The basic provisions of the U.S. Treasury Bond Futures Contract of the Chicago Board of Trade (CBOT) are summarized in Table 9.1. Since this is currently the world's most popular futures contract in terms of volume of trade (presently running at over 200,000 contracts per day and $5 trillion per year), and since it has a rich set of delivery options, it makes for an excellent case study of contract design and, in particular, delivery options. A U.S. Treasury bond is a security obligating the U.S. government to pay the bondholder semiannual interest payments fixed in advance as half the *coupon rate* of the bond, plus the face value of the bond at maturity (when the coupon payments cease). Futures contracts delivering U.S. T-bonds are currently traded on the Chicago Board of Trade, the MidAmerica Commodity Exchange (MCE), and the London International Financial Futures Exchange (LIFFE). As stated in Table 9.1, the CBOT T-Bond Futures Contract calls for delivery of a $100,000 face-value U.S. Treasury bond bearing an 8 percent coupon and having at least 15 years remaining until maturity or *first call*, the first time the issuer (in this case, the U.S. Department of the Treasury)

TABLE 9.1   The CBOT U.S. Treasury Bond Contract

Trading Unit	$100,000 face value U.S. Treasury bonds
Deliverable Grade	U.S. Treasury bonds maturing at least 15 years from the first day of the delivery month, if not callable; if callable, not so for at least 15 years from the first day of the delivery month. Coupon based on an 8 percent standard.
Delivery Method	Federal Reserve book entry wire transfer system.
Price Quotation	In points ($1,000) and thirty-seconds of a point: for example, 80–16 equals $80\frac{16}{32}$.
Tick Size	One thirty-second of a point, or $31.25 (one tick) per contract.
Daily Price Limit	3 points ($3,000) per contract above or below the previous day's settlement price.
Contract Months	March, June, September, and December.
Trading Hours	8:00 a.m.–2:00 p.m. (Chicago time), Monday through Friday. Evening trading hours are from 5:00–8:30 p.m. (Central Standard time), or 6:00–9:30 p.m. (Central Daylight Saving time), Sunday through Thursday.
Last Trading Day	Seven business days prior to the last business day of the delivery month.
Last Delivery Day	Last business day of the delivery month.
Ticker Symbol	US

Source: *1988 Contract Specifications*, Chicago Board of Trade

has the option of canceling its obligation to the bondholder by returning the face value of the bond. The short does, however, have the following delivery options:

1. *Quality option*: the option to substitute T-bonds of other coupon rates at a price adjustment to be explained shortly.

2. *Accrued interest option*: the option to make delivery on any trading day during the delivery period, with a correction for accrued interest to be explained shortly.

3. *End-of-month option*: the option to deliver during the last seven business days of the month (when the futures have ceased trading) at a price based on the last futures settlement price.

4. *Wild card option*: the option to decide, at any time from 2:00 p.m.

to 8:00 p.m. (Chicago time) whether to announce an intention to deliver at the price established that day at 2:00 p.m.

Our discussion of these delivery options is based on the more detailed analyses of Gay and Manaster (1986), Cheng (1987), Carr (1987), Hemler (1988), and Broadie and Sundaresan (1987). Each of the delivery options is a benefit to the short that, rationally speaking, is accounted for in the futures price at and before delivery. Whether or not the value of these options is properly reflected in the futures price has been a matter of much analysis. We will explain the basic provisions of each of these delivery options in turn. More details can be obtained from the above-mentioned sources and other sources indicated in the Notes.

The T-Bond Quality Option

The *invoice price* of a delivered bond is the amount the long is billed, and the short is paid, for the bond actually delivered against the futures contract. The terms of the T-bond futures contract allow the short to deliver a T-bond (having a maturity or first call of at least 15 years) at any coupon rate. Neglecting the other delivery provisions for the present, the invoice price on a delivery date T for a T-bond of coupon rate R and maturity M is $c_T(R, M)f_T$, where f_T is the futures settlement price on the delivery date and $c_T(R, M)$ is the *conversion factor* for such a bond. The conversion factor $c_T(R, M)$ is the price per dollar of face value of a bond yielding 8 percent compounding semiannually with coupon rate R and maturity date M.

Example: Consider the U.S. T-bond with a 10 percent coupon rate that matures in May 2005. Suppose the bond is currently selling at 103-19 (bid), 103-23 (ask), meaning that the bond can be bought at $103\frac{19}{32}$ percent of face value ($103,593.75) or sold at $103\frac{23}{32}$ percent of face value ($103,718.75). This price represents a yield of 9.54 percent, calculated on a semiannual compounding basis. The conversion factor $c_T(R, M)$ can be calculated by discounting the semiannual coupon payments of 5 percent (5 cents per dollar face value), and the principal payment ($1) at the maturity date May 2005, using a discount factor of 1.04^t (8 percent on a semiannual basis) for payments t half-years away. If today is May 1989, exactly 16 years before maturity (with the current coupon having just been paid), we have

$$c_T(R, M) = \frac{0.05}{1.04} + \frac{0.05}{1.04^2} + \cdots + \frac{0.05}{1.04^{32}} + \frac{1.00}{1.04^{32}} = 1.17961.$$

If the current futures settlement price is 85-21, meaning $f_T = \$85,656.25$ per bond, then the invoice price for the 10 percent bond of May, 2005 would be

$$c_T(R, M)f_T = 1.17961 \times \$85,656.25 = \$101,040.72,$$

which is less than the current market price of the bond itself, implying that delivery of this particular bond against the futures contract is not currently profitable.

If every bond were actually priced in the market to yield 8 percent, the quality option would be worthless to the short. The futures price at delivery would be $\$100,000$ and the price $S_T(R, M)$ of the bond with maturity date M and coupon rate R would be $\$100,000 \times c_T(R, M)$. The short would pay $S_T(R, M)$ for the deliverable bond and collect the invoice price

$$c_T(R, M)f_T = c_T(R, M) \times \$100,000 = S_T(R, M),$$

for a zero delivery profit. If, in this situation of "perfect" conversion factors, the delivery futures price f_T were other than $\$100,000$, an obvious arbitrage would be possible. For example, if f_T is less than $\$100,000$, one can buy T-bonds and deliver them immediately against simultaneously executed off-setting short futures positions for a riskless profit.

Of course, not every bond is actually priced to yield 8 percent, so we know that $S_T(R, M)$ is not equal to $\$100,000 \times c_T(R, M)$ for every coupon rate R and maturity M, since the yield curve is not flat at exactly 8 percent. If we number the deliverable bonds 1 through n, and let R_i and M_i denote the coupon rate and maturity date of the i-th bond, respectively, then the delivery profit to the short delivering bond number i is

$$Y(i) = c_T(R_i, M_i)f_T - S_T(R_i, M_i).$$

The short makes the optimal delivery by choosing that bond i^* with the maximum delivery profit $Y(i^*)$. Again, in order to prevent arbitrage at delivery, it must be the case that the delivery profit $Y(i^*)$ is zero (neglecting transactions costs), so we know that, if there is no arbitrage,

$$\max_i Y(i) = Y(i^*) = c_T(R_{i^*}, M_{i^*})f_T - S_T(R_{i^*}, M_{i^*}) = 0. \qquad (1)$$

We can solve (1) for the futures price f_T, obtaining the formula

$$f_T = \min_i \; \frac{S_T(R_i, M_i)}{c_T(R_i, M_i)} = \frac{S_T(R_{i^*}, M_{i^*})}{c_T(R_{i^*}, M_{i^*})}. \qquad (2)$$

(We will later correct this formula for accrued interest.)

Before delivery, of course, it is unknown which bond i^* will be the cheapest to deliver since the yield curve changes unpredictably. Advanced techniques, however, can be used to estimate the market value at any time before delivery of the short's option to select i^*, at least under certain statistical assumptions on interest rate movements. The results of Hemler (1988) and Carr (1987) are the latest available at this time. Under their assumptions, one can calculate the theoretical futures price at any time before delivery. According to Hemler (1988), as many as 19 different issues of U.S. T-bonds have been delivered during a single delivery period; this occurred in March 1986. Figure 9.1 shows the average coupon rate and average time to maturity of the issues delivered during each delivery period from December, 1977 through June, 1986.

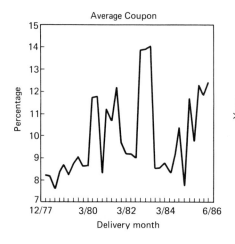 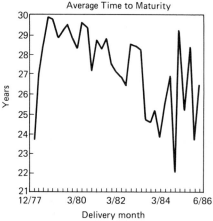

Figure 9.1(a) Average Coupon   **Figure 9.1(b)** Average Maturity

Source: Hemler (1988).

Figure 9.1   Bonds Delivered Against the CBOT T-Bond Futures Contract

In order to give the reader some idea of the magnitude of the quality option, Figure 9.2(a) shows the excess at the futures delivery date of the price of the bond that would have been the optimal issue to deliver three months earlier over the price of the cheapest-to-deliver bond at the futures delivery date. Figure 9.2(b) shows the corresponding option payoff with the originally chosen bond picked six months before delivery. The option payoff shown in Figure 9.2(a) is typically higher than that of Figure 9.2(b) since it reflects more time for changes in the yield curve to cause changes in the optimal bond to deliver. The average payoff of the option to exchange the optimal bond three months before delivery for the optimal bond at delivery is $270. With six months, the average payoff is $430, while the maximum over the study period was $3,000. These figures, provided by Hemler (1988), show the average and maximum payoffs at 12 months to be $660 and $4,400, respectively.

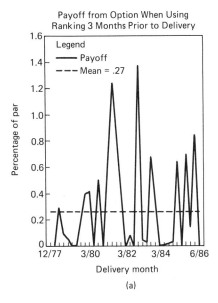

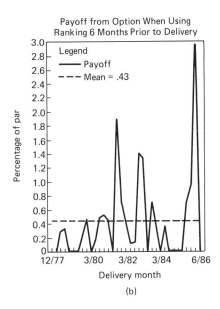

Figure 9.2(a) Choice Three Months Early   **Figure 9.2(b)** Choice Six Months Early

Source: Hemler (1988)

Figure 9.2   Excess Value of Early Cheapest Bond over Cheapest Delivery Bond

The Accrued Interest Option

In fact, the short receives not only the converted futures price $c_T(R, M)f_T$ for delivering a bond of coupon rate R and maturity M, but also any accrued interest $I_T(R, M)$ since the last coupon payment on the bond. For invoice price purposes, $I_T(R, M)$ is calculated as the total semiannual coupon payment, multiplied by the number of days since the last coupon payment, and divided by the number of days in a half-year.

Example: For the 10 percent coupon bond maturing in May 2005 (discussed in the previous example), suppose that it has been 100 days since the last coupon payment. The semiannual coupon payment of \$5,000 generates an accrued interest payment due to the short of

$$I_T(R, M) = \$5,000 \times \frac{100 \text{ days}}{180 \text{ days}} = \$2,777.78.$$

At any time during the delivery period, the optimal bond for the short to deliver is that bond i^* maximizing the difference between the total invoice price,

$$P_T(R_i, M_i) = c_T(R_i, M_i)f_T + I_T(R_i, M_i),$$

and the cost $S_T(R_i, M_i)$ of the delivered bond. It follows that, if delivery occurs on date T, then

$$f_T = \min_i \frac{S_T(R_i, M_i) - I_T(R_i, M_i)}{c_T(R_i, M_i)}. \tag{3}$$

Delivery may occur on any date T during the delivery period. The delivery period begins with the first possible date of announcement of intention to deliver by the short, which is two business days before the first business day of the delivery month. On the *announcement date*, the short's position is marked to market for the last time. On the following business day, the *invoice date*, a long is selected to accept delivery at an invoice price based on the settlement futures price of the announcement date. Finally, the delivery actually occurs on the business day following the invoice date; the short must deposit the bond by 10:00 a.m., while the long must deposit the invoice price by 1:00 p.m. Although the last trading date for the futures contract is usually seven business days before the end of the delivery month, deliveries may occur on any day of the month. The invoice price for deliveries occurring after the end of futures trading is based on the last settlement price of the contract.

For an arbitrary date T during the delivery period, equation (3) need not hold unless deliveries actually occur. In general, for any date T during the delivery period,

$$f_T \leq \min_i \frac{S_T(R_i, M_i) - I_T(R_i, M_i)}{c_T(R_i, M_i)}. \tag{4}$$

The short has the option to deliver at any date T during the delivery period. This is referred to as an *accrued interest option* since, if the coupon rate R_{i^*} of the optimal bond (i^*) to deliver is much different from prevailing short-term interest rates, it may be valuable for the short to deliver early or late during the delivery period. For example, if the short is allowed to offset only one futures position during the month and the optimal bond i^* to deliver has a coupon rate much higher than short-term interest rates, it may be valuable to delay delivery as long as possible, since the accrued interest in the invoice price is accumulating faster than the interest foregone on the cash that would otherwise be received for a delivered bond, other things being equal. Of course, other things are not equal, and in any case, the short may find it profitable to deliver early and assume another short (or long) position generating additional profits before the last delivery date. Optimal exercise of the accrued interest option is not based on a trivial comparison of coupon rate and short term interest rates.

Figure 9.3 shows the average delivery date for each delivery period in Hemler's (1988) study period, December, 1977 through June, 1986.

The End-of-Month Option

As just mentioned, if the short has not chosen to deliver before the close of trading for the contract, the short has the option to deliver at any time during the last seven business days of the delivery month at an invoice price based on the last futures settlement price. Figure 9.3, from Hemler (1988), shows that delivery often occurs during the week after the futures contract stops trading. In fact, according to data presented by Broadie and Sundaresan (1988), during the period December, 1977 to June, 1987, 75 percent of deliveries were made during the last five days of the delivery month. They also estimate the average value of the end-of-month option to the short at between 5.5/32 and 9.2/32 off the delivery cost per \$100 principal (or a total of approximately \$170 to \$290 per contract).

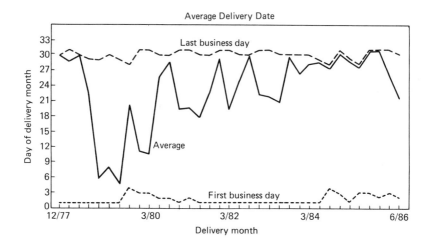

Figure 9.3   Average Delivery Date During T-Bond Futures Delivery Period

The Wild Card Option

Even though the invoice price $P_T(R_i, M_i)$ for a particular bond on any given
day during the delivery period is based on the futures settlement price f_T
established at 2:00 p.m. (Chicago time) on that day, the short can choose
whether or not to deliver the bond for that invoice price at any time until
8:00 p.m. of the same day. Since markets for bonds are still open after 2:00
p.m. Chicago time, the spot cost of a delivered bond can fluctuate before
the decision of which bond to deliver, if any, must be made. Equation (4)
need not hold, therefore, between 2:00 p.m. and 8:00 p.m., and any excess
of the invoice price over the cost of the bond is a profit to the short. (This
is not an arbitrage profit since one cannot perform the futures part of an
arbitrage after the futures market closes at 2:00 p.m.) Restricting attention
to a particular deliverable bond whose invoice price is $P_T(R_i, M_i)$ at the 2:00
p.m. settlement price, the short effectively holds a put option on the bond
with exercise price $P_T(R_i, M_i)$ and expiry at 8:00 p.m. Since there are actually
many deliverable bonds, the wild card option is somewhat more complicated,
as well as somewhat more valuable.

EXERCISES

9.1 Refer to the financial press on the first business day after this exercise is assigned for the prices, coupon rates, and maturity dates of all traded U.S. Treasury bonds maturing in 2009, as well as the price of the nearby CBOT T-bond futures price. Assuming (in order to reduce the required calcualtions) that these 2009 bonds are the only T-bonds elegible for delivery against the CBOT T-bond contract, answer the following questions:

(a) Suppose you are the short and today is a potential delivery date for the T-bond contract. Assuming you must purchase a T-bond for delivery against your short position, and ignoring the accrued interest correction, calculate the conversion factor for each of the 2009 bonds and choose the cheapest-to-deliver. Since you must purchase the bond, use the published "ask" (rather than "bid") bond prices. Assume the bonds mature at the ends of the published maturity months for your discounting calcualtions. Note that it is often easier to calculate the conversion factor c_L as of the last semi-annual coupon month (so as to discount at even numbers of half-years). Today's conversion factor is then $c_t = 1.04^t c_L$, where t is the fractional number of half-years since that date. For example, if it has been 90 days since the last coupon month, then $t = 90/180 = 0.5$, so $c_t = \sqrt{1.04}c_L$.

(b) Which of the 2009-maturity bonds are cheapest to deliver after accounting for the accrued interest?

(c) Assuming there are in fact deliveries of 2009-maturity bonds against the T-bond contract today, calculate the implied futures price. Ignoring transactions costs (aside from the bid-ask spread on bonds) and assuming that you can trade at the published bond and futures prices, is there an implied arbitrage? If so, indicate one possible arbitrage strategy. (Of course, if today is not in fact a delivery date for the contract, this is meaningful only as a conceptual exercise.)

NOTES

On the regulation of futures markets, general sources include Markham (1987), Seeger (1985), Pashigan (1986), Anderson (1986b), Edwards (1981b, 1983), Cagan (1981), Stone (1981), Fischel and Grossman (1984), and "A Study of the Effects on the Economy of Trading in Futures and Options," a report by the Fed, the CFTC, and the SEC prepared in December 1984. On the jurisdictional overlap of various federal regulators, additional sources are Kane (1984) and White (1981). A review of the Futures Trading Act of 1982 is given by Rosen (1983). The latest edition of federal futures regulations is provided by the Federal Register Office (1986) as Chapter 1 of Title 17 of the *Code of Federal Regulations*. On self-regulation, see Moylan (1981) and Saloner (1984). An example of exchange regulations is the *New York Futures Exchange Guide*, revised in December 1984. On the conditions leading to the efficiency of competitive market equilibria, one may consult any textbook on microeconomic theory, such as Varian (1984).

Edwards and Edwards (1984) survey manipulation in futures markets. Appendix 9A is based mainly on information in the staff report of the SEC titled "The Silver Crisis of 1980," prepared in October 1982. Sarnoff (1980) and Fay (1982) are popular accounts of the Silver Crisis. Barnhill and Powell (1981) analyze the volatility of silver prices during the Silver Crisis. Anderson and Gilbert (1986) study the "Tin Crisis," the collapse of the tin market on the London Metals Exchange in October 1985. A review of the Tin Crisis and of the status of other international commodity agreements is given by Stainer (1985). The coffee cartel and alleged attempts to manipulate coffee futures prices during the late 1970s are described in Greenstone (1981) and Edmunds (1982). Gordon-Ashworth (1984) reviews the control of international commodity markets, including the history and practice of regulatory and cartel agreements. Monographs by Newberry and Stiglitz (1981) and Gosh, Gilbert, and Hallet (1987) summarize the theory of commodity price stabilization. Of course, one could view the term "price stabilization" as a euphemism for price manipulation, but stabilization of commodity prices with international agreements among producer and consumer nations has been viewed as an important objective.

Miller (1988) gives a general account of futures innovation. On innovation, see also Camp (1981), Dew (1981), and Fischel (1986). Anderson (1984) reviews the regulation of futures contract innovation. Silber (1981) surveys futures innovation and competition in new contract design. Anderson (1986) is a study of exchange competition. Competition in the timing of futures innovation is modeled by Anderson and Harris (1986). The mean-variance model of innovation reviewed in Appendix 9C is simplified from Duffie and Jackson (1986). Black (1986) and Johnston and McConnell (1987) provide some statistical analysis of the success and failure of futures innovation based on hedging quality, in support of the analysis in Appendix 9C. Appendix 9B is based on Johnston and McConnell (1987).

Studies of futures contract margins include those by Gay, Hunter, and Kolb (1986), Telser (1981), Anderson (1981), Kuhn (1981), Brenner (1981), Figlewski (1984), and Tomek (1985).

General reviews of cash settlement of futures are given by Garbade and Silber (1983), Jones (1982), and Paul (1985). On stock index cash settlement, see Martell and Salzman (1981). The certificate delivery system used in live cattle futures markets is studied by Purcell and Hudson (1986). The effects of delivery substitutions on Treasury bond futures are analyzed by Kilcollin (1982), Livingston (1984), Kane and Marcus (1986), Gay and Manaster (1986), Hemler (1988), Cheng (1987), Broadie and Sundaresan (1987), Arak and Goodman (1987), and Carr (1987).

A large literature treats many other design and regulatory issues, including: price limits (Brennan [1986]), dual trading (Stanley [1981]), trading floor practices (Smidt [1985]), information systems (Spilka [1983] and Cernikovsky [1985]), dispute resolution (Moylan and Ulkman [1986]), time bracketing of execution data (Grossman and Miller [1986]), position limits (Hunt and Nissen [1981]), exchange rule approval (Teuting [1981]), reparations (Burr [1981]), customer suitability (Selmer [1981]), computerized trading (Dickins [1985]), price rounding (Ball, Torous, and Tschoegl [1985]), and the effects of inflation (Gorham [1981]). Edwards (1981) surveys the regulation of futures and forward trading by depository institutions.

Appendix 9A: The Silver Crisis of 1980

This brief review of some of the events that collectively became known as the *Silver Crisis of 1980* draws on newspaper reporting and a report by the staff of the U.S. Securities and Exchange Commission, dated October 1982. Popular accounts of the Silver Crisis are cited in the Notes.

Among the key figures in the Silver Crisis were various members of, and corporations controlled by, the "Hunt family," mainly children of the oil magnate H. L. Hunt. The principal actors were Nelson Bunker Hunt and William Herbert Hunt, the "Hunt brothers," who became active in the silver markets in the early 1970s. Hereafter we refer to the various actors in the family collectively as "the Hunts."

It is interesting to note that H.L. Hunt himself lost essentially all of his wealth by staking it on a large short cotton futures position in 1917. He recovered, of course, to become one of the richest people in the world. Moreover, even before their debacle in the silver market, Bunker and Herbert Hunt were involved in a dramatic run-up in soybean futures prices in 1977. As reported in more detail by Markham (1987), the Hunts collectively held a long position of over 4,500 contracts during a period in which soybean prices reached unusually high levels. According to Markham (1987), "estimates of their profits ranged as high as $95 million." The Hunts were ultimately brought under administrative proceedings by the CFTC for acting in concert with one another so as to violate speculative position limits, and were assessed a civil penalty of $500,000. The *soybean affair*, as it became known, was a minor event in comparison with the Silver Crisis of 1980.

The Silver Squeeze

Having taken large positions in silver spot and futures markets, particularly during 1973-1974 and 1976, the Hunts developed a pattern in the period leading up to July 1979 of rolling their futures positions into successively later contracts to deliver, always maintaining a net long position. They also bought significant interests in a number of silver producers. From a level of about $9 per ounce in July 1979, the spot and futures prices rose to approximately $35 per ounce by the end of that year. During this period, the amount of silver controlled by the Hunts was estimated to have increased from about 123 million ounces to 195 million ounces, including approximately 20,000 COMEX contract equivalents (each 5,000 ounces) on the COMEX and Chicago Board of Trade. This constituted approximately 15 percent of world silver stocks, according to Handy & Harmon, a leading market analyst, or approximately 121 percent of annual U.S. domestic silver consumption. These holdings also represented a market value of over $6 billion, presuming they could have been liquidated at year-end prices. Each increase in silver prices of $1 would have generated daily resettlement profits for the Hunts of about $97 million. The Hunts' positions were maintained at about 20 different FCMs. The Hunts purchased 6.6 percent of the stock of one of these, Bache Halsey Stuart Shields, Inc. ("Bache"), which, along with Merrill Lynch, handled over 80 percent of the Hunts' spot and futures trading positions.

The nearby futures price reached a high of over $50 per ounce in mid-January. Meanwhile, the silver futures exchanges adopted a number of measures in consultation with the CFTC including, at one or more of the exchanges:

- Increases in original margin requirements, in some cases to $60,000 per COMEX contract.
- Imposition of stricter limits on positions, or mandated 25 percent position reductions.
- *Liquidation-only trading*, a prohibition against trades increasing the size of open positions, except for hedging purposes.

During the same period, industrial demand for silver dropped markedly in response to the high price level of the metal. Production or planned production of silver increased. From mid-January, silver spot and nearby futures prices declined in various stages to under $11 per ounce on Thursday, March 27, which became known as "Silver Thursday." During this period of price declines, the Hunts borrowed heavily from many sources in order to meet margin calls. In some cases—for example, with Bache—an FCM agreed to accept physical silver in lieu of cash margin. In early January, the Hunts effected a large exchange for physicals (EFP) agreement with Phillips Brothers (also known as "Phibro"), whereby Phibro adopted a portion of the Hunts' long futures positions and sold silver forward to the Hunts. (See Appendix 2A for an explanation of EFPs.) The Hunts ultimately could not meet the obligations of this EFP, and were unable to meet a number of margin calls, including $44 million variation calls by Merrill Lynch on March 13 and Bache on March 17. The Hunts also defaulted on forward agreements in London and Zurich, and advised Bache and Merrill Lynch on March 26 that they were stopping margin payments.

On March 31, trading in the stock of Englehard Minerals and Chemicals, the owner of Phibro, was halted amid reports of Englehard's default, which had been caused by the default of the Hunts on their obligations to Phibro. This "crisis," which some felt at the time could cause a much wider financial disaster, was alleviated primarily by two transactions:

1. The Hunts agreed to forego delivery of the silver they had contracted to purchase from Phibro, and yielded to Englehard 8.5 million ounces

of silver earlier deposited as security on their EFP with Phibro, along with 20 percent of the interests of Herbert and Bunker Hunt in Beaufort Sea oil drilling licenses.

2. Largely by borrowing $1.1 billion from a consortium of 13 banks, Placid Oil, a limited partnership controlled by the Hunts, met the remaining silver-related obligations of the Hunts. The Hunt brothers in turn agreed to make periodic contributions to Placid Oil, collateralized by their remaining interests in the Beaufort Sea licenses.

The Aftermath

In assessing the Silver Crisis, the SEC staff report drew the following conclusions (limiting attention to its own domain of interest):

- There was excessive exposure by futures commission merchants to customer default risk.
- There was inappropriate valuation of customer commodity accounts by resettlement at *limit-down futures prices* (as explained below).
- The customer credit information obtained by futures commodity merchants was inadequate.
- There was inadequate financial separation between broker-dealers and their commodity subsidiaries.
- Public disclosure of customer positions was inadequate.
- NYSE surveillance was inadequate.

With regard to limit-down valuation, because of price limits on the COMEX contract, the Hunts' positions in other than nearby futures contracts were valued and resettled on the basis of limit-down futures prices that at some times were more than $10 per ounce above current spot and nearby futures prices, allowing an unrealistically favorable assessment of their positions.

The SEC report on the Silver Crisis also cites a number of other governmental reports on the Silver Crisis, including those by the CFTC. A letter by the CFTC chairman, Philip Johnson, concluded that the CFTC's initial inquiry had failed to reveal alleged conflicts of interest on the part of certain exchange governors who maintained substantial short positions during the price rise and decline. Popular accounts seriously question the appropriateness of actions taken by these and other players in the Silver Crisis of 1980.

The CFTC concluded a five year investigation in February, 1985 by bringing against the Hunts an administrative proceeding charging manipulation.

Separately, Minpeco S.A., a Peruvian government mineral marketing firm which had large short positions during the run-up in silver prices preceding the Silver Crisis, brought a $150.6 million civil suit charging the Hunts with conspiracy to corner the silver market. In August, 1988, a federal jury upheld the allegation that the Hunts and others (including a brother-in-law of the Suadi Arabian crown prince and a Bermuda firm controlled by the Hunts and two Arabian sheiks) committed fraud and and violated commodity, anti-trust, and other laws. Damages of approximately $130 million were awarded against Bunker, Herbert, as well as Lamar Hunt (a third brother who was not found to have violated certain of the charges). Lamar Hunt later settled with a payment of $17 million to Minpeco. As of this writing, Bunker and Herbert Hunt have still not settled their damages.

Two class-action suits on behalf of 17,000 investors also remain to be heard against the Hunts. According to reporting in *The Wall Street Journal* by Ann Hagedorn and Leonard Apcar (August 22, 1988), these suits, claiming $500 million in damages, also name Merrill Lynch, Prudential-Bache Securities (formerly Bache), and several other firms involved in the commodities business. In addition, Merrill Lynch, E.F. Hutton, Prudential-Bache, and a defunct unit of Donaldson, Lukin and Jenrette, had already paid a total of $64.7 million to Minpeco in pre-trial settlements of Minpeco's suit.

The Hunts' net worth has been drastically reduced by the effects of the Silver Crisis, in combination with problems with the oil and real estate markets. According to the reporting earlier cited from *The Wall Street Journal*, the Hunt brothers' net worth was at least $5 billion in 1980. In September, 1988 Bunker and Herbert Hunt filed for bankruptcy protection. As reported by *The New York Times* on November 23, 1988, documents filed with the United States Bankruptcy Court in Dallas valued their respective properties at $249.1 million and $39.7 million, while their respective debts were valued at $1.25 billion and $887.3 million.

Appendix 9B: The Rise and Fall of GNMA Futures

This appendix, summarizing the work of Johnston and McConnell (1987), relates how the design of the GNMA CDR futures contract of the Chicago Board of Trade ultimately led to the demise of the contract. Introduced in 1975, the Government National Mortgage Association Collateralized Depository Receipt (*GNMA CDR*) contract grew in popularity to the point that

TABLE 9.2   Trading Volume and Interest Rates, 1976–1986

Year	GNMA CDR Futures Volume[a]	T-Bond Futures Volume[b]	GNMA Avg. Yield[c]
1975	20,125	—	8.52
1976	128,537	—	8.17
1977	422,421	32,101	8.04
1978	953,161	555,350	8.98
1979	1,371,078	2,059,594	10.22
1980	2,326,292	6,489,555	12.55
1981	2,292,882	13,907,988	15.29
1982	2,055,648	16,739,695	14.68
1983	1,692,017	19,550,535	12.25
1984	862,450	29,963,280	13.13
1985	84,396	40,448,367	11.61
1986	24,078	52,598,811	9.30
1987	7,583	66,841,474	9.42

[a] CDR Contract Volume. Source: Chicago Board of Trade.
[b] Contract Volume. Source: Chicago Board of Trade.
[c] Assumes pre-payment in 12 years, current 30-yr. certificate.
Source: *Federal Reserve Bulletin*, various issues.

its volume of trade in 1980 was over 2.3 million contracts. Trading volume subsequently dropped to almost nothing, as shown in Table 9.2.

Each GNMA futures contract delivers a certificate promising the remaining interest and principal due on 29- or 30-year single-family mortgages insured against default by the Federal Housing Administration or the Veterans Administration. The standard deliverable certificate represents remaining principal payments of at least $100,000 and interest payments of 8.0 percent. (The standard deliverable mortgage rate is 8.5 percent; the additional 0.5 percent is paid for the cost of pooling the individual mortgages [0.44 percent to the pooler] and for default insurance [0.06 percent to GNMA].) Delivery substitutions are allowed, however, and seem to be behind the decline of futures trading volume since 1982. It appears that the formula determining the discount on delivery substitutions caused the futures price to be relatively poorly correlated with the spot price of newly issued mortgages. Since newly issued mortgages are felt to be the main source of hedging demand, the contract design in effect caused the GNMA futures contract to be a relatively poor hedge. The story is roughly as follows.

At delivery, the short may substitute any GNMA certificate for the standard deliverable certificate, provided its discounted present value, at the standard 8 percent discount rate, is at least $100,000. A deliverable certificate bearing coupons of less than 8 percent must therefore have a remaining principal of over $100,000; those paying coupons greater than 8 percent could be delivered with less than $100,000 principal remaining. In calculating the present value of the certificate for the purposes of meeting the contract's delivery requirements, it is assumed that the mortgages are repaid at the end of 12 years. Generally, the underlying deliverable mortgages may be repaid at any time by paying the remaining principal. Thus, the certificates delivered against the futures contract may actually represent mortgages with less than 12 years remaining, or may ultimately be prepaid before 12 years. Herein lies the problem.

After 1982, mortgage rates declined precipitously, as shown in Table 9.2. Under these conditions, mortgages previously issued at high interest rates have a tendency to be repaid early since the mortgage holders can replace them with new low-interest mortgages. A high-coupon mortgage with a high likelihood of being repaid early has a lower market value than the market value implicit in the futures contract's assumption of prepayment in 12 years. The holder of a short futures position will rationally deliver the cheapest allowable mortgage certificate, in this case the high-coupon grade. The futures price prior to delivery reflects the price of the cheapest-to-deliver certificates, and with the decline in interest rates, the futures price became more correlated with short term interest rates (since the high-coupon mortgages are repaid early, on average) and less highly correlated with the spot prices of newly issued GNMA mortgages.

In fact, it came to the point that returns on current-coupon GNMA certificates were more highly correlated with T-bond futures price growth rates than with GNMA CDR futures price growth rates. Johnston and McConnell (1987) demonstrated that T-bond futures were a significantly superior hedge in this regard, based on standard statistical tests. Even when both the T-bond and the GNMA CDR futures contracts were tested for their joint hedging ability, the inclusion of the GNMA CDR contract did not significantly improve the hedge. Based on liquidity considerations, the T-bond contract is also (vastly) superior, having by far the larger volume of trade. In summary, the T-bond futures contract became the superior hedging vehicle. As hedging interest in the GNMA CDR contract declined, so did the total volume of trade, in line with the theoretical analysis in Appendix 9C. Appendix 7F shows, based on more recent data than that used by Johnston and McConnell, that an even better hedge for certain types of GNMA spot price risk than that offered by T-bond futures is available in the form of a combined position in

T-bond and Eurodollar futures.

The dramatic decline in GNMA futures volume shown in Table 9.2 is thus not surprising after all. The futures contract seems to have been killed by a delivery substitution formula that did not account for the possibility of a dramatic rise and subsequent fall in interest rates.

Appendix 9C: A Mean-Variance Model of Innovation

Innovation

Probably the most important strategic business decision of a futures exchange is its basic choice of contract type: Which commodity, financial instrument, or other index should underlie its next new contract? In this context, *innovation* means the invention and marketing of new securities, and futures exchanges have been extremely active financial innovators over the last decade, especially since the introduction of financial futures. (For an interesting discussion of innovation, see Miller [1986].) Of course, every new futures contract must be approved by the CFTC. Since the stakes are large, and the first exchange to adopt trading in a particular contract type has a marked advantage because of established liquidity, the role of the CFTC in regulating the process of futures innovation has been controversial. (Since December 1982, the SEC has also had effective veto power over the innovation of stock index futures.) In the remainder of this appendix we look at a simple model for contract choice by an exchange in the simple mean-variance setting of Chapter 4. The mean-variance model is far too simple to capture many important aspects of the problem, in particular the role of liquidity in a multiperiod setting, but at least it provides a basic structure for our reasoning. Black (1986) and Johnston and McConnell (1987) give empirical support to this sort of model.

Mean-Variance Contract Choice

In suggesting a model for innovation of futures contracts, one must understand the incentives of a futures exchange vis-à-vis contract choice. After all, most U.S. exchanges are nonprofit corporations, so profit maximization in the usual sense is not an appropriate objective. As a membership association, the committee structure of an exchange will reflect the basic goals of its members:

1. To take positions in futures contracts related to the commercial interests of these members.

2. To profit from positions taken on "own account."

3. To profit from the provision of transactions services to others.

We argue here that the first motive, which is basically hedging by members, has had less and less direct influence on contract choice in recent years. Essentially, a futures contract is deemed a success for exchange members if it generates a high volume of trade. Those members supplying brokerage are clearly interested in maximizing the demand for transactions services, objective (3). Other factors held equal, those members attempting to profit from positions taken on their own accounts, motive (2), will generally prefer to work in an active (high-volume) market. This is especially true for scalpers, because, in a sense, they earn a transactions fee in the form of a bid-ask spread by, on average, buying low from the seller, holding a position for a short period until a buyer's order arrives, then selling high (or the reverse). Although it has been argued that those members trading for expected return on personal positions prefer "high-volatility" contracts, it has never been properly shown that this goes beyond the connection between volatility and volume of trade discussed in Appendix 7C. There is always a trade-off between volatility and expected return, as we have seen.

At least for the purposes of our simple model then, let us take it as given that an exchange wishes to choose that contract that maximizes its volume of trade. Of course, scaling a contract up or down in size can dramatically affect volume of trade, but we are speaking about volume of trade for a fixed contract size. In a mean-variance setting with transactions costs, Duffie and Jackson (1986) argue that a reasonable yardstick for contract size is the standard deviation of the change in the futures price over one trading period. For example, doubling the number of units of a particular commodity that a contract would deliver is the same as doubling the standard deviation of its payoff, which (if brokerage fees per contract are also doubled) has no effect on total transactions fees or on the effective positions of agents in equilibrium. For simplicity, we ignore transactions fees here.

What determines the menu of potential new contracts available to an exchange? With the advent of cash settlement and the use of index-based contract definitions, the list of alternatives goes well beyond the choice of a commodity type. Of course, limits are imposed by the need to prevent manipulation and the importance of having a legally unambiguous definition of the value of a contract held at delivery. At least for theoretical purposes, however, let us proceed as though there are indeed no limits: any given random variable could be used to define the delivery value of a contract.

Let the random variable f_1 denote the delivery value of the futures contract chosen by the exchange. We will check to see whether f_1 maximizes the volume of trade in equilibrium. We can assume (without loss of generality) that the variance of f_1 is nonzero.

As in Section 4.2, suppose the market is characterized by m agents with endowments described by random variables e^1, $e^2, \ldots, e^m$, and with mean-variance preferences having respective risk-aversion coefficients $r_1, \ldots, r_m$. We recall from Section 4.2, Equation (3), that the optimal futures position for agent i is

$$y_i = \frac{\overline{f}_1 - f_0}{2r_i \operatorname{var}(f_1)} - \frac{\operatorname{cov}(e^i, f_1)}{\operatorname{var}(f_1)},$$

and from Equation (5) of Section 4.2 that the equilibrium futures price is

$$f_0 = \overline{f}_1 - \frac{2\operatorname{cov}(e, f_1)}{\tau},$$

where $e = e^1 + \cdots + e^m$ is the total endowment, and $\tau = \frac{1}{r_1} + \cdots + \frac{1}{r_m}$ is the market risk tolerance. The equilibrium volume of trade, which we denote $V(f_1)$ to indicate its dependence on the chosen contract f_1, is given by the expression

$$V(f_1) = (y_1 + \cdots + y_L) - (y_{L+1} + \cdots + y_m),$$

where we have renumbered the agents so that the first L are long (those i with $y_i \geq 0$) and the remaining $m - L$ agents are short ($y_i < 0$). Substituting the above expression for the futures equilibrium price f_0 into the expression for y_i, and simplifying, leaves the following expression for the equilibrium volume of trade:

$$V(f_1) = K \frac{\operatorname{cov}(f_1, f^*)}{\operatorname{var}(f_1)},$$

where K is a constant depending on the identities of short and long agents,

$$f^* = \tau_L e_S - \tau_S e_L,$$

and where $\tau_L = (\frac{1}{r_1} + \cdots + \frac{1}{r_L})$ is the risk tolerance of the long agents, $e_L = e^1 + \cdots + e^L$ is the total endowment of the long agents, and likewise for τ_S and e_S. As discussed above, we can fix the variance of f_1 at any level without real consequences. For ease of calculation, we fix the variance of f_1 equal to the variance of f^*. This implies that $V(f_1) = K\operatorname{corr}(f_1, f^*)$. Two random variables X and Y are perfectly correlated if and only if $X = A + BY$ for some constants A and B, with B not equal to zero. Thus $V(f_1)$ is maximized only if $f_1 = A + Bf^*$ for some constants A and $B \neq 0$.

Duffie and Jackson (1986) go on from this point to characterize the optimal innovation by an exchange faced with a number of different futures contracts that are already traded. In a sense that can be precisely interpreted, the solution is identical to the monopolistic problem described above, once the agents' endowments are revised by subtracting that portion of the endowments that can already be hedged with the pre-existent contracts.

From this, one can characterize competition between different exchanges, at least in this simple setting, and study the question of whether volume maximizing contract choices are efficient. That is, can every agent's utility in equilibrium be improved by moving away from volume-maximizing contract choices to some other contract choices, say those dictated by regulators? For the monopolistic case $(n = 1)$, volume-maximizing contract choices are indeed efficient in this sense. Likewise, given fixed pre-existing futures contracts, the volume-maximizing innovation is also efficient. For the oligopolistic case $n > 1$, however, the outcome of exchanges competing against one another, each choosing its volume-maximizing contract given the other exchanges' contracts, is not always efficient.

Appendix 9D: Summary of Traded Contracts

The source for this and the following appendix is the 1989 Reference Guide, Trading Facts and Figures, from the periodical *Futures Magazine*, copied with permission. The intention was to make the information as complete as possible at the time it was prepared, so the tables may include some contracts that have become inactive or have not yet received final trading approval. Therefore, accuracy is not guaranteed. Changes and additional information are available from the exchanges, whose addresses are provided in Appendix 9E, and from brokers.

The contract type is indicated by (F) for futures, (O) for options on actuals or physicals, or (OF) for options on futures. The daily limit figures can vary from those shown due to provisions in many contracts, especially during the month before delivery, when the limits are eliminated for many contracts.

TABLE 9.3   U.S. Futures Contracts

Contract	Contract Months[a]	Trading Hours (Local Time)	Contract Size	Minimum Price Fluctuation	Daily Limit
American Stock Exchange					
Major Market) Index (XMI) (O) (20 stocks)	[b]	9:30–4:15	100 × Index	Premium 1/16 up to $3;1/8 above $3 (1.0 = $100	—
Institutional Index (O) (European-style) (75 stocks)	[c]	9:30–4:10	100 × Index	Premium 1/16 up to $3; 1/8 above $3 (1.0 = $100)	—
Computer Technology Index (O)	[d]	9:30–4:10	100 × Index	Premium 1/16 up to $3; 1/8 above $3 (1.0 = $100	–
Oil Index (O)	[d]	9:30–4:10	100 × Index	Premium 1/16 up to $3; 1/8 above $3 (1.0 = $100)	–
U.S. Treasury Bills (O) (90-day) (European-style)	3,6 9,12	9:30–3:00	$1 million principal	0.01 pt = $25 (1.0 = $2,500)	—
U.S. Treasury Notes (O) (10-year)	2,5 8,11	9:30–3:00	$100,000	1/32 pt. = $31.25 (1.0 = $1,000)	—

Contract	Contract Months[a]	Trading Hours (Local Time)	Contract Size	Minimum Price Fluctuation	Daily Limit
		Chicago Board of Trade			
Corn (F, OF)	3,5,7 9,12	9:30–1:15	5,000 bu.	1/4¢/bu. = $12.50	10¢/bu. = $500
Oats (F)	3,5,7 9,12	9:30–1:15	5,000 bu.	1/4¢/bu. = $12.50	6¢/bu. = $300
Soybeans (F,OF)	1,3,5,7 8,9,11	9:30–1:15	5,000 bu.	1/4¢/bu. = $12.50	30¢/bu. = $1,500
Soybean Meal (F,OF)	1,3,5,7 8,9,10,11	9:30–1:15	100 tons	10¢/ton = $10	$10/ton = $1,000
Soybean Oil (F,OF)	1,3,5,7 8,9,10,12	9:30–1:15	60,000 lb.	1/100¢/lb. = $6	1¢/lb. = $600
Wheat (F,OF) (Soft winter)	3,5,7 9,12	9:30–1:15	5,000 bu.	1/4¢/bu. = $12.50	20¢/bu. = $1,000
U.S. Treasury Bonds (F,OF)	3,6 9,12	7:20–2:00 Mon.–Fri. 5:00– 8:30 p.m.* Sun.–Thurs.	$100,000 8% coupon	1/32 pt. = $31.25	64/32 pt. = $2,000
U.S. Treasury Notes (F,OF) (6 1/2%– 10 yr.)	3,6 9,12	7:20–2:00 Mon.–Fri. 5:00– 8:30 p.m.* Sun.–Thurs.	$100,000 8% coupon	1/32 pt. = $31.25	64/32 pt. = $2,000
5-Year U.S. Treasury Notes (F,OF)	3,6 9,12	7:20–2:00	$100,000 face value U.S. T-notes	1/64 pt = $15.625	3 pt =$3,000
30-Day Interest Rate	e	7:20–2:00	$5 million	1/100 of 1% =$41.67	150 basis pt.
Japanese Government Bond (F)	3,6 9,12	7:20–2:00	20 million JY	1/100 of 1 yen	2 pt.
Municipal Bond Index (F,OF)	3,6 9,12	7:20–2:00	$1,000 × Bond Buyer Index	1/32 pt. = $31.25	64/32 pt. = $2,000

Contract	Contract Months[a]	Trading Hours (Local Time)	Contract Size	Minimum Price Fluctuation	Daily Limit
Major Market Index–Maxi (F)	f	8:15–3:15	$250 × AMEX Major Market Index	1/20 pt. = $12.50	None
Corporate Bond Index (F)	3,6 9,12	8:00-2:00	$1,000 × Corporate Bond Index	1/32 pt. = $31.25	—
CBOE 250 Index (F)	f	8:30–3:15	$500 × CBOE 250 Index	1/2 pt. = $25	12 pt.
Institutional Index (F)	g	8:15–3:15	$500 × Index	5/100 pt. = $25	None
Gold (F,OF)	h	7:20–1:40 Mon.–Fri. 5:00– 8:30 p.m.* Sun.–Thurs.	100 troy oz.	10¢/oz. = $10	$50/oz. = $5,000
Gold (F)	2,4 8,10,12	7:20–1:40	1 kilogram = 32.15 oz.	10¢/oz. = $3.22	$50/oz. = $1,607.50
Silver (F,OF)	h	7:25– 1:25 Mon.–Fri. 5:00– 8:30 p.m.* Sun.–Thurs.	5,000 troy oz.	1/10¢/oz. = $5	$1/oz. = $5,000
Silver (F,OF)	2,3,6 8,10,12	7:25– 1:25	1,000 troy oz.	1/10¢/oz. = $5	50¢/oz. = $500

*CST; 6:00-9:30 CDT.
Note: Mortgage-backed securities futures and options (redesigned GNMA) and the CBOE 50 Stock Index contracts have been approved but are not yet listed.

Chicago Board of Options Exchange					
S&P 100 Stock Index (O)	i	8:30–3:15	100 × Index	Premium 1/16 up to $3; 1/8 above $3 (1.0 = $100)	—
S&P 500 Stock Index (O)	j	8:30–3:15	100 × Index	Premium 1/16 up to $3; 1/8 above $3 (1.0 = $100)	—

Contract	Contract Months[a]	Trading Hours (Local Time)	Contract Size	Minimum Price Fluctuation	Daily Limit
U.S. 30-Year Treasury Bonds (O) (7 1/4%, 9 1/4%, 9 7/8%)	3,6 9,12	8:00–2:00	$100,000	1/32 pt. = $31.25 (1.0 = $1,000)	—
U.S. 5-Year Treasury Notes (O) (7 1/2%, 8 1/8%, 9 1/8%)	3,6 9,12	8:00–2:00	$100,000	1/32 pt.	–

Note: The CBOE 250 Stock Index is a CBOT contract but trades on the CBOE floor.

Chicago Mercantile Exchange					
Cattle, Feeder (F,OF)	1,3,4,5 8,9,10,11	9:05–1:00	44,000 lb.	2.5¢/cwt. = $11	1.5¢/lb. = $660
Cattle, Live (F,OF)	2,4,6 8,10,12	9:05–1:00	40,000 lb.	2.5¢/cwt. = $10	1.5¢/lb. = $600
Hogs, Live (F,OF)	2,4,6,7 8,10,12	9:10–1:00	30,000 lb.	2.5¢/cwt. = $7.50	1.5¢/lb. = $450
Pork Bellies (F,OF)	2,3,5 7,8	9:10–1:00	40,000 lb.	2.5¢/cwt. = $10	2¢/lb. = $800
Lumber (F,OF) (Random length)	1,3,5 7,9,11	9:00–1:05	150,000 bd. ft.	10¢/1,000 bd.ft. =$15	$5/1,000 bd. ft. =$750

Chicago Mercantile Exchange International Monetary Market Division					
Deutsche Mark (F,OF)	*k*	7:20–1:20	125,000 DM	$0.0001/DM = $12.50	150 pt.*
Canadian Dollar (F,OF)	*k*	7:20–1:26	100,000 CD	$0.0001/CD = $10	100 pt.*
French Franc (F)	*k*	7:20–1:28	250,000 FF	$0.00005/FF = $12.50	500 pt.*
Swiss Franc (F,OF)	*k*	7:20–1:16	125,000 SF	$0.0001/SF = $12.50	150 pt.*

Contract	Contract Months[a]	Trading Hours (Local Time)	Contract Size	Minimum Price Fluctuation	Daily Limit
British Pound (F,OF)	k	7:20–1:24	62,500 BP	$0.0005/BP = $12.50	400 pt.*
Japanese Yen (F,OF)	k	7:20–1:22	12,500,000 JY	$0.000001/JY = $12.50	150 pt.*
Australian Dollar (F,OF)	k	7:20-1:18	100,000 AD	$0.0001/AD = $12.50	150 pt.*
European Currency Unit (ECU) (F)	3,6 9,12	7:10–1:30	125,000 ECU	$0.0001/ECU = $12.50	150 pt.*
Treasury Bills (F,OF) (90-day)	3,6 9,12	7:20–2:00	$1,000,000	1 pt. = $25	None
Eurodollar Time Deposit (F,OF) (3-month)	k	7:20–2:00	$1,000,000	1 pt. = $25	None
Gold (F,OF)	1,3,5 7,9,12	7:20–2:00	100 oz.	10¢/oz. = $10	None

*Opening limit between 7:20-7:35 a.m.; no limit after 7:35 a.m.
Note: 5,000 oz. silver futures have been approved but are not yet listed.

Chicago Mercantile Exchange
Index and Option Market Division

Contract	Contract Months	Trading Hours (Local Time)	Contract Size	Minimum Price Fluctuation	Daily Limit
Standard & Poor's 500 Stock Index (F,OF)	3,6 9,12	8:30–3:15	500 × S&P 500 Stock Index	5 pt. = $25	Varies*
Nikkei Stock Average (F)	3,6 9,12	—	500 JY × Index	5 pt. = 2,500 JY	Varies**

*5 pt. first 10 minutes; 12 pt. next 30 min., then 30 pt. (expanding to 50 pt. if there is a trading halt.
**1000 pt. from 0-20000; 1500 pt. from 20005-30000, and 2000 pt. from 30005 and over.
Note: CME Treasury Index futures have been approved but are not yet listed.

Contract	Contract Months[a]	Trading Hours (Local Time)	Contract Size	Minimum Price Fluctuation	Daily Limit
Chicago Rice and Cotton Exchange					
Rough Rice (F)	1,3,5 9,11	9:15–1:30	2,000 cwt. (200,000 lb.)	0.5¢/cwt. = $10	30¢/cwt. = $600
Coffee, Sugar & Cocoa Exchange, Inc.					
Cocoa (F,OF)	3,5,7 9,12	9:30–2:15	10 metric tons	$1/metric ton = $10	$88/metric ton = $880
Coffee "C" (F,OF)	3,5,7 9,12	9:45–2:28 (2:30 closing call)	37,500 lb.	1/100¢/lb. = $3.75	6¢/lb. = $2,250
Sugar No. 11 (F,OF) (World)	1,3,5 7,10	10:00–1:43 (1:45 closing call)	112,000 lb.	1/100¢/lb. = $11.20	1/2¢/lb. =$560
Sugar No. 14 (F)	1,3,5 7,9,11	9:45–1:43 (Closing call begins when white sugar's closing call is completed.)	112,000 lb.	1/100¢/lb. = $11.20	1/2¢/lb. = $560
Sugar (F) (White)	1,3,5 7,10	9:45–1:43 (Closing call begins when Sugar No. 11's closing call is completed.)	50 metric tons	20¢/metric ton = $10	$10/metric ton
Consumer Price-Index (CPI-U) (F)	1,4 7,10	9:30–2:30	1,000 × CPI-U	0.01 pt. = $10	3.00 pt. = $3,000
Commodity Exchange, Inc.					
Aluminum (F)	l	9:30–2:10	44,000 lb.	5/100¢/lb. = $20	None
Copper (F,OF)	l	9:25–2:00	25,000 lb.	5/100¢/lb. = $12.50	None

Contract	Contract Months[a]	Trading Hours (Local Time)	Contract Size	Minimum Price Fluctuation	Daily Limit
High-grade Copper (F)	l	9:25–2:00	25,000 lb.	5/100¢/lb. =$12.50	None
Silver (F,OF)	l	8:25–2:25	5,000 troy oz.	10/100¢/oz. = $5	None
Gold (F,OF) (Linked to Sydney Futures Exchange)	m	8:20–2:30	100 troy oz.	10¢/oz. = $10	None
Moody's Corporate Bond Index (F) (Cash-settled) (Inactive)	3,6 9,12	8:40–3:00	$500 × Moody's Index	5/100 of 1 pt. = $25	None

Kansas City Board of Trade

Contract	Contract Months[a]	Trading Hours (Local Time)	Contract Size	Minimum Price Fluctuation	Daily Limit
Wheat (F,OF) (F,OF) (Hard red winter)	3,5,7 9,12	9:30–1:15	5,000 bu.	1/4¢/bu. =$12.50	25¢/bu. =$1,250
Value Line Stock Index (F)	3,6 9,12	8:30–3:15	500 × the futures price	0.05 = $25	Consult the exchange
Mini Value Line Stock Index (F)	3,6 9,12	8:30–3:15	100 × the futures price	0.05 = $5	Consult the exchange

MidAmerica Commodity Exchange

Contract	Contract Months[a]	Trading Hours (Local Time)	Contract Size	Minimum Price Fluctuation	Daily Limit
Cattle, Live (F)	2,4,6 8,10,12	9:05–1:15	20,000 lb.	2.5/100¢/lb. = $5	1.5¢/lb = $300
Hogs, Live (F)	2,4,6 7,8,10,12	9:10–1:15	15,000 lb.	2.5/100¢/lb. = $3.75	1.5¢/lb. = $225
Corn (F)	3,5,7 9,12	9:30–1:30	1,000 bu.	1/8¢/bu. = $1.25	10¢/bu. = $100
Oats (F)	3,5,7 9,12	9:30–1:30	1,000 bu.	1/8¢/bu. = $1.25	10¢/bu. = $100

Contract	Contract Months[a]	Trading Hours (Local Time)	Contract Size	Minimum Price Fluctuation	Daily Limit
Soybeans (F,OF)	1,3,5 7,8,9,11	9:30–1:30	1,000 bu.	1/8¢/bu. = $1.25	30¢/bu. = $300
Soybean Meal (F)	1,3,5,7 8,9,10,12	9:30–1:30	20 tons	10¢/ton = $2	$10/ton = $200
Wheat (F,OF) (Soft-winter)	3,5,7 9,12	9:30–1:30	1,000 bu.	1/8¢/bu. = $1.25	20¢/bu. = $200
New York Gold (F,OF)	e	7:20–1:40	33.2 fine troy oz.	10¢/oz. = $3.32	None
New York Silver (F)	e	7:25–1:40	1,000 troy oz.	10/100¢/oz. = $1	None
Platinum (F)	n	7:20–1:40	25 fine troy oz.	10¢/oz. = $2.50	$25/oz. = $625
U.S. Treasury Bonds (F)	3,6 9,12	7:20–3:15	$50,000 face value	1/32 pt. = $15.62	96/32 pt. = $1,500
U.S. Treasury Bills (F) (90-day)	3,6 9,12	7:20–2:15	$500,000 face value	1 pt. = $12.50	None
U.S. Treasury Notes (F)	3,6 9,12	7:20-3:15	$50,000 face value	1/32 pt. = $15.62	96/32 pt. = $1,500
British Pound (F)	3,6 9,12	7:20–1:34	12,500 BP	$0.0002/BP = $2.50	None
Canadian Dollar (F)	3,6 9,12	7:20–1:36	50,000 CD	$0.0001/CD = $5	None
Deutsche Mark (F)	3,6 9,12	7:20–1:30	62,500 DM	$0.0001/DM = $6.25	None
Japanese Yen (F)	3,6 9,12	7:20–1:32	6,250,000 JY	$0.000001/ JY = $6.25	None
Swiss Franc (F)	3,6 9,12	7:20–1:26	62,500 SF	$0.0001/SF = $6.25	None

Note: Australian dollar futures have been approved but are not yet listed.

Contract	Contract Months[a]	Trading Hours (Local Time)	Contract Size	Minimum Price Fluctuation	Daily Limit
Minneapolis Grain Exchange					
Wheat (F,OF) (Hard red spring)	3,5,7 9,12	9:30–1:15	5,000 bu.	1/8¢/bu. = $6.25	20¢/bu. = $1,000
High Fructose Corn Syrup (F)	3,5,7 9,12	9:00–1:25	37,000 lb. (dry)	2¢/cwt. = $7.40	$1/cwt. = $370
Oats (F)	3,5,7 9,12	9:30–1:15	5,000 bu.	1/4¢/bu.	10¢
New York Cotton Exchange					
Cotton No. 2 (F,OF)	3,5,7 10,12	10:30–3:00	50,000 lb. (approx. 100 bales)	1/100¢/lb. = $5	2¢/lb. = $1,000
Citrus Associates of the New York Cotton Exchange, Inc.					
Orange Juice (F,OF)	1,3,5 7,9,11	10:15–2:45	15,000 lb.	5/100¢/lb. = $7.50	5¢/lb. = $750
Financial Instrument Exchange (FINEX) Division of New York Cotton Exchange					
U.S. Dollar Index (F,OF)	3,6 9,12	8:20–3:00	$500 × U.S. Dollar Index	0.01 (1 basis pt.) = $5	None
European Currency Unit (ECU) (F)	3,6 9,12	8:20–3:00	100,000 ECU	0.01¢/ECU = $10	None
5-Year U.S. Treasury Note (FYTR) (F,OF)	3,6 9,12	8:20–3:00	U.S. Treasury notes with face values at maturity of $100,000	1/2 of 1/32 pt. = $15.625	None

Contract	Contract Months[a]	Trading Hours (Local Time)	Contract Size	Minimum Price Fluctuation	Daily Limit
New York Futures Exchange
NYSE Composite Stock Index (F,OF)	3,6 9,12	9:30–4:15	$500 × NYSE Index	0.05 pt. = $25	None
CRB Futures Price Index (F,OF)	3,5,7 9,12	9:00–3:15	$500 × CRB Index	0.05 pt. = $25	None
Russell 2000 Index (F)	3,6 9,12	9:15–4:10	$500 × Russell 2000 Index	0.05 pt. = $25	None
Russell 3000 Index (F)	3,6 9,12	9:30–4:15	$500 × Russell 3000 Index	0.05 pt. = $25	None
New York Mercantile Exchange
Palladium (F)	e	8:10–2:20	100 troy oz.	5¢/oz. = $5	$6/oz. = $600
Platinum (F)	e	8:20–2:30	50 troy oz.	10¢/oz. = $5	$25/oz. = $1,250
No. 2 Heating Oil (F,OF) (New York)	e	9:50–3:10	42,000 gal.	1/100¢/gal. = $4.20	2¢/gal. = $840
Unleaded Gasoline (F)	e	9:50–3:10	42,000 gal.	1/100¢/gal. = $4.20	2¢/gal. = $840
Crude Oil (F,OF) (Light sweet)	e	9:45–3:10	1,000 barrels (42,000 gal.)	1¢/barrel = $10	$1/barrel = $1,000
Propane (F)	e	9:40–3:10	42,000 gal.	1/100¢/gal. = $4.20	2¢/gal. = $840

Note: Options on unleaded gasoline futures have been approved but are not yet listed.

Contract	Contract Months[a]	Trading Hours (Local Time)	Contract Size	Minimum Price Fluctuation	Daily Limit
New York Stock Exchange					
NYSE **Composite** **Index** (O)	o	9:30–4:15	100 × Index	1/16 pt. (1.0 = $100)	—
Pacific Stock Exchange					
Financial **News** **Composite** **Index** **(FNCI)** (O)	p	6:30–1:15	100 × Index	None	—
Philadelphia Board of Trade					
National **Over-The-** **Counter** **Index** (F)	q	9:30–4:15	$500 × Index	0.05 pt. = $25	None
British **Pound** (F)	q	8:00–2:30* 7:00– 11:00 p.m. **	62,500 BP	$0.0001/BP = $6.25	None
Canadian **Dollar** (F)	q	8:00–2:30	100,000 CD	$0.0001/CD = $10	None
Deutsche **Mark** (F)	q	8:00–2:30* 7:00– 11:00 p.m. **	125,000 DM	$0.0001/DM = $12.50	None
Swiss **Franc** (F)	q	8:00–2:30* 7:00– 11:00 p.m. **	125,000 SF	$0.0001/SF = $12.50	None
French **Franc** (F)	q	8:00–2:30	250,000 FF	$0.00005/FF = $12.50	None

Contract	Contract Months[a]	Trading Hours (Local Time)	Contract Size	Minimum Price Fluctuation	Daily Limit
Japanese Yen (F)	q	8:00–2:30* 7:00– 11:00 p.m. **	12,500,000 JY	$0.000001/JY = $12.50	None
European Currency Unit (ECU) (F)	q	8:00–2:30	125,000 ECU	$0.0001/ECU = $12.50	None
Australian Dollar (F)	q	8:00–2:30* 7:00– 11:00 p.m. **	100,000 AD	$0.0001/AD = $10	None

*Scheduled to trade at 4:30 a.m. starting in January 1989.
**EDT, Sun.–Thurs.; 6:00–10:00 p.m. EST.

Philadelphia Stock Exchange					
Deutsche Mark (O)	r	8:00–2:30* 7:00– 11:00 p.m. **	62,500 DM	$0.0001/DM = $6.25 (1.0 = $625)	—
European Currency Unit (ECU) (O)	r	8:00–2:30	62.500 ECU	$0.0001/ECU = $6.25 (1.0 = $625)	—
Swiss Franc (O)	r	8:00–2:30* 7:00– 11:00 p.m. **&	62,500 SF $625)cr	$0.0001/SF = $6.25 (1.0 =	—
Canadian Dollar (O)	r	8:00–2:30	50,000 CD	$0.0001/CD = $5 (1.0 = $500)	—
British Pound (O)	r	8:00–2:30* 7:00– 11:00 p.m. **	31,250 BP	$0.0001/BP = $3.125 (1.0 = $312.50)	—
Japanese Yen (O)	r	8:00–2:30* 7:00– 11:00 p.m. **	6,250,000 JY	$0.000001/ JY = $6.25 (1.0 = $625	—

Contract	Contract Months[a]	Trading Hours (Local Time)	Contract Size	Minimum Price Fluctuation	Daily Limit
French Franc (O)	r	8:00–2:30	125,000 FF	$0.00005/FF = $6.25 (1.0 = $125)	—
Australian Dollar (O)	r	8:00–2:30* 7:00– 11:00 p.m. **	50,000 AD	$0.0001/AD = $5 (1.0 = $500	—
Value Line Index (O) (European-style)	s	9:30–4:15	100 × Index	1/16 pt. (1.0 = $100	—
Utility Index (O)	s	9:30–4:10	100 × Index	1/16 pt. (1.0 = $100)	—
Gold/Silver Stock Index (O)	g	9:30–4:10	100 × Index	1/16 pt. (1.0 = $100)	—
National Over-The-Counter Index (O)	g	9:30–4:15	100 × Index	1/16 pt. (1.0 = $100	—

*Scheduled to trade at 4:30 a.m. starting in January 1989.
**EDT, Sun.–Thurs.; 6:00–10:00 p.m. EST.

[a] Numbers correspond to months of the year (e.g., 1 = January, 2 = February, ...).
[b] Three consecutive near-term expiration months.
[c] Three consecutive near-term expiration months plus two months
from March cycle.
[d] Three consecutive near-term expiration months plus next
nearest month in January cycle.
[e] All months.
[f] March cycle plus next three consecutive months.
[g] Next three months plus March cycle.
[h] Current month and next two months plus February/April/June.
[i] Four consecutive near-term expiration months.
[j] Two consecutive near-term expiration months plus three months
from March cyle.
[k] March/June/September/December and spot month.
[l] Current calendar month, next two months, and January/March/May/July/
September/December.
[m] Current calendar month, next two months, and February/April/June/August/
October/December.
[n] Current three months and January/April/July/October.
[o] Next three months.
[p] Four sequential months.
[q] March/June/September/December plus two near months.
[r] Next two months and March/June/September/December.
[s] Next three months and March cycle plus two near months.

TABLE 9.4   Canadian Futures Contracts

Contract	Contract Months[a]	Trading Hours (Local Time)	Contract Size	Minimum Price Fluctuation	Daily Limit
The Montreal Exchange					
Canadian Bankers' Acceptances (F)	[b]	8:30–3:00	1,000,000 CD face value	0.01 = 25 CD	—
Canadian Government Bonds (O)	[c]	9:00–4:00	25,000 CD face value	$0.01 × 250 per contract	—
Toronto Futures Exchange					
Canadian Bonds (F) (15-year)	3,6 9,12	9:00–3:15	100,000 CD	1/32 pt.= $31.25	2 pt. = $2,000
Canadian T-Bills (F) (13-week)	[d]	9:00–3:15	1,000,000 CD	0.01 pt. = $24	0.60 pt. = $1,440
TSE 300 Spot Contract (F)	[e]	9:20–4:10	$10 × Index	1 pt. = $10	None
Toronto 35 Index (F)	[f]	9:15–4:15	$500 × Index	.02 pt. = $10	13.5 pt. = $6,750
Silver (O)	[g]	9:05–4:00	100 oz.	5¢below $2; 12 1/2¢ above $2	—
Toronto Stock Exchange					
Toronto 35 Index (O)	[f]	9:15–4:15	100 × Index	1¢ under 10 ¢; 5¢ under $5; 12 1/2¢ for $5 and above	—

Contract	Contract Months[a]	Trading Hours (Local Time)	Contract Size	Minimum Price Fluctuation	Daily Limit
The Winnipeg Commodity Exchange					
Domestic Feed Barley (F)	3,5,7 10,11,12	9:30–1:15	100 metric tons	10¢/ton = $10	$5/ton = $500
Alberta Domestic Feed Barley (F)	2,4,6 9,11	9:30–1:15	20 metric tons	10¢/ton = $2	$5/ton = $100
Flaxseed (F)	3,5,7 10,12	9:30–1:15	100 metric tons	10¢/ton = $10	$10/ton = $1,000
Domestic Feed Oats (F)	3,5,7 10,11,12	9:30–1:15	100 metric tons	10¢/ton = $10	$5/ton = $500
Canola/ Rapeseed (F)	1,3,6 9,11	9:30–1:15	100 metric tons	10¢/ton = $10	$10/ton = $1,000
Rye (F)	3,5,7 10,12	9:30–1:15	100 metric tons	10¢/ton = $10	$5/ton = $500
Domestic Feed Wheat (F)	3,5,7 10,11,12	9:30–1:15	100 metric tons	10¢/ton = $10	$5/ton = $500

[a] Numbers correspond to months of the year (e.g., 1 = January, 2 = February, ...).
[b] March/June/September/December over two years.
[c] Next three months plus two on March cycle.
[d] Four consecutive near months plus March/June/September/December.
[e] Daily.
[f] Three consecutive near months.
[g] Three consecutive near months plus six and nine months.

TABLE 9.5 London Futures Contracts

Contract	Contract Months[a]	Contract Size	Minimum Price Fluctuation	Trading Hours (Local Time)
Baltic Futures Exchange				
Baltic International Freight Futures Exchange (BIFFEX)				
Baltic Freight Index (F)	1,4 7,10	$10 × Baltic Freight Index	0.05 pt. = $5	10:15–12:30, 2:30–4:15
London Grain Futures Market				
EEC Wheat (F,OF)	1,3,5 6,9,11	100 metric tons	5 pence/ton = £5	11:00–12:30, 2:45–4:00
EEC Barley (F,OF)	1,3,5 9,11	100 metric tons	5 pence/ton =£5	11:00–12:30, 2:45–4:00
London Meat Futures Exchange				
Live Cattle (F) (Cash-settled)	1,2,4,6 8,10,11	5,000 kg.	0.1 pence/kg. =£5	10:30–12:00, 2:45–4:30
Pig (F) (Cash-settled)	2,4,6 8,10,11	3,250 kg.	0.1 pence/kg. =£3.25	10:30–12:00, 2:45–4:30
The London Potato Futures Market				
Potatoes (F,OF)	2,4 5,11	40 metric tons	10 pence/ton =£4	11:00–12:30, 2:45–4:00
Potatoes (F) (Cash-settled)	3,7 8,9	40 metric tons	10 pence/ton =£4	11:00–12:30, 2:45–4:00
The Soya Bean Meal Futures Association Ltd.				
Soya Bean Meal (F)	2,4,6 8,10,12	20 metric tons	10 pence/ton =£2	—
International Petroleum Exchange of London Ltd.				
Gas Oil (F,OF)	[b]	100 metric tons	U.S. 25¢/ton = $25	9:15–12:24, 2:30–5:24
Heavy Fuel Oil (F)	[b]	100 metric tons	U.S. 25¢/ton = $25	9:30–12:19, 2:40–5:14

Contract	Contract Months[a]	Contract Size	Minimum Price Fluctuation	Trading Hours (Local Time)
Brent Crude Oil (F)	c	1,000 barrels	U.S. 1¢/barrel = $10	9:25–12:30 2:15–5:30

The London Futures & Options Exchange (FOX)

Contract	Contract Months[a]	Contract Size	Minimum Price Fluctuation	Trading Hours (Local Time)
Cocoa No. 6 (F,OF)	3,5,7 9,12	10 metric tons	£1/ton	10:00–1:00, 2:30–5:00
Coffee (F,OF) (Robusta)	1,3,5 7,9,11	5 metric tons	£1/ton	9:45–12:30, 2:30–5:00
Sugar No. 6 (F,OF)(Raw)	3,5,8 10,12	50 metric tons	$0.20/ton	10:30–12:30, 2:30–7:00
Sugar No. 5 (F) (White)	3,5,8 10,12	50 metric tons	$0.20/ton	9:45–7:10,

London International Financial Futures Exchange Ltd. (LIFFE)

Contract	Contract Months[a]	Contract Size	Minimum Price Fluctuation	Trading Hours (Local Time)
20-Year UK Gilt Interest Rate (F,OF) (Goverment stock)	3,6 9,12	£50,000 nominal value (9% coupon)	£1/32 per £100 nominal = £15.625	9:00–4:15
Short Gilt (F)	3,6 9,12	£100,000 (10% coupon)	£1/64 = £15.625	9:05–4:20
Medium Gilt (F)	3,6 9,12	£50,000 (9% coupon)	£1/32 =£15.625	8:55–4:10
German Goverment Bond (Bund) (F)	3,6 9,12	250,000 DM (6% coupon)	0.01 DM	8:10–4:00
3-Month Eurodollar Interest Rate (F,OF)	3,6 9,12	U.S. $1,000,000	1 pt. (0.01%) = U.S. $25	8:30–4:00
3-Month Sterling Interest Rate (F,OF)	3,6 9,12	£500,000	1 pt. (0.01%) = £12.50	8:20–4:02
British Pound (F,O)	3,6 9,12*	£25,000 traded against U.S. $	0.01¢/£= U.S. $2.50	8:32– 4:02
Deutsche Mark (F)	3,6 9,12	125,000 DM	0.01¢/DM = U.S. $12.50	8:34–4:04
Swiss Franc (F)	3,6 9,12	125,000 SF	0.01¢/SF = U.S. $12.50	8:36–4:06

Contract	Contract Months[a]	Contract Size	Minimum Price Fluctuation	Trading Hours (Local Time)
Japanese Yen (F)	3,6 9,12	12,500,000 JY	0.01¢/100 JY = U.S. $12.50	8:30–4:00
Dollar-Mark Currency (F,O)	3,6 9,12 *	U.S. $50,000 traded against DM	$0.0001 DM/ U.S. $1	8:34–4:04
U.S. Treasury Bonds (F,OF)	3,6 9,12	U.S. $100,000 (8% coupon)	1/32 pt.	8:15–4:10
Financial Times Stock Exchange 100 Index (FTSE) (F,OF)	3,6 9,12	£25 × FTSE Index	0.05 pt. = £12.50	9:05–4:05
Japanese Government Bond (JGB) (F)	3,6 9,12	100,000,000 JY (6% coupon)	0.01 JY/ 10,000 JY	8:10–4:05

*Add three nearby months for options.

London Metal Exchange

Contract	Contract Months[a]	Contract Size	Minimum Price Fluctuation	Trading Hours (Local Time)
Aluminum (F,OF) (F,OF) (High-grade)	d	25 metric tons	50¢/ton	11:55–12:00, 1:00–1:05, 3:40-3:45, 4:25–4:30
Copper (F,OF) (Grade A)	d	25 metric tons	50 pence/ton	12:00–12:05, 12:30–12:35, 3:30–3:35, 4:15–4:20
Lead (F,OF)	d	25 metric tons	50 pence/ton	12:05–12:10, 12:40–12:45, 3:20–3:25, 4:00–4:05
Nickel (F,OF)	d	6 metric tons	$1/ton	12:15–12:20, 1:00–1:05, 3:45–3:50, 4:30–4:35
Silver* (F,OF)	d	10,000 troy oz.	1/10¢/oz.	11:45–11:50, 1:05–1:10, 3:50–3:55, 4:35–4:40

Contract	Contract Months[a]	Contract Size	Minimum Price Fluctuation	Trading Hours (Local Time)
Silver* (F)	d	2,000 troy oz.	1/10¢/oz.	11:45–11:50, 1:05–1:10, 3:50–3:55, 4:35–4:40
Zinc (F,OF) (High-grade)	d	25 metric tons	25 pence/ton	12:10–12:15, 12:45–12:50, 3:25–3:30, 4:05–4:10
Zinc (F) (Special high grade)	d	25 metric tons	50¢/ton	12:10–12:15, 12:50–12:55, 3:25–3:30, 4:10–4:15

*10,000 oz. and 2,000 oz. silver contracts will discontinue trading in June 1989.

London Traded Options Market				
Financial Times Stock Exchange 100 Index (FTSE) (O)	e	£10 × Index	1 pt.	9:05–4:05
Treasury (O) (12%, redeemed 1995)	2,5 8,11	£50,000	1/32 pt./ £100	9:05–4:05
Treasury (O) (9 1/2%, redeemed 2005)	2,5 8,11	£50,000	1/32 pt./ £100	9:05–4:05
U.S.- Sterling (O)	f	£12,500	0.05¢	9:00–4:05
U.S. $- Deutsche Mark (O)	f	62,500 DM	0.01¢	9:00–4:05

[a]Numbers correspond to months of the year (e.g., 1 = January, 2 = February, ...).
[b]Nine consecutive months including current month.
[c]Six consecutive months following current month.
[d]Any single market day between current day–spot and 3 months forward.
[e]Next four months.
[f] Next three months and March/June/September/December.

TABLE 9.6   Other Contracts

Contract	Contract Months[a]	Contract Size	Minimum Price Fluctuation	Trading Hours (Local Time)
Bolsa Brasileira de Futuros **(Brazilian Futures Exchange)**				
Gold (F)	2,4,6 8,10,12	250 grams	Cz$10¢/gram	11:00–4:00
Deutsche Mark (F)	1,3,4 6,7 9,10,12	25,000 DM	U.S. $0.0001/ DM	9:20–11:30, 2:30–3:20
Japanese Yen (F)	1,3,4 6,7 9,10,12	2.5 million JY	U.S. $0.000001/ JY	9:20–11:30, 2:30–3:20
U.S. Dollar (F)	b	U.S. $5,000	Cz$0.01	9:20–11:30, 2:30–3:20
OTN—Nominal (F) (Treasury bond)	b	2,000 OTN	1 pt. = Cz$0.01	9:30–4:00,
IBV—12 Rio de Janeiro Stock Exchange Index (F)	b	Cz$1 × Index	1 pt. = Cz$1	9:30–1:15
Bolsa de Mercadorias de São Paulo **(São Paulo Commodities Exchange)**				
Cattle (F)	2,4,6 8,10,12	330 units of 15 kg.	Cz$0.50/15 kg.	3:15–4:15
Cattle, Feeder (F)	1,3,5 7,9,11	27 head	Cz$1/head	3:15–4:15
Cotton (F)	3,5,7 10,12	500 units of 15 kg.	Cz$1/15 kg.	11:00–12:00
Coffee (F,OF) (Arabic)	3,5,7 9,12	100 60-kg. bags	Cz$5/bag	10:45–3:30, 12:30–2:00
Coffee (F) (Robusta)	3,5,7 9,12	100 60-kg. bags	Cz$5/bag	10:45–3:30, 12:30–2:30
Cocoa (F)	3,5,7 9,12	50 60-kg. type II bags	Cz$1/bag	2:00–3:00

Contract	Contract Months[a]	Contract Size	Minimum Price Fluctuation	Trading Hours (Local Time)
Corn (F)	1,3,5 7,9,11	60 metric tons	—	—
Frozen Chicken (F)	2,4,6 8,10,12	12 tons	Cz$5/ton	9:45–10:45
Soybeans (F)	1,3,5 7,9,11	30 metric tons	Cz$1/60 kg.	11:30–3:15
Soybean Meal (F)	1,3,5 7,9,11	25 metric tons	—	11:30–3:15
Soybean Oil (F)	1,3,5 7,9,11	12.5 metric tons	—	11:30–3:15
Gold (F,OF,O)	2,4,6 8,10,12*	250 grams	Cz$1/gram	10:00–4:30
U.S. Dollar (F,OF)	b	U.S. $5,000	Cz$0.05/ U.S. $1	10:20–3:50,
Deutsche Mark (F)	b	10,000 DM	Cz$0.05/ 10 DM	10:20–3:50
Japanese Yen (F)	b	1,000,000 JY	Cz$0.05/ 1,000 JY	10:20–3:50
British Pound (F)	b	£5,000	Cz$0.01/£1	10:20–3:50
FGV-100 Stock Index (F)	b	Cz$5 × Index	10 pt.	9:30–1:30
Brazilian Certificate of Deposit (CDB) (F)	1,3,5 7,9,11	Cz$500,000	Cz$10/ Cz$100,000	10:00–3:00

*January/March/May/July/September/November for gold options.

Bolsa Mercantil & de Futuros (BM&F)				
Bovespa) Index (F)	2,4,6 8,10,12	Cz$5 × Index	5 pt.	9:30–1:15
Gold* (F,OF)	2,4,6 8,10,12	250 grams	Cz$1/gram	10:00–4:30
Coffee (F,OF)	3,5,7 9,12	50 60-kg. bags	Cz$10/bag	11:00–1:00

Contract	Contract Months[a]	Contract Size	Minimum Price Fluctuation	Trading Hours (Local Time)
U.S. Dollar (F,OF)	[b]	U.S. $5,000	Cz$0.01/U.S.$	10:30–3:45
Deutsche Mark (F)	[b]	10,000 DM	Cz$0.05/DM	10:30–3:45
Japanese Yen (F)	[b]	1,000,000 JY	Cz$0.05/ 1,000 JY	10:30–3:45
Domestic CD (F) (60-, 90-day)	—	Cz$1,000,000	—	11:15–12:30
Central Bank of Brazil Bills (F)	[b]	Cz$1,000,000	—	3:15–4:00
Brazilian Treasury Bonds (F,OF)	[b]	1,000 bonds	Cz$0.01/OTN	10:30–4:00
Broilers (F)	2,4,6 8,10,12	12 tons	Cz$0.01/kg.	2:40–3:00
Live Cattle (F)	2,4,6 8,10,12	330 units of 15 kg.	Cz$0.10/15 kg.	2:40–3:00
Live Hogs (F)	2,4,6 8,10,12	8,000 kg.	Cz$0.01/kg.	2:40–3:00

*Also trades spot and forward contracts on 250-gram and 1-kg. gold.

European Options Exchange (EOE)				
Dutch Government Bonds (O)	2,5 8,11	10:00–4:30	10,000 DG (nominal value)	0.10 DG
EOE Index (O)	1,4 7,10	10:30–4:30	100 × EOE Index	0.10 DG
Major Market Index (XMI) (O) (Fungible with American Stock Exchange)	3,6 9,12	100 × Index	Premium 1/16 up to $3; 1/8 above $3	12:00–4:30
FTA Bullet Index (O)	2,5 8,11	100 × Index	0.10 DG	10:30–4:30

Contract	Contract Months[a]	Contract Size	Minimum Price Fluctuation	Trading Hours (Local Time)
Financiele Termijnmarkt Amsterdam N.V. (FTA)				
FTA Index	2,5 8,11	1,000 × FTA Index	0.01 pt.	10:45–4:30
FTB Index (Bullet Index) (F)	2,5 8,11	1,000 × Bullet Index	0.01 pt.	10:30–4:30
Finnish Options Brokers Ltd.				
Finnish Options Index (FOX) (F,O)	8,10	100 × Index	5/100 of Index	9:30–3:00
Guarantee Fond for Danish Futures and Options (Copenhagen Stock Exchange				
Danish Bonds (F,O) (9%, redeemed 2006)	1,4 6,10	$1,000,000 DEK	0.05 pt.	11:00–2:00
Hong Kong Futures Exchange Ltd.				
Sugar (F)	1,3,5 7,9,10	112,000 lb.	1/100¢/lb. = U.S. $11.20	10:30–2:00, 2:25–4:00
Soybeans (F)	c	500 60-kg. bags	HK 20¢/bag = HK $100	9:50, 10:50, 12:50, 2:50
Gold (F)	d	100 troy oz.	U.S. 10¢/troy oz. = U.S. $10	9:00–12:00, 2:30–5:30
Hang Seng Index (F)	e	HK $50 × Hang Seng Index	1 pt. = HK $50	10:00–12:30, 2:30–3:30

Contract	Contract Months[a]	Contract Size	Minimum Price Fluctuation	Trading Hours (Local Time)
		International Options Clearing Corp. (IOCC)		
Gold (O)	2,5 8,11	10 troy oz.	10¢/oz. =,$1	Amsterdam: 10:00–4:30 Montreal: 9:00–2:30 Vancouver: 11:30–4:00 Sydney: 11:00–4:30 (Nov.–Mar.); 10:30–4:00 (April–Oct.)
Silver (O)	3,6 9,12	250 troy oz.	10¢/oz. = $1	Amsterdam: 10:00–4:30 Vancouver: 7:30–4:30 Sydney: 11:00–4:30 (Nov.–Mar.); 10:30–4:00 (April–Oct.)
Platinum (O)	3,6 9,12	10 troy oz.	10¢/oz. = $1	Montreal: 9:00–2:30 Vancouver: 1 1:30–4:00 Sydney: 11:00–4:30 (Nov.–Mar); 10:30–4:00 (April–Oct.)
Canadian Dollar (O)	3,6 9,12	50,000 CD	$0.0001/CD = $5	Montreal: 8:00–2:30 Vancouver: 11:30–4:00
British Pound (O)	3,6 9,12	10,000 BP	0.05 DG	Amsterdam: 10:00–4:30
Dutch Guilder (O)	3,6 9,12	U.S. $10,000	0.05 DG	Amsterdam: 10:00–4:30

Contract	Contract Months[a]	Contract Size	Minimum Price Fluctuation	Trading Hours (Local Time)
Irish Futures and Options Exchange (IFOX)				
Long Gilt (F)	3,6	IR£50,000	IR£5	9:00–5:00
3-Month Interest Rate (F)	3,6, 9,12	IR£100,000	IR£2.50	9:00–5:00
Irish Pound/ Dollar (F)	3,6 9,12	$50,000	IR£5	9:00–5:00
Kuala Lumpur Commodity Exchange				
Crude Palm Oil (F)	f	25 metric tons	Malaysian $1/ton	11:00–12:30, 3:30–6:00
Rubber (F) (SMR 20)	g	10 metric tons	Malaysian 1¢/kg.	10:00–1:00, 4:00–6:00
Tin (F)	h	5 metric tons	U.S. $5/ton	12:15–1:00, 4:00–6:00
Cocoa (F)	1,3,5,7 9,11,12	10 metric tons	U.S. $1/ton	11:15–12:00, 4:00–7:00
Marche à Terme International de France (MATIF)				
Long-Term National Bond (F,OF)	3,6 9,12	500,000 FF	0.05%	10:00–4:00
90-Day Treasury Bill (F)	3,6 9,12	5 millions FF	0.01%	9:30–4:00
3-Month PIBOR (F)	3,6 9,12	5 million FF	0.01%	9:30–4:00
CAC 40 Stock Index (F)	i	200 FF per index pt.	0.1	10:00–5:00
White Sugar (F,OF)	3,5,8 10,12	50 metric tons in 50-kg. bags	1 FF/ton	10:45–1:00, 3:00–7:00
Cocoa Beans (F)	3,5,7 9,12	10 metric tons	0.5 FF/ 100 kg.	10:30–1:00, 3:00–6:30
Coffee (F) (Robusta)	1,3,5 7,9,11	5 metric tons	1FF/100 kg.	10:15–1:00, 3:00–6:30

Contract	Contract Months[a]	Contract Size	Minimum Price Fluctuation	Trading Hours (Local Time)
New Zealand Futures Exchange				
U.S. Dollar (F)	j	U.S. $50,000	NZ $0.0001/ U.S. $1	8:15–4:45
Kiwi Dollar (F,OF)	j	NZ$100,000	U.S. $0.0001/ NZ$1	8:15–4:45
5-Year Government Stock No. 2 (F,OF)	3,6 9,12	NZ$100,000	0.01	8:00–5:00
90-Day Bank Accepted Bills (F)	k	NZ$500,000	0.01	8:10–4:50
Barclays Share Price Index (F)	3,6 9,12	NZ$20 × Index	1 index pt.	8:10–4:50
Osaka Securities Exchange				
Osaka Stock Futures 50 (F)	3,6 9,12	Sum of number of shares representing one trading unit	0.5 JY	9:00–11:00, 1:00–3:00
Nikkei Stock Average (F)	3,6 9,12	1,000 × Nikkei Stock Average	10 JY	9:00–11:15 1:00–3:15
Singapore International Monetary Exchange (SIMEX)				
Eurodollar (F,OF) (Linked to CME)	l	$1,000,000	0.01 pt. = $25	8:30–5:20
Japanese Yen (F,OF) (linked to CME)	l	12,500,000 JY	$0.000001/JY = $12.50	8:15–5:05
Deutsche Mark (F,OF)	l	125,000 DM	$0.0001/DM = $12.50	8:20–5:10
Gold (F)	2,3,4 6,8,9 10,12	100 troy oz.	10¢/oz. = $10	9:30–5:15

Contract	Contract Months[a]	Contract Size	Minimum Price Fluctuation	Trading Hours (Local Time)
British Pound (F) (Linked to CME)	l	62,500 BP	U.S. $0.0002/BP = U.S. $12.50	8:25–5:15
Nikkei Stock Average (F)	l	500 JY × Nikkei Stock Average	5 pt. = 2,500 JY	8:00–2:15
Fuel Oil (F)	m	100 metric tons	U.S. $0.10/ton	8:00–5:30

Stockholm Options Market (OM)

Contract	Contract Months[a]	Contract Size	Minimum Price Fluctuation	Trading Hours (Local Time)
OMX Index (O)	1,3,5 7,9,11	58.000 SKR	0.05 SKR	10:00–4:00

Swedish Options & Futures Exchange (SOFE)

Contract	Contract Months[a]	Contract Size	Minimum Price Fluctuation	Trading Hours (Local Time)
SX 16 Stock Index (Forward, O)	b	100 × Index	0.05 SKR	9:45–10:00

Swiss Options and Financial Futures Exchange (SOFFEX)

Contract	Contract Months[a]	Contract Size	Minimum Price Fluctuation	Trading Hours (Local Time)
Swiss Market Index (O)	n	Five options per contract	Varies	10:30–2:30

Sydney Futures Exchange Ltd.

Contract	Contract Months[a]	Contract Size	Minimum Price Fluctuation	Trading Hours (Local Time)
Cattle, Live (F) (Cash-settled)	o	10,000 kg. liveweight	1/100¢/kg. = A$10	10:30–12:30, 2:00–4:00
Wool (F) (Cash-settled)	2,4,6 8,10,12	2,500 kg.	1¢/kg. = A$25	10:30–12:30, 2:00–4:00
Gold (F) (Linked to COMEX)	2,4,6 8,10,12	100 troy oz.	10¢/oz. = U.S. $10	8:35–4:00
90-Day Bank Accepted Bills (F,OF)	p	A$500,000 face value	.01 pt. = A$11.50	8:30–12:30, 2:00–4:30
Australian Dollar (F,OF)	q	A$100,000	$0.0001/AD = U.S. $10	8:30–4:30
All Ordinaries Share Price Index (F,OF)	r	A$100 × Index	0.1 pt. = A$10	9:30–12:30, 2:00–4:00

Contract	Contract Months[a]	Contract Size	Minimum Price Fluctuation	Trading Hours (Local Time)
10-Year Treasury Bonds (F,OF)	s	A$100,000 (12% coupon)	0.005 pt. = A$25	8:30–12:30, 2:00–4:00
3-Year Treasury Bonds (F,OF)	6,9,12	A$100,000	0.01 pt. = A$25	8:30–12:30, 2:00–4:00
U.S. Treasury Bonds (F) (Linked to LIFFE)	3,6 9,12	U.S. $100,000 (8% coupon)	1/32 pt. = U.S. $31.25	8:35–4:15
3-Month Eurodollar Interest Rates (F) (Linked to LIFFE)	3,6 9,12	U.S. $1,000,000	.01 pt. = U.S. $25	8:35–4:15

Tokyo Commodity Exchange for Industry

Contract	Contract Months[a]	Contract Size	Minimum Price Fluctuation	Trading Hours (Local Time)
Gold (F)	b	1 kg.	1 JY/gram	9:10, 10:30, 11:30, 1:10, 2:30, 3:45
Silver (F)	b	30 kg.	0.1 JY/ 10 gram	After gold
Platinum (F)	b	500 grams	1 JY/gram	After silver
Rubber (F)	b	5,000 kg.	0.1 JY/kg.	9:45, 10:45, 1:45,2:45,3:30
Cotton Yarn (F)	b	4,000 lb.	0.1 JY/lb.	8:50, 10:00, 12:50, 3:10
Woolen Yarn (F)	b	500 kg.	1 JY/gram	After cotton yarn

Tokyo Stock Exchange

Contract	Contract Months[a]	Contract Size	Minimum Price Fluctuation	Trading Hours (Local Time)
Japanese Government Bond (F)	3,6 9,12	20-year bonds with face values of 100 JY (6% coupon)	0.01 JY/ 100 JY	9:00–11:00, 1:00–3:00
Tokyo Stock Price Index (TOPIX) (F)	3,6 9,12	10,000 JY × Index	1 pt.	9:00–11:15, 1:00–3:15

[a]Numbers correspond to months of the year (e.g., 1 = January, 2 = February, . . .).
[b]All months.
[c]Six consecutive months ahead.
[d]February/April/June/August/October/December spot and next two months.
[e]Spot month and next two months.
[f]Next six months plus alternate months thereafter up to one year.
[g]Next nine months.
[h]Next four months plus alternate months thereafter up t one year.
[i]Three spot months plus one quarterly expiry month.
[j]Spot plus next three months, then quarterly.
[k]Spot plus next two months, then quarterly
[l]March/June/September/December and spot month.
[m]Six consecutive months.
[n]A cycle.
[o]All months up to 12 months ahead.
[p]Spot month plus next six consecutive months.
[q]March/June/September/December out to six months ahead.
[r]March/June/September/December up to 18 months ahead.
[s]March/June/September/December up to 12 months ahead.

Appendix 9E: Exchanges and Clearinghouses

The source of this appendix is the 1988 and 1989 Reference Guides of the periodical *Futures Magazine*. Although this information is intended to be accurate and up-to-date, changes can occur at any time. See Appendix 9D for additional notes. The clearinghouse information in Table 9.11 is from the 1988 Reference Guide.

TABLE 9.7   U. S. EXCHANGES

American Stock Exchange

86 Trinity Place, New York, NY 10006
(212) 306-1000; Fax: (212) 306-1802

Arthur Levitt Jr., chairman
Kenneth R. Leibler, president
Paul Stevens, executive vice president
Howard A. Baker, senior vice president, options
Joseph B. Stefanelli, vice president, options marketing

The American Stock Exchange is a uniquely balanced marketplace incorporating a primary equities market and a principal options market trading options on listed and over-the-counter stocks, stock indexes, and U.S. Treasury notes and bills. AMEX's flagship option on the Major Market Index (XMI) is the only U.S. index option listed in Europe: it trades on the European Options Exchange in Amsterdam from noon to 4:30 p.m. (6 a.m. to 10:30 a.m. in New York). A new proposal includes the Equity Index Participation (EIP) contract.

Chicago Board of Trade

141 W. Jackson Blvd., Chicago, IL 60604
(312) 435-3500

Karsten Mahlmann, chairman
Patrick H. Arbor, vice chairman
Thomas R. Donovan, president, chief executive officer
George Sladoje, executive vice president
Paul J. Draths, vice president, secretary
Thomas C. Coleman, vice president, director, economic analysis and planning

The CBOT is a nonprofit association providing a marketplace for agricultural, financial, metals, and stock index futures and options contracts. As the world's largest futures exchange, the CBOT accounted for 46 percent of U.S. trading volume in 1987. The CBOT is a self-regulated, federally designated futures market.

Chicago Board Options Exchange

400 S. LaSalle St., Chicago, IL 60605
(312) 786-5600; (800) OPTIONS
Fax: (312) 786-7409

Alger B. Chapman, chairman
Thomas A. Bond, vice chairman
Charles J. Henry, president
Richard G. Dufour, executive vice president, education and research
Edward J. Joyce, executive vice president, trading operations
Kruno Huitzingh, executive vice president, systems

The CBOE is a member organization established to serve the investing public. As the world's largest marketplace for options on equities and equity indexes, the CBOE accounted for nearly 60% of U.S. trading volume in 1987. In addition to options on 177 stocks, CBOE lists options on the S&P 100 (OEX) and the S&P 500 (SPX) stock indexes, and U.S. T-bonds and notes.

Chicago Mercantile Exchange

30 S. Wacker Dr., Chicago, IL 60606
(312) 930-1000; Fax: (312) 930-3439

Leo Melamed, chairman, executive committee, special counsel
John F. Sandner, chairman, board of governors
William J. Brodsky, president, chief executive officer
Michael Apatoff, executive vice president, chief operating officer

The CME has the world's largest facility for futures and options trading and has a membership of 2,724 traders. It is the second largest exchange in volume, with 84 million contracts traded in 1987. The CME's most active contract is Eurodollar futures, with over 20 million contracts changing hands in 1987. The exchange currently trades 31 futures and options contracts including stock indexes, foreign currencies, short-term interest rates and livestock. The CME currently enjoys an 80% share of the stock index market. The three divisions of the exchange include the CME, International Monetary Market (IMM) and Index and Option Market (IOM). The CME has offices in New York, Washington, D.C., London, and Tokyo.

Chicago Rice & Cotton Exchange

141 W. Jackson Blvd., Chicago, IL 60604
(312)341-3078

(For key personnel, see Chicago Board of Trade)

The CRCE, an affiliate of the MidAmerica Commodity Exchange, offers a rough rice futures contract, which is traded on the floor of the Chicago Board of Trade.

The Citrus Associates of the New York Cotton Exchange

(See New York Cotton Exchange)

Coffee, Sugar & Cocoa Exchange, Inc.

4 World Trade Center

New York, NY 10048
(212)938-2800; (800) HEDGEIT
Fax: (212) 524-9863

Bennett J. Corn, president
James Bowe, senior vice president, market development and planning
Joseph E. Ferrari, Jr., senior vice president, operations and administration
Elizabeth R. Clancy, vice president, general counsel/corporate secretary

The Coffee, Sugar & Cocoa Exchange Inc. is the world's leading marketplace for futures and options trading in these three international commodities. The CSCE also offers a futures contract based on white refined sugar in addition to its raw sugar contracts. The exchange will soon expand its presence in the international markets by offering a futures contract based on a new International Market Index.

Commodity Exchange, Inc.

4 World Trade Center, New York, NY 10048
(212) 938-2900; Fax: (212) 432-1154

John H. Hanemann, chairman
Alan J. Brody, president, chief executive officer
David A. Halperin, executive vice president
Gina Greer, senior vice president, marketing and exchange relations
Arthur D. Markowitz, senior vice president, operations and systems
James E. Goodwin, senior vice president, compliance

COMEX, the world's most active metals market, offers the opportunity to trade in a variety of products including gold, silver, copper, and aluminum futures and options on gold, silver, and copper futures.

Financial Instrument Exchange
(See New York Cotton Exchange)

International Monetary Market
(See Chicago Mercantile Exchange)

Index and Option Market
(See Chicago Mercantile Exchange)

Kansas City Board of Trade

4800 Main St., Suite 303, Kansas City, MO 64112
(816) 753-7500; (816) 753-1101 (hotline)
Fax: (816) 753-3944

Michael West, chairman
Roger Stover, first vice chairman
Al Polonyi, second vice chairman
Michael Braude, president

Established in 1856, the KCBT is the world's primary marketplace for futures and options trading in hard red winter wheat and was the first U.S. exchange to trade futures based on a stock market index, the Value Line Stock Index. The exchange has proposed to reactiviate sorghum futures trading. A daily market hotline details price activity and open interest for the contracts.

MidAmerica Commodity Exchange

141 W. Jackson Blvd., Chicago, IL 60604
(312) 341-3000; Fax: (312) 341-3027

(For key personnel, see Chicago Board of Trade)

The MidAm, an affiliate of the Chicago Board of Trade, offers futures on grain, livestock, metals, financial instruments, and foreign currencies, as well as options on wheat, soybeans, and gold futures.

Minneapolis Grain Exchange

400 S. Fourth St., Minneapolis, MN 55415
(612) 338-6212; Fax: (612) 339-1155

Donald E. Brummer, chairman
James H. Lindau, president
Gary Rask, vice president, marketing

The Minneapolis Grain Exchange trades futures and options on hard red spring wheat. The exchange reintroduced high fructose corn syrup futures in July 1988 and oats futures in October 1988.

New York Cotton Exchange

4 World Trade Center, New York, NY 10048
(212) 938-2650; Fax: (212) 839-8061
(212) 938-2652 (FINEX)

Donald B. Conlin, chairman
Joseph J. O'Neill, president
James V. Gargan, vice president, general counsel
Paul T. Jones II, chairman, FINEX division
Ann P. Bruch, director of marketing
Robert Layton, president of Citrus Associates of the NYCE Inc.

The New York Cotton Exchange, founded in 1870, is the oldest futures exchange in New York. It offers cotton futures, cotton options, and, under the Citrus Associates of the New York Cotton Exchange, Inc., frozen concentrated orange juice (FCOJ) futures and options. U.S. Dollar Index (USDX) futures and options, European Currency Unit futures, and five-year U.S. Treasury note (FYTR) futures and options are traded on the exchange's Financial Instrument Exchange (FINEX). The New York Futures Exchange is affiliated with the NYCE.

New York Futures Exchange

20 Broad St., New York, NY 10005
(212) 656-4949; (800) 221-7722
Fax: (212) 656-2925

Lewis J. Horowitz, chairman, chief executive officer
Richard A. Edgar, senior vice president
Charles B. Epstein, managing director, marketing
Roy Fairchild, director of market data

The NYFE lists futures and options on the NYSE Composite Index and Commodity Research Bureau Futures Price Index.

New York Mercantile Exchange

4 World Trade Center, New York, NY 10048
(212) 938-2222; (212) 938-2879

William M. Bradt, chairman
Rosemary T. Mcfadden, president
R. Patrick Thompson, executive vice president
Jan B. Kay, vice president, marketing

Established in 1872, NYMEX maintains a marketplace for energy and metals futures and options contracts. Its energy complex, the largest in the world, includes futures on crude oil, heating oil, unleaded gasoline and propane as well as options on crude oil and heating oil. It also offers platinum and palladium futures. Upcoming contracts include natural gas futures and unleaded gasoline options.

New York Stock Exchange

11 Wall St., New York, NY 10005
(212) 656-3000; (212) 692-6973

John J. Phelan Jr., chairman, chief executive officer
Richard Grasso, president, chief operating officer
Lewis J. Horowitz, executive vice president, derivative products
David Krell, vice president, options and index products

In addition to stocks of more than 1,650 companies, the world's leading stock exchange also trades options on its NYSE Composite Stock Index.

Pacific Stock Exchange

301 Pine St., San Francisco, CA 94104
(415) 393-4000; Fax: (415) 986-5246

Maurice Mann, chairman, chief executive officer
Herbert G. Kawahara, president
Charles A. Rogers, senior vice president, options
Larry R. Shotwell, senior vice president, chief financial officer

The Pacific Stock Exchange has equity trading floors in Los Angeles and San Francisco. It trades about 1,300 securities and offers options on over 100 underlying securities, including one index: the Financial News Composite Index (FNCI).

Philadelphia Board of Trade

1900 Market St., Philadelphia, PA 19103
(215) 496-5165

Arnold F. Staloff, president
Joseph S. Rizzello, senior vice president
Paul J. Adair, director of foreign currency products

A subsidiary of the Philadelphia Stock Exchange, the PBT offers futures contracts on Australian dollars, Deutsche marks, Swiss francs, Canadian dollars, British pounds, Japanese yen, French francs, European Currency Unit, and the National Over-the-Counter Index. Currency futures began trading in August 1986 to complement the highly successful foreign currency options program at the Philadelphia Stock Exchange.

Philadelphia Stock Exchange

1900 Market St.
Philadelphia, PA 19103
(215) 496-5357; (800) THE-PHLX
Fax: (215) 496-5653

John J. Wallace, chairman
Nicholas A. Giordano, president
Joseph S. Rizzello, senior vice president, marketing

PHLX, the nation's oldest securities exchange, trades more than 1,300 equity securities, 109 stock options, 8 foreign currency options, a Cash Index Participation (CIP) contract and 4 index options (Value Line European-style, National OTC, Gold-Silver, and Utility). The foreign currency options program, started in 1982, is the largest of its kind and offers options on Australian dollars, Deutsche marks, Swiss francs, Canadian dollars, British pounds, Japanese yen, French francs, and European Currency Unit.

Twin Cities Board of Trade

5353 Wayzata Blvd., Suite 500, Minneapolis, MN 55416
(612) 333-6742

Sean T. O'Toole, president, chief executive officer
Gregory J. Jaunich, treasurer, chief financial officer
Daniel E. Fobbe, secretary
Jeffrey R. Hohertz, director of marketing

The exchange was founded January 1, 1988, with the intention to introduce futures products not currently traded in the United States. Major areas of emphasis include interest rate futures and transportation futures. The first contract is expected to trade early fourth quarter 1989.

TABLE 9.8   CANADIAN EXCHANGES

The Montreal Exchange

800 Square Victoria, Montreal, Que., Canada H4Z 1A9
(514) 871-2424; Fax: (514) 871-3530

Terence Reid, chairman
Bruno Riverin, president
Marcel Barthe, vice president, public relations
Bich N. Pham, director, derivative products

The ME is Canada's leading futures and options market with international exposure. The exchange trades Canadian equity options, Canada Bond options, International Options Clearing Corp. (IOCC) gold and platinum options, and Canadian Bankers' Acceptance futures. Its options and futures are cleared by Trans Canada Options Inc., except for its precious metal options, which are cleared by the IOCC.

The Toronto Futures Exchange

2 First Canadian Place
The Exchange Tower, Toronto, Ont.
Canada M5X 1J2
(416) 947-4487; (416) 947-4700
Fax: (416) 947-4585

Tristan Lett, chairman
Andrew Clademenos, president,
Warren Bock, secretary-treasurer

The TFE, formed in early 1984, lists futures on Canadian interest rates, the Toronto 35 Index, the TSE 300 Spot contract, options on silver bullion and warrants on Government of Canada bonds.

Toronto Stock Exchange

2 First Canadian Place
The Exchange Tower, Toronto, Ont.
Canada M5X 1J2
(416) 947-4700

J. P. Bunting, president
D. Scott, chairman

The TSE trades equity futures and options and Toronto 35 Stock Index options.

Vancouver Stock Exchange

609 Granville St., Stock Exchange Tower
Vancouver, B.C. Canada V7Y 1H1
(604) 689-3334; Fax: (604) 688-6051

J. L. Mathers, chairman
D. J. Hudson, president
J. M. Forbes, vice president regulation and membership
M. A. Foreman, vice president, trading operations
W. Funt, manager, trade development
D. Taylor, options coordinator

The VSE, founded in 1907, is primarily a marketplace for raising venture capital. The majority of the 2,300 companies listed are resource based, mostly mining. However, since 1980 a growing number of listings (currently 34% of total), have been high technology and junior industrial companies. In 1982, the VSE diversified into commodity options as part of the International Options Clearing Corp. (IOCC) trading network. Through the IOCC, the VSE trades gold, silver, platinum and Canadian dollar options. In 1984, the VSE expanded into equity options which are cleared by the Trans Canada Options Inc., owned equally by the VSE and Toronto and Montreal exchanges. Currently, 18 option classes are traded on the VSE.

The Winnipeg Commodity Exchange

500 Commodity Exchange Tower
360 Main St., Winnipeg, Manitoba
Canada R3C 3Z4
(204) 949-0495; Fax: (204) 943-5448

G. W. Moore, chairman

Robert Purves, president
P. K. Huffman, executive vice present
Michael Perring, secretary, director of administration

Canada's only grain futures market offers trading in canola/rapeseed, flaxseed, rye, domestic feed wheat, oats, barley, and Alberta domestic feed barley.

TABLE 9.9   LONDON EXCHANGES

The Baltic Futures Exchange (BFE)

24-28 St. Mary Axe, London, England EC3A 8EP
44-1-626-7985; Fax: 44-1-623-2917
Telex: 916434 BALFUT G

P. Elmer, chairman
S. M. Carter, general secretary
W. J. Englebright, director of futures markets
P. A. Freeman, futures markets manager
R. P. S. Neave, company secretary

The Baltic Futures Exchange was formed from the merger of the agricultural and freight futures markets trading on the floor of the Baltic Exchange in London.

The following markets are located at the Baltic Exchange address:

The Baltic International Freight
   Futures Exchange Ltd. (BIFFEX)

A. Harper, chairman
P. Neave, information

BIFFEX is the world's first open-outcry freight futures exchange and operates on the floor of the Baltic Exchange in London, the world's only international shipping exchange. BIFFEX offers futures contracts for dry bulk carriers. Settlement is based on the Baltic Freight Index, compiled daily by the Baltic Exchange from a specified number of voyages with spot freight rates input by London's top shipbroking firms.

London Grain Futures Markets

R. Moore, chairman
P. A. Freeman, information

The exchange began trading as the London Corn Trade Association in 1929 and merged in 1971 with the Cattle Food Trade Association. Originally, business was confined to imported grains, but that changed after World War II to homegrown barley and wheat, and subsequently to the present European Economic Community barley and wheat futures and options.

London Meat Futures Exchange

P. Elmer, chairman
P. A. Freeman, information

Cash-settled pig and live cattle futures are offered.

London Potato Futures Market

R. Harris, chairman
W. J. Englebrecht, information

Contracts include potato futures and options and cash-settled potato futures.

Soya Bean Meal Futures Market

D. Wilkins, chairman
P. A. Freeman, information

Futures market for soybean meal established in 1975.

The International Petroleum Exchange of London Ltd.

1 International House, St. Katherine's Way
London, England E1 9UN
44-1-481-0643; Fax: 44-1-481-8485

Derek Whiting, chairman
Peter Wildblood, chief executive

IPE opened in April 1981 with a gas oil futures contract. It now trades on Brent crude oil and heavy fuel oil as well as options on gas oil.

The London Futures and Options Exchange (FOX)

1 Commodity Quay, St. Katherine's Docks
London, England E1 9AX
44-1-481-2080; Fax: 44-1-702-9923

Saxon Tate, chairman
Antony Rucker, director of operations
Con Lenan, director of marketing
Beverly Eatough, marketing communications manager

The London FOX trades futures and options on a range of soft commodities, enabling commercial users to hedge against the risk of adverse price movements while providing additional trading opportunities to both commercial and noncommercial interests. In 1987, various organizational changes took place: the introduction of "locals," a Traded Option Market, and the launch of a white sugar contract on an Automated Trading System (ATS).

The London International Financial Futures Exchange Ltd. (LIFFE)

The Royal Exchange, London, England EC3V 3PJ
44-1-623-0444; Fax: 44-1-588-3624

A. D. Burton, chairman
M. N. H. Jenkins, chief executive
G. P. Rodgers, deputy chief executive
J. L. Foyle, market secretary
K. Albright, managing director, business development
R. Barton, director, technical services

LIFFE members include the leading organizations that participate in London's international monetary, securities, and commodity markets, including all major U.S. and Japanese banks and brokers. New contracts introduced in the last year include medium gilt futures, German government bond futures and options on three-month sterling interest rate futures.

The London Metal Exchange

Plantation House, Fenchurch St.
London, England EC3M 3AP
44-1-626-3311; Fax: 44-1-626-1703
Telex: 895 1367

J. K. Lion, president
C. J. B. Green, chairman
J. P. A. Wolff, vice chairman
M. E. Brown, chief executive
D. E. King, R. K. Millett, R. A. Edwards, B. S. Dorkings, secretariat

Established in 1877, the LME is a major world metals market for copper, lead, silver, aluminum, nickel, and zinc. The LME accounts for about half of all the futures trading in London. All market transactions are now recorded on a centralized clearing system operated by the International Commodities Clearing House (ICCH).

London Traded Options Market

Old Broad St., London, England EC2N 1 HP
44-1-628-1054; Fax: 44-1-374-0451

Geoffrey Chamberlain, chairman, options committee
Tony De Guingand, director
Neil McGeown, head of business development
Chris Royal, marketing manager

The London Traded Options Market, part of the International Stock Exchange, offers traded options on 63 stocks, the Financial Times Stock Exchange 100 Index (FTSE), two currency exchange rates, three French equities, and long- and short-term UK Treasury instruments. The market was established in 1978.

TABLE 9.10 OTHER EXCHANGES

The Australian Stock Exchange (Sydney) Ltd.

Options Department, 20 Bridge St., Sydney, N.S.W. 2000, Australia
61-2-227-0000; Fax: 61-2-251-5525

Bruce Donoghoe, manager

Established in 1976 with calls only; puts were introduced in 1982. The exchange currently trades options on over 20 underlying stocks and clears through the Options Clearing House Pty. Ltd.

Bolsa Barsileira de Futuros (Brazilian Futures Exchange)

Rua Do Mercado, 7-2 Andar E. Sobreloja, Rio de Janeiro, Brazil 20010
55-21-224-6062

Eduardo Roscoe Bicahlo, president
Francisco Borges De Souza Dantas, vice president
Antoinio Alexandre Da Silva, Joao Batista Fraga,
  Roberto Augusto Meireles Rocha, directors

The BBF opened on November 30, 1984, with a 250-gram gold futures contract. Exchange members are banks, stockbrokers, commodity brokers, locals etc. Camara Brasileira De Compensacao SA is the independent clearinghouse to BBF. The most successful contracts have been the financial futures (stock index, T-bonds, etc.).

Bolsa de Mercadorias de São Paulo (São Paulo Commodities Exchange)

Rua Libero Badaro, 471 Fourth Floor, São Paulo, Brazil 01009
55-11-32-3101; Fax: 55-11-32-4244

Ney Castro Alves, president
Francisco J. Monteiro Esperante, general superintendent
Irene Goldenberg, research

The Sao Paulo Commodities Exchange was founded in 1971. Until the middle of the last decade, cotton was the most traded commodity. After 1978, new contracts were introduced; there are now 27 contracts including agricultural products, financials, options and premiums. Gold (futures and spot) was launched in 1982; its fast acceptance by market participants now has made it one of the most traded commodities. Recently, the exchange started operations on FGV-100 Stock Index futures based on stocks of the 100 best private performing enterprises.

Bolsa Mercantil & de Futuros (BM&F)

Praca Antoinio Prado, 48, São Paulo, Brazil 01010
55-11-239-5511; 55-11-36-6182

Luis Masagao Riberio, chairman
Fernando Rosa Carramaschi, vice president
Dorival Rodrigues Alves, chief executive officer

Luiz F. Forbes, director

The BM&F, an affiliate of the Sao Paulo exchange, is the leading futures exchange in Brazil, trading more than 35,000 contracts daily. Total trading volume from its opening in January 1986 until June 1988 was 13.3 million contracts. The most liquid contracts are stock index futures, Brazilian bond (inflation rate) futures and gold futures and options.

Bourse De Bruxells
(Brussels Stock Exchange)

Rue Henri Maus 2, Brussels, Belgium
32-2-509-1276; Fax: 32-2-513-7275

Peter Broeck, president
Robert Urbanowicz, public relations

Deutsche Terminborse

Bethmann St. 50-54, 6000 Frankfurt, W. Germany
49-69-298902-0; Fax: 49-69-298902-98

Jorg Franke, chief executive officer

The Deutsche Terminborse, scheduled to open in December 1989, is a fully automated exchange with integrated clearinghouse. Products will include a stock option and bond and index futures.

European Mercantile Exchange

Shell House, 20/22 Lr. Hatch St., Dublin 2, Ireland
353-1-61-58-55; Fax: 353-1-61-50-12

Joseph S. Sims, managing director

The EME will open trading in futures and options on foreign currencies, interest rates, precious metals, stock indexes and energy in May 1989.

European Options Exchange (EOE)

Rokin 65, Amsterdam, The Netherlands 1012 KK
31-20-5504550; Fax: 31-20-230012

P. C. Maas, chairman
T. E. Westerterp, president
F. J. L. M. Cremer, managing director
U. L. Doornbos, J. W. van de Water, deputy managing directors

The EOE lists options on stocks, the EOE stock index, the FTA Bullet Index, Dutch Government bonds, and, as part of the International Options Clearing Corp. (IOCC) network, on gold and silver as well as the U.S. dollar and British pound both quoted in Dutch guilders. The EOE also lists options on the Major Market Index (XMI) that are fungible with the XMI options listed on the American Stock Exchange and cleared by the Options Clearing Corp.

Financiele Termijnmarkt Amsterdam N.V. (FTA)

Nes 49, Amsterdam, The Netherlands 1012 KD
31-20-5504550; Fax: 31-20-236659

R. F. Sandelowsky, managing director

The FTA, EOE's daughter organization, lists two types of guilder bond futures, one based on an index of eight Dutch Government bonds and the other based on an index of ten Dutch Government bonds, all bullet loans.

Finnish Options Brokers Ltd.

Keskuskatu 7, Helsinki, Finland 00100
358-0-131211; Fax: 358-0-13121211

Asko Schrey, president
Timo Laitinen, vice president
Osmo Jauri, vice president, options development
Matti Byman, vice president, marketing
Alexander Odrischinsky, chief dealer

Finnish Options Brokers Ltd. (SOM) is a marketplace and a clearinghouse jointly owned by the market participants. Trading is arranged via two systems, electronic and telephone. SOM began trading stock index futures and options on May 2, 1988. Stock options were introduced in the fall of 1988 and interest rate futures and options will be launched later.

Futures and Options Exchange in Luxembourg (FOXIL)

Price Waterhouse, 1 London Bridge, London, England SE1 9QL
44-1-407-8989

Ian Marshall, managing consultant

Guarantee Fond for Danish Options and Futures (GDOF) (Copenhagen Stock Exchange) (CSE)

Kompagnistrade 13, Copenhagen, Denmark 1208
45-1-93-33-11; Fax: 45-1-93-49-80

Jens Otto Veile, chairman (GDOF)
Tyge Vorstrup Rasmussen, managing director (GDOF)
Christen Sorensen, chairman (CSE)
Bent Mebus, president (CSE)

GDOF is the clearing and guarantee fond for the offical market. The official marketplace is CSE. The market is under establishment with 37 clearing members. Trading started in the fall of 1988 with futures and call options on the major Danish bond, a 9% annuity redeemable in 2006. Options are European-style; both futures and options are cash settled.

Hong Kong Futures Exchange Ltd.

Room 911, Ninth Floor, New World Tower, 16-18 Queen's Rd., Hong Kong
852-5-251005; Fax: 852-5-8105089

Wilfrid Newton, chairman
Douglas O. Ford, vice chairman, chief executive
Steven Yau, general manager

The HKFE offers futures contracts in sugar, soybeans, gold, and the Hang Seng Stock Index and plans to introduce other new financial contracts in the near future.

International Options Clearing Corp. (IOCC)

(Contact EOE or The Montreal Exchange)

Andre Desaulniers, chairman
Ted Westerterp, vice chairman
Arthur Payman, Guy Berard, Bruce Donoghoe, John Forbes, managing directors

The IOCC is jointly owned by four exchanges: the European Options Exchange, three-sevenths; the Montreal Exchange, two-sevenths; Vancouver Stock Exchange, one-seventh; and the Australian Stock Exchange (Sydney) Ltd., one-seventh. The network "passes the book" from one exchange to the other around the globe to offer the longest continuous trading day in gold, silver, and platinum options. Member exchanges also trade currency options.

Irish Futures and Options Exchange (IFOX)

Ferry House, Lr. Mount St., Dublin 2, Ireland
353-1-614977; Fax: 353-1-607870

Dermoy Desmond, chairman
Diarmuid Bradley, managing director
Kieran Luddy, operations director

IFOX is scheduled to open in February 1989 and will trade futures and options on domestic (Irish pound-denominated) instruments. An automated trading system will be used. Initially, three futures contracts will be traded: 20-year Government bond, 3-month interest rate and Irish pound/U.S. dollar.

Johannesburg Stock Exchange

P.O. Box 1174, 2000 Johannesburg, South Africa
27-11-833-6580

Tony Norton, president

Kuala Lumpur Commodity Exchange

Fourth Floor, Podium Block, P.O. Box 11260
50740 Kuala Lumpur, Malaysia
60-3-2936822; Fax: 60-3-2742215

Lee Boon Chin, chairman

The exchange was established in July 1980 as a company limited by guarantee. In 1985, the exchange went through a major restructuring exercise involving changes of its membership, tracing system and clearing and guaranteeing arrangements. A new clearinghouse was set up; the exchange and its clearing members own 70% of the equity and the balance is owned by a consortium of banks.

Manila International Futures Exchange

Producers Bank Bldg, Seventh Floor, Paseo de Roxas, Makati, Philippines
63-818-5496; Fax: 63-2-818-5525

Patrick Poon, executive manager

Marche a Terme International de France (MATIF)

108 rue de Richelieu, Paris, France 75002
33-1-40-15-20-01; Fax: 33-1-42-96-83-16

Gerard Pfauwadel, chairman
Gilbert Durieux, general manager
Jean Sicard, head, communications department

Established in 1986, the MATIF specializes in financial futures and traded options. It includes 100 members (French and foreign) from the banking and stockbroking communities. Its rapid rate of growth on the long French interest rate instrument made it the most successful new exchange in 1987. Traded volume expanded from 1.6 million traded contracts in 1986 to 12.0 million in 1987. Several changes were made in 1988 including the merger of financial and commodities futures markets under the MATIF structure.

New Zealand Futures Exchange Ltd.

P.O. Box 6734, Wellesley St., Auckland, New Zealand
64-9-398-308; Fax: 64-9-398-817

Len Ward, managing director
Lincoln Gould, marketing manager
Wendie Hall, manager, finance and operations
Steve Dickson, market development

The fully computerized New Zealand Futures Exchange is the first exchange in the world to open each day and trades four financial futures contracts, Barclays Share Price Stock Index futures and two options on futures contracts. Through its automated trading system, the NZFE operates with 17 trading members and 20 affiliate members located throughout the country. The International Commodities Clearing House serves as a clearinghouse and operates the trading system for the exchange.

Norwegian Options Market (NOM)

P.O. Box 1494 Vika, Tordenskioldsgt. 8-10, Oslo 1, Norway N-0116
47-2-331550; Fax: 47-2-332793

Dag Holler, managing director, president
Carl Fredrik Morken, vice president, marketing and information

NOM was established October 1, 1987, and is owned by major Norwegian banks, insurance companies, stockbrokers and the Stockholm Options Market (OM). Due to lack of rules and regulations from the Ministry of Finance, the exchange is waiting for permission to open. Stock options will be the first contracts to trade.

Osaka Securities Exchange

2-1 Kitahama, Higashi-ku, Osaka, 541, Japan
81-6-229-8643; Fax: 81-6-229-8138

Hiroshi Yamanouchi, president
Yoichiro Tomochika, senior executive governor

Trades the Osaka Stock Futures 50 contract, the first stock index traded in Japan. Launched the Nikkei Stock Average on September 3, 1988.

Paris Options Market

52 Ave. Champfelysees, Paris 75008, France
33-1-42-25-66-25

Edward Von Hertsen, project director

The Singapore International Monetary Exchange Ltd. (SIMEX)

1 Maritime Square, No. 09-39, World Trade Centre, Singapore 0409
65-278-6363; Fax: 65-273-0241

Elizabeth Sam, chairman
Ang Swee Tian, general manager
Aw Wah Soon, marketing director

SIMEX, the first financial futures exchange in Asia, is also the first exchange to be involved in a mutual offset trading arrangement with another exchange, the Chicago Mercantile Exchange. With the successful introduction of Nikkei Stock Average futures, the exchange will launch fuel oil futures in January 1989 and plans to introduce options on existing futures.

Stockholm Options Market (OM)

Box 16305, Stockholm, Sweden S-10326
46-8-700-06-00; Fax: 46-8-723-10-92

Olof Stenhammar, president
Dag Sehlin, executive vice president
Per Larsson, vice president, Swedish market
Anders Nyren, president, OM International
Mikael Stenbom, vice president, marketing and communications

OM is an options and futures exchange with integrated clearing facilities based on an electronic trading system combined with neutral telephone broking. Sweden's leading options exchange, OM started in June 1985 and opened for foreign trading in August 1987. OM is owned by all banks and brokers active on the exchange plus a number of Swedish institutions.

Swedish Options and Futures Exchange (SOFE)

P.O. Box 7267, Stockholm, Sweden 103 89
46-8-791-4080; Fax: 46-8-791-4075

Michael Hasselquist, chairman
Dan Stridsberg, president
Henrik Waereborn, vice president
Pia Soederhorn, administration manager
Magnus Lindholm, Ulrika Kjellstroem, information officers

Anne Hoerlin, clearinghouse operations manager

SOFE offers options and forwards on the SX16 Index and stock options on six underlying stocks. The fundamental principle of SOFE is to provide a number of equal order-routing systems: automated trading system; an electronic order book through which orders are routed directly to the marketplace; Independent Interbank Broker, banks and brokerage firms may route orders through brokers independent from the exchange; Broker, the clearing members' own respresentative at SOFE, and System 2000, a two-way telecommunication system.

Swiss Options and Financial Futures Exchange AG (SOFFEX)

Neumattstrasse 7, Dietikon, Switzerland 8953
41-1-740-30-20; Fax: 41-1-741-18-00
Telex: 828392 SOFX CH

Ernst Mollet, chairman
Otto E. Naegeli, chief executive officer
Karin Wagner, information

The implementation of index options was scheduled for the fourth quarter of 1988. The underlying index, Swiss Market Index (SMI), consists of 24 stocks which are permanently negotiated at the three main Swiss exchanges.

Sydney Futures Exchange Ltd.

13-15 O'Connell St., Sydney, N.S.W. 2000, Australia
61-2-233-7633

Leslie V. Hosking, chief executive
A. John Oliver, chairman
Bruce C. Hudson, deputy chairman

Established in 1960, the SFE has expanded rapidly in recent years and now trades a wide range of futures contracts including All Ordinaries Share Price Index futures, 90-day bank bills, 10-year and 3-year Australian Treasury bonds and Australian dollars. At the end of 1986, SFE established links with COMEX (gold) and LIFFE (U.S. Treasury bonds and Eurodollars), enabling traders to establish or offset positions in these contracts at times when the world's major markets are closed.

Tokyo Commodity Exchange for Industry

10-8 Nihonbashi Horidomecho 1 chome, Chuo-ku, Tokyo, Japan
81-3-661-9191

Naozo Mabuchi, chairman

The Tokyo Commodity Exchange was organized on November 1, 1984, by consolidating the Tokyo Gold Exchange, the Tokyo Rubber Exchange and the Tokyo Textile Commodities Exchange.

Tokyo Stock Exchange

2-1-1, Nihombashi Kabuto-cho, Chuo-ku, Tokyo, 103, Japan
81-3-666-0141; Fax: 81-3-663-0625

Michio Takeuchi, president, chief executive officer
Shiro Uramatsu, executive vice president
Mitsuo Sato, managing director

Trades Japanese government bond and Tokyo Stock Price Index (TOPIX) futures.

TABLE 9.11   CLEARINGHOUSES

Note: This table is from the previous year's Trading Facts and Figures, *Futures Magazine*; some of the facts may be out of date.

Board of Trade Clearing Corporation

141 W. Jackson Blvd., Suite 1460, Chicago, IL 60604
(312) 786-5700

Roger D. Rutz, president, chief executive officer
Delbert Heath Jr., executive vice president
Maureen Brehm, manager of member services

Futures and options accounting, trade entry, and risk analysis software for exchanges, FCMs, IBs, brokers, institutional traders, and dealers.

Chambre de Compensation des Instruments Financiers de Paris (CCIFP)

15, rue de la Banque, Paris, France 75002
33-1-42-96-53-65

Gilbert Durieux, general director

Financial futures market clearinghouse responsible for MATIF's market and floor management, traders' contract clearance, and control of open interest positions.

Chicago Mercantile Exchange Clearinghouse

30 S. Wacker Dr., Chicago, IL 60606
(312) 930-3170

John P. Davidson, vice president
Mary S. Biers, director of risk management
Christine Ehrke, director of business development

COMEX Clearing Association Inc.

4 World Trade Center, Suite 7300-D, New York, NY 10048
(212) 775-1480

Vernon W. Pherson, president

Commodity Clearing Corp.

4 World Trade Center, Suite 7300-C, New York, NY 10048
(212) 775-0190

Phil Saponara, president

Clears for the New York Cotton Exchange.

CSC Clearing Corp.

4 World Trade Center, Suite 7300-A, New York, NY 10048
(212) 775-0090

Harry J. Furey, president

Clearinghouse for the Coffee, Sugar & Cocoa Exchange.

European Stock Options Clearing Corp. (ESCC)

Nes 49, Amsterdam, The Netherlands 1012 KD
31-20-550-4550

G. J. P. Okkema, A. L. Payman, managing directors

The ESCC clears the European Options Exchange's stock, bond, and EOE Index options contracts. Its subsidiary, the European Futures Clearing Corp. (EFCC), is responsible for the registration and settlement of futures contracts on the FTA, EOE's daughter organization.

Intermarket Clearing Corp.

(See Options Clearing Corp.)

International Commodities Clearing House Ltd. (ICCH)

Roman Wall House, 1-2 Crutched, Friars, London, England EC3N 2AN
44-1-488-3200

ICCH provides clearing and guaranteeing services to exchanges in London, Hong Kong, Paris, Sydney, New Zealand, and a number of other cities. The ICCH is owned by six London banks. Membership is open to companies and partnerships whose application has been approved by the ICCH board. Only a member may have contracts registered in its name and receive the ICCH guarantee.

International Options Clearing Corp. (IOCC)

(Contact EOE or the Montreal Exchange)

G. J. P. Okkema, A. L. Payman, B. J. Donoghoe, J. M. Forbes, R. Schweitzer,
  managing directors

The IOCC is jointly owned by four exchanges: the European Options Exchange, three-sevenths; Montreal Exchange, two-sevenths; Vancouver Stock Exchange, one-seventh; and the Australian Stock Exchange (Sydney) Ltd., one-seventh. The network "passes the book" from one exchange to the other around the globe to offer the longest continuous trading day in gold, silver, and platinum options. Member exchanges also trade currency options.

KCBT Clearing Corp.

4800 Main St., Suite 270, Kansas City, MO 64112
(816) 931-8964

A. S. Polonyi, president

Minneapolis Grain Exchange Clearinghouse

400 S. Fourth, Rm. 150, Minneapolis, MN 55415
(612) 333-1623

Kris W. Nelson, assistant vice president

NYMEX Clearinghouse

4 World Trade Center, Suite 744, New York, NY 10048
(212) 938-2222

Charles Bebel, vice president

Options Clearing Corp.

200 S. Wacker Dr., Suite 2700, Chicago, IL 60606
(312) 322-2060

Wayne Luthringshausen, chairman
Clearing services for BCOE, AMEX, NYSE, PHLX, and the Pacific Stock Exchange. Intermarket Clearing Corp., a subsidiary of OCC, clears for the AMEX Commodities Corp., PBT, and NYFE.

Trans-Canada Options Corp.

The Exchange Tower, First Canadian Place
Toronto, Ontario, Canada M5X 1B1
(416) 367-2466

Clears all equity options in Canada.

BIBLIOGRAPHY

A. Admati and P. Pfleiderer (1988). "A Theory of Intraday Patterns: Volume and Price Variability," *Rview of Financial Studies.* **1**, pp. 3–40.

B. Allaz (1986). "Imperfect Competition and Futures Markets—The Duopoly Case," Princeton University.

B. Allaz and J.L. Vila (1986). "Futures Markets Improve Competition," Princeton University.

T. Amemiya (1985). *Advanced Econometrics.* Cambridge: Harvard University Press.

Y. Amihud and H. Mendelson (1985). "An Integrated Computerized Trading System." In Y. Amihud, T. Ho, and R. Schwartz, *Market Making and the Changing Structure of the Securities Industry.* Lexington: Lexington Books.

R. Anderson (1981). "Comments on 'Margins and Futures Contracts'," *Journal of Futures Markets.* **1**, pp. 259–264.

————(1984a). "Market Power and Futures Trading for Durable Goods," City University of New York, Graduate Center.

————(1984b). "The Regulation of Futures Contract Innovations in the United States," *Journal of Futures Markets.* **4**, pp. 297–332.

————(1985). "Some Determinants of the Volatility of Futures Prices," *Journal of Futures Markets.* **5**, pp. 331–348.

————(1986a). "Exchange Competition in the Futures Industry," Unpublished. City University of New York.

————(1986b). "Regulation of Futures Trading in the United States and the United Kingdom," *Oxford Review of Economic Policy.* **2**, pp. 41–58.

R. Anderson and J.-P. Danthine (1983a). "Hedger Diversity in Futures Markets," *Economic Journal.* **93**, pp. 370–389.

————(1983b). "The Time Pattern of Hedging and the Volatility of Futures Prices," *Review of Economic Studies.* **50**, pp. 249–266.

R. Anderson and C. Gilbert (1986). "Commodity Agreements and Commodity Markets: Lessons from Tin," Working Paper CSFM-141. Columbia Business School.

R. Anderson and C. Harris (1986). "A Model of Financial Innovation," Unpublished. City University of New York.

M. Arak and L. Goodman (1987). "Treasury Bond Futures: Valuing the Delivery Options," *Journal of Futures Markets.* **7**, pp. 269–286.

M. Asay and C. Edelsberg (1986). "Can a Dynamic Strategy Replicate the Returns of an Option?," *Journal of Futures Markets.* **6**, pp. 63–70.

C. Ball, W. Torous, and A. Tschoegl (1985). "The Degree of Price Resolution: The Case of the Gold Market," *Journal of Futures Markets.* **5**, pp. 29–43.

395

T. Barnhill and J. Powell (1981). "Silver Price Volatility: A Perspective on the July 1979 — April 1980 Period," *Journal of Futures Markets.* 1, pp. 619–647.

V. Bawa, S. Brown, and R. Klein (1979). *Estimation Risk and Optimal Portfolio Choice.* Amsterdam: North-Holland.

R. Bear (1972). "Margin Levels and the Behavior of Futures Prices," *Journal of Financial and Quantitative Analysis.* 4, pp. 1907–1930.

W. Beaver (1981). "Accounting for Interest Rate Futures Contracts," Working Paper 11. Center for the Study of Futures Markets.

S. Benninga and M. Blume (1985). "On the Optimality of Portfolio Insurance," *Journal of Finance.* 40, pp. 1341–1352.

D. Black (1986). *Success and Failure of Futures Contracts: Theory and Empirical Evidence.* New York: New York University.

F. Black (1976). "The Pricing of Commodity Contracts," *Journal of Financial Economics.* 3, pp. 167–179.

F. Black and R. Jones (1987). "Simplifying Portfolio Insurance," *Journal of Portfolio Management.* 14, pp. 48–51.

F. Black and M. Scholes (1973). "The Pricing of Options and Corporate Liabilities," *Journal of Political Economy.* 3, pp. 637–654.

D. Breeden (1979). "An Intertemporal Asset Pricing Model with Stochastic Consumption and Investment Opportunities," *Journal of Financial Economics.* 7, pp. 265–296.

————(1980). "Consumption Risk in Futures Markets," *Journal of Finance.* 35, pp. 503–520.

D. Breeden and M. Giarla (1987). "Hedging Interest Rate Risks with Futures, Swaps and Options," Working Paper 87–108. Fuqua School of Business, Duke University, Durham North Carolina.

D. Breeden, M. Gibbons, and R. Litzenberger (1986). "Empirical Tests of the Consumption–Oriented CAPM," Research Paper 879. Graduate School of Business, Stanford University.

M. Brennan (1986a). "A Theory of Price Limits in Futures Markets," *Journal of Financial Economics.* 16, pp. 213–233.

————(1986b). "The Cost of Convenience and the Pricing of Commodity Contingent Claims," Unpublished. University of British Columbia.

M. Brennan and E. Schwartz (1986). "Optimal Arbitrage Strategies under Basis Variability," Working Paper 21–86. Graduate School of Management, University of California, Los Angeles.

————(1987a). "Arbitrage in Stock Index Futures," Working Paper 9–87. Graduate School of Management, University of California, Los Angeles.

————(1987b). "Stationary Portfolio Insurance Strategies," Unpublished. Graduate School of Management, University of California, Los Angeles.

T.W. Brenner (1981). "Margin Authority: No Reason for a Change," *Journal of Futures Markets.* 1, pp. 487–490.

C. Brinegar (1970). "A Statistical Analysis of Speculative Price Behavior," *Food Resewarch Institute Studies.* 9, pp. 1–58 (Supplement).

M. Broadie and S. Sundaresan (1987). "The Pricing of Timing and Quality Options: An Application to Treasury Bond and Treasury Note Futures Markets," Unpublished. Columbia University.

L. Burr (1981). "Reparations," *Journal of Futures Markets.* 1, pp. 505–513.

P. Cagan (1981). "Financial Futures Markets: Is More Regulation Needed?," *Journal of Futures Markets.* 1, pp. 169–189.

K. Camp (1981). "The Public Interest Test: An Anticompetitive Anomoly," *Journal of Futures Markets.* 1, pp. 475–478.

D. Capozza and B. Cornell (1979). "Treasury Bill Pricing in the Spot and Futures Markets," *Journal of Finance.* 34, pp. 513–520.

T. Cargill and G. Rausser (1975). "Temporal Price Behavior in Commodity Futures Markets," *Journal of Finance.* 30, pp. 1043–1053.

D. Carlton (1984). "Futures Markets: Their Purpose, Their History, Their Growth, Their Successes and Failures," *Journal of Futures Markets.* **4**, pp. 237–271.

P. Carr (1987). "Treasury Bond Futures and the Quality Option," Unpublished. Graduate School of Management, University of California at Los Angeles.

C. Carter, G. Rausser, and A. Schmitz (1983). "Efficient Asset Portfolios and the Theory of Normal Backwardation," *Journal of Political Economy.* **91**, pp. 319–331.

T. Cernikovsky (1985). "Real–Time Information and Market Growth." In J. Buckley, *Guide to World Commodity Markets, Fifth Edition.* New York: Nichols Publishing Company.

E. Chang and C. Kim (1988). "Day of the Week Effects and Commodity Price Changes," *Journal of Futures Markets.* **8**, pp. 229–241.

S. Cheng (1982). "A Preliminary Study of the Variability of Rates of Return for Futures Contracts," Unpublished. Stanford University.

—————(1987). "Multiple Factor Contingent Claims in a Stochastic Interest Rate Environment," Unpublished. Graduate School of Business, Columbia University.

Chicago Board of Trade (1985). *Statistical Annual.* Chicago: Chicago Board of Trade.

—————(1986). *Commodity Trading Manual.* Chicago: Chicago Board of Trade.

Chicago Mercantile Exchange (1986). *Clearing House Manual of Operations.* Chicago, Illinois: Chicago Mercantile Exchange.

K.L. Chung (1974). *Elementary Probability Theory with Stochastic Processes.* Berlin: Springer-Verlag.

P. Clark (1973). "A Subordinated Stochastic Process Model with Finite Variance for Speculative Prices," *Econometrica.* **41**, pp. 135–155.

—————(1975). "The Use of Operational Time to Correct for Sampling Interval Misspecification," *Review of Economics and Statistics.* **57**, pp. 225–230.

Commodity Futures Trading Commission (1987). *Annual Report.* Washington: Government Printing Office.

Commodity Futures Trading Commission, Division of Trading and Markets (1987). "Report on Exchanges of Futures for Physicals," Washington, D.C.: U.S. Government Printers.

P. Cootner (1960). "Returns to Speculators: Telser vs Keynes," *Journal of Political Economy.* **68**, pp. 396–404.

B. Cornell (1977). "Spot Rates, Forward Rates and Exchange Market Efficiency," *Journal of Financial Economics.* **5**, pp. 55–65.

—————(1981). "The Relationship between Volume and Price Variability in Futures Markets," *Journal of Futures Markets.* **1**, pp. 303–316.

B. Cornell and M. Reinganum (1981). "Forward and Futures Prices: Evidence from the Foreign Exchange Markets," *Journal of Finance.* **36**, pp. 1035–1045.

J. Cox, J. Ingersoll, and S. Ross (1981). "The Relation Between Forward Prices and Futures Prices," *Journal of Financial Economics.* **9**, pp. 321–346.

—————(1985). "A Theory of the Term Structure of Interest Rates," *Econometrica.* **53**, pp. 385–408.

J. Cox and M. Rubinstein (1985). *Options Markets.* Englewood Cliffs, New Jersey: Prentice–Hall.

J. Danthine (1978). "Information, Futures Prices, and Stabilizing Speculation," *Journal of Economic Theory.* **17**, pp. 78–98.

P. DeMarzo (1988). "An Extension of the Modigliani–Miller Theorem to Stochastic Economies with Incomplete Markets and Interdependent Securities," *Journal of Economic Theory.* **45**, pp. 353–369.

P. DeMarzo and D. Duffie (1988). "Corporate Financial Hedging with Proprietary Information," Unpublished. Department of Economics, Stanford University.

J. Dew (1981). "Comments on 'Innovation, Competition, and New Contract Design in Futures Markets'," *Journal of Futures Markets.* **1**, pp. 161–167.

P. Dickins (1985). "Computerized Trading." **In** J. Buckley, *Guide to World Commodity Markets*. New York: Nichols Publishing Company.

D. Duffie (1987). "The Risk–Neutral Value of the Early Arbitrage Option," Unpublished. Graduate School of Business, Stanford University.

————(1988). *Security Markets: Stochastic Models*. Boston: Academic Press.

D. Duffie and M. Jackson (1986). "Optimal Hedging and Equilibrium in a Dynamic Futures Market," Research Paper 814. Graduate School of Business, Stanford University.

————(1986). "Optimal Innovation of Futures Contracts," Research Paper 917. Graduate School of Business, Stanford University.

D. Duffie and W. Shafer (1986). "Equilibrium and the Role of the Firm in Incomplete Markets," Research Paper 915. Graduate School of Business, Stanford University.

D. Duffie and R. Stanton (1988). "Pricing Continuously Resettled Contingent Claims," Unpublished. Graduate School of Business, Stanford University.

D. Duffie and W. Zame (1987). "The Consumption-Based Capital Asset Pricing Model," Research Paper 922. Graduate School of Business, Stanford University, forthcoming: *Econometrica*.

K. Dusak (1973). "Futures Trading and Investors' Returns: An Investigation of Commodity Market Risk Premiums," *Journal of Political Economy*. **81**, pp. 1387–1406.

E. Dyl and E. Maberly (1986). "The Daily Distribution of Changes in the Price of Stock Index Futures," *Journal of Futures Markets*. **6**, pp. 513–521.

F. Easterbrook (1986). "Monopoly, Manipulation, and the Regulation of Futures Markets," *Journal of Business*. **59**, pp. S103–S127.

J. Edmunds (1982). "A Comment on Greenstone's 'The Coffee Cartel: Manipulation in the Public Interest'," *Journal of Futures Markets*. **2**, pp. 19–24.

F. Edwards (1981a). "The Regulation of Futures and Forward Trading by Depository Institutions: A Legal and Economic Analysis," *Journal of Futures Markets*. **1**, pp. 201–218.

————(1981b). "The Regulation of Futures Markets: A Conceptual Framework," *Journal of Futures Markets*. **1**, pp. 417–439.

————(1983). "Futures Markets In Transition: The Uneasy Balance Between Government and Self-Regulation," *Journal of Futures Markets*. **3**, pp. 191–205.

————(1984). "The Clearing Association in Futures Markets: Guarantor and Regulator." **In** R. Anderson, *The Industrial Organization of Futures Markets*. Lexington: Lexington Books.

L. Edwards and F. Edwards (1984). "A Legal and Economic Analysis of Manipulation in Futures Markets," *Journal of Futures Markets*. **4**, pp. 333–366.

E. Elton, M. Gruber, and J. Rentzel (1987). "Professionally Managed, Publicly Traded Commodity Funds," *Journal of Business*. **60**, pp. 175–200.

E. Elton, M. Gruber, and J. Rentzler (1988). "New Public Offerings, Information and Investor Rationality: The Case of Publicly Offered Commodity Funds," Unpublished. Graduate School of Business Administration, New York University.

R. Erickson and G. Steinhart (1985). *The Language of Commodities*. New York: New York Institute of Finance.

E. Fama (1963). "Mandelbrot and the Stable Paretian Hypothesis," *Journal of Business*. **36**, pp. 420-429.

————(1976). "Forward Rates as Predictors of Future Spot Rates," *Journal of Financial Economics*. **3**, pp. 361–377.

S. Fay (1982). *Beyond Greed*. New York: The Viking Press.

Federal Reserve System Board of Governors, Commodity Futures Trading Commission, and The Securities and Exchange Commission (1984). "A Study of the Effects on the Economy of Trading in Futures and Options," Washington: Government Printing Office.

R. Feduniak and R. Fink (1988). *Futures Trading: Concepts and Strategies*. New York: New York Institute of Finance and Prentice–Hall.

S. Figlewski (1981). "Futures Trading and Volatility in the GNMA Market," *Journal of Finance*. **36**, pp. 445–456.

——————(1984). "Margins and Market Integrity: Margin Setting for Stock Index Futures and Options," *Journal of Futures Markets*. **4**, pp. 385–416.

——————(1986). *Hedging with Financial Futures for Institutional Investors*. Cambridge, Massachusetts: Ballinger.

Financial Accounting Standards Board (1984). "Statement of Financial Accounting Standards No. 80 — Accounting for Futures Contracts," *Journal of Accountancy*. **1984**, pp. 174–182.

——————(1987). *Accounting Standards—Current Text General Standards*. Stamford Connecticut: FASB.

D. Fischel (1986). "Regulatory Conflict and Entry Regulation of New Futures Contracts," *Journal of Business*. **59**, pp. S85–S102.

D. Fischel and S. Grossman (1984). "Customer Protection in Futures and Securities Markets," *Journal of Futures Markets*. **4**, pp. 273–295.

D. Fitzgerald (1987). *Financial Options*. London: Euromoney Publications.

K. French (1983). "A Comparison of Futures and Forward Prices," *Journal of Financial Economics*. **12**, pp. 311–342.

B. Friedman (1979). "Interest Rate Expectations versus Forward Rates: Evidence from an Expectations Survey," *Journal of Finance*. **34**, pp. 965–973.

K. Garbade and W. Silber (1979). "Structural Organization of Secondary Markets: Clearing Frequency, Dealer Activity and Liquidity Risk," *Journal of Finance*. **34**, pp. 577–593.

——————(1983a). "Cash Settlement of Futures Contracts: An Economic Analysis," *Journal of Futures Markets*. **3**, pp. 451–472.

——————(1983b). "Price Movements and Price Discovery in Futures and Cash Markets," *Review of Economics and Statistics*. **65**, pp. 289–297.

G. Gastineau (1988). *The Options Manual, Third Edition*. New York: McGraw-Hill.

G. Gay, W. Hunter, and R. Kolb (1986). "A Comparative Analysis of Futures Contract Margins," *Journal of Futures Markets*. **6**, pp. 307–324.

G. Gay and T. Kim (1987). "An Investigation into Seasonality in the Futures Market," *Journal of Futures Markets*. **7**, pp. 169–181.

G. Gay and S. Manaster (1984). "The Quality Option Implicit in Futures Contracts," *Journal of Financial Economics*. **13**, pp. 353–370.

——————(1986). "Implicit Delivery Options and Optimal Delivery Strategies for Financial Futures Contracts," *Journal of Financial Economics*. **16**, pp. 41–72.

R. Geske and W. Torous (1987). "Volatility and Mispricing: Robust Variance Estimation and Black–Scholes Option Pricing," Unpublished. UCLA.

T. Goodwin and S. Sheffrin (1982). "Testing the Rational Expectations Hypothesis in an Agricultural Market," *Review of Economics and Statistics*. **64**, pp. 658–667.

F. Gordon-Ashworth (1984). *International Commodity Control – A Contemporary History and Appraisal*. New York: St. Martin's Press.

M. Gorham (1981). "The Effect of Inflation on the Rules of Futures Exchanges: A Case Study of the Chicago Mercantile Exchange," *Journal of Futures Markets*. **1**, pp. 337–345.

S. Gosh, C. Gilbert, and A. H. Hallett (1987). *Stabilizing Speculative Commodity Markets*. Oxford: Clarendon Press.

O. Grabbe (1986). *International Financial Markets*. New York: Elsevier.

F. Grauer (1977). *Equilibrium in Commodity Futures Markets, PhD Thesis*. Graduate School of Business, Stanford University.

F. Grauer and R. Litzenberger (1979). "The Pricing of Commodity Futures Contracts, Nominal Bonds and Other Risky Assets under Commodity Price Uncertainty," *Journal of Finance*. **34**, pp. 69–83.

W. Greenstone (1981). "The Coffee Cartel: Manipulation in the Public Interest," *Journal of Futures Markets*. 1, pp. 3–16.

R. Grieves (1986). "Hedging Corporate Bond Portfolios," *Journal of Portfolio Management*. 1986, pp. 23–25.

S. Grossman (1977). "The Existence of Futures Markets, Noisy Rational Expectations and Informational Externalities," *Review of Economic Studies*. 64, pp. 431–449.

——————(1988a). "An Analysis of the Implications for Stock and Futures Price Volatility of Program Trading and Dynamic Hedging Strategies," *Journal of Business*. 61, pp. 275–298.

——————(1988b). "Program Trading and Stock and Futures Price Volatility," *Journal of Futures Markets*. 8, pp. 413–420.

S. Grossman and M. Miller (1986a). "Economic Costs and Benefits of the Proposed One-Minute Time Bracketing Regulation," *Journal of Futures Markets*. 6, pp. 141–166.

——————(1986b). "The Determinants of Market Liquidity," Unpublished. Graduate School of Business, University of Chicago.

——————(1988). "Liquidity and Market Structure," *Journal of Finance*. 43, pp. 617–637.

S. Grossman and J.-L. Vila (1988a). "Optimal Dynamic Hedging," Financial Research Center Memorandum Number 93, Department of Economics, Princeton University.

——————(1988b). "Portfolio Insurance in Complete Markets: A Note," Financial Research Center Memorandum Number 94, Department of Economics, Princeton University.

L. Hansen and R. Hodrick (1980). "Forward Exchange Rates as Optimal Predictors of Future Spot Rates: An Econometric Analysis," *Journal of Political Economy*. 88, pp. 829–853.

O. Hart (1975). "On the Optimality of Equilibrium when the Market Structure is Incomplete," *Journal of Economic Theory*. 11, pp. 418–443.

L. Harris (1987). "Nonsynchronous Trading and the S&P 500 Stock-Futures Basis in October 1987," Unpublished. University of Southern California.

B. Helms, F. Kaen, and R. Rosenman (1984). "Memory in Commodity Futures Contracts," *Journal of Futures Markets*. 4, pp. 559–567.

B. Helms and T. Martell (1985). "An Examination of the Distribution of Price Changes," *Journal of Futures Markets*. 5, pp. 259–272.

J. Helmuth (1981). "A Report on the Systematic Downward Bias in Live Cattle Futures Prices," *Journal of Futures Markets*. 1, pp. 347–358.

M. Hemler (1988). "The Quality Delivery Option in Treasury Bond Futures Contracts," Unpublished. Ph.D. Dissertation, University of Chicago.

J. Hicks (1939). *Value and Capital*. Oxford: Clarendon Press.

T. Hieronymus (1977). *Economics of Futures Trading For Commercial and Personal Profit*. New York: Commodity Research Bureau, Inc.

J. Hill and F. Jones (1988). "Equity Trading, Program Trading, Portfolio Insurance, Computer Trading and All That," *Financial Analysts Journal*. 1988, pp. 29–38.

D. Hirshleifer (1986a). "A Multiperiod Model of Storage and Futures Markets," Research Paper 4-86. University of California at Los Angeles, Graduate School of Management.

——————(1986b). "Commodity Futures Hedging and Price Bias—A Mean-Variance Synthesis," Working Paper 24-86. University of California at Los Angeles, Graduate School of Management.

——————(1986c). "Futures Market Equilibrium and the Structure of Production in Commodity Markets," Working Paper 22-86. University of California at Los Angeles, Graduate School of Management.

——————(1988). "Residual Risk, Trading Costs and Commodity Futures Risk Premia," *Review of Financial Studies*. 1, pp. 173–193.

R. Hodrick and S. Srivastava (1984). "An Investigation of Risk and Return in Forward Foreign Exchange," *Journal of International Money and Finance*. 3, pp. 5–29.

D. Holthausen (1979). "Hedging and the Competitive Firm under Price Uncertainty," *American Economic Review.* **69**, pp. 989–995.

J. Hore (1985). *Trading on Canadian Futures Markets, Second Edition.* Toronto: Canadian Securities Institute.

F. Horn and V. Farah (1979). *Trading in Commodity Futures, Second Edition.* New York: New York Institute of Finance.

H. Houthakker (1961). "Systematic and Random Elements in Short-Term Price Movements," *American Economic Review.* **51**, pp. 164–172.

—————(1968). "Normal Backwardation." In J. N. Wolfe, *Value, Capital, and Growth.* Edinburgh, Scotland: Aldine Publishing Company, pp. 193–214.

—————(1975). "Can Speculators Forecast Prices?," *Review of Economics and Statistics.* **39**, pp. 143–151.

L. Hunt and W. Nissen (1981). "Section 4a(1) Should be Revised," *Journal of Futures Markets.* **1**, pp. 461–464.

International Commodities Clearing House (1985). *General Regulations for Future Delivery Business and Bylaws for Options.* International Commodities Clearing House Limited.

INTEX (1986). *General Information and User's Guide for Members.* Bermuda: The International Futures Exchange.

S. Irwin and W. Brorsen (1985). "Public Futures Funds," *Journal of Futures Markets.* **5**, pp. 149–171.

M. Jackson (1986). "Market Efficiency and the Return on Gold Futures," Unpublished. Graduate School of Business, Stanford University.

—————(1988). *Private Information and Exchange: The Implications of Strategic Behavior,* PhD Thesis. Graduate School of Business, Stanford University.

R. Jacobs (1982). "Restructuring the Maturity of Regulated Deposits with Treasury-Bill Futures," *Journal of Futures Markets.* **2**, pp. 183–193.

R. Jacobs and R. Jones (1980). "The Treasury Bill Futures Market," *Journal of Political Economy.* **88**, pp. 699–721.

B. Jarnigan and J. Booker (1986). *Financial Accounting Standards — Explanations and Analysis (Eighth Edition).* Chicago: Commerce Clearing House.

R. Jarrow and G. Oldfield (1981). "Forward Contracts and Futures Contracts," *Journal of Financial Economics.* **9**, pp. 373–382.

R. Jarrow and A. Rudd (1983). *Option Pricing.* Homewood, Illinois, Richard D. Irwin.

E. Johnston, W. Kracaw, and J. McConnell (1988). "Day-of-the-Week Effects in Financial Futures: An Analysis of GNMA, T-Bond and T-Bill Contracts," Unpublished. Department of Finance, University of Utah.

E. Johnston and J. McConnell (1988). "Requiem for a Market: An Analysis of the Rise and Fall of a Financial Futures Contract," Unpublished. Purdue University, forthcoming: Review of Financial Studies.

J. Johnston (1972). *Econometric Methods, Second Edition.* New York: McGraw-Hill.

F. Jones (1982). "The Economics of Futures and Options Contracts Based on Cash Settlement," *Journal of Futures Markets.* **2**, pp. 63–82.

N. Kaldor (1940). "A Note on the Theory of The Forward Market," *Review of Economic Studies.* **8**, pp. 196–201.

A. Kamara (1982). "Issues in Futures Markets: A Survey," *Journal of Futures Markets.* **2**, pp. 261–294.

A. Kamara and C. Lawrence (1986). "Trading Systems, Liquidity and Default: Evidence from the Treasury Bill Markets," Unpublished. University of Washington.

A. Kane and A. Marcus (1986). "Valuation and Optimal Exercise of the Wild Card Option in the Treasury Bond Futures Market," *Journal of Finance.* **37**, pp. 1183–1197.

E. Kane (1984). "Regulatory Structure in Futures Markets: Jurisdictional Competition between the SEC, the CFTC, and Other Agencies," *Journal of Futures Markets.* **4**, pp. 367–384.

M. Kawai (1983). "Spot and Futures Prices of Nonstorable Commodities Under Rational Expectations," *Quarterly Journal of Economics.* **98**, pp. 235–254.

D. Kenyon, K. Kling, J. Jordan, W. Seale, and N. McCabe (1987). "Factors Affecting Agricultural Futures Price Variance," *Journal of Futures Markets.* **7**, pp. 73–91.

J.M. Keynes (1930). *A Treatise on Money, Volume II, The Applied Theory of Money.* London: Macmillan and Company.

Kidder, Peabody, and Company (1987). "Applications of Duration and Convexity to the Analysis of Callable Bonds," Fixed Income Group.

A. Kleidon (1988). "Arbitrage, Nontrading, and Stale Prices: October, 1987," Unpublished. Graduate School of Business, Stanford University.

R. Klein and V. Bawa (1976). "The Effect of Estimation Risk on Optimal Portfolio Choice," *Journal of Financial Economics.* **3**, pp. 215–231.

R. Klotz (1985). "Convexity of Fixed-Income Securities," Bond Portfolio Analysis Group, Salomon Brothers Inc.

R. Kolb (1988). *Understanding Futures Markets, Second Edition.* Glenview, Illinois: Scott, Foresman and Company.

R. Kopprasch (1985). "Understanding Duration and Volatility," Bond Portfolio Analysis Group, Salomon Brothers Inc.

R. Korajczyk (1985). "The Pricing of Forward Contracts for Foreign Exchange," *Journal of Political Economy.* **93**, pp. 346–368.

B. Kuhn (1981). "Margins: A Review of the Literature." In Lloyd Besant, *Research on Speculation: Seminar Report.* Chicago Board of Trade.

A. Kyle (1984). "Market Structure, Information, Futures Markets and Price Formation." In G. Storey, A. Schmitz, and A. Sarris, *International Agricultural Trade: Advanced Readings in Price Formation, Market Structure, and Price Stability.* Boulder: Westview Press.

————(1985). "Continuous Auctions and Insider Trading," *Econometrica.* **53**, pp. 1315–1335.

W. Labys and C.W.J. Granger (1970). *Speculation, Hedging, and Commodity Price Forecasts.* Lexington, Massachusetts: D.C. Heath and Co..

A. Larson (1960). "Measurement of a Random Process in Futures Prices," *Food Research Institute Studies.* **1**, pp. 313–324.

H. Leland (1970). "Optimal Forward Exchange Positions," *Journal of Political Economy.* **78**, pp. 257–269.

————(1980). "Who Should Buy Portfolio Insurance," *Journal of Finance.* **35**, pp. 581–594..

————(1987). "On the Stock Market Crash and Portfolio Insurance," Unpublished. University of California, Berkeley.

D. Lien (1987). "The Inventory Effect in Commodity Futures Markets: An Empirical Study," *Journal of Futures Markets.* **7**, pp. 637–652.

J. Lintner (1965). "The Valuation of Risky Assets and the Selection of Risky Investment in Stock Portfolios and Capital Budgets," *Review of Economics and Statistics.* **47**, pp. 13–37.

A. Lo and C. MacKinlay (1986). "The Size and Power of the Variance Ratio Test in Finite Samples: A Monte Carlo Investigation," Unpublished. Wharton School, University of Pennsylvania.

D. Luenberger (1984). *Introduction to Linear and Nonlinear Programming, Second Edition.* Reading, Massachusetts: Addison-Wesley.

C. MacKinlay and K. Ramaswamy (1988). "Index-Futures Arbitrage and the Behavior of Stock Index Futures Prices," *Review of Finanical Studies.* **1**, pp. 137–158.

B. Mandelbrot (1963). "The Variation of Certain Speculative Prices," *Journal of Business.* **36**, pp. 394-419.

————(1969). "Long-Run Linearity, Locally Gaussian Processes, H-Spectra and Infinite Variances," *International Economic Review.* **10**, pp. 82–111.

T. Maness (1979). "A Direct Test of the Efficiency of the T-Bill Futures Market," *Baylor Business Studies*. **120**, pp. 7–15.

J. Mann and R. Heifner (1976). "The Distribution of Short Run Commodity Price Movements," Technical Report 1536. Economic Research Service, U.S. Department of Agriculture.

A. Marcus and D. Modest (1984). "Futures Markets and Production Decisions," *Journal of Political Economy*. **92**, pp. 409–426.

J. Markham (1987). *The History of Commodity Futures Trading and its Regulation*. New York: Praeger.

T. Martell and J. Salzman (1981). "Cash Settlement for Futures Contracts Based on Common Stock Indices: An Economic and Legal Perspective," *Journal of Futures Markets*. **1**, pp. 291–301.

T. Martell and A. Wolf (1987). "Determinants of Trading Volume in Futures Markets," *Journal of Futures Markets*. **7**, pp. 233–244.

L. McMillan (1986). *Options as a Strategic Investment, Second Edition*. New York: New York Institute of Finance.

J. Merrick and S. Figlewski (1984). "An Introduction to Financial Futures," Unpublished. Occasional Papers in Business and Finance, New York University.

R. Merton (1971). "Optimum Consumption and Portfolio Rules in a Continuous Time Model," *Journal of Economic Theory*. **3**, pp. 373–413.

——————(1973). "The Theory of Rational Option Pricing," *Bell Journal of Economics and Management Science*. **4**, pp. 141–183.

M. Miller (1986). "Finanical Innovations: The Last Twenty Years and the Next," *Journal of Finanical and Quantitative Analysis*. **21**, pp. 459–471.

M. Miller, B. Malkiel, M. Scholes, and J. Hawke (1988). "Draft of Final Report of the Committee of Inquiry Appointed by the CME to Examine the Events Surrounding October 19, 1987," Unpublished. Chicago Mercantile Exchange.

M. Miller and R. McCormick (1988). "The Modigliani–Miller Propositions After Thiry Years," Unpublished. Graduate School of Business, University of Chicago, forthcoming: *Journal of Economic Perspectives*.

S. Miller (1986). "Forward Cash Contracting of Cotton," *Journal of Futures Markets*. **6**, pp. 249–259.

N. Milonas (1986). "Price Variability and the Maturity Effect in Futures Markets," *Journal of Futures Markets*. **6**, pp. 443–460.

F. Modigliani and M. Miller (1958). "The Cost of Capital, Corporation Finance, and the Theory of Investment," *American Economic Review*. **48**, pp. 261–297.

D. Morrison (1976). *Multivariate Statistical Methods*. New York: McGraw–Hill.

J. Moylan (1981). "Self-Regulation in the Commodity Futures Industry," *Journal of Futures Markets*. **1**, pp. 501–504.

J. Moylan and L. Ulkman (1986). "Dispute Resolution Systems in the Commodity Futures Industry," *Journal of Futures Markets*. **6**, pp. 659–670.

P. Munter, D. Clancy, and T. Moores (1985). "Accounting for Futures Contracts," *CPA Journal*. **55**, pp. 18–25.

New York Futures Exchange (1984). *Guide*. Commerce Clearing House.

D. Newberry and J. Stiglitz (1981). *The Theory of Commodity Price Stabilization*. Oxford: Clarendon Press.

L. Palme and J. Graham (1981). "The Systematic Downward Bias in Live Cattle Futures: An Evaluation," *Journal of Futures Markets*. **1**, pp. 359–366.

H. Park and A. Chen (1985). "Differences between Futures and Forward Prices: A Further Investigation of the Marking-to-Market Effects," *Journal of Futures Markets*. **5**, pp. 77–88.

J. Parry (1982). *Guide to World Commodity Markets*. New York: Nichols Publishing Company.

P. Pashigan (1986). "The Political Economy of Futures Market Regulation," *Journal of Business*. **59**, pp. S55–S84.

A. Perold and W. Sharpe (1987). "Dynamic Strategies for Asset Allocation," Unpublished. Harvard Business School.

T. Petzel (1980). "The Time Series Behavior of Corn and Soybean Prices," Unpublished. Food Research Institute, Stanford University.

T. Petzel and H. Working (1980). "Cowlesian and Kendallian Autocorrelation Coefficients and the IT Variance Ratio, and their Sampling Variances," Unpublished. Food Research Institute, Stanford University.

P. Praetz (1976). "On the Methodology of Testing for Independence in Futures Prices: Comment," *Journal of Finance.* **31**, pp. 977–979.

Presidential Task Force on Market Mechanisms (1988). "Written Presentation," Washington, D.C., U.S. Government Printers.

W. Purcell and M. Hudson (1986). "The Certificate System for Delivery in Live Cattle: Conceptual Issues and Measures of Performance," *Journal of Futures Markets.* **6**, pp. 461–475.

I. Rajaraman (1986). "Testing the Rationality of Futures Prices for Selected LDC Agricultural Exports," *Journal of Futures Markets.* **6**, pp. 523–540.

K. Ramaswamy and S. Sundaresan (1985). "The Valuation of Options on Futures Contracts," *Journal of Finance.* **11**, pp. 1319–1340.

G. Rausser and C. Carter (1983). "Futures Market Efficiency in the Soybean Complex," *Review of Economics and Statistics.* **65**, pp. 469–478.

J. Raynauld and J. Tessier (1984). "Risk Premiums in Futures Markets: An Empirical Investigation," *Journal of Futures Markets.* **4**, pp. 189–211.

G. Rees (1972). *Britain's Commodity Markets.* London: Paul Elek Books.

S. Richard and S. Sundaresan (1981). "A Continuous–Time Equilibrium Model of Forward Prices in a Multigood Economy," *Journal of Financial Economics.* **9**, pp. 347–392.

L. Rocca (1970). *Time Series Analysis of Commodity Futures Prices,* PhD Thesis. University of California, Berkeley.

J. Rolfo (1980). "Optimal Hedging Under Price and Quantity Uncertainty: The Case of a Cocoa Producer," *Journal of Political Economy.* **88**, pp. 100–116.

J. Rosen (1983). "The Impact of the Futures Trading Act of 1982 Upon Commodity Regulation," *Journal of Futures Markets.* **3**, pp. 235–258.

M. Rubinstein (1976). "The Valuation of Uncertain Income Streams and the Pricing of Options," *Bell Journal of Economics.* **7**, pp. 407–425.

—————(1985). "Alternative Paths to Portfolio Insurance," *Financial Analysts Journal.* **41**, pp. 42–52.

—————(1987). "Derivative Asset Analysis," *Journal of Economic Perspectives.* **1**, pp. 73–93.

—————(1988). "Portfolio Insurance and the Market Crash," *Financial Analysts Journal.* **44**, pp. 38–47.

D. Rutledge (1976). "A Note on the Variability of Futures Prices," *Review of Economics and Statistics.* **58**, pp. 118–120.

G. Saloner (1984). "Self-Regulating Commodity Futures Exchanges." In R. Anderson, *The Industrial Organization of Futures Markets.* Lexington: Lexington Books.

P. Samuelson (1965). "Proof that Properly Anticipated Prices Fluctuate Randomly," *Industrial Management Review.* **6**, pp. 41–50.

P. Sarnoff (1980). *Silver Bulls.* Westport, Connecticut: Arlington House Publishers.

M. Scholes (1981). "The Economics of Hedging and Spreading in Futures Markets," *Journal of Futures Markets.* **1**, pp. 265–286.

E. Schwarz, J. Mill, and T. Schneeweis (1986). *Financial Futures—Fundamentals, Strategies, and Applications.* Homewood, Illinois: Dow Jones-Irwin.

Securities and Exchange Commission (1982). *The Silver Crisis of 1980.* Washington: U.S. Government Printers.

—————(1988). "The October 1987 Market Break," February, Washington, D.C.: U.S. Government Printers.

C. Seeger (1985). "The Development of Congressional Concern about Financial Futures Markets." **In** A. Peck, *Futures Market Regulatory Issues.* Washington: American Enterprise Institute.

D. Selmer (1981). "Customer 'Suitability'," *Journal of Futures Markets.* 1, pp. 527–530.

W. Sharpe (1964). "Capital Asset Prices: A Theory of Market Equilibrium Under Conditions of Risk," *Journal of Finance.* 19, pp. 425–442.

————(1985). *Investments, Third Edition.* Englewood Cliffs, New Jersey: Prentice-Hall.

H. Shefrin (1981). "Transaction Costs, Uncertainty and Generally Inactive Futures Markets," *Review of Economic Studies.* **XLVIII**, pp. 131–137.

W. Silber (1981). "Innovation, Competition, and New Contract Design in Futures Markets," *Journal of Futures Markets.* 1, pp. 123–155.

————(1984). "Marketmaker Behavior in an Auction Market: An Analysis of Scalpers in Futures Markets," *Journal of Finance.* **39**, pp. 937–953.

S. Smidt (1965). "A Test of the Serial Independence of Price Changes in Soybean Futures," *Food Research Institute Studies.* 5, pp. 117–136.

————(1985). "Trading Floor Practices on Futures and Securities Exchanges: Economics, Regulation, and Policy." **In** A. Peck, *Futures Markets: Regulatory Issues.* Washington: American Enterprise Institute.

C. Smith, C. Smithson, and L. Wakeman (1987). "The Market for Interest Rate Swaps," Unpublished. University of Rochester.

J. So (1987). "The Sub-Gaussian Distribution of Currency Futures: Stable Paretian or Non-Stationary," *Review of Economics and Statistics.* , pp. 100–107.

B. Solnik (1988). *International Investments.* Reading, Massachusetts: Addison–Wesley.

W. Spilka (1983). "An Overview of the USDA Crop and Livestock Information System," *Journal of Futures Markets.* 3, pp. 167–176.

R. Stainer (1985). "Commodity Agreements." **In** J. Buckley, *Guide to World Commodity Markets.* New York: Nichols Publishing Company.

K. Stanley (1981). "Measuring the Operational Costs of Dual Trading: An Analytical Framework," *Journal of Futures Markets.* 1, pp. 329–336.

J. Stein (1986). *The Economics of Futures Markets.* Oxford: Basil Blackwell.

R. Stevenson and R. Bear (1970). "Commodity Futures: Trends or Random Walks?," *Journal of Finance.* **25**, pp. 65–81.

J. Stone (1981). "Principles of the Regulation of Futures Markets," *Journal of Futures Markets.* 1, pp. 117–121.

S. Taylor (1985). "The Behavior of Futures Prices over Time," *Applied Economics.* **17**, pp. 713–734.

L. Telser (1958). "Futures Trading and the Storage of Cotton and Wheat," *Journal of Political Economy.* **66**, pp. 233–255.

————(1960). "Returns to Speculators: Telser versus Keynes: Reply," *Journal of Ploitical Economy.* **68**, pp. 404–415.

————(1981). "Margins and Futures Contracts," *Journal of Futures Markets.* 1, pp. 225–253.

L. Telser and H. Higginbotham (1977). "Organized Futures Markets: Costs and Benefits," *Journal of Political Economy.* **85**, pp. 969–1000.

A. Toevs and D. Jacobs (1984). "Interest Rate Futures: A Comparison of Alternative Hedge Ratio Methodologies," Fixed Income Group, Morgan Stanley and Company.

W. Tueting (1981). "Section 5a(12) Rule Approval: A Ponderous Partner in Echange Managagement," *Journal of Futures Markets.* 1, pp. 469–473.

S. Turnovsky (1983). "The Determination of Spot and Futures Prices with Storable Commodities," *Econometrica.* **51**, pp. 1363–1387.

C. Tygier (1988). *Basic Handbook of Foreign Exchange, Second Edition.* London: Euromoney Publications.

H. Varian (1987). "The Arbitrage Principle in Financial Economics," *Journal of Economic Perspectives*. **1**, pp. 55–72.

J.-L. Vila (1986). "The Role of Information in Futures Market Manipulations," Unpublished. Princeton University.

F. White (1981). "Jurisdiction over Commodity Futures Contracts: Vertical versus Horizontal Regulation," *Journal of Futures Markets*. **1**, pp. 441–443.

J. Williams (1986). *The Economic Function of Futures Markets*. Cambridge University Press.

H. Witt, T. Schroeder, and M. Hayenga (1987). "Comparison of Analytical Approaches for Estimating Hedge Ratios for Agricultural Commodities," *Journal of Futures Markets*. **7**, pp. 135–146.

J. Yawitz (1986). "Convexity: An Introduction," Financial Strategies Group, Goldman Sachs.

INDEX